WASHINGTON

WASHINGTON

The Making of the American Capital

FERGUS M. BORDEWICH

Amistad

An Imprint of *HarperCollins*Publishers

HarperCollins books may be purchased for educational, business, or sales promotional use. For information please write: Special Markets Department, HarperCollins Publishers, 10 East 53rd Street, New York, NY 10022.

FIRST EDITION

Designed by Judith Stagnitto Abbate/Abbate Design

Library of Congress Cataloging-in-Publication Data has been applied for.

ISBN 978-0-06-084238-3

08 09 10 11 12 OV/RRD 10 9 8 7 6 5 4 3 2 1

For Richard H. Parvin and Marjorie Allen Parvin

"A great city would really and absolutely be raised up, as if by magic."

—"A Citizen of the World," in *The Maryland Journal and Baltimore Advertiser*, 1789

"This place is the mere whim of the President of the United States. During his life, it may out of compliment to him be carried on in a slow manner, but I am apprehensive as soon as he is defunct, the city, which is to be the boasted monument of his greatness, will also be the same."

—An immigrant stonemason, 1795

CONTENTS

Acknowledgments

In the course of writing *Washington: The Making of the American Capital*, I benefited from the accumulated wisdom of many people who opened unsuspected windows onto the political battles and sometimes elusive personalities of the early republic. I am especially grateful to the members of the First Federal Congress Project, who generously shared both their scholarly resources and their enthusiasm for the politics of the 1790s. Above all, I am indebted to Kenneth R. Bowling, coeditor of the project, for his wise suggestions and provocative insights, which improved this book in more ways than I can count.

Bob Arnebeck's exhaustive chronicle of the capital's early years, *Through a Fiery Trial*, lit my path into the dense thickets of politics on the Potomac. He responded to my many queries with unfailing good humor, and counseled skepticism toward conventional thinking about the capital's birth. Felicia A. Bell of the U.S. Capitol Historical Society pointed me toward invaluable documents illuminating the role that slaves played in the capital's construction.

C. M. Harris, the editor of William Thornton's papers, greatly enriched my understanding of the designer of the Capitol. William C.

Allen, historian of the United States Capitol, revealed to me the ghostly vestiges of Thornton's building beneath the fabric of the modern Capitol. Mrs. Ermin Penn was an eloquent guide to the poignant locales of Thornton's life on the lovely Caribbean island of Tortola, his original home.

Elizabeth M. Nuxoll, currently the editor of the John Jay Papers, piloted me through the papers of Robert Morris, her former bailiwick, and helped me to understand the character of the larger-than-life financier who played such a great role in the capital's birth. Christopher Densmore, director of the Friends Historical Library at Swarthmore College, fielded questions regarding Quakers and the antislavery movement with his usual precision and graciousness. Anna Coxe Toogood of the National Park Service brought alive Philadelphia during its years as the nation's capital. David A. Smith of the New York Public Library helped me to ferret out invaluable editions of early newspapers.

Anna M. Lynch and Leslie Morales were of exceptionally valuable assistance during my research in Alexandria, Virginia. Patsy M. Fletcher, of the City of Washington's Office of Planning, unearthed many useful sources of local information in the District of Columbia. Chris Cole of Stone Ridge, New York, took time from a busy workday to explain to me with a craftsman's delight the use of the historic tools that were employed by laborers in the 1790s.

Without the unflagging commitment of my editor, Dawn Davis, and my agent, Elyse Cheney, this book would never have come to fruition. They have, as ever, my gratitude.

Nor could I have succeeded without the support of my wife, Jean, and my daughter, Chloe, whose love and patience I can only hope to repay with this book.

WASHINGTON

As the last decade of the eighteenth century dawned, the United States was the third world of its time, less a nation than a weak and disorderly congeries of semi-independent states, more like the rickety Yugoslavia of the 1990s than to the superpower of today. Settlement extended only from the Atlantic seacoast to the wilderness of Tennessee, Kentucky, and Ohio. Philadelphia, its largest city, had a population of just forty-five thousand; and New York, only about thirty thousand. With native industry in its infancy, Americans still imported from Europe such necessities as shoe buckles, spurs and stirrups, pistols, razor strops, paint, fishing hooks, buttons, toothbrushes, and paper. It took three days to travel the one hundred miles from Philadelphia to George Town, Maryland, on corrugated roads so afflicted with stones, stumps, and ruts that it was customary for drivers to call to their passengers to act as ballast by first leaning to one side and then to the other, to keep the coach from overturning. A crazy quilt of state jurisdictions maddeningly compounded the difficulty of travel. When Thomas Jefferson journeyed from Richmond to New York in March 1790 to take up his duties as secretary of state, he had to juggle three different state currencies—those of Virginia, Maryland, and Pennsylvania—in order to pay his expenses along the way.

For a decade, the frail government of the United States had tee-tered on the brink of financial default and depended on foreign lenders for its financial survival. Annual interest on national and state debts was $4.5 million, at a time when the federal operating budget was about $600,000 per year. Worthless paper money had made a wreck of busi-ness obligations. States ignored congressional requisitions. Unem-ployed workmen wandered the streets of the cities. Farmers complained of crushing taxation. Even a friendly observer, the French traveler J.-P. Brissot de Warville, lamented that the states "were just falling to ruin. They had no government left, the constitution was detestable; there was no confidence to be placed in the Americans, the public debt would never be paid; and there was no faith, no justice among them."

No one really knew if the system that was established at the Consti-tutional Convention in 1787 would actually function. How would the checks and balances work? Who would control foreign policy? Who had the authority to interpret the Constitution? How was the president to be addressed? (Some seriously suggested "His Exalted High Mighti-ness"; others contemptuously dismissed the proposed title "president" as appropriate to a fire company or a cricket club.) Would the Northern states help defend the Southern against a slave uprising? Would the South come to the aid of the North in the event of a foreign invasion? None of the answers was obvious. Local officials were incompetent, or worse. Congress seemed little better. Full democracy repelled virtually all the men who were charged with making it work. "The people should have as little to do as may be about the government," Connecticut Senator Roger Sherman warned. "They lack information and are constantly liable to be misled." James Jackson, a congressman from Georgia, was alleged to have once waved his pistols at visitors in the public gallery and threat-ened to shoot them if they made too much noise. Jackson at least took his job seriously. During debates, many of his colleagues could typically be seen reading newspapers and exchanging bawdy limericks with one another. Of eighty-six senators who served during the 1790s, one-third would depart in boredom or disgust before their terms expired.

Only a small percentage of the country's four million inhabitants had any role in political life. Just under seven hundred thousand were slaves, who had no rights to liberty or property at all. And it would be a generation before any woman was heard to express her opinions in a political forum. About half of all free white men were disenfranchised by property qualifications, and many others lived too far from polling places to actually vote. In the elections to select delegates to the state conventions that debated ratification of the Constitution, only about one hundred sixty thousand people had voted, just one twenty-fifth of the population. Rules for participation in government varied widely from state to state. In Pennsylvania, all taxpayers were eligible to hold office; in Virginia, the requirement was ownership of at least twenty-five acres of improved land; and in South Carolina, candidates had to prove that they were worth a minimum of $8,500 to stand for a seat. In some states, presidential electors were selected by popular vote, in others by the state legislature, and in at least one, New Jersey, by the governor and his cabinet.

Inside Congress and out, there was a pervasive sense of anxiety that at any moment the whole jerry-built system might break down and shatter. The threat of rebellion and coups was in the air. Everyone remembered how, in June 1783, four hundred soldiers with fixed bayonets had mobbed Pennsylvania governing council at Independence Hall in Philadelphia, in a dispute with the state over unpaid wages, and how the national Congress, gathered in the chamber below, had ignominiously stalked off to New Jersey. Debtors burned courthouses in Virginia. In Massachusetts, Revolutionary War veterans embittered by high taxes and oligarchic rule had taken up arms against the government and were barely prevented from seizing the arsenal at Springfield by an army of hastily assembled militia. Thomas Jefferson feared that the states, "these separate independencies, like the petty States of Greece, would be eternally at war with each other, & would become at length the mere partisans & satellites of the leading powers of Europe."

Then there was the question of the capital.

Washington, D.C., is today as much a site of national pilgrimage as it is a seat of government. For schoolchildren disembarking by the hundreds of thousands each year along the Mall, and for millions of other Americans and foreign visitors, to travel to Washington is to seek some kind of communion with the secular civic religion that is embodied in its templelike buildings and the democratic institutions they enshrine. Viewed from the top of the Washington Monument, the sepulchral monuments to past presidents and to wars won and lost, the massive government buildings, museums, foreign embassies, and the taut axis of republican power formed by the Capitol and the White House, shape a cityscape that emanates both national self-confidence and imperial grandeur like no other in the world.

It was not always thus. At the dawn of the last decade of the eighteenth century, few questions agitated the new country's leaders as much as the site of its permanent capital. The very idea was deeply controversial. A driving impetus for revolution had been the inspiring republican vision of frugal citizens devoted to individual liberty and the mutual good governing themselves through popularly elected and incorruptible legislators whose power overshadowed weak executives. By the 1790s, as the nation recovered from war and began to flex its economic muscles, this idealized republican vision came under assault from the new and unpredictable effects of rapid urbanization, big money capitalism, and the obvious efficiency of a more centralized government. To many Americans, all these issues congealed in a fear of cities as menacing nurseries of social disorder and corruption. Worse, the idea of a permanent capital evoked repellent memories of opulent European courts, with their overbearing monarchy, entrenched aristocracy, and oppressive pomp. As Kenneth R. Bowling, a leading scholar of early Washington has written, "To those Americans who worried about the survival of republicanism, the dangers of a magnificent capital were immense, particularly if it became a commercial as well as a political city."

Since the Revolutionary War, no fewer than thirty competing sites had been proposed, from New York's Hudson Valley to the Ohio frontier. Some asserted that the capital ought to be at the country's *demographic* center, others at its *geographical* center. Partisans of a more northerly site argued that since Canada was doubtless destined eventually to become part of the nation, the capital ought to lie to the north. Advocates of western expansion retorted that it should be established across the trans-Appalachian frontier. Easterners who believed that the West would inevitably secede someday, demanded a capital near the Atlantic. Philadelphians and New Yorkers maintained that for the "conveniency" of transacting public business it made the most sense to place the capital in an established city. Spokesmen for less populated areas decried the baleful influence of a large commercial and wealthy city on the public councils. Lancaster, Pennsylvania, promoted the low prices of its food and firewood. Baltimore's proponents argued that it was invincible against foreign attack. Delaware lobbied for Wilmington. Lewis Morris of New York offered his private estate in the present-day South Bronx. Some Northerners favored Princeton, but Thomas Jefferson complained that it suffered from a "deficiency of accommodation, exposing ye attending members to the danger of indignities & extortions." Annapolis, Jefferson conceded, had "the soothing tendency of so Southern a position on the temper of the S. States," but most Virginians declared that locating the government there would favor Maryland's commerce at their expense. At one point Congress actually decided to alternate nomadically between Annapolis and Trenton, prompting one disgusted correspondent to grumble in the *New-York Daily Gazette* of legislators "who talk of moving from place to place with as much indifference as a set of strolling players." One of the less likely sites was the valley of the Potomac. If not the wilderness or swamp that legend has sometimes suggested, it appealed to few but the Virginians. By 1790 the leading candidate was somewhere in rural Pennsylvania.

The epic of the capital's invention opens a window on the Founding Fathers as they struggled over what the nation was supposed to be, throwing them into stark relief, like figures caught in the flash of lightning. Washington, D.C., was born from one of the most intense political struggles in American history, one shaped by power politics, big money, the imperatives of slavery, ferocious sectional rivalry, and back-room dealing—as well as by idealism and single-minded determination. The story of its creation is thus a kind of national parable, embodying the central contradiction of America, persisting even today, between noble intentions and the sordid realities of power. The capital was more than just a big construction job. It was also an attempt—indeed, a *desperate* attempt—to create a massive symbol that would embody the spirit of a nation that barely yet existed, and which many of its Founders feared might not long survive. "It might be compared to the heart in the human body," Georgia Congressman James Jackson urgently asserted in 1790. "It was a center from which the principles of life were carried to the extremities." Greater than a mere city, the proposed seat of government was the first national capital to be established by a republic in modern times. As such, it was meant to be a sacred repository of republican values, a new Rome, "the mistress of the western world, the dispenser of freedom, justice and peace to unborn millions," in the anonymous author's expressive words. The project was stunningly ambitious for a nation with an empty treasury. The Founders believed they were initiating a "new millennium" in human history: the capital thus stood at the center of what they saw as a new spiritual world, incarnating in stone the mythic culmination of—again as Jefferson put it—"the world's progress toward its present condition of liberty." Even its ground plan was designed as a physical expression of the nation's destiny. Each street suggested a ray of light emanating from the Capitol and radiating outward toward every part of America. At one point, it was even proposed that a prime meridian of longitude be established through the Capitol's dome to replace that of Greenwich, sanctifying both the building and its city as the central node in a new cosmic order.

The city's founders intended the completion of the capital to be seen by the world as a measure of the young nation's strength. Failure, consequently, would reveal fatal weakness, emboldening enemies who, as Americans saw it, encircled the frail republic like hungry wolves. Hostile Britain ruled the seas, occupied Canada, and refused to relinquish strategic forts in the Northwest Territory. New Orleans and the trans-Mississippi country were held by unfriendly Spain. Everywhere along the Appalachian frontier, settlers trekked relentlessly beyond the authority of the federal government, provoking Indian nations into unwanted conflicts that the ill-funded and underdefended republic could not afford. Far away in the Mediterranean, North African corsairs plundered American shipping with contemptuous impunity. European intellectuals mocked the republic as a half-baked jumble of "radicals and rye coffee, slavery and green peas, bugs and statistics."

The new capital would offer proof to the outside world that the United States was here to stay. It was to be the nation's paramount unifying symbol, the brick-and-marble embodiment of its ideals and aspiration. For the time being, this unique role was filled by the most trusted man in the United States: President George Washington. Americans were painfully aware that his life was rapidly ticking away. He was fifty-eight years old in 1790, elderly by the standards of the time, and his health was a constant worry. "While we had a Washington and his virtues to cement and guard the union, it might be safe; but, when he shall leave us, who would inherit his virtues, and possess his influence?" Congressman John Vining of Delaware publicly worried. "Who would remain to embrace and draw to a centre those hearts, which the authority of his virtues alone kept in the union?" The president was a man facing a complex moral crossroads. Tired and unwell, he claimed to crave retirement beneath his "vine and fig tree," as he liked to put it, but he felt driven by his own quest for immortality to shoulder the burden of leadership that the country had thrust upon him. He believed profoundly in the republic, but possessed an almost mystical, and less than selfless, desire to advance the interests of his region.

In 1790 Congress made Washington personally responsible for bringing the new capital to completion. He was given ten years to make the chosen site habitable. The prospects for success were dim indeed. Virtually from the start, the project was hobbled by scandalous financial manipulation, and a degree of incompetence sometimes suggestive of a modern banana republic, not to mention the reluctance of officials to move to what many regarded as a "barbarous wilderness." That it actually succeeded astonished many of its main actors. If Washington failed to complete the project within the prescribed deadline—and it seemed for most of that decade that he would fail—the capital might well revert to Philadelphia or someplace else new, a prospect with immense consequences for national stability when the division between North and South, free and slave, was beginning to shape the politics of the country.

More than any other single place, Washington, D.C., embodies the lofty aspirations of the United States in physical form. But it also stands as a monument to the most disturbing truths in our racial history, for embedded in the story of its creation is the central role that slavery's protectors and enslaved African Americans played in the formative years of the nation. Slaves driven by white overseers cleared the land for the new federal city, felling trees and uprooting the stumps that clogged the future routes of streets and avenues. More slaves, hundreds of them, rented by the federal government by the month and year, laid foundations, baked bricks, quarried stone, stirred mortar, sawed lumber, and erected the walls of the grand new temples to American liberty. Without them, the federal city could not have been built. For two centuries, their presence, and their sacrifice, was largely left out of the story of the capital's creation, as if they had never been there.

Even before the foundations of the new federal city had been laid, propagandists hailed its manifest destiny as the "Metropolis of America," promising that it would be not only the seat of government, but also become the nation's greatest port, and a center of commerce and manufacturing, a city of imperial dimensions fit to rival London and Paris. An American metropolis was indeed coming into being in the 1790s, but it was not on the Potomac. It was on the Delaware, in Philadelphia, the actual national capital from 1791 to 1800. Philadelphia was the nation's first living crucible of freedom, a city that was home to a vigorous community of abolitionists, as well as growing numbers of free blacks whose independence and energy defied the assumptions upon which slavery rested. Although present-day Americans now generally acknowledge the horrific realities of slavery, they still remain largely unaware of the struggle of black Americans to create a safe and autonomous place for themselves in the virulently racist America of the early republic, when general emancipation was only a distant dream.

That struggle began in the Philadelphia of the 1790s. There, while visionaries and speculators strove to create a Potomac capital to suit the interests of slaveholding Southerners, the first generation of free African Americans was beginning the painful national process of learning how to live together in freedom with white Americans. Because one of the most powerful incentives to complete Washington, D.C., was the desire of Southern politicians to escape Philadelphia's atmosphere of tolerance for African Americans, the story of the capital's creation is thus their story, too.

Some of the players in this decade-long drama are well known, among them George Washington, Thomas Jefferson, James Madison, and Alexander Hamilton, although they may seem at times like strangers when seen through the unfamiliar lens of the capital's creation. Others are less so, such as the city's flamboyant planner, the ill-fated Peter Charles L'Enfant; the idealistic William Thornton, designer of the Capitol, who was better known in his day as the impassioned promoter of the first scheme intended to solve the nation's "race problem"; Benjamin Banneker, who charted the passage of the stars from Jones's Point and left his own distinctive imprint on the story of the capital's creation; and the buccaneer speculators Robert Morris, John Nicholson, and James Greenleaf, whose ambition nearly destroyed the federal city before it came into being.

The invention of Washington, D.C., is in part a soaring story of national aspiration, in part a cautionary tale of the first great land-grabbing boondoggle in American history, and in part a grim record of slavery's buried history. It is much more than the story of the mere physical construction of a city where none existed before, though that is dramatic enough, with its byzantine web of financial scandals, personal betrayals, and political cliff-hangers. Ultimately, it is an epic tale of the often faltering, sometimes delusional, and ultimately triumphant quest to create the first great physical symbol of the nation's identity.

Chapter 1

THE NEW MACHINE OF GOVERNMENT

"The climate of the Patowmack is not only unhealthy, but destructive to northern constitutions. Vast numbers of eastern adventurers have gone to the Southern states, and all have found their graves there."

—THEODORE SEDGWICK
OF MASSACHUSETTS

FEDERAL HALL, HOME TO the newly minted United States Congress, was inseparable from its designer, the picturesque Major Peter Charles L'Enfant, late of the Continental Army, architect extraordinaire, émigré, and a figure almost as recognizable to New York's elite as President Washington himself. For months, his tall, fastidious figure had prowled around the old city hall on Wall Street, examining its eighty-year-old brickwork, muttering to himself in French, or his syntactically challenged English, imagining—where others saw merely a tired old workhorse of a building—a blank canvas upon which to paint an architectural epic.

Few men were more in demand by the belles of New York than the celebrated L'Enfant. He was no one's idea of handsome, but his beaky face was more than compensated for by the Gallic panache that he brought to the glittery whirl of society. There was, it was true, a certain "haughtiness," an edgy volatility, to his otherwise impeccable manners, but people were willing to make allowances. He was after all, well, *French*, not to mention a favored confidant of the political luminaries who had come together here in the temporary capital on the Hudson. L'Enfant had grown up the son of a professional painter of battle scenes, in the incandescent glow of the court of Louis XV. Like his compatriot the Marquis de Lafayette, he volunteered to fight for American independence, arriving in 1777 with a shipment of guns and ammunition, a knack for making useful friends, and a most unmilitary education from the prestigious Royal Academy of Painting and Sculpture in Paris. During the brutal winter at Valley Forge, he entertained his shivering fellow officers with his sparkling conversation and pencil sketches, winning the attention and later the patronage of George Washington and his aide Alexander Hamilton. Hypersensitive though L'Enfant could be, he proved himself under fire to be a soldier of considerable courage, when he was seriously wounded storming the British fortifications at Savannah: in later years, he would often have to rely on laudanum to control the pain. Imprisonment by the British further gilded his patriotic credentials, which would shield him again and again from the consequences of his personality.

After the war, having become a citizen and changed his name from Pierre to the more American-sounding Peter, L'Enfant developed a lucrative career as New York's most sought-after architect. He remodeled the interior of St. Paul's church, planned a vast (though never built) park that would have stretched from New York's present City Hall to Greenwich Village, and staged a famously extravagant procession on the eve of New York's adoption of the Constitution, featuring along with much other exotica, a pretty eight-year-old boy dressed as Bacchus, a contingent of furriers made up to resemble Indians in sweltering animal skins, and a model frigate—christened the *Hamilton*—mounted on wheels and firing salvos from its two cannon as it was tugged through the streets of Manhattan. Perhaps not entirely by coincidence, Alexander Hamilton, who was now the secretary of the treasury, soon afterward invited L'Enfant to design the country's first coins and medals.

However, it was L'Enfant's transformation of city hall into Federal Hall, the seat of Congress and an icon of patriotic spirit, that cemented his reputation as the architectural laureate of the republic. Already redolent with history—in 1735 the printer John Peter Zenger had been tried there in a case that became a landmark of press freedom, and in 1765 delegates from the colonies had met there to denounce the Stamp Act—the dowdy structure faced south down a gentle slope, diagonally across from the present-day New York Stock Exchange. New Yorkers fairly swooned at the stylishness of L'Enfant's redesign. He erased the old Queen Anne facade and in its place erected an architectural paean to classical Rome, whose fashionable motifs served as a universal visual code for Enlightenment idealism and republican politics. Where the two wings of city hall had flanked an open courtyard, he erected a lofty balcony framed by four austere Doric columns topped by a triangular pediment where, instead of the muscled gods of the ancient world, Americans found an image of their own native eagle from which radiated the rays of the sun, proclaiming the dawn of a new age. The interior was no less impressive. The twenty-two-member Senate met in a chamber on the second floor, adjoining the "machinery room," where models of inventions were displayed. The sixty-five-member House of Representatives, regarded at the time as the more powerful of the two bodies, occupied a richly decorated, two-story octagonal chamber that opened off the central vestibule. So proud were New Yorkers of the government's new home that one popular theatrical production dramatized a mock-up of Federal Hall descending from the clouds while an actor costumed as the "genius of Columbia" poetically hailed it as a sacred temple of liberty and virtue. (To be sure, there were a few dissenters: puritanical Pennsylvania Senator William Maclay regarded the "vamped up Jimcrackery and Gingerbread" of L'Enfant's design as an insult to Congress.)

New York was the country's temporary capital more or less by default, Congress having come to rest there in 1785 after repeatedly failing to agree on a permanent seat of government. By European standards, the city was little more than an overgrown town, extending barely twenty blocks north from the Battery before petering out amid swamps and meadows. The Revolutionary War and the long British occupation had taken a heavy toll: hundreds of buildings had burned, commerce had come to a halt, and many of the most affluent citizens had gone into exile. Fortifications still scarred the suburbs. But after years of stagnation, the city was now coming back to life. In the past five years alone, the population had grown by 25 percent to just over thirty-one thousand, and it would double again before the decade was out. Bluenoses sneered at its cosmopolitanism as a "vortex of folly and dissipation" where ladies of fashion—"a bunch of bosom and bulk of Cotton," as Maclay snidely put it—promenaded in wigs and silks, stylishly bent forward "as if some disagreeable disorder prevented them from standing erect." Along its dog-legged lanes, ripe with the stench of nearby wharves, sharp-dealing merchants rubbed elbows with immigrants from the British Isles and upstate farms, turbaned West Indians, declassed French aristocrats, and visiting planters from the South who, as a British visitor dryly expressed it, "were alternately explaining the free principles of the Constitution, and reading the description of runaway slaves." Water Street wharfs groaned with new shipments of fustians and calicoes from India, choice wheat from Virginia and the Hudson Valley, cargoes of sugar and cotton from the South, New England rum, and coffee from England. Every week, it seemed, more handsome brick buildings in the stately English style replaced the shambling old step-roofed, sloping houses of the Dutch. Everywhere new streets were being laid out, marshes filled in, and shorelines extended.

New Yorkers had enthusiastically welcomed what the *New-York Daily Gazette* admiringly called "the new machine of government," as if it were speaking of a remarkable new feat of engineering, which in a sense it was. They lavished individual attention on the congressmen and senators with endless rounds of teas, soirees, and levees. And when President Washington was suffering from anthrax, the city fathers even ordered the portion of Broadway in front of his house to be blocked with a chain to spare him from the annoying rattle and clank of passing traffic. Some New Yorkers were still talking grandiosely about laying out new imperial boulevards in hope of inducing the government to settle permanently there. But as the members of Congress gathered beneath L'Enfant's stylish cupola in June 1790, it seemed clear to most that the permanent federal capital was going to be built somewhere on the Arcadian banks of the Susquehanna River, in Pennsylvania.

FOR YEARS, THE question of the capital's location had been recognized as one of explosive, potentially fatal significance for the country. Failure "will lay a foundation for animosities that no government can prevent or heal," the *Pennsylvania Gazette* had warned. But at last, on September 8, 1789, Congress had voted with apparent finality to place the nation's capital on the east bank of the Susquehanna by an apparently decisive vote of thirty-two to nineteen. Three appointed commissioners—one of them surely L'Enfant—were to select the best site, purchase land, and within four years begin constructing buildings for the federal government. In the meantime, Congress would remain quartered in New York.

The opening shots in a debate that almost sank the union were fired on August 27, when Thomas Scott of Pennsylvania rose in the House's forty-six-foot high octagonal chamber to propose that "a permanent seat for the government of the United States ought to be fixed as near the centre of wealth, population and extent of territory, as shall be consistent with the convenience of the Atlantic navigation, having also a due regard to the circumstances of the Western country"—an elliptical code, everyone knew, for Pennsylvania. The most likely site on the Susquehanna was Wright's Ferry, seventy miles west of Philadelphia by a good road, and fifty miles north of Baltimore. The climate was temperate and healthy. The setting was splendid, situated on a low bluff, with a panoramic view of the verdant Pennsylvania hinterland, and completely safe from foreign attack. In 1788 Samuel Wright had even renamed the town Columbia in hope of enticing Congress. Some wryly opined that the locals now regarded their rough-hewn hamlet as the "hub of the universe." Indeed, in 1790 speculators were busy raffling off the best lots in anticipation. In a country that took human bondage for granted, Columbia was also an island of freedom. Although slavery still existed in the state, Columbia's Quaker-dominated population of 320 included no slaves at all.

The idea of a Susquehanna capital enjoyed the support of a broad coalition from the Northern states. There was opposition, of course. New Yorkers supported by Southerners who objected to Pennsylvania's increasingly antislavery climate advocated naming New York City to continue to serve as the temporary capital. Others tenaciously promoted Baltimore. Only Virginians argued for a site on the Potomac. Their language was ostentatiously bullying and defensive. Alexandria Congressman Richard Bland Lee asserted that only a Potomac site would guarantee "perpetual union and domestic tranquillity." Behind this was a veiled warning. If these great principles were not preserved, Lee warned, it would be an unhappy fulfillment of the predictions of those who had opposed the new Constitution, and instead "one part of the Union would be depressed and trampled on, to benefit and exalt the other," adding that if they felt disregarded, "it would be an alarming circumstance to the people of the southern states." How the question was resolved would determine "whether this government is to exist for ages, or be dispersed among contending winds." He was unmistakably threatening secession, the trump card that the South would play again and again for the next seventy years, whenever it perceived that its interests, slavery paramount among them, were endangered.

Of the 3,929,827 Americans counted by the first national census in 1790, 697,647—about 18 percent—were slaves. Of these, 94 percent lived in Southern states, whose economic stake in protecting slavery was immense. Slaves comprised 43 percent of South Carolina's population, almost 40 percent of Virginia's, 35 percent of Georgia's, 32 percent of Maryland's, and 25 percent of North Carolina's. Slaves picked tobacco in Maryland and Virginia. They cultivated rice and indigo in South Carolina and Georgia. They fished off the shores of Delaware and North Carolina. Everywhere, they plowed fields, harvested crops, tended cows and hogs, labored in grist mills, foundries and tanneries, cleaned chimneys, piloted boats, staffed hotels and taverns, and served their masters as cooks, butlers, valets, coachmen, and nursemaids. Although less than 6 percent of slaves lived in the North, they were still crucial to local economies in New Jersey and New York where, in New York City, 20 percent of the households employed slaves in some capacity.

Slaves had helped to win the war for independence. Despite Southern efforts to thwart the recruitment of blacks—nothing was more terrifying than the prospect of armed slaves in states where blacks made up almost half the population—the Continental Army was the most racially integrated force the United States fielded until the Vietnam War. As much as 13 percent of its fighting force may have been black, including many slaves serving in place of their masters, and hoping for manumission after the war. Several blacks, including at least one slave, Prince Estabrook (or Easterbrooks), stood with the Minutemen on Lexington Green, when the first shots of the Revolution were fired. They fought at Bunker Hill, and at Monmouth, where George Washington's loyal body servant Billy Lee nearly took a bullet for his master, and at Yorktown, where many of the American troops under Washington's command were black. In 1781 black troops of the Rhode Island Regiment under the command of Alexander Hamilton heroically stormed the key British redoubt at Yorktown, and in hand-to-hand fighting captured it, leading to the British surrender. Many more slaves, however, put their trust in British promises of freedom and defected to the crown, perhaps as many as one hundred thousand in the course of the war, including thirty belonging to Thomas Jefferson, in what was, in effect, the greatest slave rebellion in American history. South Carolina alone hemorrhaged twenty-five thousand slaves, about one-third of its African American population. These numbers were all too soon replenished after the war by the unending chain of slave ships that carried shackled men, women, and children across the Atlantic from the coasts of Africa.

The bravery of black troops on the battlefield nonetheless spurred calls for gradual emancipation. "Blush ye pretended votaries for freedom!" Massachusetts preacher John Allen harangued his parishioners. "Ye trifling patriots! Who are making a vain parade of being advocates for the liberties of mankind, who are thus making a mockery of your profession by trampling on the sacred natural rights and privileges of Africans." Especially in the North, there was widespread optimism that slavery had become an anachronism, and that a gentle moralistic nudge from right-minded men would cause it to disappear entirely. By the mid-1780s, Pennsylvania and all the New England states had either declared slavery illegal or enacted plans for gradual abolition; New York and New Jersey would pass similar laws in 1799 and 1804. Even some Virginians were talking cautiously about emancipation. At the Constitutional Convention of 1787 Roger Sherman of Connecticut complacently asserted that "the abolition of slavery seemed to be going on in the United States, and that the good sense of the several states would probably by degrees complete it." This was just wishful thinking, of course. Manumissions increased—by 1790 the number of free African Americans would grow to 59,466, just under 8 percent of the total black population. But those who had hoped that the Revolution would lead to general emancipation were sadly disappointed. Between 1776 and 1790 the enslaved population of the United States steadily climbed by 40 percent. Bondage remained more profitable than ever.

It is stating the obvious to point out that without the Constitution, the United States as we know it would not exist. It is less well understood today that the nation wrought by the Constitution committed itself decisively to the protection and preservation of slavery. By 1787 it was obvious to virtually everyone that the Articles of Confederation, which had nominally defined the country since the end of the Revolutionary War, were a recipe for internecine conflict. That summer delegates from all the states except Rhode Island came together in Philadelphia to hammer out a more effective system of government. (Rhode Island alone rejected revision of the Articles of Confederation, and it would be the slowest to approve the Constitution.) The knottiest problem the delegates faced was inventing a system of representation in Congress that satisfied both populous states and small ones. Under the Articles of Confederation, each state had only one vote in Congress, an arrangement that made slavery politically irrelevant, since it gave Virginia, with its 100,783 slaves, no more weight than Massachusetts, which had none. The larger states were now demanding that representation reflect the size of a state's population. This produced predictable tensions between states that had enjoyed parity up to now. It also raised a new and deeply troubling dilemma: were slaves people who should be counted, or property that should not?

James Madison, whom posterity would perceive as the single most effective advocate for the Constitution, trenchantly observed that the real battle was less between large and small states, but between the North and South, and that "it was pretty well understood that the institution of slavery & its consequences formed the line of discrimination." It was perfectly clear to Madison and everyone else that if only free whites were counted, the more populous North would dominate the government and would have the power to bring an end to slavery, as states were now doing throughout that region. However, most Americans believed that the North would eventually lose its demographic advantage as new slave states were carved from the trans-Appalachian West. (No one yet foresaw that the great wave of nineteenth-century immigration would flow to industrializing Northern cities, and not to the rural South.) If the South could achieve sufficient leverage over the government in the short run, periodic reapportionment would eventually cement its hegemony.

Some delegates to the convention also proposed writing into the Constitution a ban on the overseas slave trade. This position was advocated both by antislavery Northerners—who were few in number—and by Virginians, whose "surplus" slaves would increase dramatically in value if foreign imports were banned. But delegates from the Carolinas and Georgia repeatedly threatened that unless they were guaranteed the right to import slaves from Africa, they would oppose the entire Constitution. John Rutledge, Charleston's most prestigious lawyer and an unembarrassed defender of slavery, warned the delegates, "If the Convention thinks that N.C.; S.C & Georgia will ever agree to the plan, unless their right to import slaves be untouched, the expectation is in vain. The people of those States will never be such fools as to give up so important an interest." Not coincidentally, importing more slaves would continue to augment the South's population, adding steadily to its representation and power in Congress. Rutledge added a blunt appeal to Yankee self-interest: "Religion & humanity had nothing to do with this question. Interest alone is the governing principle with Nations. If the Northern States consult their interest, they will not oppose the increase of slaves which will increase the commodities of which they will become the carriers."

The quid pro quo that was achieved was a cold-blooded one. Northerners, who mostly sought a stronger central government, won for the federal government the right to control commerce, the right (never actually used) to levy direct taxes on the states, and, more equivocally, the right to terminate the slave trade after twenty years. In addition, with Southern acquiescence, Congress approved the Northwest Ordinance, which barred slavery from the trans-Appalachian country north of the Ohio River. The small states were pacified with the creation of the Senate, where each state would enjoy equal representation. In order to secure ratification of the Constitution in the South, Yankee delegates agreed that each slave would count as three-fifths of a person—the so-called federal ratio—for the purpose of apportioning the size of a state's delegation in the House of Representatives, and consequently in the Electoral College as well, where each state's votes were the sum of its members in both houses of Congress. This meant that the slave states would have one-third more seats in Congress than their free population alone warranted. The free states were required to recognize all laws protecting slavery; they were prohibited from emancipating slaves who had fled to them for safety from other states and were mandated to restore runaways to their owners. Finally, Congress was empowered to order state militias to suppress insurrections, including slave rebellions.

Beaten antislavery delegates understood how much had been sacrificed to accommodate the slaveholders. "The admission of slaves into the representation, when fairly explained, comes to this," one-legged Gouverneur Morris of New York fairly snarled: "that the inhabitant of Georgia and South Carolina who goes to the coast of Africa and, in defiance of the most sacred laws of humanity, tears away his fellow creatures from their dearest connections and damns them to the most cruel bondage, shall have more votes in a government instituted for protection of the rights of mankind than the citizen of Pennsylvania or

New Jersey who views with a laudable horror so nefarious a practice."
Two generations later, the abolitionist William Lloyd Garrison would
forge their defeat into fiery polemics. He would curse the Constitution
as a "devil's pact" and a "covenant with death" that had fatally yoked the
people of the free states to intolerable sin. For decades to come, the federal ratio would preclude any attempt to revise the status of slaves and
ensure that the South could defend slavery as a fundamental national
institution even against a growing majority of white voters. Without
the federal ratio as the deciding factor in House votes, slavery would
have been excluded from Missouri in 1820, Andrew Jackson's removal
of Native Americans from the South in the 1830s would have failed,
slavery would have been banned in the territories won from Mexico in
the 1840s, and the Kansas-Nebraska Act of 1854 would not have been
able to open the Western territories to slavery. The federal ratio would
also give the South the power to systematically gag free debate over
slavery in Congress for more than half a century, beginning with the
First Congress in the spring of 1790.

Because the Founders failed to deal with the conundrum of slavery
in the 1790s, the South's problem would become the entire nation's.
As Joseph Ellis has put it, "We know full well what they could perceive dimly, if at all—namely, that slavery would become the central
and defining problem for the next seventy years of American history;
that the inability to take decisive action against slavery in the decades
immediately following the Revolution permitted the size of the enslaved
population to grow exponentially and the legal and political institutions
of the developing U.S. government to become entwined in compromises with slavery's persistence; and that eventually over six hundred
thousand Americans would die in the bloodiest war to resolve the crisis,
a trauma generating social shock waves that would reverberate for at
least another century."

THE SHADOW OF slavery brooded over the deliberations that
took place in Federal Hall throughout September 1789, as partisans
of the different sites attempted to reverse the vote for the Susque-

hanna. The debate proved particularly popular with spectators, who crowded into the elevated gallery—the "palladium of liberty," as it was known—where they annoyed the congressmen by loudly cracking nuts with their teeth and treading on the shells. Fissures that had opened during the Constitutional Convention yawned ever wider. Theodore Sedgwick of Massachusetts argued sarcastically that only by including slaves in the census could the Potomac be made to seem the demographic center of the country. And if slaves were to be counted, he provocatively demanded, why not count the black cattle of New England on the other side? Sedgwick added hyperbolically "that the climate of the Patowmack is not only unhealthy, but destructive to Northern constitutions. Vast numbers of eastern adventurers have gone to the Southern states, and all have found their graves there." Fisher Ames, also of Massachusetts, accurately noted that the Potomac was too shallow for navigation in the summer months. The eminent young doctor Benjamin Rush, a partisan of Philadelphia, who was earning a reputation as one of the most eloquent white advocates for the rights of his native city's African Americans, ominously warned vice president Adams: "By *delaying* the removal of Congress to Philadelphia, you will probably be dragged in a few years hence to the banks of the Potomac, where Negro slaves will be your servants by day, mosquitos your sentinels by night, and bilious fevers your companions every summer and fall, and pleurisies every spring."

In defense of the Potomac, James Madison, arguably the deftest politician in Congress, inserted himself into the debate. In contrast to war heroes like Washington and Hamilton, Madison had (like Jefferson) spent the war as a politician. At thirty-nine, he was one of American history's rare examples of a wholly political man who owed his influence more to sheer intellect than to seniority, connections, or personal charisma. Humorless and monkish in demeanor, he disappointed many who dealt with him as a "cloistered pedant," and a "gloomy, stiff creature." But none doubted his brilliance. He and fellow Virginian Jefferson had begun working to bring the capital to the Potomac as early as 1783. They believed that a Potomac site would attract immigrants and commerce to both Virginia and Maryland, not to mention guaranteeing

Southerners, as Jefferson bluntly acknowledged, "the advantages of a favorable bias in the Executive officers." George Washington joined them as an enthusiastic ally, from his retirement at Mount Vernon. His travels in the Ohio River watershed—a vast region encompassing western Pennsylvania, much of present-day West Virginia, as well as the future states of Ohio and Indiana—had strengthened his belief that the Potomac must become the nation's key highway to the West.

Madison was usually regarded as one of the staunchest advocates of vigorous central government. But against those who objected to placing the capital on the Potomac, he now rose to defend the interests of his native state, declaring with studied dismay that had Virginians heard such disparaging sentiments toward their region expressed at their ratification convention for the Constitution, they might never have joined the union at all. He was shocked that anyone should presume to call the Potomac a "Southern" river; it was really a *Western* one, since future settlement would surely flow up it to Kentucky and the Ohio country. On September 17 another Virginian, Richard Bland Lee, moved to replace the Susquehanna in the enabling legislation with the "banks of the Potomac," menacingly reiterating that should Congress dare to keep the capital in Pennsylvania, it would devastate Southerners' faith in the union. But Lee's motion failed. Congress voted once again to establish the capital on the Susquehanna. By all rights, the notion of a Potomac capital now should have been dead. But Madison had barely even begun to fight.

Of course, the bill also required the approval of the Senate. And that was where things began to go wrong. In the Senate, the leading advocate for the Susquehanna was William Maclay, of Harrisburg, Pennsylvania, whose puckered and bony face and sour disposition seemed to embody his pinched view of the larger world. But he knew the Susquehanna well, having surveyed the land along its banks, and having once served as a state commissioner responsible for clearing obstructions from its rocky bed. He also hated slavery with icy Presbyterian zeal. Unfortunately for the causes he espoused, Maclay was a man of Olympian stubbornness which ill-fitted him for the flexible, if not Machiavellian, horse trading of congressional negotiation.

The debate in the Senate pitted Maclay against his fellow Pennsylvania senator, Robert Morris, a massive, genial man of immense appetites and grandiose ambitions. Although democrats like Maclay regarded him as sly and arrogant, John Adams praised him for his "masterly understanding, an open temper, and an honest heart." Born in Liverpool, Morris was brought as a child to Maryland, where he was orphaned at the age of thirteen. He was raised by his father's friend Charles Willing, who took him into his Philadelphia trading firm, where he proved a quick study, cornering the city's flour market while still in his teens, it was said, and becoming a partner at the age of twenty-two. He invested in anything that might turn a profit: tobacco, ships, frontier back lands, indigo, slaves. Morris and Willing sometimes served as agents for masters hunting runaway slaves, and when imported white indentured laborers were scarce, they imported slaves from the West Indies and Africa, advertising in 1758, for example, "parcels of likely young Negroes" along with newly arrived shipments of rum, sugar, and cordage. In May 1762 they put on sale the largest single shipment of slaves ever to disembark in Philadelphia: 170 premium stock from the Gold Coast, all with "natural good Dispositions, and being better capable of hard Labour." Although Morris's credentials as a patriot were impeccable, he was no democrat. He deplored the politics of "the mob," regarded amendments to the Constitution with disdain, and supported lifetime appointment to the Senate, whose debates he sought to close to the general public. At the same time, he was profoundly modern in his faith in the free market, the creative use of investment capital, and new—even futuristic—technology. After the first Paris balloon ascension, in 1783, he had enthused, "Pray cannot they contrive to send Passengers with a Man to steer the course, so as to make them the means of conveyance for Dispatches from one Country to another, or must they only be sent for intelligence to the Moon and Clouds?"

As the decade advanced, Morris's life would become intimately entwined with the fate of the federal city. More than almost any other man, he would be counted on to make the fantastic plan for the national metropolis a reality, bridging the idealistic hopes of the Founders with the embryonic American faith in big money and the capitalist spirit. To Americans of his time, he was the archetypal money man, and he enjoyed a unique reputation as a man who could get things done. During the last months of the war, he served as the rebellious colonies' superintendent of finance, in effect its secretary of the treasury. He had pledged his personal fortune as collateral to pay the wages of the Continental Army, and once went from house to house in Philadelphia, rousing wealthy friends from their beds to borrow money to pay the troops. (His enemies, however, accused him of profiteering, by siphoning public money into his own accounts.) After the war, he turned to land speculation, buying and selling millions of acres of frontier land, usually with money borrowed on the strength of his name. Now he was promising to find the money to build the new city. He might well have been remembered as the man who made the capital a reality. Instead, his role has virtually been buried beneath the avalanche of disgrace that followed his thunderous fall from power. It would be a personal and political collapse of titanic proportions that would nearly wreck the plan for the capital before it was even built.

In autumn 1789 Morris's primary goal was to sabotage the plan to put the capital on the Susquehanna. While he harbored not the slightest doubt that the capital would be established in Pennsylvania, he much preferred that it be placed either at Germantown, just outside Philadelphia, or on the Delaware River near Trenton, New Jersey, where—not coincidentally—for years he had been steadily acquiring land. Maclay was furious when he realized what his fellow senator was up to. "Mr. Morris [was] running backwards and forwards like a boy, taking out one senator after another to them," he fulminated in his diary. "No business was ever treated with more barefaced partiality." Without any official sanction, Morris even promised $100,000 from the State of Pennsylvania to establish the capital at Germantown. When Maclay demanded to know on what authority Morris could promise such money, "He now came forward the Great Man and the Merchant, and pledged himself that if the state would not he would find the money." In other words, Morris would simply pay for it out of his own pocket.

The legislative ballet that now took place under Morris's direction was a tour de force of political choreography. Behind the scenes, Morris lobbied senators from several Northern states to switch their support from the Susquehanna to the Delaware. He believed, with some reason, that many Northerners didn't really care where the capital was, so long as it was north of Maryland. And he was sure that his fellow Pennsylvanians would never vote against a permanent location anywhere within their state. He promised the two New York senators that if they voted for Germantown, he and his allies would agree to block removal of the government from New York City before 1793, even if the new capital was ready sooner. On September 24 Morris moved to delete the Susquehanna from the bill, and to leave a blank space in its place, confidently anticipating that if he played his cards deftly it would be filled by Germantown. For much of the day, flurries of conflicting motions clouded the debate. First Maclay moved that Morris's proposal be ruled out of order. The Virginians then moved that the Potomac be reconsidered for the seat of government. Still another motion called for the capital to be placed on the Susquehanna in *Maryland*. Morris then repeated his promise to provide $100,000 from the State of Pennsylvania if the capital was placed at Germantown. Finally, as Morris had planned, his backroom lobbying paid off. When at last the votes were counted on his original motion, the Susquehanna was struck out. Morris immediately proposed inserting Germantown in its stead. Appalled by Morris's ploy, Maclay was so furious that he voted against the motion, leaving the Senate evenly divided, nine to nine. The fate of the Susquehanna— and, as it turned out, Pennsylvania—now rested in the hands of Vice President John Adams, who held the deciding vote.

Measured by temperament and background, at fifty-four Adams had more in common with the crusty, plain-spoken Maclay than he did with plutocrats like Morris, much less with the polished slaveholding aristocrats who wielded so much influence in the new government. A Yankee farmer's son born and bred in a pinewood farmhouse within sight of Massachusetts Bay, Adams was frugal, independent, devoid of affectation, and his own worst enemy. He could be woefully awkward in his relations with others and contentious to the point of rudeness. He enjoyed political support in New England. However, even his political ally Alexander Hamilton considered him unfit to be president. Others derided him as everything from a feebleminded crank to a closet Tory. Maclay, who truly despised him, believed that he lacked both the sound judgment and "respectability" to fill the office of vice president, cruelly but memorably writing of Adams that, "I cannot help thinking of a Monkey just put into Breeches when I see him betray such evident marks of self-conceit."

Adams now rose to cast his vote. No one knew what he would say. A brief entry in Maclay's diary is the only record of what happened. Facing the eighteen senators gathered on the second floor of Federal Hall, the vice president first praised the Potomac, in order to mollify the Virginians, Maclay thought. He then made some sort of slighting remark about the Susquehanna. Next he spoke highly of both Philadelphia and New York, suggesting that in his personal opinion Congress ought to alternate between the two cities, spending four years at a time in each. But since Pennsylvania—that is, Robert Morris—had offered $100,000, he would vote for Germantown. "Thus fell our hopes," wrote the devastated Maclay.

Although Morris did not yet know it, he had overplayed his hand. The Potomac's partisans were playing an even subtler game. Its genius was James Madison. The House took up the Senate bill on September 28. Madison knew that unless he found a way to cripple it, the capital would still go to a site somewhere in Pennsylvania. With characteristic subtlety, he discerned an oversight in the bill so hair-splitting that he surmised, correctly, no congressman would object to its correction. He pointed out that the bill failed to specify what jurisdiction would govern the Federal District until Congress took over. Would it be Pennsylvania law? Federal law? Some other law? Madison then slyly proposed a seemingly innocuous amendment. He moved that the laws of Pennsylvania remain in force in the new capital until Congress voted otherwise. He spent the weekend relentlessly lobbying his fellow representatives: when the House met on Monday, his amendment was adopted with only the most perfunctory discussion. The Pennsylvanians had been outfoxed before they caught on to what was happening. It was the end of the session. Amendment required that the whole bill now be returned to the Senate—which immediately voted to postpone it to the next session of Congress, effectively killing it. Morris would have to start the whole process again from scratch.

THE POTOMAC'S ADVOCATES realized that if they were ever to overcome Pennsylvania, they had to win the support of Americans outside the South. That autumn they launched what may have been the country's first nationwide public relations blitz. Their claims were founded for the most part on an influential essay that appeared in a Baltimore newspaper in January 1789 by George Walker, a transplanted Scottish merchant based in George Town. Walker was passionately devoted to the commercial promotion of the Potomac. Writing as "A Citizen of the World," he argued that the Potomac was the perfect location for the capital because it was equidistant between the North and South, easily defended, and naturally attractive to international investment. "Thus a connexion and energy would be given to commerce and manufactures, the arts and sciences, civilization and elegant refinement, hitherto unknown in America," he opined. Walker was the first to suggest placing the capital between Rock Creek and the Eastern Branch of the Potomac, just below George Town. He also suggested a practical plan for the city's development, including the innovative notion of using the sale of public lots to finance the construction of government buildings, a method that he predicted ought to easily raise at least $10 million at no cost to taxpayers. "A great city would be raised up as if by magic," Walker predicted.

Soon newspapers and broadsides from around the region were declaring grandiosely that the situation of George Town was "without parallel on the terraqueous globe," and predicting that if the capital were established there its manufactures would soon "clothe and cherish the perishing sufferers in the wilds of Siberia, as well as the pampered Alderman on the English Exchange." The Potomac itself, one of the "most distinguished rivers of the world," was "capacious enough to contain the fleets of the universal world." The river's propagandists made access to the West a pivotal argument, assuring settlers that traveling via the Potomac would require merely seventeen miles of land portage to reach the Ohio River. Soon the Potomac's waters would "groan under the pressure of New England manufactures" heading west. (Never mind that the Potomac's bed was a stone washboard, and far too shallow much of the year to float anything bigger than a canoe.) Although George Washington remained publicly silent, his total commitment to the scheme was well known. "It is in fact the interest of the President of the United States that pushes the Potomack," William Maclay complained to his diary. "He by means of Jefferson, Madison, [Charles] Carroll, and others urges this business." The ante was upped further when, in December, Virginia and Maryland jointly promised $192,000 for the construction of government buildings at a site to be selected anywhere on the Maryland side of the Potomac.

WHILE THE SENATORS argued, L'Enfant dreamed. It was said of him, with truth, that he always thought *en grande*—on an epic scale. A city was even now taking shape in his fertile imagination, a city unlike any that existed anywhere on the globe, compared to which Federal Hall would seem but an architectural bauble. When Americans spoke of a "seat of government," they could scarcely imagine anything much larger than the scrubby county towns that shambled around their rural crossroads. True, the Frenchman would admit, there was a handful of cities that pretended to be something more: New York, Boston, Charleston, and of course Philadelphia, although L'Enfant found the Quaker city's grid of streets boring and repulsive. Memories of Versailles and its vast symmetries flickered through his overcharged brain. Given a free hand, his would be a city for the ages, a masterwork that would make him immortal. He had already begun lobbying Washington for the commission to design the capital, telling the president, with typical immodesty, that bringing to fruition "a Federal City, which is to become the Capital of this vast Empire, offers so great an occasion for acquiring reputation that your Excellency will not be surprised that my ambition and the desire I have of becoming a useful citizen should lead me to wish to share in the undertaking." L'Enfant never shrank from self-promotion. But he believed with a passion that the capital must be something extraordinary: that it must incorporate the very spirit of the nation, that it must command the world's respect and express the future greatness of a nation yet to be. "It will be obvious," he told Washington, "that the plan should be drawn on such a scale as to leave room for that aggrandizement and embellishment which the increase of the wealth of the Nation will permit it to pursue at any period however remote."

Chapter 2

DINNER AT JEFFERSON'S

"Seize your chance now, men of the South!"

—JAMES MADISON

IN THE SPRING OF 1790 morbid curiosity drew streams of visitors to lower Broadway, in New York City, where excavations for the new president's mansion on the site of the old colonial fort had exposed the coffins of Lady and Lord Bellamont, the colony's governor a century before. Just seven years after the end of the Revolution and only three years after the adoption of the Constitution, this grisly attraction served as a graphic symbol of the uprooting of the British monarchy from its American foundations. One afternoon in late June, sightseers who came to view the coffins might have recognized two of the most powerful men in the United States walking back and forth, deep in conversation, in front of President Washington's four-story Palladian residence nearby at Exchange Place. The two were a striking physical contrast: one short, compact, and fine-boned, with startlingly blue eyes; the other much taller, red-haired, more languorous in his movements. The shorter man, the boyishly self-confident Alexander Hamilton, the secretary of the treasury, seemed overwrought. In the words of his companion, Thomas Jefferson, the secretary of state, Hamilton painted "a pathetic picture" of the infant government on the brink of collapse. For months, the secretary of the treasury fruitlessly had been urging Congress to enact a plan to stabilize the nation's battered public credit. But sectional bitterness was rapidly corroding the delicate consensus that had made the Constitution possible. Congress was at a standstill. There was even talk of secession.

Hamilton confided that he desperately needed Southern support for his scheme to have the federal government take responsibility for the war debts of the individual states, a measure that was imperative to satisfy increasingly unhappy foreign creditors. Hamilton told him, according to Jefferson, "It was probable that an appeal from me to the judgment and discretion of some of my friends might effect a change in the vote, and the machine of government, now suspended, might be again set into motion." Jefferson added, quite disingenuously, "I told him that I was really a stranger to the whole subject; not having yet informed myself of the system of finances adopted." Nevertheless, maybe he could still help, he replied; reasonable men could surely find some kind of solution, couldn't they? Jefferson invited the secretary of the treasury to dine at his home the next day, promising encouragingly that he "would invite a friend or two, bring them into conference together."

Jefferson, who had just spent the past five years as the American ambassador to France, knew perfectly well that the government was facing a financial crisis. Unpaid national debts threatened to ruin both the country's credit and its credibility at home and abroad. He also knew that he had Hamilton over a political barrel. He didn't care much for the newly appointed secretary of the treasury, whom he considered to be in thrall to New York money men, and whom he suspected of authoritarian tendencies that could undermine the republican institutions that had been won at such bloody cost. In time, Jefferson's suspicion would ripen into hatred. But at the moment Hamilton had something that Jefferson and his allies wanted: enough influence in the fractious Congress to ensure that the nation's capital was planted securely on the Potomac River.

A<small>T THE END</small> of the 1780s the nation's ramshackle financial system, such as it was, resembled that of a twentieth-century banana republic. Paper money issued by Congress during the war was virtually worthless. Liquid capital was scarce. Money that might have been invested in trade or productive agriculture was being sucked away by unbridled speculation in frontier lands and discounted securities issued during the Revolutionary War. In some states, crushing taxes stifled commerce. Elsewhere, land values and commodity prices were shriveling. Debt swarmed over the economic landscape like runaway kudzu. No one even knew the size of the public debt, or what divisions of government owed what to whom. "We are in the dark at present, inasmuch as we do not know the real amount," confessed one uneasy Pennsylvania congressman. "I do believe we are now walking on the brink of a precipice, that will be dangerous for us to step too fast upon." Hamilton was charged with the unenviable task of mapping the country's financial plight and finding a path to solvency.

The vast bulk of the debt dated from the war. First there was the foreign debt. The revolutionary government had scant resources of its own, beyond the expedient of printing reams of increasingly worthless paper money. So in order to pay its running expenses, the Continental Congress had borrowed more than $10 million from the French treasury and Dutch bankers, as well as a small amount from the Spanish monarchy. On these debts alone, Americans were now in arrears by $1.6 million on interest payments and another $1.4 million on payments of principal. Nearly $500,000 in new payments to overseas creditors was continuing to fall due annually. In addition to having printed $200 million in unsecured paper money—which was now barely redeemable even at a rate of forty to one—Congress had also raised money by issuing bonds and securities, mainly for paying and supplying the soldiers of the Continental Army. On top of this, the individual states owed their own wartime debts to private creditors at home and abroad, and to the national government itself. Complicating matters further, accounting practices in the states ranged from inadequate to incompetent to downright fraudulent. Hamilton plunged into this tangled wilderness and had emerged with some truly alarming numbers. He discovered that taken altogether, the federal government and the states owed a staggering $79 million. The total annual interest bill amounted to $4.5 million, triple the foreseeable national income. Simply paying the interest on the foreign debt alone would devour the entire yearly income from the tariff on imports, the national government's only existing tax, with nothing left over to pay the government's operating budget, much less to service the even larger domestic debt.

The challenge facing Hamilton was to craft a policy that would sufficiently restore national credit to enable the government to borrow money again in the future. Creditors had to be shown that the United States had the will to honor its debts as well as the actual funds to do so. Washington had chosen his secretary of the treasury wisely. Unlike Jefferson, Madison, and the president himself, all of whom had been born to power, and who exercised it almost in a spirit of noblesse oblige, Hamilton had claimed it by sheer force of personality. Raised in near poverty on the Caribbean sugar islands of Nevis and St. Croix, where his mother eked out a precarious existence as a shopkeeper, he had soared into the galaxy of the nation's revolutionary elite like a meteorite appearing suddenly from the outer constellations of the colonial world. In contrast to his slaveholding father, who surrendered to the casual tyranny of a planter's life, the fiercely ambitious son rejected provincial insignificance and eagerly seized the opportunity to reinvent himself on a larger stage. It was his good fortune that a philanthropic merchant recognized him early as an intellectual prodigy and underwrote his studies at King's College in New York, where he almost immediately embraced the cause of the colonies against the crown, eventually rising to become George Washington's personal aide-de-camp during the war. In 1784 he became a founder of New York's first bank, the Bank of New York. Along with Madison and John Jay, he was a principal author of the *Federalist Papers*, which had laid out the basic arguments for a strong central government and helped pave the way for the Constitutional Convention. In contrast to the many rural men who occupied seats in Congress, Hamilton believed that government could and should wield the power of money as a dynamic tool to advance the national interest.

The plan that the secretary of the treasury unveiled at the beginning of February 1790 was for most congressmen their first lesson in the alien sphere of creative capitalism. Hamilton proposed that the federal government assume responsibility for the entire consolidated federal and state war debt, and commit itself to paying off the interest in a reliable and timely fashion. He believed that once the government had regained creditworthiness, the debt could serve as a form of collateral: government bonds issued against it and backed by a trustworthy federal government could function as a vast reservoir of de facto capital, which in turn could be used to invest in national development. This would, in addition, strengthen the government itself by giving creditors a stake in its stability—precisely because it would owe them money. As reasonable as Hamilton's proposal might seem two centuries later, it was both radical and confusing to Americans in 1790, many of whom wanted to repudiate the entire debt, or at least the interest on it. So unfamiliar were the concepts he advocated that to many in Congress he might as well have been speaking Chinese. As the New Englander Fisher Ames, who understood business better than most, remarked to his fellow House-members, "The science of finance is new in America."

Hamilton's determination to repay the debts meant that a great deal of money would have to be raised somehow. The most obvious way to do so was of course to impose a new menu of federal taxes. This would be a hard sell, especially to congressmen from back country districts where currency was close to nonexistent and the reach of federal power was especially weak. In a country that had just fought a war for independence in part against unjust taxation, as well as an imperious crown, Americans were notoriously hostile toward taxation by their own elected leaders. Indeed, a few years later Hamilton's tax on distilled whiskey, a staple of the frontier economy, would provoke outright insurrection in western Pennsylvania.

Revaluing the tens of thousands of securities—essentially IOUs that had been issued to Revolutionary War soldiers in lieu of pay, to citizens who had loaned money for the war effort, and to others in exchange for confiscated property—posed another particularly thorny problem. These were now trading in the open market for as little as fifteen cents on the dollar. Speculators had bought them up wholesale from jobbers and from veterans themselves, many of whom preferred cash in hand to pie in the sky. Hamilton provoked an outcry when he affirmed that the present holders of securities must be paid full face value. Hamilton's opponents conjured up pathetic scenes of impoverished war veterans being driven penniless into the wilderness, having been plundered of their reward by greedy New York and Philadelphia financiers. "Immense sums were thus filched from the poor and ignorant," scathingly wrote Jefferson, who adhered to the popular view that only the veterans deserved to receive the securities' full value. Hamilton responded to his critics that as a matter of principle financial transactions must not be retroactively reversed. Yes, that meant that thousands of veterans would lose out. Yes, speculators—including members of Congress who had bought up discounted IOUs—would reap a windfall. But there was a larger cause at stake, he maintained. To discriminate against the present holders of securities, whoever they were, would make the paper nonnegotiable and thus cripple its value: future investors would never again have confidence in government securities and would shun them in the marketplace. However, raising the securities to market value, as the secretary of the treasury wished, would assist the process of translating the national deficit into a long-term asset by converting them from essentially junk into desirable investments.

The debate began on February 8, 1790. Hamilton seemed to be everywhere, fairly bristling with excitement, lobbying the indecisive and urging on his supporters with élan. Broadly speaking, Hamilton's plans were favored by the commercial North and opposed by the rural South—with the exception of South Carolina, which one of its representatives declared "was no more able to grapple with her enormous debt than a boy of twelve years is to grapple with a giant." Massachusetts, Connecticut, and South Carolina, which had suffered particularly badly during the war, owed almost half of the state debts and were eager to embrace federal assumption. New York and Pennsylvania were major creditors of the national government, and avidly supported any increase in federal revenues. On the other side, populists generally believed that public debt was a curse, and regarded Hamilton's plan as a kind of financial coup d'état by New York and Philadelphia designed to subvert state sovereignty in favor of federal power. Virginia and North Carolina, having paid off much of their state war debts—North Carolina had even written into its constitution an amendment barring congressional interference with its state debt—had little or nothing to gain from assumption, and resented the prospect of bailing out states that had not paid off their own. They were a bloc to be reckoned with: between them, they held nearly a fourth of the seats in the House of Representatives. Madison, the single most effective member of the House, opposed long-term debt both as a Virginian and as a matter of principle, fearing that it would fall into foreign hands. Others, including William Maclay and Thomas Jefferson, who although he was not a member of Congress nonetheless exerted a significant moral influence, feared that Hamilton's scheme would also fuel rampant speculation. Apart from the equally intractable debate over the site of the national capital, no issue inspired more passion or more insidious distrust. Some in New England threatened to leave the union if state war debts were not taken over, while some Southerners threatened to secede if they were.

SLAVERY HAD RARELY been mentioned in the debates of 1789. Then in February, it burst like a coarse and unwelcome guest onto the floor of Congress. Scarcely had the debate over Hamilton's assumption plan begun when Quakers surprised the lawmakers by submitting two petitions calling on the federal government to end the African slave trade, and urging it to "take such measures in their wisdom, as the powers with which they are invested will authorize, for promoting the abolition of slavery." In what may have been the first grassroots lobbying campaign in American history, sober-faced Quakers in their distinctive black hats and frock coats cornered congressmen in the colonnaded anteroom of Federal Hall, and appeared without warning at the doors of their private lodgings, insisting on talking about slavery. Two hundred years later, when lobbying is arguably Washington's biggest industry after government itself, it is hard to imagine the consternation that the Quakers caused. On the floor of Congress, as the *Gazette of the United States* rather understatedly put it, "a warm debate ensued." Some considered the Quakers' behavior downright subversive. "They had even obtruded themselves into the committee with a ready made report in their hands, calculated to violate the Constitution and overturn the government," sputtered William Smith, a congressman from South Carolina. Criticism of the transatlantic slave *trade* was comparatively respectable. Even many slaveholders paid public lip service to its "immorality." But talking openly about abolition was a kind of racial treason that was shocking beyond belief.

With few exceptions, congressmen of all stripes regarded the petitions as an embarrassment at best. Benjamin Huntington, of Connecticut, where slavery although in decline was still legal, warned that even well-intentioned interference with it "may excite a great degree of restlessness in the minds of those it is intended to serve, and that may be a cause for the masters to use more rigor toward them." Vice President Adams might have been expected to offer some support to the Quakers. He had never owned a slave, always made it a point to employ freemen as domestics and laborers at his home in Massachusetts, and was known to believe in gradual emancipation. But like many nominally antislavery Northerners, he also believed that slavery would disappear naturally if it were let alone. In any case, he considered poor public morals, the decline of educational standards, and "general debauchery" more worthy of his concern than the plight of black slaves. As presiding officer of the Senate, however, he had the duty of presenting the Quaker petitions to that body. He did so, William Maclay recorded, "rather with a sneer."

The debate, which stretched into March, was dominated by proslavery speakers. The case for slavery was made at length by James Jackson, a lean, hatchet-faced planter who owned a thousand acres of rice-growing land tilled by slaves on the Altamaha River in Georgia. He denounced even the slightest discussion of so incendiary a subject. If Quakers wanted to free the Negroes, they should come forth and buy them, or else "they should keep themselves quiet," he shouted. (Jackson himself was often so loud that the House was asked to shut its windows so as not to disturb the senators in their chamber.) "Slavery is an ill habit but when once contracted, there are cases where slavery is absolutely necessary," he went on. Without slaves, large tracts would remain uncultivated, and the rice trade would fall into the hands of the Spanish. Was Congress willing to abandon the revenue it derived from the rice trade just "to gratify the supposed feelings—the theoretical speculations on humanity" of the petitioners? Quakers who professed to be acting in Christian spirit didn't even understand their own religion, he sneered, since they were acting in a way "diametrically opposed to the commands of their divine master, Jesus Christ, who allowed it in his day, and his apostles after him—not to mention the Egyptians, Babylonians, Jews, and Greeks." After all, even the "purest sons of freedom in the Grecian republics" had held slaves. Slavery in America was a distinct blessing on those whom the Quakers presented as victims, since Africans "would better be imported here by millions than stay in their own country in despotic slavery." But moral issues were really beside the point. The habit of slavery was well established, and Congress could not interfere with it without endangering the whole system of government, he told the House. To challenge slavery was to attempt to subvert the government. The Quakers were veritably "blowing the trumpet of sedition." Jackson warned menacingly of civil war: "the people of the southern states will resist one tyranny as soon as another; the other parts of the continent may bear them down by force of arms, but they will never suffer themselves to be divested of their property without a struggle."

A third petition, from the Pennsylvania Abolition Society, was signed by its president Benjamin Franklin, and called explicitly for abolition. During the debate, the aged Franklin savagely mocked the hypocrisy of proslavery ideologues in a brilliant satire, literally written on his deathbed, putting Jackson's speech almost word for word into the mouth of a fictional Barbary Arab, one "Sidi Mehemet Ibrahim," who asserted that without the continued kidnapping and enslavement of white Christians, the Algerian economy would collapse: "If we forbear to make Slaves of their People, who in this hot Climate are to cultivate our Lands? Who are to perform the common Labours of our City, and in our Families? Must we not then be our own Slaves?" Freeing their white slaves would be an injustice, since they would inevitably become a burden on Algerian society, for "Men long accustom'd to Slavery will not work for a Livelihood when not compell'd." In captivity, on the other hand, they were fed, clothed, and lodged at no expense to themselves, and blessed by exposure to the splendorous sunlight of true religion—Islam. Opined "Ibrahim," "Sending the Slaves home then would be sending them out of Light into Darkness."

Meanwhile, the debate ground on. William Smith of South Carolina verbally shrugged off the horrors of the Middle Passage, blithely reminding members that "all voyages must be attended with inconveniences." But he, too, reserved his harshest words for the Quakers, who in his opinion were advocating the outright robbery of legal property from honest men. He reminded Congress that the very existence of the nation represented a compromise on both sides: "we took each other with our mutual bad habits and respective evils, for better for worse; the northern states adopted us with our slaves, we adopted them with their Quakers." Madison, like Jefferson, affected distaste for slavery, and shunned the crude rhetoric of Jackson and Smith. But he was no less determined than they to ensure that no discussion of slavery take place on the floor of Congress. Indeed, his goal was to establish a precedent that would permanently preclude any national commitment to emancipation. Under his direction, the committee assigned to report on the petitions declared explicitly that Congress had no authority to either emancipate slaves or to interfere with their treatment within any state. It was a stinging repudiation of the Quakers' hopes: legislation that they had envisioned as the beginning of a peaceful general emancipation of the nation's slaves had been captured by slavery's defenders and transformed into a ban not only on emancipation itself, but even on public discussion of it in the halls of Congress. President Washington wrote to a friend, with palpable if premature relief, that "the slave business has at last [been] put to rest and will scarce awake."

WITH THE IRRITATING anti-slavery petitions now out of the way, Congress returned to the knotty problem of Hamilton's financial reforms, and the future site of the national capital. By the end of May, Congress was doubly paralyzed, unable either to adopt Hamilton's proposals or to decide where to establish the federal city. On June 2, however, the House finally enacted most of the core elements of Hamilton's plan. New loans would be floated to pay interest on the existing debt. A sinking fund would be created to reassure creditors that the government was committed in principle to retiring the debt in full. And against Madison's stony opposition, Congress also agreed to reimburse the holders of government securities at face value. It was a watershed moment in the history of American finance, simultaneously establishing the basis for securities trading and institutionalizing public debt as a new tool of economic management.

To Hamilton's immense chagrin, however, the House deleted the bill's irreconcilably controversial section on the federal government's assumption of state debts. The secretary of the treasury was frantic with frustration. Conflicting political loyalties were a Gordian knot that defied solution. The financier Robert Morris, who was firmly committed to assumption, still wanted to place the capital on the Delaware. Maclay was an enemy of assumption, and championed the Susquehanna. Hamilton personally wished to keep the capital in New York—so closely associated was he with the city's interests that some termed it "Hamiltonopolis"—but he was committed to assumption at all costs. The South Carolinians ardently supported assumption, but were determined to block any attempt to put the capital in Pennsylvania. South Carolina Congressman Aedanus Burke fulminated that if the seat of the government capital were placed even temporarily anywhere near Philadelphia, it would be "like putting the hand into a steel trap"—the government would never get free. Maryland's representatives were divided, some favoring a Potomac capital, and others Baltimore; some were pro-assumption and others against. Jefferson opposed assumption, and was firmly committed to the Potomac. President Washington, who was wholly committed to both the Potomac and to assumption, managed to finesse every issue by projecting an impression of impassive rectitude. Madison, an advocate for the Potomac and an enemy of assumption, adroitly maintained that since the war had been a common cause its cost should be equally apportioned, but that states (like Virginia) that had paid most of their war debts should not be compelled to bail out states that had not.

A sour and helpless mood hung over Congress. Some members were urging that the whole question of a permanent capital be put aside while an agreement was reached on a new location for the temporary one. It would have made great practical sense for the government to simply remain in New York City. Congress was comfortably settled there, and it offered amenities that no city besides Philadelphia could match. But New York's supporters lacked both the passionate single-mindedness and the influence of the Pennsylvanians and the advocates for more southerly locations. The debate largely reprised the arguments of the previous autumn. Congressmen were so exhausted that they hardly knew what they were voting on anymore. Alliances shifted constantly, lasting sometimes no more than a few days. On May 30 supporters of moving the capital temporarily from New York to Philadelphia were defeated thirteen to eleven in the Senate. A few days later, removal to Philadelphia was carried in the House by thirty-eight to twenty-two. The next week, the House voted to move to Baltimore, fifty-three to six. "This was not the effect of choice, but of the confusion into which they had been brought," Jefferson wrote to his Virginia friend, George Mason. Elbridge Gerry exclaimed in exasperation, "[I]f we are to bring forward motions like the present at every session, we may be drove to Williamsburg or Marietta." (In 1790, to mention Marietta, a fortified frontier town on the Ohio River, was something like proposing that the capital be put in Alaska.) Rumors of secret deals and backroom betrayals were everywhere. Maclay, who still failed to realize that the prize had slipped through his own fingers, was also disgusted. "It was nothing but Snip, Snap & Contradiction," he wrote in his diary. "I left the Senate Chamber compleatly sickened."

By the second week in June, pressure to come to a decision was intense. On June 8 the Senate again voted down a motion to place the permanent capital on the banks of the Potomac. Baltimore and Wilmington were also voted down. The mere suggestion of placing the government in Philadelphia—the home of those obstreperous Quakers, abolitionists, growing numbers of free blacks, and money men like Robert Morris—roused such violent opposition that ailing Senator Samuel

Johnston of North Carolina was carried bodily into the chamber in a sedan chair with a nightcap on his head to cast his vote against it. Philadelphia's opponents groused that its servants were unreliable, its citizens subversive, and its climate ruinous to the health. Congressmen would have little hope of raising children there, the *New-York Daily Gazette* warned with barely disguised glee, "where it has been proved that there are from 4 to 11 funerals of children every day during the fall seasons." However, Morris remained confident that he could manage to take the capital to Germantown. He knew Hamilton to be the key to Northern votes. On June 11 he initiated a meeting, announcing in a note to Hamilton that he would be taking an early morning walk on the Battery, a 1,450-foot-long earthwork that ran from modern Battery Place to Whitehall Street, and suggesting that if the secretary of the treasury had anything to propose to him, he might meet him there "as if by accident." Hamilton had an agenda of his own. He asked Morris to secure one more vote for the federal assumption of debt in the Senate and five in the House. If he got them, Hamilton promised the permanent seat would go to either Germantown or the falls of the Delaware. Morris, overreaching once again, egregiously demanded as the price for his cooperation that Philadelphia be named not only the permanent capital, but also the temporary one as well.

Unable to meet Morris's extortionate terms, Hamilton proposed to Maclay through a go-between that Pennsylvania would have the permanent capital on the Susquehanna, if the state's delegation voted for assumption. Maclay was indignant. He could barely contain himself "within the bounds of decency." He refused to bargain with a man he deemed to be insincere. "I gave him such looks and answers, as put an End [to] this business," Maclay told his diary. "I considered assumption so politically wrong and productive of so much injustice that no offer could be made which would induce me to change my mind." This was Pennsylvania's last chance. Maclay thus finished what Morris had begun. Their stubbornness cost the North the capital.

Although Jefferson portrayed himself as a financial naïf, he knew that the opponents of assumption would have to compromise. He wrote to his son-in-law, "Congress are much embarrassed by the two questions of assumption, and residence. All proceedings seem to be arrested till these can be got over, and for the peace and continuance of the union, a mutual sacrifice of opinion & interest is become the duty of everyone: for it is evident that if every one retains inflexibly his present opinion, there will be no bill passed at all for the funding of the public debts, & if they separate without funding, there is an end of the government. The only choice is among disagreeable things." Regarding the capital, Jefferson added that one of the proposed compromises that was in the air would give the capital to Philadelphia for a fixed period of years, and then establish it permanently at George Town. "This is the best arrangement we have now any prospect of, & therefore the one to which all our wishes are at present pointed. If this does not take place, something much worse will; to wit an unqualified assumption & and the permanent seat on the Delaware."

At the end of that week Jefferson bumped into Hamilton in front of the president's house. Jefferson later described their encounter as a coincidence. It may well have been. But after months of stalemate, both men were primed to cut a deal.

WHEN JEFFERSON ARRIVED in New York in March, he had expected to find a house on Bowling Green, "the center of residence in the fashionable world," as a contemporary newspaper had described it. But all the best quarters had already been occupied by members of Congress. A little crankily, he resigned himself to make do with a small "indifferent" dwelling rented from a grocer at 57 Maiden Lane. To make it at least minimally suitable, he hired carpenters to build a book gallery on the back of the house; he also laid in stocks of madeira, claret, cider, and porter (as well as a new chamber pot), and bought two new engravings of President Washington, which would gaze down impassively on the men who gathered there on (most probably) the afternoon of June 20.

Jefferson and Hamilton may well have begun by exchanging the latest details of the shocking scandal that had just broken. A Georgian named Telfair, who may have been related to that state's governor, had cut his throat with a razor on the morning of June 19. Everyone was talking cryptically about the "astonishing attachment" of Telfair's black serving boy, who could only be separated from his master's body by force, and who could barely be restrained "from committing violence on himself." The incident hinted enigmatically at both an unsavory and illicit intimacy, a secret shame, and more reassuringly—to those who wished to think so—at slaves' childlike devotion to their owners and their quaint capacity for love and loyalty.

The men who face each other over Jefferson's dining table represent the pole stars of the republic's power elite. Picture the red-haired Jefferson at the age of forty-seven, dressed as he often is in clothes too small for his long figure, lounging characteristically on one hip with one of his shoulders elevated above the other, his face deceptively vacant. Hamilton's small-boned face is weary but concentrated, and etched with the open and martial manner that befits a genuine war hero, who nine years earlier personally led a bayonet charge over the British ramparts at Yorktown. This military crispness does not endear him to Jefferson, who has never been in battle, and who as wartime governor of Virginia ignominiously fled his capital at the approach of redcoats led by the traitor Benedict Arnold. The third figure at the table, "Little Jemmy" Madison, radiates equally an impression of intellectual incisiveness and of sickly fatigue. The three men have known each other for years, and their shifting relationships have never been more complex. Hamilton considers Jefferson a utopian dilettante. Jefferson, the administration's most radical democrat, finds the prospect of compromise with the secretary of the treasury's Northern banker friends utterly repugnant. Although Madison and Hamilton were once intimates, as Hamilton's promotion of strong central government has deepened, Madison has moved closer to Jefferson as an advocate for the interests of the rural Southern planter class to which they both belong.

There is yet another, only half-visible presence at Jefferson's table: twenty-five-year-old James Hemings, Jefferson's slave chef. He is the brother of Jefferson's enslaved mistress-to-be, Sally Hemings, as well as the illegitimate half-brother of Jefferson's dead wife, Martha, whose father sired a generation of black Hemingses upon his slaves. No one will ask his opinion about assumption of state debts or about the future national capital, of course. But his hovering figure—*"Another glass of claret, Mr. Madison?"*—speaks eloquently in its way of the obscured existence of the many thousands of African Americans who are working out their destinies alongside the great men of the age. Hemings has accompanied Jefferson to France, and watched that country's Revolution unfold before his eyes. Now, all around him in New York, he sees newly emancipated blacks inventing lives for themselves in freedom. (Although the number of slaves is growing in the city, so is that of freed people, of whom there are about one thousand in 1790.) Before the decade is out, Hemings, too, will become free, with Jefferson's resentful acquiescence. For the moment, however, poised behind three of the most powerful men in America, he stands silently for the seven hundred thousand enslaved Americans whose future hangs in the balance tonight.

They can expect little from Jefferson and Madison, both of whom own slaves. Jefferson was one of the largest slaveholders in Virginia, with two hundred men, women, and children working his estates. Jefferson's clarion assertion in the Declaration of Independence that "all men are created equal" would eventually become the battle cry of abolitionism, and he indeed condemned slavery as unjust, in principle. But he was also infected by color prejudice of the deepest dye. Although he would father several children by the very light-skinned Sally Hemings, he felt an ingrained repugnance toward black people whom—he claimed with what he imagined to be scientific objectivity—emitted "a very strong and disagreeable odor," felt less pain than whites, and were incapable of higher thought. "Among the blacks is misery enough, God knows, but no poetry," he lamented. He also harbored grotesque psychosexual fantasies of a sort that would haunt relations between the races for generations. Blacks, he wrote, were more highly sexualized, driven by an animal-like lust after whites' "elegant symmetry of form" as predictably as the orangutan supposedly craved black women over his own species. In other words, blacks were driven by unbridled, animal-like lust, along with a terrifying proclivity toward sex with white women. At bottom, he was terrified of black rebellion. "Deep rooted prejudices entertained by the whites; ten thousand recollections, by the blacks, of the injuries they have sustained" would inevitably produce "convulsions" that would finally lead to the extermination of one race or the other. Madison, too, believed that emancipation could only mean economic and political catastrophe for Virginia and the entire South.

Hamilton was something entirely different. Rare among men of his time, he grasped the basic psychology of racism and rejected the notion of black inferiority. "Their natural faculties are probably as good as ours," he wrote to his fellow New Yorker and emancipationist, John Jay, chief justice of the United States. "The contempt we have been taught to entertain for the blacks makes us fancy many things that are founded in neither reason nor experience." Hamilton was a driving force in the New York Manumission Society, and in 1785 had issued a proposal for gradual emancipation that so distressed the society's members—many of whom were slaveholders—that the society issued an official apology. He nonetheless continued to lobby the state legislature to halt the export of slaves from New York to the West Indies and the Southern states. During the war, he had even proposed recruiting a regiment of slaves to fight in return for their freedom. In words that would not have been out of place coming from Frederick Douglass or John Brown, he had argued that arming slaves would "animate their courage" and "have a good influence upon those who remain [in slavery], by opening a door to their emancipation." However, in June 1790 nothing mattered more to him than winning support for assumption.

Hamilton had it within his power to ensure that the national capital remained in the North—or to hand it to the South. As New York's leading politician, he effectively controlled most of the votes of the Northern members who were committed to assumption. Madison, on the other hand, had the votes to block Hamilton's assumption plan indefinitely. But both he and Jefferson, and their allies, wanted the capital. Madison made it clear that the Southerners were willing to bargain.

The only version of what actually happened at the dinner is Jefferson's rather self-serving one, penned more than thirty years afterward. "The discussion took place. I could take no part in it, but an exhortatory one, because I was a stranger to the circumstances which should govern it," Jefferson wrote; this was untrue, but by 1824 no one bothered to argue with him. What is clear is that the Virginians finally agreed that defeating Hamilton's financial plan would amount to a pyrrhic victory at the expense of national unity. They would compromise on this, a matter of high principal as they saw it, in order to preserve the union. Some of the plan's opponents would have to switch their votes. But compromise would come at a high price. "It was observed," wrote Jefferson, "that this pill would be especially bitter to the Southern States, and that some concomitant measure should be adopted to sweeten it a little to them."

The sweetener was to be the national capital. Madison promised to provide at least three votes for Hamilton's assumption plan, guaranteeing its passage. In return, Hamilton agreed to urge his friends not to stand in the way of the capital's establishment on the Potomac. Twisting the knife of compromise yet deeper, the Virginians forced Hamilton to agree to favorably recalibrate Virginia's debt, ensuring that assumption would cost them nothing, and that they could also proclaim that they had won the capital for the South.

To assuage the Pennsylvanians, the capital would be transferred from New York to Philadelphia for ten years, while the necessary government buildings were erected somewhere on the Potomac. This "anodyne," as Jefferson put it, was expected to calm the ferment stirred by the South's surrender on assumption. "So two of the Potomac members (White and Lee, but White with a revulsion of stomach almost convulsive) agreed to change their votes, and Hamilton undertook to carry the other point," Jefferson wrote. The two grudging turncoats were not altruists. Richard Bland Lee—who had warned of secession if the South failed to get its way—received a promise that Alexandria, the main town in his congressional district, would be included in the new Federal District. Alexander White represented Virginia from Harper's Ferry west to the Ohio, a region that was expected to enjoy a massive economic boom once the capital was built. With respect to speculators who had already bought up vast quantities of discounted securities in anticipation of the financial plan's passage, Jefferson added caustically: "The influence [Hamilton] had established with the agency of Robert Morris with those of the middle states effected his side of the engagement, and so the assumption was passed, and 20 millions of stock divided among favored states, and thrown in as pabulum to the stock-jobbing herd." Two more equally self-interested votes also switched sides, those of Daniel Carroll, whose district included George Town and the whole north shore of the Potomac, and George Gale of Maryland's Eastern Shore, another ardent partisan of the Potomac scheme. To ensure the measure's passage in the Senate, Charles Carroll, whose ten-thousand-acre estate lay near the Potomac, just south of Frederick, Maryland, agreed to flip as well.

Hamilton had attained his goal. But the sacrifice was a heavy one. He confessed, "the funding system including the assumption is the primary national object. All subordinate points which oppose it must be sacrificed." New York would now never become the London or Paris that it might well have been, had the capital remained there. Construction of the president's palace on Bowling Green would be halted. The grand plans for imperial boulevards and parks would remain stillborn. But something even greater had also been traded away over Jefferson's dinner table: the country's last real chance to root its capital in the increasingly free soil of the North.

In Congress, debate over both assumption and the residency question continued awhile longer through the withering heat of July. When some Southern members sought to replace the Potomac with Baltimore, Madison reminded them that the Potomac site represented a tremendous victory for the South, both politically and, implicitly, in the interest of slavery. "We have it now in our power to procure a southern position," he warned. "The opportunity may not again speedily present itself. If the Patowmack is struck out, are you sure of getting Baltimore? Instead of Baltimore it is not improbable we may have Susquehanna inserted, perhaps the Delaware?"—in other words, a free state. "Seize your chance now, men of the South! Act now, without further debate, lest the bill be wholly defeated and the prospect of obtaining a southern position vanish forever."

Southerners well knew what was at stake. Deepening suspicion of Northern intentions along with a wildly exaggerated fear of Northern power had percolated through the South following the debate over the Quaker petitions. From his estate in Virginia, Revolutionary War hero Henry "Lighthorse Harry" Lee—the future father of Robert E. Lee—wrote to his friend Madison that it was imperative to increase Southern influence over the federal government. "The introduction of the southern youth as clerks in the high departments of the nation seems to me to be a sure tho slow means of Aiding the southern influence," he urged, pointing out that over time such young men would inexorably rise to positions of power. "I wish our southern gentlemen would in due time attend to this material truth—if they do not a monopoly will take place from the northern hives in this, as in everything else in their power. To disunite is dreadful in my mind, but dreadful as it is, I consider it a lesser evil than union on the present conditions. I had rather submit myself to all the hazards of war & risk the loss of everything dear to me in life, than to live under the rule of a fixed insolent northern majority."

On July 16 Congress finally enacted the residence bill, as it was called. A few days later, Hamilton's assumption bill became law, with the assistance of the votes Madison had promised. In both cases, the votes broke almost completely along sectional lines, foreshadowing the rift between North and South that would only grow with time. Precisely where on the Potomac the new capital would be put the bill did not say—merely somewhere between the Anacostia River, opposite Alexandria, and Conochocheague Creek, about sixty-five miles upriver. The choice would be left up to President Washington. New Yorkers and their allies, deprived of the temporary capital, reacted with vitriol. One newspaper cartoon showed Robert Morris being led by the devil to Philadelphia, where a whore beckoned alongside a man in women's clothing, who was labeled Congress's procuress. A flood of invective filled New York newspapers, including the following poetical defense of "virtuous Yorkites," from the pen of one "T.C.":

> *Canst thou with patience see the ingrates spurn*
> *At all thou'st done, and not with fury burn?*
> *Oh call them ingrates, call them fools and knaves.*

Just in case any readers failed to identify the culprits, T.C. savaged the "wretched slaves" in Congress, who he alleged had been bribed by Robert Morris's "long purse," as well as Southern parties to the compromise:

> *Offending states with utmost freedom lash,*
> *And call Virginia's polish'd members trash—*

Let nought confine thy zeal and patriot rage,
Indulge thy fury, 'twill thy griefs assuage.

Southerners were ecstatic, however. Exclaimed Representative Michael Stone of Maryland, "Joy! Joy to myself! Joy to my Country! Joy to the United States! Joy to the lovers of Mankind!"

The act was as much Pennsylvania's failure as it was Virginia's victory. Madison and his allies had played a weak hand brilliantly. Pennsylvania had played a strong one abysmally. The capital had been well within its grasp. But instead of a Hamilton or a Jefferson to advance its cause, it had the cramped personality of William Maclay and the self-seeking Robert Morris. Maclay felt utterly defeated. "I cannot even find a single member to condole in sincerity with me, over the political calamities of my country," he brooded. "Let me deliver myself from the company of such men, for I verily believe the sun never shone upon a more abandoned composition of political characters." He knew that he had been outclassed. He also understood that a historic opportunity had been missed, and that the United States would be a different kind of country with its capital on the Potomac. "Fixed as Congress will be among men of other minds on the Potowmack, a new influence will in all probability take place," he wrote glumly. "And the men of New England, who have hitherto been held in check by the patronage and loaves and fishes of the President, combined with the firm expectation that his resignation (which is expected) will throw all power into their hands, may be refractory and endeavor to unhinge the government. I cannot however help concluding that all things would have been better on the Susquehannah."

Philadelphians rejoiced at the government's removal from New York's "sink of political vice," as the reformer Benjamin Rush termed it, to their own more sober city, which they prided themselves in believing was less in thrall to ostentation and genteel dissipation. Throughout the autumn, the Quaker city was abustle with arriving dignitaries and their entourage of clerks, secretaries, journalists, petitioners, and office seekers. (Getting to Philadelphia was not always easy: Aedanus Burke of South Carolina was shipwrecked in Delaware Bay, while James Jackson of Georgia suffered such tumultuous seas that he was convinced that he would die en route.)

The city fathers turned over Philadelphia's new county courthouse to the federal government for the use of Congress. Offices for the various federal departments were hastily acquired. President Washington settled into the luxurious townhouse of his friend, the financier Robert Morris, and the Adamses at an estate two miles outside the city, for what they considered the exorbitant rent of $400 per month. By New Year's Day 1791 the transition was complete. Philadelphians confidently assured each other that with the national government now comfortably settled on the Delaware, it would never want to relocate to cow pastures on the Potomac.

SEEN FROM THE angle of national survival, the compromise brokered over Jefferson's dinner table was a kind of success. The infant republic would survive, for the time being. As with the better known compromises that would follow in 1820 and 1850, the interests of slavery had been protected at the expense of freedom, and open sectional conflict had been postponed for a few decades more. But in the course of the bitter debates over the capital and assumption, fissures appeared that would only widen, between the interests of commerce and those of the plantation, between centralized power and the states, between North and South, and between the slave states and the (increasingly) free.

Madison was right, of course. The Potomac would prove a comfortable home for the kind of government the South wanted, and for slavery. "The capital was placed where no professors from a university, no Quakers, no sophisticated financial operatives would rub up against the slaveholding natives," Garry Wills has written. "No major harbor would give a cosmopolitan air to the place. Here president after president would preside over an executive mansion maintained by slaves. Can one imagine a succession of twelve slaveholder presidents if the capital had remained in Philadelphia? The southerners got what they wanted, a seat of government where slavery would be taken for granted, where it would not need perpetual apology, excuse or palliation, where the most honored men in the nation were not to be criticized because they practiced and defended and gave privilege to the holding of slaves."

Chapter 3

POTOMAC FEVER

"There is such an intimate connection in political and pecuniary considerations between the federal district and the inland navigation of the Potowmac that no exertions, in my opinion, shou'd be dispensed with to accomplish the latter. Public and private motives therefore combine to hasten this work."

—GEORGE WASHINGTON

THE PRESIDENT ARRIVED IN George Town on March 28, after an exhausting seven-day journey on horseback, along glutinous, mud-choked roads from Philadelphia. A few miles outside George Town, Washington was met by its "principal citizens," who escorted him to his rooms at Suter's one-story inn on High Street, the only establishment fit for such an eminent guest. The town, eight miles upriver from Alexandria, had been established at the head of navigation to serve a colony of mostly Scottish merchants who traded in tobacco and frontier commodities such as corn, pork, and iron piloted on flat boats from the upper Potomac, sugar and molasses from the West Indies, and manufactured goods from England.

The landscape through which the president traveled was a familiar one, of course: his home at Mount Vernon lay just a few miles below Alexandria. Indeed, it was so familiar that its essential bleakness escaped his attention. Although Washington and other progressive farmers were shifting to less speculative crops like wheat, most Tidewater planters still relied on tobacco, the basis of the region's economy for almost two centuries. Tobacco cultivation was the strip-mining of its day. "Their method of farming is slovenly, without any regard to continue their Land in heart, for future Crops—They plant large Quantities of Land, without any Manure, & work it very hard to make the best of the Crop, and when the Crop comes off they take away the Fences to inclose another Piece of Land for the next year's tillage, and leave this a common to be destroyed by Winter & Beasts," Philip Fithian, a Princeton divinity student who was serving as a tutor on a local plantation, recorded in his diary. By 1791 much of the area's soil was effectively ruined. Less self-interested travelers than Washington typically remarked upon the dreary expanses of scrub and the poverty of local white smallholders, who clung tenuously to a dwindling number of miserable farms amid the plantations, with their scrawny cows and dwarfish sheep.

The capital's fate, and the nation's, rested in Washington's hands. The Residence Act that Congress passed the previous summer had set in motion a race against time that would grow increasingly desperate as the decade advanced. Although the opponents of the Potomac site had lost the battle in Congress, they had succeeded in imposing a deadline: the government's most important buildings—a meeting hall for Congress and the president's mansion—must be erected and the new capital made ready for occupancy by its officials no later than December 1800. Until then, Philadelphia would serve as the temporary seat of government. In the hope of stifling further debate, Congress gave Washington complete executive authority to carry out the project. If he did not succeed, Washington and everyone else knew perfectly well that Congress could reverse its commitment to the Potomac. The Virginia statesman George Mason, for one, believed that for at least another half century Congress would never escape from the "whirlpool of Philadelphia."

For Washington, failure was simply unacceptable. No man would expend more energy and political stock on the capital than he did, immersing himself in the minutiae of hiring and firing, the construction of roads and bridges, and even the pettiest financial questions. Knowing better than anyone how politically fragile the whole project really was, Washington turned even the slightest hint of reversal into a personal affront, wielding his most powerful weapon, his prestige, to enforce his will. Later in the year, for instance, when a vital compact that he negotiated with Potomac landowners showed signs of fraying, he informed them icily: "The pain which this occurrence occasions me is the more palpably felt, as I had taken pleasure during my journey through the several states, to relate the agreement, and to speak of it, on every proper occasion." Put plainly: *You have made a fool of me. You have embarrassed me, and I will not have it!*

Could he really bring off a project this vast, this ambitious, and this expensive? Could the country? Nothing of such magnitude or such fraught symbolic importance had ever been attempted in North America. Washington's vision of a national metropolis aspired to create an entirely new kind of American city that embodied in bricks, mortar, and ashlar the soaring hopes, the latent power, and the still tenuous unity of the embryonic nation. Failure could mean national collapse. Contentious debate would resume. Sectional distrust would deepen. If predictions such as George Mason's proved correct, Southern congressmen who feared that even their own slaves would be seduced from them by the insidious propaganda of Yankee Quakers would undoubtedly renew their threats to break up the union. The task facing Washington, America's Romulus, was a daunting one indeed.

Congress had mandated only that the capital be established somewhere between George Town and the green waters of remote, tongue-twisting Conococheague (pronounced Co-no-ko-cheeg) Creek, which empties into the Potomac at Williamsport, Maryland, 65 miles to the north as the crow flies, and 150 miles via the twisting course of the river. All that Congress specified was that the district was to be no more than 100 miles square in area. The exact location was left up to the president. In October 1790 Washington had traveled upriver, ostensibly to scout

out competitive locations. Beginning at George Town, he rode north through Frederick, Maryland; Shepherdstown, Virginia; Sharpsburg and Elizabethtown (later Hagerstown), both in Maryland; and finally Williamsport, on the much mocked Conococheague. Although the preponderance of congressional sentiment clearly favored an upriver site, some members sneered that it was insane to place Congress in a place "dug out of the rocky wilderness," where it would have to take up residence in "an Indian wigwam," and that the very sound of "Conococheague" was so disturbing that it made ladies shrink. At each stop, dignitaries lavished praise on the president and on the virtues of their rustic hamlets. Washington's performance was impressively judicious. But this was really just political theater, a grand gesture to suggest that he was taking alternative sites seriously. He had in fact made up his mind long before. He was determined to place the capital close to the Eastern Branch, today known as the Anacostia River, virtually across the Potomac from his own estate at Mount Vernon.

In the spring of 1791 Washington was fifty-nine, and uneasily aware of his mortality: few Washingtons had lived beyond fifty. He was a physical giant, standing well over six feet, with broad hips and shoulders, and the famously stony, sun-reddened visage that men habitually described as "commanding." Since the war, he had also grown into a kind of secular deity, "a Roman hero or a Grecian god," in the words of the contemporary poet Philip Freneau, enjoying a personal charisma unmatched by any of his contemporaries. Many regarded him with an almost religious piety. "His mind dwells in the midst of great things, and mingles in trifles with difficulty," wrote one awestruck admirer. Another, Philadelphian Richard Rush, who as a boy once saw Washington stride solemnly through a crowd on his way to address Congress, never forgot the scene as the president paused at the entrance to Independence Hall and turned for all to see. "He stood in all his civic dignity and moral grandeur, erect, serene, majestic," Rush recalled years later. "Profound stillness reigned. Not a word was heard, not a breath. Palpitations took the place of sounds. It was a feeling infinitely beyond that which vents itself in shouts. All were gazing, in mute unutterable admiration. Every eye was riveted on that form—the greatest, purest, most exalted of mortals."

Washington had not achieved this kind of adulation as a result of battlefield brilliance, having lost more fights than he won, sometimes quite badly, most notably in his incompetent failure to hold New York, where he squandered thousands of his troops needlessly. However, he was physically brave to the point of near foolhardiness, and he reassured Americans with a manly stoicism that lent spine to a nation that repeatedly seemed on the brink of disintegration. Not everyone was awed by Washington: the ever caustic Senator William Maclay complained, "No Virginian can talk on any Subject, but the perfections of Genl. Washington it weaves itself into every conversation." And John Adams would later sarcastically mock his "strain of Shakespearean excellence at dramatic exhibitions," manifested by his taste, as president, for stagy ceremony and uniformed retainers. He was also a surprisingly poor speaker who, when he delivered a speech, "was agitated and embarrassed more than ever he was by the leveled cannon or pointed musket." Washington was, nonetheless, a truly inspired leader of men, whose devotion to the cause of independence was second to none. His stature was further enhanced when, after the war, he relinquished power and returned gracefully to civilian life. He wore power as naturally as he sat astride a horse (he was widely declared to be the best rider in all of horse-obsessed Virginia), and for a man with an only shallowly rooted sense of religion, he believed in his own destiny, and the nation's dependence upon him, with a faith that bordered on the mystical. He desired above all else immortality in the hearts of Americans yet unborn, an idea as quintessentially classical as fluted columns and Corinthian capitals, and which he would do everything in his power to promote, and risk nothing to subvert.

Throughout his career, Washington cultivated a serene acceptance of life and fate, believing that whatever befell him, he was morally bound to face it with courage and chilly dignity. Beneath his toga of public nobility, he was a creature of considerable ambiguity, cryptic by design. When a woman once casually remarked that she could read his joy in his face, he retorted, "You are wrong! My countenance never yet betrayed my feelings!" Although he detested slavery, he was one of the largest slaveholders in Virginia. His marriage to the handsome and amiable young widow Martha Custis in 1759 made him the master of her 84 slaves, and eventually of another 170 slaves who were owned by her son Jacky Custis. By 1791 nearly three hundred African Americans were at work on his farms around Mount Vernon. In his younger days, he had raffled off slaves for entertainment, and blithely packed off troublemakers to the death-camp plantations of the West Indies, without any evidence of moral reflection on the human consequences of what he was doing. But with greater moral courage than Jefferson or Madison, Washington was now beginning to face the personal hypocrisy of continuing to own slaves while espousing the revolutionary ideal of human equality, particularly since he had personally witnessed the fortitude of black troops under fire. Indeed, his own manservant Billy Lee, who accompanied him throughout the war, had nearly been killed at the battle of Monmouth by a cannonball that was intended for Washington and his staff.

Although many Americans continued to hope that slavery would wither away on its own, the facts told a different story: the number of slaves in Virginia had metastasized from 13,000 in 1700 to 105,000 in 1750, and to 292,627 in 1790. Countless masters, like George Washington's friend, neighbor, fellow slaveholder, and soon-to-be commissioner of the federal city, David Stuart, paid lip service to slavery's "evil," but assuaged whatever incipient guilt they might feel with a facile pragmatism. "Their work is worth little if they are not whipped," Stuart assured a foreign visitor. "We would all agree to free these people; but how to do it with such a great number? This unfortunate black color has made such a sharp distinction between the two races. It will always make them a separate caste which in spite of all the enlightenment of philosophy will always be regarded as an inferior class which will never mix with the society of whites."

The real question was: should you rationalize it, as Thomas Jefferson evasively did, or do something about it? Like the soldier that he was, Washington gradually decided to face up to that question and to act on what he knew to be the truth. Home at Mount Vernon, his day-to-day concerns were typical of those of any master, complaining about his slaves' malingering, sloppy work, and even occasional acts of sabotage. But he had come to believe that their shortcomings derived from the inherent degradation of slavery, not from racial inferiority. After the war, he had seriously discussed with the passionately abolitionist Marquis de Lafayette acquiring lands where freed slaves might be settled, to serve as encouragement to slaveholders to free their human property. Although this plan came to nothing, Washington himself quit buying more slaves and stopped selling those he already owned, unless they agreed. "The unfortunate condition of the persons, whose labour in part I employed, has been the only unavoidable subject of regret," Washington told his early biographer David Humphreys. "To make the adults among them as easy & comfortable in their circumstances as their actual state of ignorance & improvidence would admit; & to lay a foundation to prepare the rising generation for a destiny different from that in which they were born; afforded some satisfaction to my mind, & could not I hope be displeasing to the justice of the Creator." It would be years before he emancipated any of his own slaves, and in the meantime he would dispatch agents to hunt those who made a break for freedom. Nonetheless, Washington had profoundly changed. "In the last decade of his life Washington grasped some truth about slavery that was eluding everyone around him," historian Henry Wiencek has written. "For all its superficial benevolence, the slave regime cloaked crimes that Washington could no longer stomach."

Earlier than most Americans, Washington also understood that the nation's future would be shaped profoundly by the great tidal flow of westward settlement. Although Tidewater born and bred, Washington was in important respects a man of the West. He had learned the ways of the frontier as a youth, traveling by canoe, surveying the deep wilderness of the Ohio Country, and dealing with native tribesmen with impressive sangfroid. In 1748, at the age of sixteen, he had noted in his diary, "We were agreeably surprised at y. Sight of thirty of Indians coming from War with only one scalp. We had some Liquor with us of which we gave them Part it elevated there spirits put them in y. Humour of Dauncing." Six years later, as the leader of a company of Virginia militia, he ambushed and slaughtered a party of unsuspecting French soldiers deep in the wilderness of western Pennsylvania, thus firing the first shots of the French and Indian War. Years afterward, he boasted that the Indians had named him "Caunotaucarius"—"Towntaker." After that war, he eagerly began his insatiable lifelong quest to acquire speculative property in the West, at one point secretly employing an agent under the guise of a hunting expedition to "secure some of the most valuable lands." His avid quest for western land was not matched by a comparable affinity for its mostly poor white settlers, who with an aristocrat's disdain he contemptuously dismissed as uncouth as "dogs or cats."

Washington was the most famous victim of what the skeptical called "Potomac Fever," an obsessive conviction that the Potomac River was destined as if by the will of God to serve as the nation's gateway to its bountiful interior. "It is the River, more than any other, in my opinion, which must, in the natural progress of things, connect by its inland navigation . . . the Atlantic States with the vast region which is populating (beyond all conception) to the Westward of it," he would write in December 1791. "It is designated by law for the seat of Empire; and must, from its extensive course through a rich and populous country become, in time, the grand Emporium of North America." Using boosterish language to breezily compress the size of a vast and difficult region, Washington described a busy riverine highway that would someday carry "the whole produce of that rich and extensive vale between the Blue Ridge and the Alligany [sic] Mountains." To appreciate the president's thinking, it is necessary to reimagine an America virtually without roads, in which nearly all long-distance travel and commercial shipping takes place by water. He proposed an elaborate zigzag route that, he argued persuasively, would enable farmers in the Ohio Valley to float their whiskey, iron, and tobacco east by first taking it up the Little Kanawha River into present-day West Virginia, then southeast into Virginia, then overland to the west fork of the Monongahela, then downstream to the Cheat, then by a second portage through the Allegheny highlands to the North Branch of the Potomac, and then finally down the Potomac to Alexandria and George Town, and ultimately to the Atlantic Ocean and Europe. Wilder dreamers even envisioned links to the Missouri River, and beyond. Today, such a scheme seems to defy logic. But in an era when nothing traveled in a straight line, it made a kind of sense, if rather less than Washington imagined.

Westward migration could be a dynamic engine of growth. But unless the emigrants were anchored to the settled part of the country, they "would in a few short years be as unconnected to us, indeed more so, than we are with South America," Washington worried. This was no idle concern. Separatists in Tennessee, Kentucky, and Vermont had already pressed for outright independence, and had initiated secret negotiations for alliance with Spain and Britain. Restive pioneers on the Monongahela frontier were agitating for the creation of a new state to be called Westsylvania. There was no reason to think that there would not be more such movements as the fingers of settlement stretched ever more tenuously westward. Many Americans believed it inevitable that the country divide into two parts, with the West backed by the nation's enemies. An article the previous year in the *Maryland Journal* had warned that the momentous selection of a site for the capital would determine whether the Union would "dissolve into the horrors of civil commotion," or flourish and prosper. Washington himself wrote elsewhere, "No well informed Mind need be told, that the flanks and rear of the United territory are possessed by other powers, and formidable ones too—nor how necessary it is to apply the cement of interest to bind all parts of it together, by one indissolvable band—particularly the Middle States with the Country immediately back of them." For the moment, Spain and England posed stumbling blocks to settlement. But what if they instead offered trade and alliances? "The Western Settlers—from my own observation—stand as it were on a pivet [*sic*]—the touch of a feather would almost incline them any way," he warned.

Washington certainly believed with real conviction that a new national city on the Potomac would help to bind the West to the Atlantic seaboard. But he also had a less elevated interest in the success of the capital: he and his friends stood to make a great deal of money from it. (Indeed, he raised the rents on his lands in the area as soon as Congress approved the Potomac site.) Their vehicle was the Patowmack Navigation Company, a profit-making corporation that was chartered in 1784 by the states of Virginia and Maryland, at Washington's instigation. Its membership read like a roster of the wealthiest landowners along the river. The state of Virginia purchased fifty of the initial five hundred shares of stock for $22,000—more than $769,000 in today's dollars—and presented them to Washington as a gift. He made a modest public show of reluctance, then accepted them without further demur. He also invested in the enterprise £2,500 of his own money, worth almost $250,000 today. This stood to make him fabulously wealthy, should the Potomac become the great commercial artery that the company wished. In May 1785 he wrote to his French protégé Lafayette that development of the river would produce "the greatest returns of any speculation I know of in the world." With Washington's encouragement, James Madison, Henry Lee, and other prominent politicians invested fortunes in land speculation near George Town, which the company was touting as a future manufacturing center, along with a canal to facilitate travel around the river's many falls and rapids. If the national capital were located there too, their £4,000 investment would be multiplied many times over. Washington was elected the company's president in 1785, in effect, its chief lobbyist, tirelessly telling all who would listen that the national interest was indissolubly wedded to the prosperity of the Potomac Valley and its landholders and slave owners. Although he lowered his profile as an advocate for the company after his election as president, his conflict of interest remained an open secret among the political elite. He did not publicly advertise the fact that development of the river would also dramatically increase the value of his by now vast land holdings in the West, which included almost five thousand acres in western Pennsylvania, and more than twenty thousand acres on the Ohio and Great Kanawha rivers, in present-day West Virginia—"the cream of the country," he gloated to friends. The Patowmack Company's first project got off to a promising start in 1786, when it purchased crews of slaves and set them to digging the canal. The work was brutal, and without families to tie them down as they might on a plantation, they posed a high risk of flight. To discourage them, their hair and eyebrows were shaved off to make recapture easy, the *Maryland Chronicle* matter-of-factly noted.

The interests of the company quickly became intertwined with the fate of the federal city. Although Washington continued to keep a tight grip on the project, on-the-spot management was placed in the hands of three commissioners whom he appointed. Their rather ill-defined powers provided that they supervise architects, surveyors, and laborers, as well as accept whatever tracts of land "the President shall deem proper to the use of the United States." Washington's selections for these powerful offices were revealing. All were old cronies. David Stuart was the administrator of Washington's private business affairs and his personal doctor, as well as the husband of Martha Washington's widowed daughter-in-law. Blunt-spoken Thomas Johnson, a former governor of Maryland, had nominated Washington as commander in chief of the Continental Army during the Revolution. Daniel Carroll of Rock Creek, one of the congressmen who had switched his vote on Hamilton's assumption plan at Madison's request, was one of the largest slaveholders in Montgomery County, and owned a four-thousand-acre plantation that lay partly within what would become the Federal District. None of the three had any experience in city planning, construction, or architecture. But all three were members of the Patowmack Navigation Company. Johnson had in fact taken over as its chief executive when Washington became president. The president saw his own role as that of ultimate arbiter, a commander in chief who would reason when possible, and if not, then beat the recalcitrant forward with the metaphorical flat of his sword. "I have a mind open to information, and a disposition always to correct abuses as far as I am able," he assured one of his landowning friends in the Federal District, Benjamin Stoddert.

Throughout the autumn and early winter of 1790 the country and an army of impatient speculators waited tensely for Washington to name the site for the capital. Everyone knew that the value of land would instantly soar. On January 24, 1791, Washington officially announced his choice: the federal city would be built between George Town and the Eastern Branch—where he had secretly intended to place it all along. Washington would later maintain that the site was a veritable Gibraltar, insisting that "No place, either north or south of this, can be more effectually secured against the attack of an Enemy."

The *Pennsylvania Gazette* commented meaningfully that "the Patow-mac Navigation is likely soon to acquire powerful assistance," and that "a monied interest" was expected to invest heavily in the company. In parts of the North there were gasps of dismay. The site lay at the southernmost tip of the congressionally mandated zone. Many North-ern congressmen who believed that when they approved a Potomac location for the capital they had explicitly voted for a more northerly site were now incredulous and angry. Others protested in vain that at George Town the Potomac was still deep enough for warships, and that the site was thus dangerously vulnerable to foreign attack. These critics were of course proved prescient when the capital was easily captured and burned by the British in 1814. But the living god had spoken.

Washington did have one significant obstacle to overcome. He now wanted Congress to extend the district's limit even farther south, to bring within its boundary Alexandria, then a bustling town of thirty-two hundred. Coincidentally or not, this would incorporate into the Federal District, 1,200 acres of Washington's own land, 950 acres belonging to George Washington's aide Custis (the future site of Arlington Cemetery), and several building lots that the president owned in downtown Alexan-dria. At this point, the capital's future became entangled once more, if temporarily, with Alexander Hamilton's financial plans.

In December, Hamilton had proposed the creation of a national bank modeled on the Bank of England, with one-fifth of its capital to be provided by the federal government. Hamilton argued that the bank would benefit the country, which suffered from chronic shortages of both reliable currency and investment capital, by servicing the national debt and by creating a deep well of credit that could be drawn upon by the country's growing economy; by means of its power to control credit, the bank would also be able to prevent excessive inflation or deflation. Despite such manifest benefits, Hamilton encountered fierce, if not entirely unexpected, opposition from those who feared that such a bank would make the government hostage to Northern financial inter-ests. Southerners led by Madison asserted that Congress had no power to charter a bank at all. When the bill passed over their opposition, Thomas Jefferson and Attorney General John Randolph, both Virginians, asserted that the bank's charter was inherently unconstitutional, since the Constitution had never provided for such an institution, and was therefore null and void. There was a self-serving subtext: the Virginians also feared that the bank would be powerful enough by 1800 to prevent the government's removal from Philadelphia to the Potomac. Hamilton countered that the bank was sanctioned by Article I of the Constitution, which authorized the federal government to make laws that it considered "necessary and proper" to carry out its duties. In mid-February, in the midst of this rancorous debate, the powerful Potomac landowner Charles Carroll introduced a bill to extend the Federal District southward to accommodate the president's desire to include Alexandria. For more than a week the outcome remained unclear. Finally, as they had the previous summer in New York, the opposing forces reached a compromise: Hamilton got his bank, and Washington got Alexandria. After Washington's death, John Adams acerbically declared that the decision had raised the value of the Washington and Custis properties 1,000 percent.

THE FEDERAL DISTRICT now had to be surveyed. For this crucial task, President Washington selected the prematurely graying, portly, thirty-eight-year-old Andrew Ellicott, one of the most famous men in America. He was, in the president's words, "a man of uncommon talents." A friend of Benjamin Franklin, Ellicott had completed the surveying of the Mason-Dixon line, which had been halted by the French and Indian War, and, possibly at Franklin's instigation, had undertaken the first professional survey of the Niagara River and of the great falls itself. Raised as a Quaker, he had rejected pacifism in order to serve in the Maryland militia during the Revolutionary War, rising to the rank of major, the title by which he preferred to be addressed. "Danger had been his own daily comrade throughout long years, privation and hardship he had met at the very outset of his career, and he had long ago learned how to make friends with them," his biographer, Catharine Van Cortlandt Mathews, wrote. Ellicott needed an assistant capable of doing rarified astronomical work, who was also willing to endure the physical discomforts of life in a surveyor's camp. He would have preferred to bring along one of his usual helpers, but they were all engaged on other projects. As a replacement, his cousin George Ellicott suggested someone who, though far less famous than Andrew Ellicott himself, was widely recognized nonetheless as one of the most remarkable men of his time, the amateur astronomer Benjamin Banneker.

Before the month of February was out, Banneker was looking northward across the Potomac from his post at Jones Point toward the panorama that filled the valley before him. The scene was a microcosm of the American landscape: an expanse of tangled woodland interrupted by scattered fields and farms, barely penetrated by roads. Nearby lay the port of Alexandria, and surrounding it the plantations of the young nation's aristocracy, both symbols and repositories of the economic power of slavery. A little to the north, Banneker could see George Town, a clump of low-slung buildings afloat on the tide of greenery, and closer in, the trough of the stream that had been dubbed the Tiber, after the river that flowed through ancient Rome. Its name portentously seemed to herald the splendor of the new capital that avid promoters promised was about to rise on its banks.

Banneker was bone tired. A big-bodied man, who some people said bore a certain resemblance to Benjamin Franklin, he was heavily muscled from decades of farm work. But the years weighed on him, as if his broad frame were the result of time pressing down upon him. His white hair made him look even older than he was. The rigors of camp life aggravated his gout and tried his naturally mild and philosophic disposition. His work for Ellicott required him to get up repeatedly in the night to point a telescope through a hole in his tent, to take new readings by the stars. Still, he enjoyed the silence of the night and the time alone. For sixty years he had lived his life quietly and unobtrusively within the narrow interstices of Maryland's unforgiving distinctions of race. But as he watched the passage of the planets, taking his measurements, he retreated into the divine world of numbers, a world devoid of double standards, where there was neither black skin nor white, only truth and untruth, a cosmic order where everything had a perfect place.

He was well aware that his presence here was something extraordinary. He fit neatly into none of the convenient pigeonholes to which his era assigned African Americans: he was a free man in an era when nearly all blacks were slaves, and an intellectual in a nation were even most whites were barely literate. Although deeply religious he belonged to no church, and although he would later be embraced by abolitionists as proof of Africans' intellectual equality, he shunned involvement in politics. He had been born in 1731, the grandson of a white woman, Molly Welsh, who had been deported from England and into indentured servitude for stealing a pail of milk, and a slave whom she later purchased and manumitted. In an era before color consciousness became a national obsession, when there was more uninhibited mixture among whites, blacks, and Indians on the frontier than later generations remembered, or at least cared to admit—at the time, as many as one quarter of the illegitimate children born to white women in the Chesapeake colonies may have been mulattoes—Welsh was less unique for choosing such a relationship than she was for legitimizing it by marriage.

By the 1790s distinctions of color and caste had confined the vast majority of blacks tightly within a slave system that was defined by laws that our own age would recognize as totalitarian. Slavery within the Federal District was typical of the region. Of the 720 people who lived there in 1791, exclusive of George Town and Alexandria, 591 were slaves. Masters, and even some European travelers, asserted that Tidewater slavery was "mild," by American standards. However, under the laws of Virginia and Maryland, which governed the district, slaves were barred from learning to read or write, possessing books (including the Bible), gathering without permission, leaving home without a pass, blowing horns or beating drums, or practicing medicine. (Thomas Jefferson, who counted himself an indulgent master, believed that for utilitarian reasons slaves should be taught to read, but not to write, to ensure that they were unable to forge free papers.) Any slave found abroad without a pass was treated as a runaway; free blacks who failed to produce a certificate of freedom could be, and often were, sold into slavery for jail costs. In Maryland, a fugitive slave who resisted arrest could legally be killed on the spot. In both states no slave, and in Virginia no free black, was allowed to testify in court cases in which whites were concerned. Blacks were permitted to testify against other African Americans, however. In Maryland the penalty for perjury was to have one ear cropped and thirty-nine lashes, and the next day, to have the other ear cropped and another thirty-nine lashes; in Virginia, the prisoner's ears were first nailed to the pillory before cropping. Minor offenses like stealing and house-breaking were punishable by death.

Even on the plantations of comparatively benign masters, the labor was grueling. George Washington expected his slaves to work up to sixteen hours a day, six days a week, "and be diligent while they are at it." For clothing, Washington's slaves were periodically issued a jacket and a pair of homespun breeches per year, and were expected to wear them until they fell apart. Although the president allowed his slaves to keep chickens, he specifically barred them from raising ducks, geese, or pigs, which might have enabled them to accumulate capital. Living conditions were squalid. A European visitor to Mount Vernon was appalled to find adult slaves sleeping on mean pallets, and children on the bare ground. On the farm of Isaac Riley, just outside the Federal District in Rockville, Maryland, slaves lived "huddled, like cattle, ten or a dozen persons, men, women and children" to a room, recalled Josiah Henson, who was enslaved there as a boy, in the 1790s. "All ideas of refinement and decency were, of course, out of the question. Our beds were collections of straw and old rags, thrown down in the corners and boxed in with boards; a single blanket the only covering. The wind whistled and the rain and snow blew in through the cracks, and the damp earth soaked in the moisture till the floor was miry as a pig-sty." Typical for plantations in the region, the principal food on the Riley farm was cornmeal and salt herrings, along with vegetables that slaves raised in their own garden plots.

Slaves everywhere in the region were interwoven in the most intimate ways into the lives of the whites who owned them. They served as planters' concubines and body servants, suckled and tended their masters' white children, and gave birth to their own mulatto infants who bore the telltale print of their masters' features. Slavery distorted the lives of the enslaved and masters alike. "The whole commerce between master and slave is a perpetual exercise of the most boisterous passions, the most unremitting despotism on one part, and degrading submissions on the other," Thomas Jefferson famously observed. "Our children see this and learn to imitate it. The parent storms, the child looks on, catches the lineaments of wrath, puts on the same airs in the circle of smaller slaves, gives loose to the worst of passions, and thus nursed, educated, and daily exercised in tyranny, cannot but be stamped by it with odious peculiarities. The man must be a prodigy who can retain his manners and morals undepraved in such circumstances." Jefferson's insight into the psychology of enslavement never prompted him to embrace the cause of emancipation, however, or to free any slaves other than those of his favored concubine Sally Hemings.

Benjamin Banneker grew up sheltered from the shaming and degraded world of the plantation. Banneker—his name derived from that of his African grandfather, Bannaka, or Banneky—lived his entire life on his family's remote farm ten miles west of Baltimore, a town still so insecure as late as the 1750s that it was defended against marauding Indians by a stockade. Wolves and panthers prowled the forests around the Bannekers' log cabin. Roads were few, and carriages completely unknown. As a child, remarkably, he attended school with a mixed class of white and black children. He impressed his classmates even then. One later recalled that "all his delight was to dive into books," although Banneker never owned a book until the age of thirty-two, when he acquired a Bible. He was an acute and curious observer of everything he saw in the natural world, from the behavior of locusts to the density of snow. Often he passed the night wrapped in a cloak on the ground outside his cabin, contemplating the stars until dawn. He also exhibited an early talent for advanced mathematics. Then at the age of twenty-one, he astonished his neighbors by constructing a wooden clock from parts that he had carved by hand, with no model to work from other than a borrowed pocket watch.

Banneker's isolation was finally breached by the arrival of the worldly Ellicott family. The Ellicotts were Quakers from Pennsylvania who settled in Maryland in the early 1770s to establish a mill and general store in the craggy glen of the Patapsco River, a mile west of the

Banneker farm. The young man became something of a curiosity at the store, where the locals enjoyed testing him with difficult mathematical problems; not infrequently, he returned his answers in rhyme. Like Banneker, the Ellicotts were intellectuals of a distinctly American sort, largely self-taught, curious, inventive, and well read in whatever literature found its way into their hands. Their warm friendship across the color line was as unusual in Maryland's charged racial climate as Banneker's singular achievements. Banneker was fascinated by the advanced machinery in the Ellicotts' mill, the first in the area. But they bonded over clocks, when Joseph Ellicott—the cousin of the federal city's future surveyor, Andrew Ellicott—showed his own handmade timepieces to Banneker. Joseph's brother George, an amateur astronomer, became Banneker's best white friend, lending him books and instruments, and plunging the older man into a hectic immersion course in the celestial drama of the planets. The Ellicotts' generosity overwhelmed Banneker. As if spreading a banquet, the older man would arrange and rearrange all this rich food for his intellect on his rustic table, trying to decide what he would indulge in first. Chores were forgotten, tobacco fields left untended, apples left unpicked as his omnivorous mind devoured delicacies of abstruse calculations and reveled in the mathematical poetry of orbits and eclipses. "It is a hard matter for young Tyroes," Banneker sighed in a letter to George Ellicott, adding that although he felt stumped by the contradictory theories of different astronomers, "I hope the stagnation will not be of long duration." When he journeyed to the Potomac in 1791, Banneker was already thinking about publishing his astronomical observations. He was perhaps the only black man in North America who could entertain such a dream.

Andrew Ellicott could surely have found other men, white men, capable of carrying out the work that had been entrusted to Banneker. It is a measure of Ellicott's cocky independence of mind, and the self-confidence of a man at the pinnacle of his profession, that he hired his cousin George's candidate without reservations. Banneker was thrilled. He had never traveled much beyond the small world of the Patapsco, and he owned no clothing fit to wear in George Town or Alexandria. One of the Ellicott women was delegated to organize a respectable wardrobe for him, so that he would not feel embarrassed in the presence of the distinguished folk he was likely to meet. Turning his farm over to his sisters, he rode south toward the site of the federal city, forty miles away, farther than he had ever been from home in his life. His local fame as a mathematician preceded him. So curious was this brainy black man that his arrival was noted in the *George Town Weekly Ledger*, which reported that Ellicott was accompanied by "an Ethiopian, whose abilities, as a surveyor, and an astronomer, clearly prove that Mr. Jefferson's concluding that race of men were void of mental endowments was without foundation."

Few Americans were ready to accept that assessment in 1791. The white inventors of the new capital were promoting a national dream in which there was no sure place for blacks except as slaves. Banneker found the federal commissioners "a very civil set of gentlemen [who] overlooked his complexion on account of his attainments." However, he would spend his months in the Federal District mostly isolated from contact with local slaves and whites alike, except for Ellicott's crew. Shy, reserved, and circumspect, he preferred the company of the stars to the always problematic company of people. Invited to dine with Ellicott's men in George Town, he agreed to sit nearby, but alone at his own table, a posture that reflected perfectly his own suspension in the white man's world, the living symbol of the nation's racial divide, tolerated but never quite safe, admired but never quite understood, except perhaps by the Ellicotts.

THE PRESIDENT WAS all business on March 28, when he set up shop at John Suter's inn, a long, low building with a shady veranda on High Street (now Wisconsin Avenue). First he met with the three district commissioners, who outlined their plans for acquiring the land needed for the city from the landowners who occupied it. Then he examined the preliminary results of Ellicott's surveys, and after that the first sketches by the man he had personally engaged in January "to examine, & make a draught of the grounds" between George Town and the Eastern Branch: Peter Charles L'Enfant. The engineer had headed for the Potomac brimming with enthusiasm, certain that he was embarking on the greatest work of his career. In this he was not wrong. But it was a decision that would ruin his life. The reputation of the courtly immigrant "whose taste and talents are universally admired" (as a local newspaper put it) ran ahead of his arrival at George Town. The surveyor Andrew Ellicott found him "a most worthy French gentleman and tho' not one of the most handsome of men, he is from his good breeding, and native politeness, a first rate favorite among the ladies." At thirty-seven, L'Enfant's personality was a fusion of Gallic charm, slavish loyalty, overweening pride—"haughtiness," in the preferred language of the time—intellectual brilliance, and petulance. (Although the evidence is inconclusive, he was probably homosexual, which would make him, along with the Revolutionary War drillmaster Baron von Steuben, one of the most prominent gays involved in the nation's founding.) Where contemporaries complained of his "lofty self-regard" and inexplicable stubbornness, a later age might have diagnosed symptoms of neurosis and paranoia. The stolid Washington much admired L'Enfant's aesthetic judgment, however, and paternally returned the younger man's loyalty as one of the band of brothers who had stood fast with him during the terrible wartime winter at Valley Forge. He was willing to make allowances for L'Enfant's volatile temperament. But he clearly did not know what he was in for.

L'Enfant was awed by "the whole immensity of the business," the inspiring challenge of inventing a city "in a country devoid of internal resources . . . distant from materials and necessaries." The task was daunting indeed, especially since the federal government had appropriated no funds for the project, much less for L'Enfant's part in it. L'Enfant reported to Jefferson, whom Washington had delegated to oversee the design process. Jefferson in turn directed L'Enfant to make drawings of the land that seemed most appropriate for the "federal town," beginning at the Eastern Branch, and to "proceed from thence upwards"—that is, over present-day Capitol Hill—"laying down the hills, valleys, morasses, and waters between that, the Potomac, the Tyber, and the road leading from George Town."

On March 11, L'Enfant wrote to Jefferson that he had arrived late the previous Wednesday, after an apparently irksome journey, "having travelled part of the way on foot and part on horseback leaving the broken stage coach behind." In the days that followed, he slogged over rain-soaked hills that seemed to rise and sink "as the waves of a tempestuous sea," and thrashed across marshy bottomland, sketching as best he could. "As far as I was able to judge through a thick fog I passed on many spots which appeared to me raly [sic] beautiful and which seem to dispute with each other who command," he wrote to Jefferson, in his vivid, idiosyncratic English. In spite of the fog, he began to visualize "a situation most advantageous to run streets and prolong them on grand and far distant point of view."

Jefferson did not really want a *city* at all. In fact, he had personally drawn up a plan for a government village of just twenty square blocks between Rock Creek and the Tiber, in the area known as Foggy Bottom, an austere capital that he thought appropriate for a nation of farmers who shunned the pretensions of Europe. A simple grid of streets would be sufficient, he thought, as an expression of modern rationalism, in an age when towns on both sides of the Atlantic were messy and illogical warrens of straggling lanes. L'Enfant considered a grid "tiresome and insipid," although he may not have told Jefferson so in quite those terms. As the engineer soldiered through the mud and mist, something very different from Jefferson's hamlet took shape in his mind, a city that would capture both the spacious grandeur and the revolutionary idealism of the new nation. Looking out across these fog-shrouded plantations and rain-soaked pine flats, he saw avenues branching out from "every principle place, to which they will serve as does the main veins in the animal body to diffuse life through smaller vessels in quickening the active motion to the heart." Where others saw vacant farmland, he saw grand classical symmetries, an almost mystical geometry of lines, angles, squares, and circles, a shimmering architectural fantasy that would someday rival the capitals of Europe.

When Washington met with L'Enfant on March 28, the engineer apologized profusely for having nothing to offer except some rough pencil sketches. But the president was thrilled at what he saw, or at least imagined that he saw. The two men were soon thinking along the same grandiose lines. Washington too wanted an imperial city for a future when the United States would stand boldly among the powers of the world. At 7:00 AM on the morning of March 29, they set off to examine the ground in person. They made an imposing picture, these two tall and command-ing men in a country of short people, heavily cloaked against the raw weather, sharing visions of the metropolis they intended to spread across the scrubby plain, animatedly talking of obelisks and squares, philosophi-cal academies—"such sort of places as may be attractive to the learned and afford diversion to the idle"—and streets that radiated like sunbursts from the stately centers of government.

In L'Enfant's company, Washington was free to luxuriate in the realm of dreams. Back at Suter's, he reentered the world of politi-cal reality. Hints of the trouble that lay ahead were already present. The district's landowners were at odds with one another. No one but Washington yet knew what L'Enfant had in mind. The landowners still imagined a Jeffersonian town of a few hundred acres centered on a small cluster of government buildings. But they all knew that where those buildings were erected, land values would skyrocket. "Some were so wild as to suppose that the Government might pave the streets with ingots of gold or silver," one landowner would recall many years later. Proprietors on the western side of the district emphasized the conve-nience of their proximity to George Town and its markets, those close to the Potomac the benefit of access from the river, and those to the east the superior anchorage of the Eastern Branch. Confronting them in his lodgings, Washington was patient—these were his own neigh-bors, after all—but quite forceful. He told them that their competition threatened to undermine the entire project, as well as their own inter-est, for "whilst they were contending for the shadow they might lose the substance." He explained that the federal city was to be far more magnificent than they imagined. Instead of competing, they should combine their efforts and "make a common cause of it."

The city was ultimately to fill the land between Rock Creek and the Eastern Branch. Acquiring the land for it presented an obstacle, how-ever: the government didn't want to pay for it. Congress had appropri-ated no money at all for the acquisition of land and erection of buildings, voting only to provide a "sufficient sum" to physically remove government property to the Potomac in 1800. This ominous vagueness would cause no end of trouble, as would all too soon become clear. Virginia, it was true, had pledged $120,000 and Maryland another $72,000. But none of this money had yet been paid out, and with Virginia's treasury apparently bare, Washington seriously worried that the funds might not be forthcoming at all. Without money, work would quickly come to a halt, and the capital would never leave Philadelphia.

Washington probably had in mind George Walker's clever plan for financing the city when he proposed to the landowners that they give half their land to the government outright. (Back in 1789, writing as "Citizen of the World," the George Town businessman had advocated land sales as a politically painless device to raise development capital.) The president explained that once L'Enfant had properly mapped the district, the tobacco fields, and oak forest, and scrubby swathes of alder would be properly surveyed and divided into building lots. The owners, Washington suggested—told them, really—might keep every other lot for themselves. The government would pay them $66.67 per acre for any additional parcels that were taken for public use, apart from that needed for streets and squares, for which they would be paid nothing. The landowners were to be remunerated for the loss of the land they gave up by the increasing value of the property that remained to them as the capital grew. Meanwhile, the government would auction off its lots to pay for the construction of the federal buildings, streets, squares, and obelisks that were swimming in L'Enfant's fertile imagination. Washington never doubted that buyers would flock to the city, and that the forces of the marketplace would ensure that dwellings and businesses would be erected in no time. It was a brilliant plan. So it seemed, at any rate. There would be no need to go beg for financing from a reluctant Congress. The capital would be built virtually free of cost to the public and by private initiative, a formula that was expected to magically produce the effect that enlightened thought and high ideals did not want to actually pay for.

The landowners liked the idea. Or at least they were overawed by the president. On March 30 they agreed to combine their efforts and to yield the land that he had asked for. The United States thus acquired 10,136 lots and miles of streets at no cost to itself and over five hundred acres of land reserved for the public for the bargain price of $36,099. Washington remained anxious about the agreement falling apart, as he had good reason to. He wrote to the commissioners to have it put into effect without delay, "leaving nothing to chance." The "old and the new towns would be blended and assimilated," he ordered, and Major L'Enfant was to "lay out the whole accordingly."

When Washington left George Town later that day for his home at Mount Vernon, he had reason to feel confident. He had brought round the recalcitrant landowners. With a little luck, the project would finance itself. Ellicott's survey was progressing well. And he heartily approved of L'Enfant's magnificent plan. As the ferry slid across the Potomac toward Virginia, his eyes could not help but take in the "wavy" hills, as he called them, across which he had ridden with L'Enfant. Perhaps his mind's eye painted the misty green landscape with streets and stately brick homes, with imaginary fountains spuming from hillsides, with canals channeling commerce across the plain, with white-sailed schooners from the ports of the world scudding into bustling docks with, in short, the future. The sketchy signs of occupation that he saw before him—the tobacco sheds, the shambling slave quarters, the plantation houses—seemed, perhaps, as insubstantial as the mist, destined to yield in a few short years, so he deeply hoped, to the Metropolis of America.

THE SURVEYOR ANDREW Ellicott was nothing if not a hands-on superintendent, personally overseeing every aspect of the continuing fieldwork. He arrived at the surveyors' ever-shifting field camp before dawn every morning, breakfasted by candlelight, and remained with his men until nightfall, frequently skipping dinner, before riding miles back to his residence in George Town. Although he presented a stoic face to others, he hated the crepuscular weather and the soggy, impoverished countryside. And he was ill. "I have met with many difficulties for want of my old hands, and have in consequence a most severe attack of influenza worked for many days in extreme pain," he had confessed in a letter to his wife in mid-March. (Gruff though he could be with his men, Ellicott was also a man of deep sentiment; with the same letter, he sent her "a pair of black silk mitts, and a small smelling bottle, which I hope you will receive as a small testimony of as pure affection as ever had place in the Human Breast.")

Congress had decreed that the district as a whole should form a square of up to ten miles on each side. First Ellicott laid out a north-south longitudinal meridian from his first base camp at Jones Point, at the square's southern apex. Measuring an angle of forty-five degrees to the northwest, he then traced a straight line for ten miles in that direction, taking in all but a small corner of Alexandria. Moving camp as they progressed, Ellicott's men marked out the line on the ground with a chain, dropping a plumb where the ground was uneven, as it often was. Where the first line ended, just beyond the upper reaches of Four Mile Run, well into Virginia, he measured a right angle to the northeast, and drew a line ten miles in that direction, across the river into Maryland, terminating a little beyond the main bed of Rock Creek. There he made a right-angle turn to the southeast, carrying his line for another ten miles, about two miles beyond the Eastern Branch. He then angled southwest, to connect with another straight line back to his starting point at Jones Point. The city itself was, of course, intended to occupy only a relatively small portion of the district, the valley between Rock Creek and the Eastern Branch, and to extend inland about as far as present-day Florida Avenue.

Ellicott drove his crew hard. Once the boundary had been defined, he dispatched crews of woodsmen to chop away timber and brush in a twenty-foot-wide corridor along the boundary line, whacking down trees with three-feet-long, double-bladed steel axes, manhandling the felled logs with ring-dogs—steel bars each with an S-shaped hook attached—and dragging them clear with chains hitched to oxen and mules. It was dangerous work; at least several workmen would die before the job was done. The laborers who undertook this backbreaking task may have been slaves hired from local masters, most likely for about fifteen cents a day. Since Ellicott's field notes were lost long ago, nothing is known about these men, except that they existed, and that for weeks on end they hacked and chopped their way through rain and snow in a steady trek around the rim of the district. Ellicott, although unfriendly to slavery, was forced to work with whomever was available. Free workers were exceedingly hard to find in the area, a problem that would plague the project throughout the decade. Slaves would be as essential to the capital's birth as were the surveyors' transit and chains, the bricks and mortar of the buildings that would eventually arise along the Potomac, and indeed even the engineers, architects, and political leaders who would reap the glory.

Benjamin Banneker spent most of his time at the base camp, which had now shifted to the Maryland side of the river, where he monitored several instruments whose exceptionally precise measurements Ellicott relied on to help plot the boundaries, and later the lines of streets and avenues, without error. This required continuing measurement of latitude, as the boundary line was carried forward. To accomplish this, Banneker hauled himself from his cot several times each night to observe the course of several stars through a massive six-foot zenith sector, a type of telescope, which angled up through an opening in his tent. The readings for each star had to be repeated nightly, then averaged and corrected for refraction, a challenge for the self-taught astronomer, for whom mathematical calculation had until now mainly been a form of home entertainment. As part of his job, he also monitored Ellicott's astronomical clock, timing the speed of the stars as they moved through the heavens. Banneker had to keep the clock wound, and check its rate of movement by measuring the sun's altitude, a trickier task than one might assume, because variations in temperature and vibrations from movements on the ground could distort its speed, and therefore its readings. Given the cold and humidity, the clock demanded almost constant attention, as well as patience. Since many of the readings had to be taken at night, Banneker never really slept. Then in the morning, Ellicott would typically appear from his lodgings in George Town to rouse him, in order to collect the previous night's data.

In what little time he had to spare, Banneker returned with a homing instinct to the idea that had been percolating in his mind all these weeks, the creation of something great and original, an almanac that would serve up the exquisitely calculated journeyings of the planets to a public that was hungry for scientific information. Through such an almanac, perhaps, he might speak to the larger America, the new nation that was cohering around him, in the spare language of numbers and measurements, where he might be granted an attentive ear, and a degree of respect, that no black man could expect in the flesh.

Exhausted as he was, Banneker would have liked to continue working with Ellicott. But in April, Ellicott's brothers Benjamin and Joseph arrived as planned, to assist with the surveying. Both were experienced surveyors and much younger than Banneker. In all, Banneker had spent a bit more than two months working in the Federal District. Later, fanciful legends would claim that he had helped to select and plan the federal city, and that after L'Enfant's untimely departure the rustic mathematician had reconstructed the architect's entire map from memory. His actual role was more modest. Nevertheless, it was rich in symbolic importance. As the earliest free African American to participate in the creation of the capital, he was a harbinger of the emerging class of men and women who were just beginning to invent the first free black communities in the United States. In Northern states, the first wave of emancipation was already under way. White Americans were being forced to ask themselves: Did the ringing assertions of human rights embodied in the nation's founding documents also apply to blacks? Even to slaves? Were blacks destined by God and biology to serve as slaves forever? Or were they—like Benjamin Banneker—to be permitted to step into the new world of free citizens?

More would be heard from Banneker. Remarkably, he would fulfill his own dreams, to the astonishment of white Americans. He would become famous in a country that rejected even the possibility of intellect in African Americans who, as Thomas Jefferson had confidently expressed it, were "in reason much inferior" to whites, and "could scarcely be found capable of tracing and comprehending the investigations of Euclid." But for the moment Banneker was just a tired, overweight black man on a horse, heading home to the valley of the Patapsco. According to Martha Tyson, George Ellicott's daughter, who as a girl had known Banneker, and wrote about him in later life, "He arrived on horseback, dressed in his usual costume, a full suit of drab cloth, surmounted by a large beaver hat. He was in fine spirits, seeming to have been reanimated by the kindness of the distinguished men with whom he had mingled. With his usual humility he estimated his services at a low rate."

Chapter 4

A Cloudy Business

"There is a current in this city which sets so strongly against everything that relates to the Federal District, that it is next to impossible to stem it."

—George Washington

L'ENFANT'S LANKY FIGURE BECAME a familiar sight, swathed in a military greatcoat, stalking with a clinical eye over the ground between Rock Creek and the Eastern Branch. His restless imagination soon settled on the steep, wooded eminence known as Jenkins Hill, about half a mile from the Potomac, as "the most desirable position offer for to Erect the Publique Edifices." From this topographical root, he wrote to Washington, "the Federal City would soon grow of itself and spread as the branches of a tree do towards where they meet with most nourishment." The west end of Jenkins Hill attracted him particularly: it stood "like a pedestal waiting for a superstructure." Here he would plant the "Congress House," as he called it, since no one had yet settled on a name for the building that would house the Senate and the House of Representatives. A mile to the west of Jenkins Hill he would site the "President's mansion," a magnificent edifice, as he envisioned it, with "the sumptuousness of a palace, the convenience of a house, and the agreeableness of a country seat." A magnificent boulevard wider than any road that then existed in North America—the future Pennsylvania Avenue—would connect the two poles of democratic government in an ensemble "as grand as it will be agreeable and convenient." East of the Capitol would lie the "populouz" commercial center of the city. George Walker, the capital's most ardent local propagandist, heaped praise on L'Enfant's plan, which, he enthused, "exhibits such striking proofs of an exalted genius, elegance of taste, extensive imagination and comprehension, as will not only produce amazement in Europe, but will meet the admiration of all future ages."

The summer was a happy time for the engineer. Washington offered him lavish encouragement. But there was a problem, one that would soon become very nasty. L'Enfant believed that the president had delegated him alone to create the federal city, and to design its most important buildings, without restriction. Enraptured by his own ideas, he forgot how intimately the success of the project was interwoven with the president's personal reputation, and how critical Washington believed its achievement was to the larger project of the nation's survival. Not everyone was as enamored of the plan as were Washington and L'Enfant. Some close to the grandiose project wondered whether there would ever be money enough to pay for it, while Washington's friend Commissioner David Stuart dared to say that the vast size of the projected square in front of the President's House—the future Lafayette Square—seemed more fitting to "the genius of a Despotic government" than to that of a republic.

Andrew Ellicott, who traversed the land every day that spring and summer, surveying the district's boundaries, found the whole site impoverished and depressing. "For near seven miles, on it there is not one house that has any floor except the earth. We find but little fruit, except huckleberries," he wrote to his wife, cautioning her: "As the president is so much attached to this country, I would not be willing that he should know my real sentiments about it. But this country bears no more proportion to the country about Philadelphia, than a Crane does to a stall-fed Ox!" Ellicott was under unrelenting pressure to complete his work before the first, much-heralded sale of city lots in October. He lived in a state of constant exhaustion, "hurried off my legs and bothered out of my senses." The district's three commissioners failed to tell him what lots they wanted laid off for the sale, on October 17. A chaos of felled timbers made surveying streets a constant headache. One of his best men was crushed by a falling tree. And just finding workers was a problem. Thousands of men would be needed to build the city, it was predicted, but skilled, free labor was in such short supply in the district that Ellicott could find only six men to assist with the surveying when he wanted twenty. Meanwhile, because Virginia and Maryland had failed to make their promised payments, he had not even been paid. Ellicott sounded like a man on the edge of a breakdown: "Do not my dear send me any bad news, my present frame of mind would only suffer extremely by it."

Feverish excitement filled the air on the eve of the sale. Desirable properties that used to be worth $13 or $14 per acre were already said to be changing hands for six times that amount. Speculators predicted that land values throughout the district would easily double within the next two years. The ever-optimistic George Walker confidently predicted that the city would "grow up with a degree of rapidity hitherto unparalleled in the annals of cities, and will soon become the admiration and delight of the world." In September, the commissioners decided to name the city "Washington"—no surprise to anyone, including the president—and the larger Federal District "Columbia."

By the time of the sale, the beleaguered Ellicott had succeeded in blocking out ten squares into 40-by-100-foot building lots, just north of the future site of the President's House. The plan called for fifteen thousand lots to eventually become available for auction, once streets and squares had been subtracted from the public share of the capital's land. The total value of this land was potentially immense. The first sale alone was expected to earn at least $800,000 for the government, which along with the $192,000 pledged by Virginia and Maryland would comfortably pay for land clearance, road building, the quarrying of stone, and the construction of the government buildings.

But now, precisely when it would do the most damage, L'Enfant's inner turbulence now burst its dike. The engineer did not like speculators, and he did not want the land auctioned off to them. "For to look upon the property at this moment as a source of supply and to use it to defray the first expenses would be to destroy the capital from the very beginning," he warned Washington, urging him to borrow the money instead, and then sell the land later at a higher value. Work could thus be done "without the restraint of petty saving." Underselling property in this city that was to incorporate in stone the loftiest principles of the nation would be a disgrace. "A sale this fall is premature, for the land will not bring a tenth part of what it will later," he insisted.

Washington listened to the engineer's opinion, and then overruled it. The president was of course a speculator himself; he also knew that political support for the Potomac site was so thin that going to Congress for a loan to build a capital where few Americans really wanted it was out of the question. But L'Enfant held a trump card. Potential buyers, who naturally wanted desirable locations, needed to know where the available lots were going to fit into the city's overall design. For this, they needed—and had been promised—a detailed map. L'Enfant's plan was exquisite, everyone agreed. But there was only one copy. Washington had explicitly asked L'Enfant to provide a published version for general distribution. Despite months of prodding, he failed to deliver it. He unconvincingly blamed the Philadelphia engraver, one Narcisse Pigalle, who he claimed could not find a sheet of copper. L'Enfant later confessed to Washington's personal secretary with astonishing insouciance that he had deliberately taken care "to prevent the exhibition of the general plan at the spot where the sale is made."

The sale was scheduled to last for three days. It was over in an afternoon. But not because there was any mad rush to buy lots. Hopeful investors had come with high expectations from as far away as Boston, New York, and Philadelphia. The day began poorly when bad weather forced everyone indoors, into Suter's inn. Next, Washington, Jefferson, and Madison left early because the president's secretary discovered that he had got the opening date for Congress wrong by a week, and they had to rush off to Philadelphia. The auction itself, once it finally got under way, was a complete fiasco. Although a deposit of only 8 percent was required, with the remainder to be secured by bonds payable in three yearly installments, barely more than thirty lots were sold, at an average price of $265 apiece, for a total of $8,756—barely 1 percent of the expected take. Commissioner David Stuart glumly reported to Washington, "We have thought it proper, as the business seemed to flag a little to discontinue the sale." This was an understatement. Washington blamed it all on L'Enfant's failure to deliver a map. He put a good public face on things to Congress, speaking disingenuously of "ample funds" and the "expectation of progress," but in private he frustratedly demanded of the commissioners, how could bidders be "induced to buy, to borrow an old adage, a pig in a poke?"

Washington was not only angry, he felt personally betrayed. As a man not given to introspection, L'Enfant's behavior made no sense to him, except as a sort of moral dysfunction. Washington had regarded him as "a scientific man," a cool-headed professional, a man of facts like himself. The flaw, he supposed, must lie somehow in the engineer's artistic temperament. "Men who possess talents which fit them for peculiar purposes," as the president clumsily put it in a letter to his friend Commissioner David Stuart, invariably seemed to fall "under the influence of an untoward disposition, or are sottish, idle, or possessed of some other disqualification, by which they plague all those with whom they are concerned. But I did not expect to have met with such perverseness in Major L'Enfant." Now Washington's job was to control the damage, and to protect the city at all costs. There was no time to lose. The failed land sale had given new life to rumors that the government would never leave Philadelphia. Washington directed Stuart to see that Ellicott and his surveyors laid out squares and lots as fast as possible, without waiting for the next sale. The city's irreconcilable enemies were poised to attack, "aiming all the side blows in their power at it," he warned. They must not be given the chance. The great project must at least *seem* to be going forward.

The abortive auction was a warning sign that the capital's enthusiasts were living a delusion. The capital was essentially an abstraction, an act of political imagination imposed on a blank space. There was no compelling reason to live there, apart from the presumably seasonal activities of Congress. Nor could anyone be forced to move there, as Peter the Great had compelled the docile peasants and merchants of Russia to relocate to his new capital of St. Petersburg in the 1720s. Fractious Americans would never have stood for it, and the government did not even consider such a course. Instead, Washington and the promoters of the Potomac had determined to tap the public's self-interest, or more bluntly its greed. With the faith of true believers, they had committed themselves and implicitly the nation to real estate speculation as the engine that would finance the city's development. They barely considered the possibility that it might fail, and they would continue to cling to a doomed policy with a tenacity that with hindsight seems suicidally irrational. Reliance on largely unsuccessful land sales crimped the flow of money from the start, and created political consequences that only Washington's imperviousness to criticism could conceal. For it meant that Congress and the American public would repeatedly have to be deceived in order to suppress damaging rumors, and to avoid undermining the confidence of the speculators to whom the project was in thrall.

For L'Enfant, the debacle of the land sale was the beginning of the end. What happened next would have been laughable except that it exposed still deeper flaws in the character of the man to whom the president had entrusted the capital's design. One of the district's wealthiest landowners, Daniel Carroll of Duddington (who, like other members of the numerous Carroll clan, was usually known by the name of his estate), had begun erecting a new home on a shoulder of Jenkins Hill, protruding into the line of New Jersey Avenue. L'Enfant could with just a little effort have tweaked his plan to accommodate the politically powerful Carroll's house. Instead, on November 20 he imperiously ordered his assistant Isaac Roberdeau to dismantle it. Washington was mortified. "The conduct of Major L'Enfant and those employed under him astonishes me beyond measure," Washington wrote to Jefferson. The demolition threatened to turn the landowners and their well-connected cronies against the entire project. To mollify the engineer, Washington flatteringly wrote him, "Having the beauty and regularity only of your plan in view, you pursue it as if every other person or thing were obliged to yield to it." But he added pointedly: "In future I must strictly enjoin you to touch no man's property without his consent, or the previous order of the Commissioners." It was a warning shot. Certain that he was indispensable, L'Enfant failed to heed it. Instead, L'Enfant characteristically blamed the crisis on someone else, this time on Carroll's "manifest disposition to oppose the progress of operations."

Washington recognized the affair as a public relations disaster that created an incendiary impression of both arrogance and incompetence at the highest level of leadership—his own. He wanted everyone to believe that things were going smoothly on the Potomac. Although he considered Carroll at least partly to blame for the debacle, he soothingly assured the landowner, "It would be unfortunate in my opinion, if disputes among the friends of the federal city, should arm the enemies of it, with weapons to wound it." If only L'Enfant would get a grip on himself, all might yet turn out all right. But L'Enfant remained unrepentant. He was now talking about razing the home of the wealthiest local landowner of all, Notley Young. "I hope the maj. does [not] proceed to the demolition of this also," Washington told the commissioners. One can almost hear his groan resonating across the centuries.

L'Enfant ignored the chill that increasingly frosted Washington's messages in the early winter of 1791. Acting as if nothing had happened, he continued refining his plan of the city, while still managing to keep it from publication, to everyone's chagrin. He officiously reminded the president that before work could begin in earnest in the spring, quantities of timber would have to be purchased from the local landowners, hundreds of wheelbarrows needed to be acquired, and barracks built for the multitudes of workers who would be needed: "Axe-men must also be kept in constant employment in cutting down and clearing timber from the streets that are now run," and diggers set to work leveling the crown of Jenkins Hill for the foundation of the Congress House. In January he blithely advised Washington to place the entire project under a single decisive person—a czar, as it were. Naturally he was thinking of himself.

Meanwhile, he still had not published his plan of the city. "What his motives were, God knows," sighed the exasperated Andrew Ellicott. Finally, apparently without informing L'Enfant, Jefferson handed over responsibility for engraving the elusive map to Ellicott himself, who undertook to complete it with his usual efficiency. Working from L'Enfant's drawings, Ellicott slightly realigned avenues, diminished the large green space which the engineer had placed just north of the President's House, and reconfigured certain visual perspectives that L'Enfant had created to exploit the undulating topography. The result was less elegant than L'Enfant's vision, but it was at least complete. Ellicott's map was at last received by Washington in late February. Either from oversight or opportunism on Ellicott's part, the map in its published form failed even to mention L'Enfant's name. When L'Enfant saw what Ellicott had done he raged with an implacable fury that his art had been "unmercifully spoiled and altered," proclaiming that were it ever to be made public he would be utterly disgraced.

L'Enfant began to complain to Washington cryptically of imagined "intrigues and injuries" against him, and charged that the Ellicotts had stolen his drawings, enabling "others to reap reputation and profit from my labors." The president tried placating: "Every mode had been tried to accommodate your wishes," short of firing the commissioners, he wrote L'Enfant, who declared them "ignorant and unfit," and tainted by "pride of office." He even accused agents of the commissioners, and of Secretary of State Jefferson, of having stolen letters supporting him from the landowners to the president. Washington repeatedly begged him to calm down and to submit to the commissioners' guidance.

By January 1792 the commissioners, for their part, had lost whatever inhibitions had restrained their language, and were charging that the engineer had become "insubordinate" and "insufferable." David Stuart told Washington that all three commissioners would resign "rather than be any longer subject to the caprices and malicious suggestions of Major L'Enfant." Stuart then added a further complaint about the irresponsible and high-handed manner in which the work had been carried on, asserting that L'Enfant had capriciously ordered the laborers to excavate an assortment of "long, deep, wide ditches" for no rational purpose. Beneath such sniping lay a real fear that L'Enfant's disdain for political realities, love of "ornament," and imperial vision might bankrupt the project. Jefferson, who had disliked the scale of L'Enfant's plan from the beginning, now accused him of a tendency to "chicane and raise opposition."

At the end of February, Washington reiterated that L'Enfant could only continue on the job if he submitted himself to the authority of the commissioners. "Every mode has been tried to accommodate your wishes," the president told him. "Five months have elapsed and are lost, by the compliment which was intended to be paid you in depending alone upon your plans." But the engineer's pride would permit him nothing more to do with the great project, on what he considered the most demeaning terms. Without him, the federal city was doomed to failure, he proclaimed to all who cared to listen. He could no longer share responsibility for its fate. He told the president, in syntax even more tortured than usual, "Fearing that by my continuance, you might indulge a fallacious hope of success, by which in the end you must have been deceived, under these impressions do I renounce all concern in it."

Washington, in his iciest mode, wrote to Jefferson. "No farther overtures will *ever* be made to this Gentn." On March 6 Jefferson wrote to the commissioners that L'Enfant's "services were at an end." A few days later, on March 14, Ellicott was placed in overall charge of the project. By then, L'Enfant had already left the Potomac for Philadelphia, where Washington and Jefferson worried that "the enemies of the project will take advantage of Lenfant to trumpet an abortion of the whole." The president authorized the commissioners to offer L'Enfant up to $3,000 in what was, in effect, hush money for his services over the past year. This was too much for the unrepentant commissioners, who offered him half as much, plus a city lot. L'Enfant proudly declined the payoff and kept his silence. Bruised and bitter as he was, he would never turn on the president he adored. He would not visit the site again in the 1790s, except to pass through during a journey to Virginia later in the decade. As time passed the delusional aspect of his personality would become steadily more pronounced. Increasingly out of touch, he would try with scant success to promote a succession of grandiose, ill-starred engineering projects as he slid inexorably toward penurious obscurity.

The long-suffering Ellicott had his own problems with the commissioners. At the best of times, he found Thomas Johnson brusque and impetuous, and the aristocratic Daniel Carroll "dictatorial in tone." The elderly David Stuart he damned with faint praise as a "benevolent gentleman, fond of quoting the classics." The grueling pace of the fieldwork, L'Enfant's ranting accusations, pressure from the commissioners to work faster, nagging complaints from proprietors that he was favoring one part of the city over others, all were taking an emotional toll on him. "I have scarcely had time to either shave, or comb my head," he groaned to his wife, Sally, confessing that he couldn't stand the company of anyone except his four assistants, and had taken to eating alone in his office like a bear holed up in his den for the winter. Adding insult to injury, a disgruntled former assistant named James Dermott began spreading rumors that Ellicott was incompetent, and fraudulently altered measurements on the surveyor's plats in an effort to undermine him. Swayed by Dermott's scheming, the commissioners demanded that Ellicott surrender all the documents in his possession, along with his surveying equipment. "Our demand is all," the commissioners belligerently told him. For weeks Ellicott teetered on the brink of quitting his job and abandoning the federal city altogether. In a letter to Washington, he furiously accused Dermott of drunkenness, and Commissioner David Stuart of leading a cabal to destroy his character. Washington well knew that the city couldn't afford such discord: if Ellicott took his complaints to the newspapers, the president worried, it would give new ammunition to the city's enemies in Philadelphia. In the end, Ellicott was reinstated in the commissioners' good graces, but he never forgave them. "Neither credit, not reputation, will ever be the lot of a single person who enters their service," he wrote to Sally, praying that he would soon be restored to her loving embrace. "I dislike the place, and every day adds to my disgust."

WASHINGTON HAD OTHER things to worry about as well. No work at all had been done on either the President's House or the home of Congress. Rumors circulated that New Englanders were secretly bribing the federal commissioners to slow down the work. The discouraged George Town businessman George Walker reported that "a melancholy languor now reigns." Time to organize crews for the summer season of 1792 was growing desperately short. Foundations had to be laid. Terraces were needed to shore up the top of Jenkins Hill. Wharfs and bridges had to be built. Streets had to be graded. Aqueducts had to be constructed to convey water to the city. Mills had to be erected to grind plaster, pound clay, and saw wood. Tons of stone had to be cut and ferried up the Potomac from the Aquia quarries. Bricks had to be made in prodigious quantities. More than a thousand workmen were needed, if construction was to start on schedule—masons, laborers, teamsters, wheelwrights, carpenters, quarrymen, stonecutters, and men skilled at working with lime. Instead, for lack of money, the commissioners had fired virtually all the workmen still on hand, except for Ellicott's small team of surveyors. Instead of progressing, they were regressing. Crops were being planted in the streets that Ellicott had laid out the previous year. Public confidence was disintegrating. Soured landowners circulated unfounded rumors that the commissioners had taken bribes to scuttle the entire project.

Meanwhile, in Philadelphia, where physical work on accommodations for the temporary capital was progressing rapidly, the rumor mill was already treating the federal city as a virtual dead letter. The Potomac's political enemies, like "a Congress of fiends met in Pandemonium," were demanding that the project be canceled immediately. The Federalist Congressman Egbert Benson of New York, for one, was planning to propose a repeal of the Residence Act. Pressure was building to keep the capital in Philadelphia. Washington worried, "There is a current in this City which sets so strongly against everything that relates to the federal District, that is next to impossible to stem it." He flailed the commissioners for their inactivity "whilst action on the part of [Pennsylvania] is displayed in providing commodious buildings for Congress." Vividly punctuating his anxieties, on May 10 the cornerstone was laid in Philadelphia for what that city hoped would be the President's mansion, if the government gave up its pipe dream on the Potomac.

Just as the capital's future seemed uncertain, that of the United States itself seemed shakier than ever. Dangers loomed on every side. The nation's trans-Appalachian frontier, which extended from western Pennsylvania and Virginia into the new state of Kentucky and the future ones of Tennessee, Ohio, Michigan, and beyond was as wild as—if not even wilder than—the Dakotas of the 1870s, a vast zone of sketchy settlement, weak loyalty to the federal government, class conflict, and incredible violence. All along the frontier, which in Pennsylvania began two hundred and fifty miles west of Philadelphia at Pittsburgh, irate settlers were defying federal attempts to impose Alexander Hamilton's tax on locally produced whiskey, assaulting government agents sent to collect it and, at least in the anxious minds of federal officials in Philadelphia, threatening outright revolution. Already at a boil by the summer of 1791, this agitation would climax three years later with the political upheaval known as the Whiskey Rebellion.

Meanwhile, full-scale war with Britain over western claims seemed a very real possibility. The British still held a chain of outposts, including Detroit, in direct contravention of the treaty that ended the American Revolution, and were conspiring with both Indians and disaffected settlers to subvert American authority in the Ohio River Valley. Hard-pressed Indian tribes had good reason for resisting the ever-increasing pressure of American settlement, and with clandestine British support they achieved considerable success, at least initially. In the course of interminable skirmishing along the frontier, hundreds of settlers were killed and many others kidnapped from their homes. Thousands were abandoning the Ohio Country and fleeing east. One ill-fated military expedition had already been lost in 1790, in a failed attempt to pacify what Washington called "the deluded tribes." In the summer of 1791 a second expedition under General Arthur St. Clair was sent west, comprised largely of Kentucky militia, "whose enterprize, intrepidity and good conduct are entitled to peculiar commendation," Washington optimistically assured Congress. In fact, the campaign was an encyclopedia of incompetence. Contractors failed to provide the troops with enough tents, kettles, knapsacks, or weapons. Most of the soldiers were inexperienced—allegedly "collected from the streets . . . from the stews and brothels of the cities"— and they were often drunk on the march. A company of those "enterprizing" Kentuckians deserted and attempted to loot the wagon train on their way home. The tragic climax came in the predawn hours of November 4, when St. Clair's force was ambushed on the Wabash by a smaller force of Indians led by the Shawnee war chief Tecumseh. The Americans panicked. Hundreds threw down their rifles and ran for their lives. St. Clair was so crippled by gout that he gave orders from his hands and knees, all too apt a metaphor for the ineffectual posture of the United States. When it was over, more than nine hundred Americans—two-thirds of St. Clair's army—were dead. Indian losses were just sixty-six killed and nine wounded. It was the worst defeat that the United States ever suffered at the hands of Native Americans, dwarfing the far more famous but strategically insignificant slaughter of General Custer and his 268 men in 1876. When Washington heard the news, he reportedly exclaimed, "To suffer that army to be cut to pieces, hacked, butchered, tomahawked by a surprise! Oh, God! Oh, God! The curse of Heaven!" Panic raced through the settlements on the Pennsylvania frontier. Blockhouses were overrun, families massacred, captives tomahawked on the trail. Community leaders in Pittsburgh feared the complete depopulation of the country. "The present line of frontier will give way, unless supported by the government," one desperate western correspondent wrote to a Philadelphia newspaper. "For God's sake, interest yourself in this business."

On the high seas, the United States was also painfully vulnerable. Even more humiliating to the tattered national sense of honor than American helplessness in the West, North African pirates were seizing American merchant ships and enslaving their crews without fear of retaliation. The constant threat of attack was crippling American commerce in the Mediterranean. In 1786 the United States had managed to buy off the Emperor of Morocco for $20,000, sending the protection money with a fawning letter that flattered the "noble" monarch for deigning to grant the United States his "friendly regards" across the ocean. Tunis, Tripoli, and Algiers remained at war with the United States, however. In 1792 the Dey of Algiers alone held more than one hundred Americans prisoner, along with a dozen American ships, and was demanding $60,000 in ransom. The survivors sent Congress a pathetic petition pleading that if nothing was done for them, they would be forced to abandon both Christianity and their country, and convert to Islam. Without a navy, American military action was impossible. The United States was thus forced to beg and bargain for the captives' release. Missions sent to negotiate their release came away empty-handed. In February Secretary of State Jefferson proposed a peace offering of $100,000 to the Dey, plus $13,500 in annual tribute, and $27,000 in ransom for the American prisoners, but it came to naught: instead, the money went to finance another campaign against the Indians. Sporadic negotiations would go on for years while Americans toiled at the Dey's public works and died chained in his war galleys. Antislavery Americans could hardly fail to see the irony of the U.S. government bribing dusky Muslim pirates for the release of white slaves, even as they suppressed debate over slavery in Congress, and enshrined in law the bondage of blacks. "For this practice of buying and selling slaves, we are not entitled to charge the Algerines with any exclusive degree of barbarity," the Philadelphia pamphleteer Mathew Carey admonished. "The Christians of Europe and America carry on this commerce an hundred time more extensively." While there were three thousand white slaves in Algiers, there were nearly seven hundred thousand black ones in the United States.

Another threatening sequence of events was simultaneously taking place on the French island of Sainte-Domingue, later Haiti. The slave-led revolution that began there in the summer of 1791 engulfed what once was the wealthiest colony in the Caribbean, inspiring visions of unspeakable horror in American slaveholders, who feared a bloodbath if slaves rose up on their own plantations. Armies of black former slaves, whites, and mulattoes struggled for supremacy in a war of ever-shifting alliances that was complicated still further by the factional politics of the French Revolution. Newspapers carried horrific reports of fanatical black armies on the march, of ravaged plantations, of slave masters torn limb from limb with red-hot pincers, and stockades adorned with the heads of white victims. Hideous atrocities were perpetrated against the rebels, too: at Le Cap, whites broke twenty or thirty captured blacks on the wheel every day and commonly massacred all slaves they encountered, even those who had not revolted. "The country is filled with dead bodies, which lie unburied," the *Philadelphia General Advertiser* reported in October 1791. "The negroes have left the whites, with stakes, &c. drove through them into the ground; and the white troops, who now take no prisoners, but kill everything black or yellow, leave the negroes dead upon the field." This was America's worst nightmare come to life. Jefferson, for one, predicted that the "revolutionary storm" would sweep through the United States. Panicky American slaveholders united to support the embattled French. In September 1791 Washington provided an American loan of up to $40,000 to the whites, along with the offer of more money and arms to help quell the "alarming insurrection of the Negroes." By the following spring four thousand Haitian whites and two thousand of their loyal slaves had arrived in American ports, bearing tales of slaughter and rapine that would resonate terrifyingly through slaveholders' psyches for years to come.

In this climate of roiling danger, completion of the federal city took on a special urgency. Hardly a decade earlier, the United States had astonished a doubtful world by winning the American Revolution. Now, in peace, the country advertised its impotence to its citizens and enemies alike by its inability to lay even a few streets or erect a pair of buildings for its own government. Washington needed a miracle. It arrived, so the president believed, in the charismatic person of a thirty-six-year-old financier by the name of Samuel Blodget, who inspired great confidence in Washington and his friends as a man of big ideas, a sort of Donald Trump of the 1790s, a man who *got things done.* Born in Woburn, Massachusetts, Blodget had served on Washington's staff during the war. He went on to make a fortune in the East India trade, acquiring the reputation of a canny money man, along with intimate connections among the rich, powerful, and fashionable, including the renowned designer Charles Bulfinch. His credentials, or at least his polish and his promises, impressed the commissioners, who praised him lavishly for his "fertility of genius," and "very pretty taste." Although the president had only a slight acquaintance with him, Blodget was yet another of those bright young men who like Hamilton and L'Enfant had shared with Washington the hardships of war, and whose ambitions he was predisposed to nurture. He had high hopes for Blodget. In search of "some active and competent character" to take complete charge of the capital's development, he considered Blodget the man for the job.

In his way, Blodget was indeed a man of genius. He played Washington, Jefferson, and the commissioners like a pitchman hustling a crowd of hayseeds at a county fair. Blodget had bought several lots at the first land sale, on October 17. Alert to the capital's precarious prospects, he now offered to put together a $500,000 loan that he would raise among private investors. Washington acknowledged that borrowing was now essential if work was ever to begin on the key government buildings, not to mention basic public works that were essential to attract investors to the federal city. But he was still determined that the project be financed by private enterprise rather than public appropriations. Blodget's formula perfectly matched the president's hopes. Boston and New York were awash in speculative money looking for someplace to go, Blodget explained. He promised the commissioners $50,000 by mid-May, another $50,000 in November, and annual payments of $100,000 through 1794, plus a steady income of $30,000 per year interest. The commissioners would in return pledge publicly owned lots as security. Meanwhile, this massive investment would drive up the value of city lots by more than 40 percent, he assured them. In the course of things, it would also make Blodget very, very rich. It seemed a winning proposition for everyone. From the scrubby wastes of the moribund Federal District, Blodget's magic wand would conjure up the city of which Washington dreamed.

Whether Blodget could really have brought off his financial sleight of hand will never be known, for yet another calamity intervened. New York's unregulated financial market was in the throes of what contemporaries called "bancomania," a hurricane of speculation in government bonds that had prompted the instantaneous birth of a brood of flimsily financed banks. This bubble, Alexander Hamilton later reported, "was in fact artificial and violent such as no discreet calculation of probabilities could have supposed." The master manipulator at the eye of the hurricane was William Duer, Hamilton's former assistant secretary of the treasury, who before he was forced to resign had exploited insider information gleaned from his official position to corner the bond market for himself and his partners. In March 1792 the market finally collapsed. "The extraordinary crush" [*sic*], Jefferson wrote to the commissioners, toppled the "persons dealing in paper." Many of the city's biggest money men went bankrupt, including Duer, who was almost lynched. The collapse shocked financial markets, scaring away those investors who survived. The money upon which Blodget had pinned his hopes, and the national capital's, suddenly evaporated into thin air.

The great loan would have to be deferred, Blodget reported. Jefferson, who was helpless in money matters, reluctantly agreed, concluding that nothing better was to be done than to leave the matter in Blodget's hands. Blodget remained sanguine that he would be able to raise the whole amount by summer. He would even advance $10,000 of his own money by way of reassurance. But after that: silence. In late June the commissioners were still waiting for the $10,000. "Not having heard from you, I take the liberty of asking a line from you," Jefferson plaintively begged—an uncharacteristic and no doubt painful posture for the dignified secretary of state. Blodget cheerily replied, from Boston, "I have found everyone much disposed to favour the Plan of the City, & believe we shall obtain many good Citizens from this place." (This was complete fiction.) He had sold off some lots, dumped them really, at bargain prices in order to give the capital "general notoriety," and he reassured Jefferson that once construction began on the principal buildings settlers would flock to the capital. Moreover, a new bank that he was promoting would soon be able to generate more investment capital. So—*sorry, Mr. Jefferson*—at the moment he could only offer $5,000 of the $10,000 he had promised. Although Blodget did pay the remainder later, only the fortuitous arrival of $24,000 from the state of Maryland, part of its promised contribution, saved the project from collapse.

The second land sale was held on October 8, 1792. It was another flop. It raised only $20,000, just $5,000 of which was in cash, the rest in promissory notes. Two months later, the commissioners were bemoaning "a great want of punctuality among those who purchased at the first sale, in their second payments." In other words, buyers refused to pay what they had promised. (The only real winner was, no surprise, Samuel Blodget, who acquired at a secretly discounted price the most valuable piece of real estate on offer, which he would later exploit in the capital's most bizarre fund-raising scheme of all.) Washington's steadfastness in the face of yet another disappointment was impressive. But he was a man who had suffered many more battlefield reverses than successes. As he had during the war, he simply acted as if every defeat was really a victory. In effect, he declared "mission accomplished" when it was patently clear that if the capital was to be completed at all, it would require a long, hard financial and political slog. He ignored the project's critics. And he refused to compromise on even the smallest details. He insisted that the project continue to be portrayed to the public as immutable, brilliantly conceived, and an ongoing success. Speaking of the president, Jefferson wrote to the commissioners, "He thinks it best to decline making any alterations in the plan of the city. The considerations which weigh with him are the expediency of fixing the public opinion on the thing as stable & unalterable."

Like so much of the official discourse swirling around the capital, the president was practicing what a later generation would call "spin." Widespread scuttlebutt had it that "everything was going to the devil from the mismanagement of the gentlemen who have the direction." In fact, they were finding it impossible to recruit the labor they needed. Skilled workers were not interested in coming to the federal city. Jefferson and the commissioners had tried with little success to lure masons and other workers from as far away as New England, and even Europe. Failure to obtain workers, Washington wrote to the commissioners in November, with a rather military flourish, "fills me with *real* concern; for I am apprehensive if your next campaign in the Federal City is not marked with vigor, it will cast such a cloud over this business and will so arm the enemies of the measure, as to enable them to give it (if not its death blow) a wound from which it will not easily recover. Nothing short of the absolute want of money ought to retard the work."

Slaves would be the salvation of the federal city. They had been present from the beginning, in crews of a half-dozen or a dozen, hewing trees to open the streets that would someday become the thoroughfares of the city, prying up stumps, driving teams, hauling logs, and cutting the fine-grained brown sandstone for the future buildings of government. The commissioners would later brag that they "could not have done without slaves." They were not exaggerating. There would be free white, and a few free black, wage earners who contributed their sweat to the creation of the capital. But much of the work that would make the city a reality would be done by men who were hired out to the commissioners and their agents, and who were rewarded with nothing but bread, sardines, and salt pork. The capital would become, at least in part, a slave labor camp.

———

Aɴ ᴜɴꜰʀɪᴇɴᴅʟʏ ᴏʙsᴇʀᴠᴇʀ might have used the same words to describe Secretary of State Jefferson's magnificent estate at Monticello, where two hundred enslaved African American men, women, and children tilled his fields and staffed his workshops. Despite Jefferson's professed hatred of slavery—"the most unremitting despotism on one part, and degrading submissions on the other"—he expressed no discomfort that the capital of the world's first nation dedicated to human freedom was being built by slaves. He regarded himself as an indulgent master, and was seen so by others. In contrast to fire-breathers like James Jackson of Georgia, who showered the First Congress with his proslavery venom, Jefferson never seriously claimed that slavery was a blessing for the enslaved. (On the other hand, he lacked Jackson's blunt honesty in admitting that their class owed its wealth and privileges to slavery.) As Lucia Stanton has amply shown, his antislavery posture was essentially just that, a rhetorical pose that enabled him to express lofty moral sentiments while profiting from the labor of slaves. Of masters and slaves, he reflected, "providence has made our interest and our duties coincide perfectly." Although, in Europe, he had been repulsed by the sight of European women performing heavy manual work, calling it "a barbarous perversion of the natural destination of the two sexes," the same sentiment never crossed his mind with respect to the black women who labored in his own fields. And though physical brutality offended his sensibilities, he saw to it that slaves who ran away from him were pursued, caught, flogged, and sometimes sold away to the Deep South, where he knew that disease and exposure exacted a terrible toll. Slaves made him the gentleman that he was. And in this summer of 1792 slave labor was a key component of the human engine that permitted him to preoccupy himself with the invention of a classical tradition for a government that had no precedent at all.

That preoccupation is captured perfectly by one small but still resonating symbolic amendment that he made in the plan for the capital. On the original plan, L'Enfant had written "Congress House" where he placed the national legislature, on Jenkins Hill. Jefferson crossed out those two words, and wrote "Capitol" instead. Taken for granted today,

Jefferson's innovative name self-consciously invoked the famous temple of Jupiter Optimus Maximus on the Capitoline Hill, in ancient Rome, and by extension claimed for the infant United States the hoary mantle of the Roman Republic, with its political freedoms and precedent of popular government. The home of Congress was to be a kind of national temple to the secular religion of democracy, a physical counterpart to the Constitution, a civics lesson in stone as it were. Where others saw a work site, Jefferson saw a moral landscape, though one in which the monstrosity of slavery did not really count, of course. Steeped in the classics, he believed with an almost religious passion in the transformative power of colonnades, domes, and marble porticoes to ennoble the human spirit and sharpen the intellect, even urging the commissioners to replicate the dimensions of ancient Roman brick—twenty-two inches long, eleven inches wide, and two inches thick—in the Capitol's construction.

Americans of Jefferson's generation embraced their idealized vision of Rome with a credulity that, from a twenty-first-century vantage point, itself seems quaintly antique. They gave their favorite horses names like Gracchus and Plutarch, and called their slaves Venus, Caesar, Juno, Pompey, Claudius, and Jupiter. For models of stoicism and honor, patriotism and statecraft they looked to the works of Homer, and historians like Thucydides, Livy, and Plutarch. Washington was forever claiming that he wished to escape the cares of his office and return home like the Roman farmer-turned-warrior Cincinnatus; and when retired officers founded a postwar association to assert their considerable political influence, they dubbed it the Society of the Cincinnati. The eagle on the national seal was itself a quintessential emblem of ancient Rome, and the words engraved upon it, "e pluribus unum"—out of many, one—were meant to uplift all the more by virtue of their rendering in Latin; on the seal's reverse, two even more inspiring mottoes proclaimed, to those who could read them, that the United States represented no less than the rebirth of the ancient world's Golden Age: "annuit coeptis" and "novus ordo seculorum": "the world's great age begins anew/the golden years return."

For all Americans, it was a decade of dizzying, even chaotic, transformation. The degree of social stress was evident in the shocking spike in the nation's consumption of alcohol, which during the 1790s was two and a half times greater per capita than in the decade before national Prohibition was imposed in 1920. The Revolution had wrought an abrupt and violent break with the colonial past. Old loyalties to caste and class were foundering. British traditions no longer sufficed, at least in their outward form. Old patterns of thought, old symbols of power, old ways of relating to government, all had to be destroyed, and new ones created. City-dwelling workmen and hardscrabble farmers were demanding for themselves rights that the mostly patrician Founders hadn't bargained for. The nation faced a complex challenge indeed: how to both draw strength from the past, and at the same time break radically with it. Having rejected the British past, the Founders embraced the symbolism—the eagles, the Latin mottoes, the marble colonnades—of a far more ancient, semifictional past: they tailored Rome to fit their own needs.

In the spring of 1792 designs were solicited for the Capitol and the President's House. For the Capitol, Washington imagined something both "chaste" and "capacious," while the commissioners envisioned something more "on a grand scale." The winner of each competition would receive a city lot and $500, about $20,000 in today's dollars. Jefferson, the administration's resident aesthete, was delegated to judge the submissions. Perhaps because the presidency was then generally regarded as the lesser branch of government after Congress, less symbolic importance was attached to the design of the executive mansion. There, Jefferson expressed a desire for something "modern," perhaps resembling the Louvre or some other Parisian landmark. The contest was won, without significant controversy, by James Hoban, a ruddy-faced, thirty-four-year-old Irish-born builder whom the president had met and been impressed by a few months earlier. In an era when British law discouraged teaching Irish Catholics to read or write, Hoban had received a liberal education, as well as training in architecture. Professional discrimination drove him from his native country, however. He sailed to America in 1785 and eventually settled in Charleston, where he soon acquired a reputation as a talented "house carpenter," as he deprecatingly advertised himself, along with possession of a team of enslaved craftsmen at his command. For the President's House, L'Enfant had intended to erect what quite literally would have been a palace stretching seven hundred feet from east to west, and two hundred feet from north to south. Hoban's much smaller plan was roughly based on the home of the Duke of Leinster, in Dublin, an imposing but rather austere two-story pile whose most distinguishing details were four doric columns surmounted by a pyramidal pediment framed over the front door. Washington liked it well enough, but wanted something a bit more, well, majestic, a bit more ornate. Hoban, whose "even temper" soothed the president after L'Enfant's artistic tantrums, would be happy to oblige.

The competition for the Capitol was far more fraught: if the federal city was a physical symbol of the new nation, the Capitol was its political and, in Jefferson's terms, its moral anchor. Not surprisingly, Jefferson turned like a tropism to the architectural vocabulary of Rome, explicitly declaring that, "I should prefer the adoption of some of the models of antiquity which have had the approbation of thousands of years." Designs began to arrive in July, at least eighteen in all. Two came from British veterans of the Revolutionary War, one from a New York schoolteacher, another from a furniture maker, still another from the ubiquitous Samuel Blodget. James Diamond's design included a gigantic, turkeylike bird perched atop a cupola. Jefferson himself anonymously submitted a remarkable plan based on the circular Pantheon, the most famous surviving temple in Rome, with four oval rooms for the various branches of government. (Jefferson was a talented amateur architect, who had designed his own splendid neo-classical home at Monticello, and considered the colonial Georgian mansions of the Tidewater country simply "rude, misshapen piles.") Washington was disappointed by all the submissions, however, informing the commissioners that "if none more elegant than these should appear . . . the exhibition of architecture will be a very dull one indeed."

Jefferson settled somewhat reluctantly on the one design that had been submitted by a professional architect, Stephen Hallet, whose overly ornate rendering—Jefferson referred to it as the "fancy piece"— was dominated by a two-story colonnade. Hallet had been at work for months refining his design when, in December, the commissioners unexpectedly received yet another submission, a surprise entry sent from the Caribbean island of Tortola. On principle, they should have ignored it, since the deadline was long past. But the man who sent it was not to be dismissed lightly.

Chapter 5

THE METROPOLIS
OF AMERICA

"I would be as soon pitch my tent beneath a tree in which was a hornet's nest, as I would, as a delegate from South Carolina, vote for placing the government in a settlement of Quakers."

—CONGRESSMAN AEDANUS BURKE

ALTHOUGH ALMOST TOTALLY FORGOTTEN today, Dr. William Thornton was one of the most celebrated men of his time, a polymath, inventor, and inspired idealist whose amazing range of interests incorporated natural history, botany, mechanics, linguistics, architecture, speech therapy, racial theory, government, and an addiction to fast horses. Born the son of a wealthy Quaker sugar planter on the island of Joost Van Dyck, in the British Virgin Islands, and trained as a doctor, the thirty-one-year-old Thornton loved the United States with romantic abandon. In America, he wrote, "virtue and talents were alone sufficient to elevate to office, instead of men whose meanness or vices were the principal causes of their grandeur"; men who, he vividly added, were permitted "to suck the honey of industry, and leave nothing but the wax to the labourers." Within a few years of his arrival in America he would count Hamilton, Jefferson, and Madison as personal friends, and he would be in attendance at Washington's bedside when the great man died in 1799. He was also a passionate radical in the Jeffersonian mold, who wished for the subversion of the British government, and rejoiced at the France's overthrow of despotic European regimes.

THERE SEEMED NO end to Thornton's achievements. It would later be said of him that "when explaining to some members of Congress his noble and splendid conceptions of mind on various subjects, they coolly answered him 'ah Doctor you have lived a hundred years too soon!'" He had worked with Benjamin Franklin in London on experiments in electricity, and he corresponded with the renowned astronomer William Herschel. He would help finance the first experimental steamboat and design its boiler, develop plans for a steam-operated gun, and propose "a *speaking organ* to be worked by water or steam and to *preach* to the whole city." He speculated about installing steam engines, ventilators, and devices for the distillation of salt water into fresh in naval ships. He was the author of a treatise on comets, and of another that advocated a system of universal orthography to speed the teaching of language.

This last resulted from an ugly incident that revealed Thornton simultaneously at his worst and his best. With characteristically good intentions, while on Tortola, he had set out to teach a slave named Tatham how to read. Becoming frustrated at Tatham's lack of progress, Thornton literally threw the grammar book at him, saying, "If I can't drive learning into you I'll drive it at you—begone you are too stupid to be taught." After Tatham left, Thornton was overtaken by remorse, and began to analyze the word that had been the stumbling block, becoming convinced that it was not the slave's shortcoming but the difficulty of the language that was at fault. He went on to propose an enlarged alphabet of thirty letters, including a square and several tweaked Greek letters. In his excitement, he predicted that dialects would disappear, that spelling would cease to be confusing, and that any language could be learned in no more than a few weeks. He explained, with an enthusiasm that was probably less conceited than it sounds, "There is no language that I cannot write perfectly (with regard to sound I mean) nor indeed is there a dialect I cannot reduce to writing." To prove his point, he produced the first-ever written transcription of the Miami Indian tongue.

Thornton was also a skilled artist and had won a prize for his design of Philadelphia's Library Hall. His earliest apparent plan for the United States Capitol, the so-called "Tortola Scheme," was less ostentatious than either Hallet's or L'Enfant's, although it was still gigantic, with a front 500 feet in length. (Some dissenting scholars hold that Thornton's first design was lost, and that the Tortola Scheme is actually the mislabeled work of another contestant, George Turner.) Two grand staircases led to a raised terrace and the focal point of the building, a templelike portico based on the Pantheon—Jefferson's influence there—and supported by six Corinthian columns. Symmetrically proportioned wings to the north and south provided quarters for the Senate and the House of Representatives. Atop the main building rose a wooden cupola, which in later versions would eventually grow into the majestic dome that distinguishes the Capitol today. As for the interior, the central part of the Capitol was organized around a "grand vestibule," or rotunda. There, Thornton proposed a spectacular white marble equestrian statue of Washington "in a very high stile," and beneath it a crypt to house Washington's remains, completing his sanctification as the nation's presiding deity. In January 1793, Thornton revised the design into a form that closely prefigured the Capitol as it is known today, with more graceful classical lines, a broad dome, and a more modest frontage of 352 feet. The good doctor's work overwhelmed Washington—who had just been reelected without opposition to his second term—with its "grandeur, simplicity, and beauty." And it captivated Jefferson, who described it euphorically as "Athenian" in taste, but appropriately embellished for a nation "looking far beyond the range of Athenian destinies." Washington made clear to the commissioners that this was the one he wanted:

"I have no doubt of its meeting with that approbation from you which I have given it upon an attentive inspection." Emblematic images placed strategically around the building would include buffalo, elk, Indians, Hercules, and Atlas, "an allusion to the members assembled in this house bearing the whole weight of government," thus wedding ancient symbolism with the unique American iconography of the wilderness and westward expansion. It was an innovative design in other ways, too, providing hidden service stairs and storage for the unobtrusive supply of fuel, and even water closets for both members and visitors on all levels. The design would of course evolve over time. Since Thornton had no experience making working drawings, that task was assigned to none other than "poor Hallet," whose own design had just missed being selected, and whose feelings, Washington wrote with some embarrassment, would have to be "sa[l]ved and soothed to prepare him for the prospect that the dr's plan will be preferred to his."

For Thornton, the selection of his design was of course a transcendent personal triumph, although he likely received at least some coaching from a professional architect on the final version of his plan. In so far as his name is still known at all today, it is for his Capitol design, and among architectural historians for a pair of more modest dwellings that survive in Washington. His other, more equivocal, contribution to the United States has largely been erased from the national memory, scrubbed away by the politics of later generations and the Civil War. Thornton was one of the first Americans—and he was an American, having officially been granted citizenship by the state of Delaware in 1786—to attempt to come to grips with the dawning prospect of a biracial America. With the same passionate single-mindedness that he applied to his work on the Capitol, he proposed a radical solution that he believed could save the nation from the race war that Jefferson and so many other Americans feared if ever slaves were emancipated en masse.

THORNTON'S INVOLVEMENT WITH the Capitol still lay in the future when he stepped ashore at Philadelphia in October 1786 after a voyage from England, an open-faced man "full of hope, and of a cheerful temper," with lace-trimmed clothes that belied his Quaker origins, and a messianic belief that it was his destiny to lead the enslaved blacks of America back to Africa. Thornton was preoccupied with slavery to the point of obsession, and what he said about it would influence elite American thinking for decades to come. From Philadelphia, he traveled to New York, Boston, Newport, and then back to Philadelphia, seeking out black community leaders and white abolitionists, condemning the evils of the slave trade, feelingly evoking the "groans of a hundred men, the sighs of a hundred women," of bodies thrown from slave ships to the watchful sharks, and of the "flinty hearts" of traders who bought and sold the survivors in the markets of the America, and crying out with a sincerity that wrenched his listeners, "O Christianity! Christ has seen his name rejected—the cause is before him, for his eye is upon all flesh!"

Thornton's native Tortola, in the late eighteenth century, was a rough, wild place not much removed from the days when it was a haunt of pirates who preyed on the Spanish colonial fleets. Ten thousand slaves toiled upon its corrugated landscape of precipitous bays and terraced, razorback mountains sown with sugarcane, turpentine trees, and spiky indigo. Breathtaking brutality was commonplace: Thornton's doctor cousin John Coakley Lettsom was once ordered to cut the leg off a slave for attempting to escape. Sent to England to be educated, Thornton fell under the influence of humanitarian reformers at the University of Edinburgh. There he came to believe that the only reason for Negroes' apparent "apathy" or "indolence" was denial of their equal rights, a very radical view at that time. If they were excluded from all offices merely because of their color, he would argue, what inducement did they have to develop their character or acquire learning: "If they are so lazy, why do men abduct them from their homeland and condemn them to the hardest and most painful kind of work?" Surprisingly, given British Quakers' opposition to slavery, Thornton also began to drift away from his familial religion. By the time he arrived in America, "not having parted yet with my Quakerism, though not in unity with the Quakers," as he put it, he had shed the solemn garb and rigid manners of his parents' faith for a more lightly worn piety that did not impinge on his empirical, scientific bent. On the subject of slavery, however, Thornton was as steadfast as any Quaker of his generation, in principle. "A total and immediate abolition of slavery may indeed be pregnant with some danger to society, but there can be no inconvenience in a gradual emancipation to commence as soon as general safety will permit it," he proclaimed.

Thornton had a serious problem, however. He was heir to between seventy and eighty slaves who worked his family's plantation in Tortola. He wanted to free them. But he discovered that emancipation was not as simple as it seemed. "I am induced to render free all that I am possessed of, by the dictates of conscience, and the uncommon desire I have to see them a happy people," he wrote to a friend in England, in August 1786. "My inclination is however in some degree counter to the prejudices of my parents—prejudices absorbed by a West Indian education, and which by the continued habit of slavery, are now become shackles to the mind." If he was determined to free the slaves that were in his name, his family told him, he must remove them from Tortola, lest their freedom corrupt the loyalty of their other slaves. "My own feelings plead for their liberty; and in that case my parents for their being taken away entirely," Thornton wrote. "I can do both; but then I ask myself the question—to what place can they be carried?"

In the United States, even among whites who condemned slavery, opposition to general emancipation was widespread. Many feared that it would lead to unbridled miscegenation—usually failing to admit that the main cause of race-mixing was masters' sexual exploitation of their female slaves. (For all his aching sensitivity over slavery, Thornton too harbored a visceral disgust at race-mixing, opining that "If the taste of a white man should be so depraved as to prefer a black to a white they ought to be joined, for it would be injustice to permit such depravity to contaminate a white woman.") With more reason, slaveholders complained that emancipation made their remaining slaves "less submissive and more turbulent," and warned (with much less evidence) that freeing large numbers would result in a massive crime wave, if not a bloodbath worse than anything yet seen in Haiti or other Caribbean islands. Minor slave rebellions in Virginia and South Carolina, ineffectual as they were, filled whites with foreboding. Even in the North, anxiety was never far from the surface. In 1741, well within living memory, more than two hundred New York slaves had been arrested and thirty executed, many of them burned at the stake for their part in an alleged plot to torch the city and murder whites.

Nevertheless, in spite of fear and prejudice, emancipation was slowly gaining ground in the Northern states. Quakers and Methodists vigorously challenged slavery on humanitarian principles, while others found slavery impossible to square with the ideals of the Revolution. "If we persevere in this wicked practice, when we have done so much to rescue ourselves from the hands of oppression, will not the world call us liars and hypocrites?" asked one pamphleteer. Mercantile self-interest lent edge to the softer appeals of religion and sentiment. Modern capitalism's prophet Adam Smith argued that slave labor was simply too costly and inefficient. "The experience of all ages and nations demonstrates that the work done by slaves, though it appears to cost only their maintenance, is in the end the dearest of any," Smith wrote in *The Wealth of Nations.* "A person who can acquire no property can have no other interest but to eat as much and to labour as little as possible." By the 1780s, slavery had been terminated in Massachusetts and New Hampshire, while Rhode Island, Connecticut, and Pennsylvania had all initiated the process of gradual emancipation. New York and New Jersey would follow suit at the end of the decade. In addition, the Northwest Ordinance of 1787 had barred slavery from the new states that eventually would be carved from the vast, still only sparsely settled region between the Ohio River and the Great Lakes. A Virginian, St. George Tucker, had even proposed a plan to gradually emancipate all the slaves in the United States, beginning with children born to enslaved mothers after 1800, estimating that slavery would peacefully disappear within fifty years. Tucker's farsighted proposal, unfortunately, would find no support in the South.

In contrast to most early abolitionists, for whom persuasive empathy was an end in itself, Thornton saw himself as a man of action. He conceived a solution that was vast in scope, one that would span the Atlantic Ocean, and transform the greatest sin of Anglo-Saxon man into a humanitarian triumph. He would emancipate his slaves and lead them—and eventually, he hoped, all the slaves of British North America—back to "their own country," Africa. He envisioned a model colony that would be a sort of African Philadelphia, a beacon of civilization in a benighted continent. It would have courts and laws on the Anglo-American model. (Thornton proposed to write those laws himself.) Taxes would be assessed to support churches, schools, and "societies for the encouragement of science," as well as for buying the freedom of Africans in the hands of slave dealers. "Thus by proper encouragement and perseverance, a most valuable country would soon become the seat of commerce, of arts, and manufactures, of plenty, of liberty, of peace, and happiness!" Trade would naturally flourish. Cotton, indigo, gold dust, sugar, cocoa, and coffee would be exported to Europe and the Americas. Meanwhile, Christianized American Negroes would "bring to industrious lives the ignorant and slothful of the warm country of Africa." A later age would call this a win-win proposition. Former slaves would enjoy full play for their talents and intelligence, Thornton asserted, as he traveled through the United States. Whites would no longer have to worry about assimilating free blacks. And Africans would become civilized with the help of their American cousins. Even Europe would benefit, by the opening up of a new market for its manufactures. Financial assistance would surely be forthcoming from abolitionists in Europe and America. He was persuaded that once his plan was widely known, thousands of the Negroes would eagerly follow him.

Colonization was the racial liberalism of its day. "Deportation," as its critics more harshly termed it, would always be rejected by the vast majority of African Americans; in the nineteenth century, Frederick Douglass and other radical abolitionists would argue that American-born blacks had no deeper roots in Africa than white Americans did. Nonetheless in an era when almost all whites considered black inferiority self-evident, and the prospect of free blacks set loose upon their former masters filled Americans with terror, colonization was a doctrine that even slaveholders could comfortably embrace, and many did. In time, it would supply political cover for proslavery politicians who were much less interested in emancipation than they were in expelling free blacks from the United States. Although

Thornton's scheme was the first practical plan for organizing the return of black Americans to Africa, he was not the first to advocate colonization. Thomas Jefferson had suggested a similar idea in *Notes on the State of Virginia*, in 1784. And thousands of freed British slaves were even now being shipped to Sierra Leone, where they were struggling to establish a settlement under the nominal guidance of philanthropists.

Thornton meant to leave nothing to chance. He was determined to personally go to Africa to lead his colony. "Few may be better fitted to undertake a project of the kind than myself, none more willing; my acquaintance with the culture of the tropical productions, with medicine, with many necessary arts, which the Africans do not understand; my disposition to serve them, and willingness to give up every pleasure of society, every tie of relationship, for a while, on their account," he wrote to a friend. There was nothing to hold him back: he was young, active, and single: "It is vain for any of my friends to attempt to persuade me from it." Soon he was hard at work learning coastal languages of West Africa, working up a law code, and searching for an army officer to write a book on military tactics for his settlers.

Thornton's thinking represented one of the first halting attempts to come to grips with the dawning racial realities of the postrevolutionary era. It presented no end of conundrums. Were blacks Africans, or Americans? How would slavery and free blacks fit into the future of the United States? Could blacks ever become citizens? Hardly anyone thought so. Was slavery compatible with democracy? Southerners certainly thought so. Many, like James Jackson of Georgia, and John Calhoun in a later generation, argued that slavery was essential to provide the leisure for a ruling elite to put republican government into practice. There was no precedent at all for abolition. How could it ever be accomplished? Nowhere in all of human history had there ever been a mass emancipation of slaves. The sheer originality of the idea was mind-boggling. Would whites ever agree to it? Could blacks and whites ever live together in peace? Or, as Jefferson warned, did freedom for blacks doom society to insurrection, warfare, and slaughter? No one knew the answers. All that was certain, at least to those who were willing to face reality, was that a racial revolution was already taking place, if in slow motion, and that Americans would have to find answers that they had never sought before.

Nowhere was that revolution taking place with more vigor, or with more astonishing speed, than under the noses of the country's governing elite, in the temporary capital of Philadelphia. By declaring that "all servitude for life . . . hereby is utterly taken away, extinguished and for ever abolished," Pennsylvania's gradual emancipation law of 1780 had set the stage for the development of the first large free black community in the United States, and for the ongoing struggle of white and black Americans to discover how to live with each other in freedom. The law was not perfect. It abolished the Black Codes, which had limited the rights of free blacks, and explicitly banned the importation of slaves into Pennsylvania. But it did not immediately emancipate any adult slaves. Rather, children born to enslaved parents would henceforth be free in principle, although they were required to work for their parents' masters as indentured servants until they reached the age of twenty-eight. The law ordered all slaveholders to register their human property, stipulating that if they failed to do so, the slaves in question would be deemed free, thus leaving a loophole through which many blacks would slip to freedom. To accommodate slaveholding politicians, the law also exempted from its provisions members of Congress, as well as foreign dignitaries, and it permitted visitors from other states to bring their slaves into Pennsylvania without penalty for up to six months. Even with its limitations, the law's significance was tremendous. What Massachusetts or New Hampshire did about slavery made relatively little difference to Southern masters. But Philadelphia was the national seat of government. Indeed, it would likely become the permanent capital, if construction of the new city on the Potomac faltered. A Southern capital would proclaim to all that slavery was as fundamental to the new nation as its Constitution. A Pennsylvania capital would establish freedom as the national paradigm.

PROMOTERS OF THE new city on the Potomac incessantly and windily proclaimed it to be the "Metropolis of America." But Philadelphia was the real thing. The temporary capital hummed with political excitement and cosmopolitan fizz. With forty-three thousand inhabitants—far more than New York's thirty-three thousand, and Boston's eighteen thousand—it was the country's unchallenged financial, commercial, and cultural epicenter. "Philadelphia may be considered the metropolis of the United States," the French traveler Jacques-Pierre Brissot de Warville wrote in 1788. "It is certainly the most beautiful and best-built city in the nation, and also the wealthiest, though not the most ostentatious. Here you find more well-educated men, more knowledge of politics and literature, more political and learned societies than anywhere else in the United States."

Staid Quaker and Yankee businessmen mingled on its pebble-paved streets with immigrants from Germany, Holland, and Ireland, French refugees, fashionable women in high-waisted gowns, bustling workmen in thigh-length brown or gray vests, feathered Shawnees and Miamis from across the Ohio, and an ever-swelling African American population that was itself a dizzying babel of the newly emancipated, the still-enslaved, and recently escaped fugitives speaking a cacophony of English, French, Jersey Dutch, Caribbean patois, and the cadences of the West African coast. Countryfolk could only marvel at the liveried servants and elegant carriages that plied the cobbled streets, and at the phantasmagoria of urban professions that included such exotics as mustard and chocolate makers, soap boilers, and men who earned their living guarding sedan chairs while their owners went to the theater. To this hectic mix, the arrival of the federal government brought with it regiments of official secretaries and clerks, master chefs and dancing masters, tailors, wig makers, caterers, portrait painters, actors, and cohorts of speculators and sharpers. Not everyone liked it. "The inhabitants indulged themselves in all the gratifications of luxury and dissipation to be procured in the Western hemisphere," grumbled one disgruntled Philadelphian nostalgic for bygone Quaker austerity. And Senator Jeremiah Smith of New Hampshire harrumphed, "You cannot turn around without paying a dollar."

"Everywhere there is activity, industry, and competition," wrote Brissot de Warville. On the city's landward side, new stage lines seemed to spring up every week, linking the capital with the burgeoning settlements to the west and south, while forward-looking investors were already planning the nation's first paved highway—an "artificial road," they called it—from Philadelphia to Lancaster. Philadelphia's port was the biggest in the United States. The Delaware River docks from Arch Street to Chestnut Street teemed with sweating stevedores, haggling merchants, swaggering sailors, clerks, and apprentices climbing like alpine mountaineers amid bales of tea from China and muslins from the looms of Britain, crates of Cuban sugar, and barrels of molasses from Caribbean plantations. The city's driving spirit was perfectly embodied in the person of Senator Robert Morris, whose ships carried the American flag around the globe, and who was about to cap a lifetime of wheeling and dealing by attempting to corner the Federal District's real estate market.

No other American city even came close to Philadelphia's opulence of amenities. Its streets were lighted at night by lamps placed at regular intervals, and flanked on each side by brick sidewalks and gutters of brick or wood. There were more printing presses, more newssheets, more bookstores in Philadelphia than in any other city in America. On Lombard Street, the painter Charles Willson Peale had recently opened the country's first museum, displaying his collection of exotic stuffed birds and animals, American Indian regalia, silk slippers made for a Chinese woman's bound feet, a shark's jawbone, rare shells, outlandish weapons, a live bear, and a chicken with four legs. Philadelphia's multitude of benevolent societies distributed free medicines to the poor, offered care to needy mothers in labor, provided for the mentally ill, and lent assistance to prisoners in the city's model penitentiary, where inmates enjoyed the startling luxury of flush toilets. Ten thousand books were available in the public library, the nation's first, "an elegant building lately erected, in a modern stile." Many of the country's finest scholars taught at the University of Pennsylvania. Schools for the young were plentiful and free. There were academies for girls, and a Quaker school for blacks, and even a school for orphans, under the personal patronage of Robert Morris, who had himself been left parentless as a boy in Maryland.

There was also a darker side to life in the capital. For the poor—including most of the city's blacks, many of whom lived in crude sheds, cabins, and "mean low box[es] of wood"—life was precarious at best. Homeless men and women pleaded for handouts on the streets. For the working poor, jobs were always insecure, and with no safety net downturns in business sent hundreds cascading into penury. Many wound up in the poorhouse, where they or their children might be sold into indentured servitude. Bodies gave way early from exhaustion and disease. Alcoholism, an illegitimate birth, or a husband's sudden death drove women to prostitution. Respectable folk complained about the "lawless and wandering banditti of wheelbarrow-men, and the unwholesome effluvia of dirty streets," not to mention shameless citizens "going into the river to bathe in utter disregard of all the sentiments of decency."

Sanitation was primitive or nonexistent. Much of the city smelled of manure, sewage, rotting hides, and the refuse of slaughterhouses. One of the main avenues into the city, the *Pennsylvania Gazette* complained, was "the receptacle of stagnant waters, of dung, human excrement, and all kinds of filth—so that a stranger passing into the city, instead of being saluted with the beautiful appearance of groves, meets what is offensive to the eye and most of his other senses." Cesspools were rarely emptied, and seeped into wells. Dock Creek, which meandered through the center of town, was a sludge of poisonous waste that spawned vast aerial flotillas of disease-carrying flies and mosquitoes. Lice crawled everywhere. Epidemics remorselessly swept the city without warning. In 1791 Clement Biddle's city directory fulsomely proclaimed that in recent years the city had enjoyed "a remarkable revolution in respect to the healthiness of its inhabitants," thanks to an "increase in horticulture," the closure of several sources of "putrid exhalations," and the "improved state of physic." In this, Biddle was far too optimistic. The city would soon endure a catastrophe of unimagined proportions, one that would wreak havoc on its hope to retain the national capital.

Philadelphians of all classes took immense pride in their place at the heart of the nation's political life, and felt that their city deserved to remain the capital, no matter what happened at the upstart site on the Potomac. Senator William Maclay sarcastically observed, "The citizens of Philada. (Such is the Strange infatuation of self-love) believe That ten Years is Eternity to them with respect to the residence. & that Congress Will in That Time be so enamoured of them As never to leave them." Many remembered South Carolina Congressman Aedanus Burke's prophecy during the First Congress: that once Pennsylvanians obtained the government, along with the national treasury and all the public offices, they would "laugh at the idea of building palaces in the woods." Indeed, the national government was even more entertaining than Peale's Museum. On any given day, one might see George Washington dressed in black silk and a cocked hat passing by in his cream-colored "chariot," or meet him at his weekly public reception, or at one of Martha Washington's Friday ice cream parties. Or simply knock on the front door of his home: there were no barriers to fend off ordinary citizens.

The federal government carried on its business in quarters that it had begged, borrowed, and rented from the locals. The sixty-five congressmen met on the ground floor of the county courthouse on Sixth Street, and the thirty senators up a painfully steep flight of stairs in a second-floor chamber that was generously lit, at least on sunny days, by tall arched windows. The Supreme Court camped in the mayor's courtroom in City Hall, at the corner of Fifth and Chestnut; the Treasury Department was housed a short distance east on Chestnut, War at Fifth and Chestnut, and State two blocks away on High Street, close to the president's residence at High and Fifth. Although everyone was cramped, access to officials was easy, and politicians from distant corners of the country were exposed to the sophisticated international culture of the city. Indeed, everything in Philadelphia was so convenient that Washington worried that he could never persuade members of the government to leave for the Potomac. "There is a current in this city which sets so strongly against everything that relates to the Federal District, that it is next to impossible to stem it," Washington confided to the district's commissioners. When Pennsylvania voted to erect a $45,000 domed Palladian mansion for the president, fueling Washington's anxiety that the state meant to hold on to the capital, he refused to live in it, believing that if he did so the public would think he had abandoned his dream city on the Potomac. (The mansion would eventually be sold to the University of Pennsylvania to provide quarters for its medical school.)

Instead, Washington ostentatiously made clear that he intended to continue to live in the rented townhouse belonging to his friend, Robert Morris. This elegant, ocher, four-story mansion doubled as the seat of the executive branch of government, establishing a tradition that persists to the present day. Elegant though it was, Washington complained that it was smaller than his former residence in New York, requiring visitors to climb two sets of stairs and pass his private rooms to reach his study, the equivalent of today's Oval Office, which was located in a converted bathroom. The house and its outbuildings were crammed with the president's entourage, housing as many as thirty people at any given time: the president, his wife, and her two grandchildren; Washington's chief secretary, Tobias Lear, and his wife, Polly; three additional secretaries, and assorted valets, coachmen, footmen, porters, maids, housekeepers, and their families, all wedged into quarters that were carefully subdivided to separate free whites from enslaved blacks.

In the early 1790s the presidential household included eight or nine slaves, and about twice that number of white servants. Tobias Lear observed, the president's "negroes are not treated as blacks in general are in their Country, they are clothed and fed as well as any labouring people whatever and they are not subject to the lash of a domineering overseer—*but they still are slaves.*" Pennsylvania's emancipation law posed the same problem for the president that it did for other slaveholders. Any out-of-state slave who remained in Pennsylvania for more than six months automatically became free, apart from those owned by members of Congress, who were specifically exempted from the law. Washington was careful to take no chances. "The idea of freedom might be too great a temptation for them to resist," he advised Lear. "At any rate it might, if they conceived they had a right to it, make them insolent in a State of Slavery." He ordered his secretary to see that each of his slaves was temporarily rotated out of Pennsylvania before the expiration of the legal time limit. Lear was to lie to the slaves, if necessary, to ensure their compliance. "I wish to have it accomplished under the pretext that may deceive both them and the Public," the president directed, "and none I think would so effectually do this as Mrs. Washington coming to Virginia next month."

WASHINGTON HAD REASON to worry. Thanks to the city's large Quaker population, and to the legal protections enshrined in state law, no place in the United States was more hospitable to blacks than Philadelphia. Free and fugitive alike, they flocked to the capital from the Pennsylvania hinterland, from New Jersey, Maryland, and Delaware. As early as 1688 Quakers in nearby Germantown had lodged the first formal protest against slavery in the colonies, asserting, "Tho' they are black, we cannot conceive that there is more liberty to have them as slaves, as there is to have other white ones," and that those who traded in them were no better than thieves. Through the next century, as Philadelphia's population swelled, the number of slaveholders steadily declined, while the enslaved population plummeted, dropping from about fourteen hundred to seven hundred in the years just before the Revolutionary War. Admittedly, slavery was still a part of Philadelphia's life: in 1790, 273 of the city's 2,100 blacks were still enslaved. However, among whites a complacent tolerance of slavery was rapidly giving way to angry disdain. The French traveler Brissot de Warville, a passionate abolitionist, could exclaim after visiting the capital, "There exists, then, a land where these poor Negroes are believed to have souls and intelligence, where there is felt an obligation to shape their character to virtue and to give them instruction . . . where Negroes, by their virtue and diligence, disprove the slanderous lies which their oppressors utter about them elsewhere."

Philadelphia was headquarters to the Pennsylvania Abolition Society (its full jaw-breaking title was the Pennsylvania Society for Promoting the Abolition of Slavery and the Relief of Free Negroes Unlawfully Held in Bondage and for Improving the Condition of the African Race), which was founded in 1775 and became the model for similar groups that proliferated from New England to Virginia during the postwar period. The society's charter demanded of all who considered themselves Christians "to use such means as are in their power to extend the blessings of freedom to every part of the human race," in particular to those of them "who are detained in bondage by fraud or violence." After a hiatus during the war, the society reorganized in 1787 with the aged Benjamin Franklin as nominal president, and the self-effacing philanthropist James Pemberton, of whom it was said that "his coat was threadbare but spotless," as its de facto leader. Members included many of the most eminent professionals in the city, providing a reservoir of political clout as well as a genteel, Quakerly style of operation that was guided by obedience to the law and optimism that emancipation would soon win out through patient moral persuasion. Not all opponents of slavery were quite so mild mannered. Perhaps the slave trade might best be restrained by the confiscation of slave ships, and the execution of their captains, suggested one implacable correspondent to the *Pennsylvania Gazette*. "But death were too mild a punishment! Let the wretch be loaded with chains, and sunk to the middle of one of the swamps of Carolina or Georgia, there to plant rice for the remainder of his days, under the control of one of his own Negro passengers, who shall be authorised to use the cowskin at discretion." This was precisely the kind of thinking that Southern enemies of prolonging the government's sojourn in Philadelphia most feared.

THE SOCIETY ALSO TURNED Benjamin Banneker into the nation's first African American celebrity. True, there had been the enslaved Boston poet Phyllis Wheatley, who had penned a hymn of praise to George Washington, and the illiterate "African Calculator" Thomas Fuller, who amazed visitors to the Virginia plantation where he was enslaved by performing dazzling numerical feats in his head. But Banneker was something else entirely: a self-made scholar in the classic American mold, who just happened to be black. Without the support of Philadelphia abolitionists, he would have lapsed back into rural oblivion; but his patron Andrew Ellicott, after his return from the Federal District, sent a copy of Banneker's calculations to James Pemberton, who recognized their importance immediately. What better proof could there be of Africans' intellectual equality than an almanac based on the computations that Banneker had made during his long winter nights in the Federal District: the logarithms of the sun's distance from the earth, the longitude of the moon at the beginning of each year, geometrical diagrams of eclipses—in short, a wealth of information that eighteenth-century farmers required for planting their crops, and sailors for piloting their ships by the stars. With Pemberton's assistance, a publisher was found, and the almanac went on sale at the end of 1791, promising an accurate account of the motions of the sun and moon, "the true places and aspects of the planets, Conjunctions, Eclipses, Judgments of the Weather, Festivals," plus court calendars for Pennsylvania, Maryland, Delaware, and Virginia, "several valuable recipes," and selections from the musings of a homegrown "Kentucky philosopher." It was the first work of its kind by a black man in American history, and it was an instant best seller.

Banneker sent a copy of his almanac to Thomas Jefferson. Had not the chasm of race intervened, the two men might well have become friends. They shared a farmer's deep emotional connection to the land, coupled to an engineer's fascination with the workings of things, as well as passion for the realm of pure intellect. Instead, this epistolary encounter—the two men never met in person—laid bare Jefferson's fundamental anxiety about race. Jefferson responded to Banneker's letter with interest, and sent the almanac with its "elegant solutions of Geometrical problems" on to his friend the Marquis de Condorcet, the secretary of the Academy of Sciences in Paris, inviting his assessment. "I shall be delighted to see these examples of moral eminence so multiplied as to prove that the want of talents observed in [blacks] is merely the effect of their degraded condition, and not proceeding from any difference in the structure of the parts on which intellect depends," Jefferson wrote to Condorcet. Jefferson pursued the matter no further. Banneker's brilliance shook Jefferson's racism at its core, but failed to topple it. Jefferson knew that unless slavery was abolished there would be few, if any, more Bannekers. But he would do nothing to subvert the institution upon which his own way of life depended. Meanwhile, Banneker's health steadily deteriorated. "I have a constant pain in my head, a palpitation in my flesh, and I may say I am attended with a complication of disorders," he wrote to an admirer, gently refusing her request for a few lines of verse from what he described as his "trembling hands." Oblivious to physical discomfort and visitors alike, and preoccupied with his fruit trees, beekeeping, and the stars, he continued to crank out new editions of his almanac into the early years of the nineteenth century, until his death in 1806 at the age of seventy-five.

In practical terms, the Pennsylvania Abolition Society fought for the education, employment, social welfare, and legal defense of former slaves with considerable vigor. As one of its lawyers proudly expressed it, "In Pennsylvania at least it will not be thought fanatical to protect a man though black." Slave masters often learned the hard way that Pennsylvania courts would not readily cave in to their demands, and that in order to recover their human property, they would have to hire lawyers, and spend money and time traveling to appear in court, with no guarantee of winning in the end. Indeed, they might even face prosecution themselves for failing to comply with the technicalities of Pennsylvania law. No slaveholders were immune. In April 1791 George Washington's secretary Tobias Lear warned the president himself that, in Philadelphia, "there were not wanting persons who would not only give them (the Slaves) advice; but would use any means to entice them from their masters." (This was not an idle concern: Martha Washington's maid and the president's personal chef, two of the most prized slaves in the presidential household, would make successful breaks for freedom, much to Washington's chagrin.)

The same conditions that made Philadelphia the preferred destination for free blacks and fugitive slaves also made it a magnet for slave catchers, with its support industry of venal ship's captains, thugs for hire, and innkeepers like Lewis Bender, who for a fee helpfully held recaptured slaves for their masters at the Black Horse tavern, on North Second Street. Newspapers bulged with ads for runaways like "Joe," a "tawney" six-foot giant from rural Chester County, who was "much given to drink, playing on the fiddle, dancing and frolicking," and was supposed to be en route to Philadelphia, where his free brother lived, and "Peter," a New Jersey mulatto with "large glaring eyes" who was supposed to be "lurking" somewhere in the city; and "Dick," a twenty-eight-year-old from Trenton, with "tolerable black smooth skin" and "a bunch of bushy hair behind," who was also last seen on the Philadelphia road. Dick's master Abraham Hunt added, by way of further identification, that the fugitive slave "has scars on his back, having been several times flogg'd at the whipping post."

Kidnappers flourished, too. Within hours, a free man or woman kidnapped in Philadelphia would become a valuable slave in Baltimore or Wilmington. Andrew Ellicott, the Federal District's surveyor, would later testify eloquently before Congress about how "these poor, unprotected victims have been claimed as fugitive slaves, have been suddenly and secretly dragged before some magistrate selected for the special purpose." Some were literally snatched from the streets, and others—especially children—lured aboard sloops in the Delaware River with promises of work, clothes, or food, and then carried south for sale. Still others, like the unfortunate Moses White, were thrown in jail as suspected fugitives and ultimately reenslaved. "Says he is free," an ad placed by the Lancaster, Pennsylvania, jailer noted. "His master, if he has any, is requested to come and take him away, otherwise he will be sold in three weeks from this date, for his expenses."

As the activists of the Pennsylvania Abolition Society worked to create a place for freed slaves in America, William Thornton continued to dream of leading them back to Africa in clouds of glory. In October 1790 he left his new fifteen-year-old wife, Anna Maria, in Philadelphia and returned to Tortola to see his dying mother; he remained there for two years. There had been changes since his boyhood. Quaker influence had faded, weakened by isolation, intermarriage with non-Quakers, and the growing conflict between Quaker antislavery and the economic imperatives of the plantation economy. The atmosphere was tense. Just before Thornton's return, slaves on a local plantation had rioted when false reports of a general emancipation circulated and were savagely put down. Thornton shocked the island's colonial council by attempting to convince them to enact an emancipation plan for the island's slaves. They "hint me to be a dangerous member of society when I mention things concerning the blacks," he wrote with a twinge of amusement (and perhaps pride) to the British abolitionist Granville Sharp.

While on Tortola, Thornton received the unwelcome news from friends in England that the colony of former British slaves they had dispatched to the coast of Sierra Leone had proved a disaster of monumental proportions. Of the first contingent of 450 settlers, 84 had died from sickness before the ships even left England. Another 96 had died from illness and exposure soon after their arrival. Others were captured by native rulers and sold back into slavery. Many of the settlers who remained had abandoned the colony and relocated for safety—to the unutterable dismay of the philanthropists who had organized the settlement—to slave factories elsewhere on the coast. Even the whites who had been sent out to serve the colony had entered the service of slave traders, lured by large salaries. Sharp warned Thornton that this catastrophe must dissuade him from all thought of moving to Africa. But Thornton's unquenchable optimism remained undiminished. Destiny had touched his shoulder. Nothing, including his most amiable and affectionate wife, he wrote back to Sharp, could "have any effect in staying my soul in any part of the world except Africa."

It was also at this time that Thornton learned of the design competition for the United States Capitol. He threw himself into the project, which brought him welcome distraction from the continuing mockery of his fellow island whites. The pungent smell of sugar being rendered into molasses and rum filled the humid air as, day and night, he worked at his sketches, oblivious to the thrum of rain on the giant bulletwood trees, and the thud of waves on the shore of nearby Sea Cow Bay. From his room, he could see beyond the plantation's wattle-and-daub slave quarters and squat whitewashed warehouses to mountainsides silvery and undulating with sugarcane, and the turquoise expanse of the Caribbean, where islands shimmered like dream images in the haze. Thornton later described his creative process to a friend, Anthony Fothergill: "First I thought of the amazing extent of our country, and of the apartments that the representatives of a very numerous people would one day require. Secondly, I consulted the dignity of appearance, and made minutiae give way to a grand outline, full of broad prominent lights and broad deep shadows. Thirdly, I sought for all the variety of architecture that could be embraced in the forms I had lain down, without mixing small parts of the large of the same kind; and keeping the whole regular, in range, throughout the building. Finally I attended to the minute parts; that we might not be deemed deficient in those touches which a painter would require in the finishing."

In his lively imagination, the clean classical lines of democracy's temple-to-be on the Potomac perhaps lent something of their grandeur to his dreamlike vision of a black colony on the African coast: twinned images of better worlds, one white, one black, united by idealism, but bifurcated irrevocably by race. For Thornton, as for his friend Thomas Jefferson, the vision was a comforting refuge from sordid reality, and from the guilt and fear that freighted every scheme for emancipation. As long as Thornton conceived of African Americans as a problem to be solved, like the design of the Capitol's entablature, or the disposition of its water closets, he felt himself on firm moral and emotional ground. Like nearly all white men of his time, he could not see former slaves as people capable of charting their own destiny, with their own voices that deserved to be heard. Blinkered by his own ambitions for black Americans, he failed to understand the extraordinary revolution that was taking place in Philadelphia, which would become the national capital by default if the promoters on the Potomac failed to achieve their goal. There, former slaves were making clear that they had much to say indeed.

Chapter 6

AN ALARMING AND SERIOUS TIME

"We found a freedom to go forth, confiding in Him
who had preserved us in the midst of a burning fiery
furnace, sensible that it was our duty to do all the good
we could to our suffering fellow mortals. We set out to
see where we could be useful."

—RICHARD ALLEN AND
ABSALOM JONES

ON A SUNDAY MORNING in the autumn of 1792, four
African Americans entered St. George's Church at Fourth and Vine, in
Philadelphia. They were conservative, pious men, and scrupulously def-
erential, in the way that all black men who lived among whites cultivated
for their own safety. All four had been raised in slavery. Two of them,
Absalom Jones and Richard Allen, were preachers in their own right,
and probably wore the solemn black frock coats and knee breeches
appropriate to their vocation. St. George's congregation was largely
white, of course, like that of all the churches in Philadelphia. However,

it took pride in accommodating free blacks and slaves, with whom in the spirit of Christian generosity it patronizingly shared the word of the Lord preached from its carved oak pulpit. The four black men had their own reason to be proud. They and the other African American members of St. George's flock had contributed their labor, and even money—shillings painstakingly saved from their labor as sweeps, cartmen, and household servants—to enlarging the church to accommodate its growing membership. Their efforts reflected not only their personal devotion, but also their quiet determination to wrest a dignified place for black Philadelphians in the life of the city that was their home.

But all was not well at St. George's. It had at least been hinted to the blacks that in spite of their contributions they were to be assigned isolated seats in the new upstairs gallery, making it plain that whites meant to keep them separate rather than draw them into more intimate fellowship. What Jones, Allen, Caesar Cranch, and William White thought about this is not recorded. What they did, however, made their sentiments perfectly clear: they staged the first sit-in protest in American history. Allen later described the scene: "We expected to take the seats over the ones we formerly occupied below, not knowing any better. We took those seats; meeting had begun, and they were nearly done singing, and just as we got to the seats, the [white] Elder said, 'Let us pray.' We had not been long upon our knees before I heard considerable scuffling and loud talking. I raised my head up and saw one of the trustees having hold of the Rev. Absalom Jones, pulling him off his knees, and saying, 'You must get up, you must not kneel here.' Mr. Jones replied, 'Wait until the prayer is over, and I will get up, and trouble you no more.' With that he beckoned to one of the [white] trustees to come to his assistance. He came and went to William White to pull him up. By this time prayer was over, and we all went out of the church in a body, and they were no more plagued by us in the church." The walkout went unmentioned in the local newspapers. Although it meant little or nothing to white Philadelphians, its meaning for blacks was profound, for here in the teeming metropolis where people of all kinds were inventing what it was to be American it announced that African Americans intended to be part of that process.

On his quest to recruit settlers for his proposed colony in Africa, William Thornton had arrived in Philadelphia in 1787 hopeful that he would find many there "very desirous of reaching the coast of Guinea." To his surprise, he received a chilly reception. His "vast plan" held little appeal to men and women who were creating a free world for themselves right where they were. Philadelphia in the 1790s was not only the capital of the United States: it was the capital of black America, and the embryo of an African American culture that would grow and flourish for centuries to come. It would give birth to the nation's first black churches, schools, and mutual aid societies; to its first black middle class; and eventually to its first black political activists.

Former slaves were emerging from a world where no relationship had been safe from white interference, and in which they were dependent for their every need on the self-interest or indulgence of their owners. In Philadelphia, to a far greater degree than in any other place in the country, blacks were free to come together on their own, to explore for themselves what it meant to be black in America, and for the first time in North America, to create community as they desired it to be. Legal emancipation was only the first step toward real freedom. Even harder, perhaps, was the interior liberation that challenged every man and woman to think like a free person. Questions that no slave ever faced suddenly had to be answered: How were they to find work and negotiate wages? Where would they live? Could they learn to read and write? Could they ascend to the higher professions? Could they become citizens? None of the answers was clear in a society that was controlled by whites, most of whom were at best indifferent to black aspirations, and who wondered if blacks were mentally and morally capable of surviving on their own.

Even in Philadelphia, freedom was a relative term. For blacks everywhere in the country the perimeter of freedom shrank abruptly in February 1793 when Congress, meeting in its cramped quarters on Sixth Street, enacted the first Fugitive Slave Law by a lopsided vote of forty-eight to seven. The law—it might better have been called the Slavery Protection Act—made it a federal crime to help a fleeing slave, and empowered a master or his hired slave catcher to seize a fugitive and take him or her before any local magistrate, who required only oral testimony from the master or his agent to send the fugitive back to the place from which he or she had allegedly fled. The supposed fugitives had no right to speak on their own behalf, much less to demand a lawyer, while anyone who obstructed the process was subject to a draconian fine of $500, about $21,000 in present-day currency. The ads for runaway slaves that appeared in Philadelphia newspapers constantly reminded blacks just how tenuous their safety was. Any man or woman, freeborn or fugitive, could easily see a child, parent, or sibling, not to mention himself, in the plight of Cuff, who had run off in a white jacket, red vest, and olive-colored trousers, and whose mistress warned local families against concealing him, demanding that "every one act the honest part, and see a certificate of freedom before they employ a Negro."

Quite apart from their vulnerability to slave hunters and kidnappers, free black Philadelphians were liable to be bound into servitude for offenses as innocuous as vagrancy, and typically they were condemned to harsher punishment than whites who committed the same crimes. They were completely excluded from the political process. They were unwelcome in almost all theaters, reading rooms, and other public institutions. And although they were permitted to attend public schools, they were explicitly barred from institutions of higher learning. It was also close to impossible for them to develop any but the smallest businesses since banks, with only the rarest exceptions, refused to lend black shopkeepers money to expand, and white firms declined to hire blacks for jobs where they might learn the accounting and financial skills needed to manage larger enterprises.

Difficult though life was for the majority of black Philadelphians, the door of opportunity had opened a crack. A new kind of man—at this point, those who were pushing open the door of freedom were virtually all men—walked the city's cobbled streets, uncowed by racism, alert to his own talents, and eager to work his way upward in a society that scarcely knew what to make of him. At a time when few blacks had access to print, one of the few who made his voice heard was an otherwise anonymous correspondent to the *Gazette of the United States*—he identified himself only as "Africanus," who proclaimed, "The American and the African are one species—the law of nature declares it. And I, a sheep hairy African negro, being free and in some degree enlightened, feel myself equal to the duties of [any] spirited, noble, and generous American freeman." Another was freeborn James Forten, who had served bravely on an American privateer during the war, and patriotically accepted imprisonment rather than turn traitor and join the British. After the war, Forten apprenticed himself to a white sailmaker named Robert Bridges, bringing with him hands-on expertise from his years at sea that proved invaluable to his employer. In 1798 Bridges would transfer the business to Forten, and help ensure that his clients continued to do business with him. Forten himself would eventually become one of the wealthiest black businessmen in the city, employing both white and African American craftsmen in his sail loft, trading in real estate, and forcefully speaking out on behalf of civil rights and abolition.

Like plants straining toward the sunlight through fissures in a rock, African Americans asserted their independence in spite of white disdain and the low expectations of their friends. By the end of the decade, there would be seventeen black businessmen, including James Forten and Richard Allen, listed in Philadelphia's city directory. There would be black teachers and preachers, black Masons, black charities, and even a school organized and managed by African Americans, the nation's first. Today, in an age when the term "black community" has become a widely used convention of journalists and political leaders, the revolutionary originality of what black Philadelphians were doing can easily be missed. They were truly creating the first free black *community* in America, in which members, often at considerable personal sacrifice and cost, invented a shared spiritual world, shared responsibility, a shared sense of identity as free men and women, and a shared determination to maintain their self-respect in the face of discrimination and outright hostility.

At the heart of this awakening pulsed the faith of a handful of inspired men, foremost among them Absalom Jones and Richard Allen. At a time when politics was a closed avenue to blacks, religion paved the way toward what a much later era would call personal empowerment.

Spiritual questions were imperatives to men and women desperate to discover their individuality and a sense of inner purpose. Was there salvation for men and women with black skin, and how could they achieve it? How could they find God in churches governed by hostile whites? How were they to preserve their humanity, indeed their sanity, in this unfolding era of compromised and always threatened freedom? The enslaved New York pamphleteer Jupiter Hammon had asserted that "getting our liberty in this world, is nothing to our having the liberty of the children of God. Heaven is a place for those who are born again, and who love God; and it is a place where they will be happy forever." Jones and Allen, however, believed that not only were both earthly and spiritual liberty possible, but that they were inextricably intertwined. They knew from harsh personal experience that white Americans could not be trusted to respect the freedom of blacks. (A few years later, Allen would be seized on a Philadelphia street in broad daylight by slave catchers, and nearly shipped south into slavery before he was rescued.) And they understood that it required a great leap of faith to obey the commands of people whose power over them they knew to be unjust. But even the oppressed, slave and free, had the power to cultivate moral autonomy: they were free every waking moment to think for themselves, and to choose between good and evil, no matter what powerful whites demanded of them.

If Philadelphia was the capital of free black America, Jones and Allen were its copresidents, so to speak. Jones, the older of the two, was forty years old in 1787, an introspective, intellectual man endowed with a reserve of quiet fortitude as large as his rotund body. Born and raised a slave in Delaware, he was relatively fortunate in his master, who permitted him to become literate by begging lessons from anyone who would help him. However, this same master, with a callousness that would have been breathtaking were it not so commonplace, sold Jones's mother and his six brothers and sisters, and moved to Philadelphia, where he put Absalom to work in his store. For the next twenty-two years, he denied Jones's pleas to be allowed to purchase his freedom, although Jones did eventually succeed in saving enough money to buy two houses, to marry, and to buy freedom for his wife and himself.

Jones left no record of the emotional toll that these events must have taken upon him. But the pattern of his life shows an extraordinary tenacity rooted in his Episcopalian faith, which again and again caused powerful white men to yield to his determination to forge a freer life for the greater community of African Americans. Jones's persistence was finally rewarded with freedom in 1784. He was already a leading member of Philadelphia's tiny black elite when Richard Allen arrived there in 1786.

Allen, thirteen years Jones's junior and leaner of build, was, in the words of W. E. B. DuBois, "a shrewd, quick, popular leader, positive and dogged and yet far-seeing in his knowledge of Negro character." Allen had also grown up in slavery, the property of a Philadelphia lawyer who owned a plantation in Delaware. Both master and slave were swept up in the hurricane of revivalist Methodism that blew across the region in the late 1770s, and it left them transformed. Whites and blacks who were put off by the staid rigidity and cerebral sermonizing of the Episcopal church were drawn to Methodism's promise of immediate spiritual rebirth and the uninhibited emotionalism of its revivals. (The more reserved were shocked by the sight of ecstatic crowds who "leapt and swayed in every direction and dashed themselves to the ground, pounding with hands and feet, gnashing their teeth.") Although Methodists would soon begin to trim their principles to gain wider acceptance among more respectable segments of the white population, they then doctrinally held slavery to be "repugnant to the unalienable rights of mankind, and to the spirit of the Christian religion." Allen's master embraced the gospel of emancipation, and allowed him to buy his freedom. For his part, Allen discovered in himself an unsuspected talent for preaching that would shape the rest of his life, and leave an indelible imprint on African American religious history. As a free man, he evangelized on street corners and in rural groves from New York to the Carolinas, earning his way as a sawyer, teamster, and shoemaker. Absalom Jones heard him in Philadelphia in 1786, and the two men soon formed a mutual bond, despite their sectarian differences.

In April 1787 eight black men led by Jones and Allen met at the Quakers' Negro School to establish what they decided to call the Free

African Society, "the first wavering step of a people toward an organized social life," as DuBois put it. They had originally hoped to form "some kind of religious society." But African Americans were dispersed among the Episcopalians, Methodists, Presbyterians, and Quakers, not to mention the "irreligious and uncivilized," in Jones's words, who belonged to no church at all. When it proved impossible to find common doctrinal ground, Jones and Allen declared the society to be dedicated to mutual welfare "without regard to religious tenets," with a mandate to provide aid to sick members and to widows and orphans. Each member agreed to contribute to the general fund "one silver shilling in Pennsylvania currency" per month, and to provide the "orderly and sober" needy with a weekly stipend of up to three shillings and nine pence, as needed.

Jones and Allen were not radicals: they had nothing in common with the rebellious Gabriels, Denmark Veseys, and Nat Turners* who led bloody and self-destructive revolts against white power. Rather, embedded in faith, they urged followers to offer gratitude to God for leading them from the pagan darkness of Africa to "a land of Gospel light," from slavery to liberty, and from guilt to salvation. They reminded their followers that they lived under constant scrutiny. "Remember, that you have enemies, as well as friends; that you will be narrowly watched; and that less allowance will be made for your failings, than for those of other people," they warned. "Peaceableness among yourselves, and with all men, is indispensable to a fair character; as also truth in your dealings, in your words, and in your inner man," along with diligence, honesty, temperance, and "an obliging, friendly, meek conversation." This was hardly a call for revolution, but it was a viable recipe for survival in an America where all the levers of power were controlled by whites. If they were to thrive at all, free black com-

---

*Gabriel Prosser led an abortive revolt among slaves in several counties near Richmond, Virginia, in August 1800. Denmark Vesey, a free black, was accused of fomenting rebellion among slaves in Charleston, South Carolina, in 1822. Nat Turner organized a violent slave revolt in Southampton County, Virginia, in 1831. All three events resulted in bloody reprisals against innocent blacks.

munities would have to thread themselves circumspectly between the narrow interstices of white tolerance.

The two men never abandoned their mutual dream of a black church, a spiritual community "so general as to embrace all, and yet so orthodox in cardinal points as to offend none," where blacks would be free to pray in a way of their own choosing, among their own people, away from the disapproving eyes and well-intentioned bullying of white authorities. Their unceremonious eviction from St. George's in the autumn of 1792 spurred them to redouble their efforts. Land was acquired on Fifth Street. A fine two-story brick meeting house was planned. Funds were sought from African Americans and from white supporters, prominent among them the eminent abolitionist Benjamin Rush, who at the request of Jones and Allen also sketched out "sundry articles of faith and a plan for church government," which provided that none but "men of colour" could be elected to any church office, except that of minister. At first, contributions flowed in. Then, in the spring of 1793 an utterly unforeseen catastrophe occurred. Boatloads of penniless whites began arriving from Sainte-Domingue, fleeing butchery by their rebellious slaves. Refugee ships spilled at least 750 "French unfortunates" into the city. Homes were thrown open to them "without any form of ceremony," and donors abruptly diverted their pledges from the African church to the Haitian whites. It seemed, with pitiless irony, that the legacy of Haitian slavery was about to doom the hopes of Philadelphia's freemen when, like the deus ex machina of classical theater, one of the richest men in Pennsylvania, Rush's friend the land speculator and philanthropist John Nicholson—who would soon play a leading role in the effort to develop the new capital on the Potomac—stepped in with a $1,000 loan, sufficient to complete the church.

On August 22, 1793, more than one hundred black Philadelphians gathered in the leafy shade of broad-boughed oaks a little outside the city, to celebrate the roof-raising of the church of St. Thomas the Apostle, which Jones and Allen had named after the first disciple to recognize the divinity of Christ. Several respected blacks personally served the handful of loyal white friends in attendance, who included Rush and Nicholson. Then the whites rose, and served their black hosts. Extraordinary scene!

"The dinner was plentiful—the liquors were of the first quality—and the dessert, which consisted only of melons, was very good," Rush wrote to his wife, Julia. "Never did I witness such a scene of innocent—nay more—such virtuous and philanthropic joy." Rush stood to offer a toast: "May African churches everywhere soon succeed to African bondage!" A black man named Billy Grey attempted to express his gratitude to the whites present, but broke down in a flood of tears. Later, after everyone had dined, Jones, Allen, and several other blacks came up to Nicholson and took him by the hand, and thanked him for the loan that had made the church possible. One of them told the speculator, "May you live long, sir, and when you die, may you not die eternally."

THE DAY AFTER the picnic, August 23, the wealthy Quaker Elizabeth Drinker noted in her diary, "A Fever prevails in the City of the malignant kind, numbers have died of it. Some say it was occasioned by damaged Coffee, and fish." Seventy people were already sick with what Drinker called "putrid fever." Some speculated that the mysterious illness was brought on a vessel from Sainte-Domingue, or was spread by a "noxious miasma" emanating from polluted marshes and drains, or rotted foodstuffs, or the infested wood of old houses; others that it resulted from drunkenness and dissolution, or perhaps from excessive fear or grief; others that it was God's just punishment for Philadelphians' sinful pride. "Tis really an alarming and serious time," Drinker wrote. The contagion was yellow fever, and it would take more than a century for medical researchers to discover that it was carried by infected mosquitoes.

President Washington, like many residents of the city, at first tried to ignore the "spreading disorder." Epidemics were simply a fact of life in eighteenth-century America. The president had other things to worry about, such as the irritating new French ambassador, who was arousing the urban rabble with his revolutionary ideas, and the increasingly cutting personal attacks to which he was subjected from democrats pressing for a military alliance with France. (Washington found some moments of solace in letters from more conservative citizens who praised him for steering a neutral course between the warring European powers.) Then there were the usual problems in the Federal District. At the president's request, the Irish architect James Hoban had come back with plans for a more imposing presidential residence. Washington liked what he saw, a bigger footprint for the mansion and an abundance of frills—roses, garlands, acanthus leaves, acorns, griffons—that would awe Americans and impress the most fashionable European visitors. But when he looked at the price tag he blanched. "I had no idea that it would carry the expence of that building to anything like the sum of 77,900 pounds," he (at least figuratively) gasped to the commissioners. Raising money to build the capital was already threatening to become a crisis. Finally he advised the commissioners to swallow the cost and just get started. This was to be the home of presidents yet unborn. It must serve the needs of men who would someday govern an empire. The whole building need not be built at once. *Just get started.* By September, work had begun on the basement walls.

There were other upsetting reports from the Potomac: serious defects had apparently been found in Thornton's plan for the Capitol. Among other problems, according to Jefferson, the interior colonnade would obstruct congressmen's lines of sight, the floor of the central peristyle was too wide to support itself, stairways were too low, and many parts of the building lacked light and air. These criticisms originated with the young French architect Stephen Hallet, who was nothing if not self-interested, his own design for the Capitol having been shoved aside when Thornton's was accepted. However, if Hallet was right, it would be folly to proceed with the building's construction. "I was governed by the beauty of the exterior," Washington defensively admitted to Jefferson. "I had no knowledge of the rules or principles of architecture." Hallet proposed a revised plan that would erase almost everything in Thornton's design that the president had liked in the first place—and would increase the cost of the Capitol by one-third. Eventually Thornton would regain the president's confidence, and a compromise design would incorporate a modest version of some of Hallet's suggestions. In the meantime, it added up to one more headache for the beleaguered president. To ease his anxiety, Washington's thoughts turned to Mount Vernon and to farming, as they so often did in times of stress: Had the English oats planted in the spring come up yet? Wasn't it time to thresh the timothy grass and clover? By the second week in September, however, the horror of what was happening in Philadelphia was inescapable.

The summer had been hot and humid, and the muggy air was acrid with the smell of "excrementous substances in a state of putrefaction" that clogged the city's stagnant drains and nurtured clouds of mosquitoes. Hot weather always brought fevers. This was different, however. Terrifyingly different. Philadelphia was on the cusp of one of the worst catastrophes in American history, a sudden and devastating attack by an alien, invisible, and utterly terrifying enemy, striking savagely without respect to class, sex, or education, slaughtering alike the strong and the weak, the generous and the mean, the pious and the profane. The first to die were a number of unfortunates who crowded in hovels on Water Street. Then several foreign sailors. Then an oyster-seller on Front Street. Then respectable people like Mary Shewell, the young wife of a Baptist minister. Day after day, Drinker recorded the relentlessly mounting toll of the dead: Sally Mifflin in Walnut Street, the Hodges' maid, "a man at the shoemaker's," John Morgan who had married the Smiths' daughter, "and many whose names we did not hear."

Typically, victims first felt a chill, then a headache and upset stomach, then pains in their limbs and back. The next stage was peculiarly horrible and disgusting. Victims turned yellow and began hemorrhaging from their nose, gums, ears, stomach, and bowels. Hideous lesions disfigured the skin. Finally the flesh turned purple, as if it had been savagely bruised. Some victims lingered for a week or more, others appeared to recover just hours before they died. "Some lost their reason and raged with all the fury madness could produce, and died in strong convulsions," Absalom Jones and Richard Allen wrote in their extraordinary account of the epidemic. "Others retained their reason to the last, and seemed rather to fall asleep than die." Corpses leaked so much black fluid that coffins had to be lined with tar. With the utmost seriousness, medical authorities proposed all kinds of exotic preventive measures. Tobacco smoke would ward off infection, it was asserted, and sprinkling vinegar through the house, or wearing camphor around the neck, or burning gunpowder to blast the miasma from the corrupted air. Desperate Philadelphians shot off guns inside their homes. For a time, soldiers rolled cannon around the city, firing every few yards. Elizabeth Drinker dosed her husband with Daffy's Elixir, a spongeful of vinegar, and a sprig of wormwood. But nothing seemed to work. By the end of August, hundreds had died. Like grim fates, cartmen loitered in front of city hall, waiting for business, and feeding their horses from the coffins they would use later that day. So many were the dead that the tolling of bells to mark their passing was forbidden so as not to demoralize the living.

Panic spread. The city's trim cobbled streets emptied. Families barred their doors in a pathetic effort to fend off infection, then watched each other sicken and die. Those who could—judges and constables, bankers and clerks, chimney sweeps, printers, even the night watchmen—fled to the countryside. The financier Robert Morris, like most of the city's elite, holed up at his estate in the suburbs. Fear traveled with them, first along the stage routes, then up and down the Atlantic seaboard. Terrified, and often infected, they jammed roads from the city with their possessions piled into everything from gilded carriages to sedan chairs. In the midst of social and moral breakdown, paranoid rumors proliferated: a French army had captured New York and was marching on Philadelphia; Negroes had poisoned the wells. Rural vigilantes ordered refugees off stagecoaches and ran them out of town, and in at least a few instances beat hapless strangers to death. Starving travelers dropped dead by the roadside. Postmasters in New Jersey and Maryland dipped letters from Philadelphia in vinegar with tongs. At distant ports, Philadelphia ships were quarantined, or ordered back to sea. At New York, mobs forced passengers back into boats arriving from New Jersey.

Philadelphia's port, fell silent as commerce ground to a halt. Perishables rotted on the docks. Businesses collapsed. Each morning yielded a new crop of corpses. The city itself was dying. Day by day, first the bonds of public civility, and then the most intimate family ties, frayed and snapped. Doctors and nurses, fearing for their own lives, abandoned the ill. The poorhouse turned away the needy from its doors. Hundreds died simply for lack of treatment, "without a human being to hand them a drink of water, to administer medicines, or to perform any charitable office for them," according to the contemporary journalist Mathew Carey. Desperate officials unceremoniously dumped the helpless sick and dying at a suburban mansion once occupied by Vice President Adams, quickly turning it into what one diarist grimly termed "a great human slaughter-house." Parents abandoned their infected children, and children their parents, husbands their wives, and wives their husbands. "Tis very afflicting to walk through the streets of our once flourishing and happy city," wrote Drinker with Quaker understatement.

A handful of doctors remained in the city. Among them, none was more respected than Benjamin Rush, he who during the debates over the seat of government back in 1790 had warned against the "bilious fevers" of the Potomac. His finely chiseled features and pale blue eyes radiated a commanding fusion of charismatic intelligence, compassion, and fatally unbreachable self-confidence. For Rush, medicine, morality, and politics were inextricably intertwined: a confidante of Tom Paine, he was an outspoken advocate of virtually every progressive cause of his time from improved sanitation and prison reform, to public education, women's education, and temperance. Friends called him "Mr. Great Heart." His reforming impulse, like his irrepressible optimism, was deeply rooted in evangelical Christianity. As his biographer Alyn Brodsky elegantly put it, although baptized in the Church of England, he "moved through a number of the Protestant factions like a migratory animal in quest of the most gratifying habitat."

No cause inspired Rush to loftier flights than emancipation. "I love even the name of Africa, and never see a slave or freeman without emotions which I seldom feel in the same degree towards my unfortunate fellow creatures of a fairer complexion," he exclaimed. "Let us continue to love and serve them, for they are our brethren not only by creation, but by redemption." He, even more decisively than William Thornton, was one of the few early abolitionists who went beyond opposition to the institution of slavery, to attack racism itself. He fiercely rejected the prevalent belief that blacks were by nature mentally and morally inferior to whites. "All the vices which are charged upon the Negroes in the Southern colonies and the West-Indies, such as Idelness, Treachery, Theft, and the like, are the genuine offspring of slavery, and serve as an argument to prove that they were not intended for it." He also dismissed the Biblical argument advanced by proslavery ideologues that as the supposed children of Cain, Africans had been cursed with black skin by God, and were destined to atone forever for his sins. "The vulgar notion of their being descended from Cain, who was supposed to have been marked with this color, is too absurd to need a refutation," he wrote. Indeed, he went so far as to say that far from being a curse, black skin was an obvious asset that "qualifies them for that part of the Globe in which Providence has placed them," adding that "when we exclude variety of color from our ideas of Beauty, they may be said to possess everything necessary to constitute it in common with white people." This was shocking stuff indeed.

In many ways, then, Rush was a man ahead of his time. Unfortunately, his grasp of the human organism and its ailments was positively medieval. He believed in bloodletting with a furiously buoyant dogmatism that transcended all reason. Worse yet, he also believed—with dreadful consequences, that terrible autumn of 1793—that the human body contained about twice as much blood as it actually did. Many of Rush's contemporaries shared these misconceptions, but no other Philadelphia doctor exerted remotely as much influence during the epidemic. Some dosed patients with a mixture of water, laudanum, and Madeira, or with a concoction of vegetable soup and camphor. Rush's mercurial sweating purge, as he called it, prescribed a grueling treatment of violent purges, a "gentle vomit of ipecacuanha," frequent and egregious bloodletting, and the application of focused heat to blister the head, limbs, and back of the neck. (He bled one patient no fewer than 22 times, and drained him of 176 ounces of blood.) When this still failed to stem contagion, Rush abandoned his "ill-timed scrupulousness about the weakness of the body," and instituted an even more horrific treatment, which he termed the "heroic cure." He purged and bled still more aggressively, prescribed what one critical colleague described as murderous doses of mercury, and ordered that buckets of cold water be thrown over patients who were already ravaged by illness and blood loss. Thornton, who also witnessed the epidemic, believed that more victims were killed by bleeding and violent purges than would have died if nothing at all had been done for them. He contemptuously referred to Rush's disciples as the "bloody Russians," since they slaughtered with as much abandon as the czar's troops. (Thornton also correctly speculated that the spreading of the disease had some connection with the filthy cesspits under the foundations of most houses.) Rush conceded only that while aggressive bleeding indeed might be too much for the monarchical British, who were debilitated by excessive luxury, his manly "Republican" treatment was entirely appropriate for hearty, well-fed Americans.

Rush worked virtually around the clock, his sleepless mind elevated to a state of enthusiasm bordering on frenzy. He was seeing more than one hundred patients a day—sometimes half as many again—at his home at Third and Walnut. They pressed upon him in such numbers that sometimes he bled them standing up in the front yard. Every room in his home was contaminated. "Streams of miasmata were constantly poured into my house, and conveyed into my body by the air, during every hour of the day or night," he later wrote. Four of his assistants collapsed and died. When Rush himself fell ill, he had himself drained of twenty ounces of blood, and continued to see patients. Miraculously, he survived.

Meanwhile, the bodies of the dead crawled with maggots behind the doors of mansions and tenements alike and lay crumpled where they fell in doorways, ditches, and lanes, petrifying in their black vomit, blood, and excrement. It was next to impossible to find anyone willing to nurse the sick, much less remove the corpses. Although Rush knew nothing of germ theory, he understood well enough that as a source of poisonous "miasmata," hundreds of unburied bodies only deepened the threat to the reeling city. He had observed (or at least thought he had) that the plague rarely struck blacks, and reasoned that they must therefore be immune. Suddenly the solution to the dearth of nurses and grave diggers was obvious: the men with whom he had picnicked just a few short weeks before, at the roof-raising for St. Thomas's church.

Rush went to Absalom Jones and Richard Allen, and told them that the fate of the city depended on them. He explained that blacks alone were unsusceptible to the fever. He begged them as Christians to step forward "to assist the distressed, perishing, and neglected sick." He added, as an abolitionist, that "a noble opportunity is now put into their hands, of manifesting their gratitude to the inhabitants of that city which first planned their emancipation, and who have since afforded them so much protection and support." They stood at a turning point. If blacks acted now, when the epidemic had run its course, as it surely must, whites would abandon their prejudices and fears, and embrace them as brothers and neighbors. The simple human respect that blacks craved, and that was denied them as a matter of course, would be granted without stint. Never again would they have to beg support for their schools and churches. It would be given gladly, as from brother to brother. Whites would welcome them to work side by side. Rights of citizenship that seemed like the remotest of dreams would soon undoubtedly be theirs.

There was perhaps no white man in Philadelphia whom Jones and Allen trusted more than Rush who, after all, had interceded on their behalf with white Philadelphians on countless occasions. They called together the leading members of the Free African Society. There is no verbatim record of the meeting. But in their memoir of the epidemic Jones and Allen expressed views that may be very close to what they said to their followers that day in September. "Much depends upon us for the help of our colour more than many are aware," they wrote. "We intreat you to consider the obligations we lay under, to help forward the cause of freedom." Instead of rancor for bad treatment they may have received from whites, the preachers urged kindliness "toward the compassionate masters" who had set them free: "There is much gratitude due from our colour towards the white people, very many of them are instruments in the hand of God for our good, even such as have held us in captivity." They concluded, "After some conversation, we found a freedom to go forth, confiding in Him who had preserved us in the midst of a burning fiery furnace, sensible that it was our duty to do all the good we could to our suffering fellow mortals." Trusting in their faith and in Benjamin Rush, they walked out into the living apocalypse of the fever-ravaged city.

"We visited upwards of twenty families that day—they were scenes of woe indeed!" Jones and Allen recorded. "The Lord was pleased to strengthen us, and remove all fear from us, and disposed our hearts to be as useful as possible." At the society's expense, they also hired five men who "with great reluctance" agreed to put the bodies of the dead in coffins, and haul them to graveyards, and recruited black prisoners from the city jail, who labored with conspicuous devotion in the death camp at Bush Hill, where "the ordure and other evacuations of the sick, were allowed to remain in the most offensive state imaginable." More blacks volunteered to serve without pay. With many of the remaining physicians struck down by sickness, Rush taught Jones and Allen how to bleed, and to prepare medicine, possibly the first instance of blacks delivering organized medical treatment to whites in American history.

In pairs, their teams trudged through the vast, reeking charnal house that Philadelphia had become. They saw to it that the infected were fed and kept clean, and that the dead were provided with coffins and delivered to graveyards with at least the minimum of respect. It was revolting work. "We have found them in various situations, some laying on the floor, as bloody as if they had been dipt in it," the two preachers recalled. Within days, it became evident that Rush's assurances of immunity had no basis in fact. Blacks began to fall ill. The survivors nonetheless continued to fulfill the commitment they had made to Rush, and to themselves. They witnessed countless scenes of heartrending tragedy. In many houses, windows were nailed down and doors locked to prevent victims from jumping out and running away. "Others lay vomiting blood, and screaming enough to chill them with horror." Nurses spent a week or more with victims until they died, then went on to another home, to do the same thing again, without rest, sometimes with their own families suffering from want or illness. Sometimes they arrived to find parents dead, "and none but little innocent babes to be seen, whose ignorance led them to think their parent was asleep; on account of their little prattle, we have been so wounded and our feelings so hurt, that we almost concluded to withdraw from our undertaking, but seeing others so backward, we still went on."

To many of the whites they tended, they remained human shadows, only half visible, like tools to be used and then laid aside when no longer needed. "Our distress hath been very great, but much unknown to the white people," Jones and Allen wrote, in an unusual admission of their personal feelings. "Few have been the whites that paid attention to us while the blacks were engaged in the others' service." Blacks may not have been seen in sharp focus, but they saw: the disintegration of white Philadelphia before their eyes stripped away the aura of infallibility and invulnerability that had enveloped it. They saw former masters babble helplessly like children. They saw patrician men and women turn into savages overnight. Even friends when they passed in the streets looked away from each other in fear. Whites' manifest fear and selfishness demolished trust in their authority, along with embedded notions that whites deserved to set moral standards for their servants and former bondsmen. "Many of the white people, that ought to be patterns for us to follow after, have acted in a manner that would make humanity shudder," they wrote.

Lawyers, magistrates, and public officials died. Schools and newspapers closed. The Post Office ceased to function. The city recorder fled. Civic administration broke down. The mayor begged ordinary citizens— anyone at all—to help manage the city. (Those who responded included an umbrella maker, a cabinet maker, a chair maker, a music teacher, and a shoemaker.) For most of two months, the United States was virtually without a government. The threats from England, France, and the Barbary pirates, the Indians' encroachments, were all but forgotten. Treasury Secretary Hamilton came down with the fever. Six treasury clerks fell ill and fled. Two members of the president's household died: his secretary Tobias Lear's wife, Polly, and his personal valet, William. Washington himself stayed on in the city until September 10, when Martha Washington finally convinced him to retreat to Mount Vernon. The president left Secretary of War Henry Knox in charge of the government. But within days, Knox himself panicked and decamped for New York. But because that city had imposed a quarantine against travelers from Philadelphia, he was stuck for weeks in Elizabeth, New Jersey. He tried to buy passage to Newport, Rhode Island, but no ship would take him. Had the government collapsed? demoralized citizens wondered. Was there still a United States? There was fresh talk of moving the capital somewhere else—anywhere!—to Lancaster, Trenton, Annapolis. Writing from Mount Vernon, Washington suggested Germantown, outside Philadelphia, which seemed relatively safe from contagion. But Jefferson and Madison warned that since the president had no constitutional authority to move the capital, it would set a potentially despotic precedent for future chief executives who might do so at their whim. They also feared that relocating the government, even temporarily, would make it easier to remove the national capital from the Potomac, an outcome that neither man wanted to risk. Just the rumor of relocation threatened to provoke "local partialities," and reawaken the vituperative sectional debate that the agreement of 1790 had seemingly put to rest. "I think we must have nothing to do with the question, and that Congress must meet in Philadelphia, even if it be in the open fields," Jefferson wrote the president.

Rush estimated that no fewer than six thousand people were now ill. The number of deaths continued to climb daily. More than fourteen hundred died in September alone. On a single block in Shippen Street, where the black sailmaker James Forten lived, twenty-seven people died. William Thornton contracted the fever but miraculously survived, possibly because he rejected Rush's lethal advice, instead trusting the so-called "West Indian cure" of quinine bark, wine, and cold baths. "This has been a long night of silence and death," Thornton wrote to a friend in England. "The air was here one mass of infection." The plague continued to worsen into October. Benjamin Rush's sister died on October 1. In just six days, a single pastor lost 130 of his church members. Among the survivors, delirium became the norm. People saw angels hovering in the humid night and heard disembodied voices crying doom through the desolate streets.

In the third week in October, the weather turned cold, and the number of deaths at last began to abate, dropping to thirteen on the twenty-seventh, which would have stunned back in August but was now negligible. Ravaged survivors slowly began to reappear from the houses that they had pathetically barricaded against the invisible miasma. Many were yellow with jaundice, and spoke through mouths weirdly blackened from Benjamin Rush's mercury treatment. The first boats that Philadelphians had seen in weeks began venturing cautiously into the harbor. A few stores opened their doors, and farmers began bringing their produce to market. Commerce had for so long been paralyzed that weeds grew in the streets. The stink of death and decay was everywhere.

On November 10 the president returned to the city, bowing majestically from his white horse to the feeble and ghostly figures who turned out to greet him. Washington was back! The government lived! He must have seemed like a creature from another world, so crisp and well-fed and untouched by illness, with his magnificent martial bearing, his very presence a promise of return to order and stability. In Washington's wake, congressmen followed. The city was numb, and it was crippled. But it had not died.

The epidemic probably killed more than five thousand Philadelphians, and many more in surrounding areas. About twenty thousand people, almost half the population, fled the city. Ten doctors died, ten ministers, a former mayor. Benjamin Rush, one of the handful of medical men who remained in the city throughout the epidemic, was hailed as a hero, and was so regarded for generations afterward. The great historian of the epidemic J. M. Powell credited Rush with dampening the atmosphere of panic with his constant reassurance and his steadfast confidence that the epidemic would eventually be overcome. The high mortality rate from the fever itself obscured the fact that his monstrous treatment probably killed more victims than it saved. It never even occurred to Rush that he might be mistaken.

Rush was also wrong about the fever's impact on African Americans. In September he had assured Absalom Jones and Richard Allen that their people could safely handle the dead and nurse the dying. In the end, at least three hundred black Philadelphians died, a proportion only slightly lower than the toll among whites. Rush also promised them that their service would earn them the respect and love of white Philadelphians. Though Philadelphia's mayor publicly commended Jones and Allen for their "diligency, attention and decency of deportment" during the crisis, they were nonetheless attacked by racist broadsides that turned their self-sacrifice against them.

As early as October 7, Rush's enemy William Cobbett caustically declared in his newspaper *Porcupine's Gazette*, that the doctor had "appointed two illiterate Negro men and sent them into all the alleys and by places in the city, with orders to bleed, and give his sweating purges, as he empirically called them, to all they could find sick, without regard to age, sex, or constitution; and bloody and dirty work they made among the poor miserable creatures that fell in their way." Soon afterward and to even greater effect, Mathew Carey, a journalist who had safely sat out the epidemic in Germantown, published a widely circulated account in which he accused blacks of robbing and vilely extorting money from the dying and dead.

Stung by the criticism, Jones and Allen published a public rebuttal, which stands as one of the most eloquent declarations of the dignity and humanity of blacks in early American history. They reminded whites who regarded African Americans as less than human "that a black man, although reduced to the most abject state human nature is capable of, short of real madness, can think, reflect, and feel injuries, although it may not be with the same degree of keen resentment and revenge, that you who have been and are our great oppressors, would manifest if reduced to the pitiable condition of a slave." The booklet was a tour de force. Only in Philadelphia could African Americans challenge white men not only for their prejudice and lack of compassion, but also for irresponsible reporting, and still hope for a fair hearing from white readers. The two preachers first provided a detailed accounting of the money that had been advanced to them, and what they had spent: they had received £233 for burying the dead, and had paid out, for coffins and for wages for their five assistants, a total of £411. Far from aggrandizing themselves, they were left out of pocket by £178, apart from the expense of supporting their own families, and gifts of money they had given to the most poor, both white and black. They took pride in having personally bled upward of eight hundred people, without accepting any payment. However, they admitted that at the height of the plague, nurses who had been engaged for $6 per week were sometimes offered, and accepted, as much as $4 per day for their services. But for each black who may have accepted more than he deserved, there were many more who were motivated by nothing but Christian charity. They asserted that theft by whites was twenty times as great as among blacks, and they cited numerous examples. Six pounds was demanded by one white nurse just for putting a corpse in a coffin, and $40 more by four white men for carrying it downstairs to the street. On another occasion, when Jones and Allen came to collect the corpse of one Mrs. Malony, they found her white nurse lying drunk on the floor with the dead woman's rings on her fingers. When black nurses were seized with illness, the churchmen pointedly noted, they were typically turned out of the houses, and left to die. "Thus were *our services extorted at the peril of our lives, yet you accuse us of extorting a* little money from you," they wrote, with unconcealed sarcasm.

The accusations leveled against a few blacks would inescapably taint the reputation of all, they knew. Jones and Allen urged their followers as free men and women to remain unbowed by either false report or irrational prejudice. Sacrifice had not erased indignity or contempt, but it had forged in the city's blacks a determination to go forward with courage, and to fight bigotry with the greater power of faith and compassion. In the epidemic of 1793, African Americans had discovered in themselves a capacity for courage, self-sacrifice, and moral action that far transcended the moralizing pretensions of their former masters. Indeed, amid the most horrifying crisis that any of them would live to see, they had proved themselves more civilized than the whites to whom they had always been taught to defer and obey.

In the months after the epidemic, Philadelphia's African Americans continued to enlarge the sphere of their freedom. In 1794 they would dedicate the completed church of St. Thomas. Inside its vestibule was written: "The people that walked in darkness have seen a great light." Two years later, Richard Allen and his followers would erect Bethel Church, the mother church of the African Methodist Episcopal faith, which for generations to come would represent the largest island of autonomy for blacks in white America. Absalom Jones would eventually become the first ordained black rector of the Episcopal Church in America. Soon there would be more black churches, schools, and businesses, like James Forten's sail loft, the best in the city. Proslavery congressmen could hardly help but see that the realities of life in the nation's temporary capital made nonsense of their claims that Africans were too childlike, too incompetent—too *subhuman*—to be permitted to be free. They could also see all too clearly that the growing abolitionist consensus in Pennsylvania would make it ever harder to enforce the new Fugitive Slave Law. Philadelphia indeed was, as Congressman Smith of South Carolina had memorably put it during the 1790 debate over the location of the capital, "a dangerous place for Southerners." The nation would be kept much safer for slavery by a government ensconced on the Potomac.

The epidemic had also deeply shaken white Philadelphia's imperious self-confidence. The city's boosters had long complained that the Potomac region was too unhealthy to be the nation's capital. Some doubtless remembered with bitter irony the dire speeches made during the debates over the seat of government, back in 1790, in which Northern partisans had asserted that the climate of the Potomac was so destructive to Northern constitutions that vast numbers of Yankee settlers had already "found their graves there." As Philadelphians emerged devastated from the holocaust of 1793, such warnings seemed hollow indeed. Yellow fever would intermittently return throughout the remaining years of the decade, though never with such severity, feeding the arguments of those who had always insisted that the capital must be placed anywhere but in Philadelphia.

Chapter 7

IRRESISTIBLE
TEMPTATIONS

"In America, where more than in any other country in the world, a desire for wealth is the prevailing passion, there are few schemes which are not made the means of extensive speculations; and that of erecting the Federal City presented irresistible temptations."

—FRANÇOIS-ALEXANDRE-FRÉDÉRIC,
DUC DE LA ROCHEFOUCAULD-LIANCOURT

O<small>N</small> S<small>EPTEMBER</small> 18, 1793, while Philadelphians cowered from the yellow fever, a scene medieval in its panoply unfolded on the banks of the Potomac. Like tapestry figures come to life, Brother George Washington and his fellow Masons from Alexandria stepped from their boat onto the north bank of the Potomac in eye-filling regalia of satin aprons, badges, and sashes. Flourishing ceremonial truncheons and wands, preceded by a military band, and trailed by the crisply uniformed soldiers of the Alexandria Volunteer Artillery, they trod with solemn step along the sketchy streets of what was mostly still a city of the imagination. One carried the Bible on a satin cushion, another a ceremonial sword, still others symbolic offerings of corn, wine, and oil. Along the way, they were joined by contingents of Masons from Maryland, the city's surveyors, the federal commissioners, stonecutters, and "mechanics," and assorted leading citizens, among them the Capitol's architect William Thornton; James Hoban, who had designed the President's House; Andrew Ellicott, the surveyor; and the Boston financier Samuel Blodget. Two abreast, with drums beating and flags snapping in the warm breeze, they marched past the foundations of the President's House, picking their way around potholes and tree stumps, through cornfields, along the route of what one day would be Pennsylvania Avenue, toward Capitol Hill, where the eye might make out, just barely, the heaps of stone and brick where hired slaves and white craftsmen were at work on the future home of Congress.

Washington had been a devoted Mason for thirty-seven years, and Grand Master of Alexandria Lodge No. 22 for five, and he saw no more conflict of interest in shrouding the Capitol's dedication in Masonic ritual than he had in manipulating the federal city's location to favor the interest of his friends in the Patowmack Company. "I shall always be happy to advance the interests of the Society," he had told a Masonic gathering, in 1790. "Being persuaded that a just application of the principles on which the Masonic Fraternity is founded, must be promotive of private virtue and public prosperity." To Washington, as to many of his friends in the governing elite, the goals of republican government and Masonry were congruent: to be a good Mason was to be a good American. (While other aspects of the Brotherhood's influence on the Founders have largely been forgotten, the cryptic Masonic symbol of a pyramid topped by the Deity's all-seeing eye continues to adorn the national currency.)

Masonry claimed descent from secret Hebrew principles handed down by the master mason of King Solomon's temple, an assertion that seemed less outlandish in an era when even the educated possessed a shaky grasp of historical chronology, and generally believed the earth itself to be but a few thousand years old. The brotherhood's actual roots lay in a workmen's guild of the later Middle Ages, which by the eighteenth century had evolved into an elite fraternity propounding Enlightenment ideals of rationality, fellowship, and generalized benevolence. During the Revolutionary War, Masonry served as a powerful bonding force among the officers of the Continental Army, fostering among them a sense of common purpose, and helping to overcome the centrifugal force of local loyalties. It seemed to many in the leadership class that too much democracy would lead to anarchy, unless official firmness coupled to principles of gentlemanly honor restrained men's baser impulses. In 1796 Washington would proclaim with deep conviction that the entire nation must become like Masonry, "a lodge for the virtues."

It has been said that if the Capitol was a temple to the state religion of republican government, then the Masons represented a kind of national priesthood. This was never more vividly illustrated than on that hot, bright September day in 1793. As the cavalcade approached Capitol Hill, each file of marchers paused and then hieratically stepped to the side, creating a human corridor through which now advanced the Grand Sword Bearer alongside Brother Washington, wearing the ornately embroidered apron given him by Madame de Lafayette. The procession finally halted at the southeast corner of what would be the north wing of the Capitol. There the artillerymen unlimbered their guns and fired a cannonade that resounded across the sun-swept plain. A high-ranking Mason named Joseph Clarke brandished aloft a silver plate engraved with "the year of Masonry 5793" and a paean to Washington, "whose virtues in the civil administration of his country have been as conspicuous and beneficial as his military valor and prudence have been useful in establishing her liberties." Washington, Clarke, and two other Masons then climbed down into the trench, where they laid the plate atop the Capitol's cornerstone, and then placed upon it the offerings of corn, wine, and oil, doubly symbolizing in accordance with Masonic belief nourishment, refreshment, and joy, and on a loftier plane science, virtue, and the Brotherhood itself. The entire crowd now joined in prayer, followed by a round of Masonic chants, and another of fifteen-round cannonade. Afterward, the assembly retired to a covered "booth" where they banqueted on a barbecued five-hundred-pound ox.

There was about the cornerstone-laying, for all its triumphal trappings, if not an atmosphere of desperation exactly, then at least one of anxiety, a nervous hope that it would prick the enthusiasm of investors, who so far had shown disconcertingly little interest in the federal city. After three disappointing land auctions, the last held only the day before, the project was starving for lack of funds. Not only had few buyers appeared, but many of the winning bidders failed to make good on their notes for the lots they had bought. As the commissioners delicately put it, there was "a great want of punctuality among those who purchased at the first sale." The consequences of the backroom deals of 1790 were now coming home to roost. Washington and the Potomac lobby had never asked Congress for money either to acquire land for the Federal District, or for the public buildings, knowing that Congress would never have given its approval. Instead, construction was left to the creative inspiration of private enterprise, assisted by modest grants from Maryland and Virginia. (Maryland was prompt in its payments, but the commissioners wrested installments from Virginia's tight-fisted treasury only after repeated episodes of pathetic pleading.) This hopeful strategy, such as it was, virtually ensured that the project would eventually fall prey to speculators and insiders. Voices would soon be heard grumbling, with good reason, that "Bankrupts, Land and Stock Jobbers" were taking control. Washington's strategy, like L'Enfant's plan—which had extravagantly predicted six hundred thousand residents within a decade—was based on the belief that the capital's destiny as a national commercial hub as well as its seat of government would instantly attract investors. Instead, the development of the federal city would become, behind its lofty facade of austere public purpose, an exercise in opportunism on a grandiose scale.

Washington felt time growing short. He had reluctantly agreed to run for a second term, to which he had been reelected without opposition a year earlier; he felt tired and old and frustrated. On the Potomac, nothing seemed to be going right. Land sales were stalled: something was necessary to put the wheels in motion again. Investors held back because there were no settlers. Prospective settlers held back because building lots remained undeveloped. Inflated land prices were one deterrent; another was Washington's stipulation that houses be built only of brick, and be at least two stories high, which precluded purchase by the less affluent. Some way had to be found to spur construction. The commissioners thought they found the solution to their worries in the ingratiating person of Samuel Blodget, who had been the biggest bidder at the first auction, in September 1792. For the second auction, in October, Blodget negotiated a secret deal personally approved by the president—"it would be best for the circumstance not to be publicly known," Washington cautioned—which permitted Blodget to bid at an artificially low, that is rigged, price of $3,648 for one of the most valuable pieces of real estate on Capitol Hill. So infatuated were the commissioners with Blodget that they handed him the direction of the entire project, at the generous salary of $1,600 annually. "You are retained for one year commencing the first Instant, as supervisor of the Buildings and in general of the affairs committed to our care," they wrote him, with a sigh of collective relief. "You are to be next in power to ourselves. We have more pleasure in advising than in giving orders."

But Blodget had in mind something much simpler, and more profitable, than the thankless labor of meeting budgets, procuring materials, placating irritable landowners, and actually erecting buildings. "He has great confidence in a lottery," the commissioners reported to Secretary of State Jefferson. "We find ourselves at Liberty and agree to it." This was hardly the dignified development model that the president had in mind. But it was imperative that the project move forward somehow. Washington's personal secretary, Tobias Lear, was pressed into service as a propagandist, painting in a widely distributed pamphlet a heady picture of "chaste, magnificent and beautiful" public buildings already under construction alongside a "superb hotel"—Blodget's—and promising that, thanks to the sale of thousands of lots to defray the city's expenses, the city's future residents and their property would be "forever free from a heavy tax, which is unavoidable in other large cities."

Lotteries had been used before to raise money for public works: New York had held one to finance the construction of Federal Hall, as had Philadelphia for its new city hall. And in 1790 the promoters of Columbia, Pennsylvania as the prospective Federal District had "chanced off" lots to hapless investors, who wound up owning cow pasture instead of the national capital. But fraud was all too common, notoriously epitomized by the illegal lotteries, which flourished from "offshore" bases on islands in the Delaware River, outside the jurisdictions of New Jersey, Pennsylvania, and Delaware. Blodget's actions would do nothing to burnish the reputation of the lottery as a respectable instrument of fundraising. He was already deft at telling the commissioners what they wanted to hear. First, he had proposed sending agents through the states hawking city lots. Then he had assured them that he could obtain a loan large enough to pay for major construction, using unsold city lots as security. After a visit to Boston, he breezily declared that "we shall obtain many good Citizens from this place." These pioneers, like the loan, existed nowhere but in Blodget's sales pitch, and like his other promises it too came to naught. He proposed to offer fifty thousand tickets at $7 apiece, with a top cash prize of $25,000, and a grand prize of "1 Superb Hotel with Baths, out houses, etc. to cost $50,000." In all, $350,000 in awards would be handed out.

Blodget may have been a huckster, but he was an inspired one. The hotel, at Eighth and E Streets NW, between the Capitol and the President's House, was yet to be built of course, but when it was, he promised, it would be the grandest in the United States, with an expansive frontage of 120 feet. Its style, the starry-eyed commissioners effused, "will far exceed any building at present known in America." Blodget declared a contest to select the hotel's design, and publicized it nationwide. The winner turned out to be none other than James Hoban, the architect of the President's House, a choice that lent cachet to Blodget's scheme. Fifteen hundred people attended the laying of the hotel's cornerstone on the Fourth of July.

Once again, all was not as it seemed, however. The commissioners still had no money. They urgently begged Virginia Governor Henry Lee to forward the next portion of his state's contribution: "We entreat, Sir, throw the balance into our hands. [Without it] we shall not be able to carry on the public buildings." Blodget, although he was the capital's official superintendent, largely ignored such mundane concerns, preferring to travel the country hustling his real estate and lottery tickets. However, even his consummate salesmanship could not convince Americans to move to the Potomac. He too was losing money. Thousands of tickets had to be recalled because of legal problems, while many Philadelphians who had bought lottery tickets on credit had died from yellow fever, making it impossible to collect payment. With characteristic insouciance, however, he promised the commissioners that he would pay off the prizes from his own estate, a nearly impossible feat since it depended on collecting debts owed him by insolvent creditors.

The lottery drawing proved to be an excruciatingly slow-motion affair. Weeks after it began, so many tickets still remained unsold that, with the commissioners' approval, George Town merchants quietly bought up blocks of them to create the impression of high demand. By October, no one had yet drawn any of the big prizes. Disgruntled ticket holders complained that Blodget was deliberately dragging out the drawing in order to inflate the value of the tickets that remained unsold. But Blodget blithely replied, "In a short time it will appear that no lottery was ever better paid in this country than ours, & this will secure success to future lotteries without which the city will never go on with spirit." When someone finally won the $25,000 prize, Blodget had only $4,000 on hand to pay him.

Undismayed, the irrepressible promoter was already talking about yet another scheme, called a "tontine," whose payout was contingent on the longevity of its participants. Investors would purchase shares at $100 apiece, to pay for the development of city lots. Over time, dividends would be paid into a collective fund from income generated by the properties. When enough shareholders had died off so that the number of survivors equaled the number of lots owned by the fund, the assets would be divided among them. Naturally Blodget himself would oversee the fund, manage the sales, and deploy his own agents to sell shares around the country.

By the end of the year, the commissioners finally decided that they had been taken in, and that far from attracting either settlers or serious investors, Blodget's machinations were deterring them and tainting the reputation of the whole federal city. Blodget, the disillusioned commissioners gloomily informed the president, "wants judgment and steadiness. We all wish to part from him, and that quietly." Washington disingenuously sneered, "Speculation has been his primary object from the beginning," lamenting of the ingratiating promoter. "I was at a loss how to account for a conduct so distant from any of the ideas I had entertained of the duties of a Superintendent." On December 15, the commissioners ordered Blodget "to forbear the publication of any lottery for the present, for we are rather inclined not to have another." Blodget simply ignored them. Safely ensconced in Philadelphia, he told them that he would carry on with his lottery with or without their approval. "Altho' you may understand the building of federal cities, capitals, painting, botany, the Belles Lettres, *and such trifles* give me leave to assure you that you are not instructed in the *more noble and more exalted science of lottery making*," he impertinently wrote to William Thornton. The commissioners first pleaded, writing, "[We] beg you sir to Stop the Business as soon as possible." Then five days later, they wrote Blodget again, this time fulminating that "no further steps should be taken," toothlessly warning him "not [to] drive us to the necessity of a public disavowal."

THE CITY NEEDED a new savior, and the commissioners believed they had found him. Among the Masons who had dined on ox shank at the Capitol's cornerstone with the president was another young New Englander upon whom the president and the commissioners now pinned their hopes. The sudden appearance of James Greenleaf, and his rapid ascent into the commissioners' favor, freed them (or at least so they thought) from the obnoxious Blodget. Greenleaf first showed up in the Federal District in September 1793 with a letter of personal recommendation from the president: "He has been represented to me as a Gentleman of large property and having the command of much money in this Country & in Europe. I have reason to believe that if you can find it consistent with your duty to the public to attract Mr. Greenleaf to the federal city, he will be a valuable acquisition." This wasn't exactly an order, but it was close. The commissioners never failed to do Washington's bidding.

With his chubby face and bedroom eyes, Greenleaf looked more like a pampered schoolboy than a power broker. His appearance was misleading. Greenleaf was a virtual epitome of the nation's swaggering postwar commercial spirit: fiercely determined, irrationally optimistic, risk-taking, vast in his ambition, and eager to profit. On paper, at least, he was one of the most successful financial men in America. Radiating charm, he dazzled everyone he met. Only thirty-two years old, he had already amassed a fortune in transatlantic shipping, and won the trust of key Dutch banking firms, through one of which he had successfully negotiated major loans for the United States government. His stature was further enhanced by his appointment as the U.S. consul at Amsterdam, and by his glamorous marriage to a Dutch baroness. His patriotic credentials were also impeccable. His father, as the High Sheriff of Boston, was an early and ardent revolutionist, and had in July 1776 personally read out the Declaration of Independence from the balcony of the Massachusetts Statehouse. In the summer of 1793 Greenleaf returned home from Holland to prospect for investment opportunities. In Philadelphia, he encountered Samuel Blodget, who despite his fall from the commissioners' grace, showered him with his effervescent optimism about the federal city, and about the opportunity for quick profit that it offered a clever man like himself.

Five days after the cornerstone-laying at the Capitol, Greenleaf contracted to buy three thousand lots at $66.50 apiece, for a total of $200,000. Within days, he had lined up as partners two of the boldest speculators in the United States: Senator Robert Morris and John Nicholson, Pennsylvania's comptroller-general. (Politics was no barrier to anticipated profits: Morris and Nicholson were the respective leaders of bitterly opposed parties in Pennsylvania.) On Christmas Eve, the three inked a second contract with the commissioners to buy an *additional* three thousand lots, this time at $95.10 per lot, for a total of nearly $950,000. Combining their purchases, the three partners committed themselves to paying the commissioners seven annual interest-free installments of $68,000 each, beginning on May 1, 1794. The partners also took on Greenleaf's commitment to build ten houses each year for the next decade. If they sold any land before January 1, 1796, they would still be responsible for erecting one house on every third lot that Greenleaf sold within four years after the sale. Further, they agreed to lend the commissioners $2,600 monthly, at 6 percent interest, until all the public buildings were finished. (As security, the commissioners gave Greenleaf a mortgage on additional lots.). A few months later, the partners would buy another twelve hundred lots from local landowners. In all, the partners would eventually acquire a total of 7,235 lots, 42 percent of the lots available in the federal city. To pay for all this, Greenleaf would float a giant loan of $1.2 million through his contacts in Holland, using the lots themselves as collateral. Writing in the 1930s, the economic historian A. M. Sakolski would call them "the greatest land-grabbing triumvirate that ever operated in America."

It seemed like a winning proposition all around. The partners stood to reap a fortune. The commissioners believed that well-respected financial men would ensure that the city receive the funding that it needed. There need be no more coaxing of unwilling investors, no more crawling to the governor of Virginia, no more embarrassing lotteries. "Be fully assured that we have the most perfect disposition to meet your wishes," the commissioners assured Greenleaf. To Blodget, they patronizingly wrote, "We have no fears that Mr. Greenleaf, after contracting to build ten houses a year, will think his contract is executed on building fewer."

The president thought that the trio had gotten their lots a bit too cheaply. But he was impressed by Greenleaf. The young financier, he wrote to his former secretary Tobias Lear, had "dipped deeply into the concerns of the Federal City—I think he has done so on very advantageous terms for himself, and I am pleased with it notwithstanding on public ground; as it may give facility to the operation at that place, at the same time that it is embarking him and his friends in a measure which although could not well fail under any circumstances that are likely to happen, may considerably be promoted by men of Spirit with large Capitals." From the laconic Washington, this was lavish praise. In other words, Greenleaf would at last make clear to Americans, and in particular to investors—those "men of Spirit"—that the city was soon to become a reality, and that plenty of money could be made in the process. Greenleaf had at last succeeded in harnessing the engine of profit to the president's unbreachable faith in the destiny of his pet project.

Not everyone was quite so impressed. The aristocratic French exile François-Alexandre-Frédéric, duc de la Rochefoucauld-Liancourt would reflect with worldly skepticism on the new burst of excitement that seemed to have overtaken everyone with an interest in the federal city: "In America, where more than in any other country in the world, a desire for wealth is the prevailing passion there are few schemes which are not made the means of extensive speculations; and that of the erecting of the Federal City presented irresistible temptations. The public papers were filled with exaggerated praises of the new city; accounts of the rapidity of its progress toward completion; in a word, with all the artifices with which trading people in every part of the world are accustomed to employ in the disposal of their wares, and which are perfectly known, and amply practiced in this new world."

Greenleaf could not have found two better-connected collaborators. Legend held that Senator Robert Morris had virtually single-handedly saved the patriot government during the Revolutionary War by stabilizing its chaotic finances. An awed creditor once described him as the "Hannibal" of finance, an unconquerable warrior of the balance sheet. He was also an intimate of the president, who was renting Morris's Philadelphia mansion. John Nicholson was Pennsylvania's highest-ranking financial officer, a position he had held since 1781, and which provided him with insider information that facilitated his prodigious speculations in frontier land. At thirty-five, the long-jawed, sharp-featured Nicholson was another young man on the make. Frontier-reared, he had taught himself French and Dutch, acquired manners, and ridden his talent for numbers from a clerk's job in the accounts department of the Continental Congress into the monied world of Philadelphia's elite. Like Greenleaf, he was a living embodiment of the acquisitive energy that was being unleashed in the new republic, having made a fortune with astonishing speed in a country where most people counted their earnings in shillings and pennies. When he turned his appraising eye toward the federal city's real estate, he heard the clink of coins, a great many of them. "All other places have risen by slow degrees," he opined.

"This will astonish the world by its rapidity, the people are all ready and only wait for houses to rush in."

Robert Morris's presence on the team was even more valuable. Although the commissioners had agreed to Greenleaf's proposals partly in "consideration of the uncertainty of settled times and an unembarrassed commerce," it was "Mr. Morris's Capital, influence, and activity" that had ultimately swayed them. Morris was widely believed to be one of the richest men in America. And in the autumn of 1793 he towered over his partners like a colossus. A mountainous man of large girth, heart, and appetites, and standing over six feet in height, his gregarious personality and florid complexion spoke eloquently of his taste for good company and the pleasures of the table. He was attended in all his needs by a small army of liveried table servants and footmen, several of them enslaved. His hospitality was famous. "No badly cooked or cold dinners at their table; no pinched fires upon their hearths; no paucity of waiters; no awkward loons in their drawing rooms," sighed one contented guest.

During the Revolutionary War, Morris had served first as the Continental Congress's chief commercial agent, and then as superintendent of finance. So vast was his wealth that when the embattled revolutionaries' finances were at a low point in the early 1780s, he kept the rebel government afloat by assigning its debts to his own personal line of credit. Critics, and he had many, accused him even then of misusing public funds, and of profiteering: the line between his public and private financial activities was murky at best. However, conflict of interest worried him no more than it did Nicholson, or for that matter President Washington.

In 1793 Morris was at a turning point. Although he never completely abandoned commerce—he had financed the first American ship to trade with China—increasingly he was engaging in bolder and riskier speculations. Challenged by Washington to exercise restraint, he replied heartily, "I can never do things in the small; I must be either a man or a mouse." In the 1780s he had attempted to corner the French tobacco market, a costly failure that severely damaged his credit, and from which he was still financially reeling. The answer, he decided, lay in the expanding land market. Everyone down to the commonest stable hand seemed to be trying to buy land in Ohio or Kentucky. From Vermont to Georgia, Americans were hitching their oxen and trekking westward in an almost unbroken line. They all wanted land, and they would have to buy it from someone.

"Were I to characterize the United States, it would be by the appellation of the land of speculation," the British traveler William Priest wrote in 1796. Tens of millions of acres were being added to the public domain as new lands bought or seized from the Indians were opened for settlement. The phenomenon of the "land rush" was becoming a fixture of American life, as the states speedily sought to convert wilderness into cash. Syndicates bought and sold Western lands by the thousands, then tens of thousands, then hundreds of thousands of acres. Almost every politician seemed to be scrambling to get in on one deal or another: members of the Supreme Court, the cabinet, the Senate, the House of Representatives, not to mention the president himself. Washington, having been raised in a colonial world where the acquisition of back lands was the surest route to riches, acquired patents on some twenty thousand acres in the Ohio Country before the Revolutionary War, and he would own seventy thousand acres from upstate New York to Kentucky by the time of his death, in 1799.

Frontier speculation was a buccaneer's game that fostered misrepresentation and fraud. Rochefoucauld-Liancourt wrote, "Every class of men, even watch makers, hairdressers, and mechanics of all descriptions, eagerly ran after this deception." Plungers like Morris and Nicholson bought giant parcels of land on credit, usually sight unseen. "The men that say so much in favour of the land know no more of the land than a horse—nor perhaps so much, as they do not eat grass," wrote another gimlet-eyed English traveler, Richard Parkinson. Employing a legal but risky technique then known as "dodging," and today as "flipping," speculators sought to resell vast tracts to European buyers before they had paid for them in the United States, then use part of the profits to pay for the original purchase, and use the remainder to reinvest in new property. Surveys were often haphazard. Deeds might never be filed. Titles were clouded by unpaid taxes and Indian claims. Agents shamelessly hawked land that didn't exist, or was impossible to reach, or had been sold several times over in different states. Complicating matters further, agents commonly sold not actual land, but rather "warrants," or claim certificates, which were themselves fiercely traded in bulk by speculators. John Nicholson, for instance, was said to have acquired *85 percent* of the warrants that had been issued to Revolutionary War veterans, in lieu of back wages, while his office was supervising the disposal of Pennsylvania's vast undeveloped interior. Nicholson also speculated heavily in state loan certificates, which he used to buy up still more state land until he became the largest landowner in Pennsylvania, with title to almost four million acres, much of it purchased under fictitious names. When later threatened with impeachment, he freely admitted that "the necessity of using borrowed names as was usual in the Land Office." Morris also achieved stunning success in his first attempt at speculation on a grand scale, buying five million acres in the Genesee country of western New York for $75,000 in 1790 and then doubling his investment less than two years later by reselling it to syndicates in England and Holland. Afterward, in debtors' prison, he would lament, "If I had contented myself with these Genesee purchases, and employed myself in disposing of the land to the best advantage, I believe that at this day I should have been the wealthiest citizen of the United States."

Morris and Nicholson teamed up in the autumn of 1793 to sell two hundred thousand acres on the upper Susquehanna to royalist refugees from France. Throughout their partnership, they regularly endorsed each others' notes, so entangling each in the other's obligations that their financial fates would become inextricably intertwined. They soon expanded their collaboration to begin acquiring what would eventually grow to more than six million acres scattered along the frontier from New York to Kentucky, and as far south as the Carolinas and Georgia, a sprawling empire of real estate, tangled deals, and jerry-rigged credit. In October, Greenleaf's personal agent Sylvanus Bourne, who also served as the American vice-consul in Holland, was dispatched to Amsterdam, Europe's financial capital, with the contract for Greenleaf's purchase of three thousand city lots, which he was to offer as collateral for the $1.2 million loan. Bourne also carried deeds for half a million acres of Morris and Nicholson land in Pennsylvania and Georgia. The trio was so confident that Greenleaf's Dutch associates would give them what they desired—"we know that their credit and respectability is such that the said loan will undoubtedly fill under their influence"—that they began circulating drafts on the loan with abandon before they had any actual commitment from the bankers in hand.

Meanwhile, the commissioners needed $82,000 to complete the construction, surveying, and quarrying work that was already planned through the end of 1794. Everyone waited eagerly for the good news from Holland. But the Dutch were proving considerably less pliant than Greenleaf anticipated. The bankers realized of course that Greenleaf was offering them as "security" land that he didn't actually own: all the agent Bourne had to offer were promissory notes, not deeds. The Dutch wanted titles before they loaned money. However, in accordance with their contract, the speculators were to receive title to their lots only in proportion to their payment in cash of each installment of the purchase price. Their first $68,000 payment to the commissioners was already late. Complicating matters further, Greenleaf now asked for deeds for five thousand of the lots, in return for which he and Morris "pledged their personal security, united with that of Mr. Nicholson."

Ultimately, the speculators had the commissioners over a barrel, and everyone knew it. No deeds, no loan; no loan, no money for construction. At the end of April, the president reluctantly agreed to approve surrender of title to one thousand lots. To further sweeten the pot for the Dutch, the Americans offered to put up as collateral sufficient U.S. bonds to pay the annual interest on the loan until the principal was paid off. With this, Bourne at last managed to negotiate, in principle, a loan of $780,000 through the Amsterdam firm of Daniel Crommelin & Sons. This was far less than the partners were counting on. In addition, Bourne had to settle for 6 percent interest instead of the 5 percent that Greenleaf had told him to expect, along with an assortment of costly premiums. Still more disappointing, leading loan brokers declined to participate in the deal at all, compelling Crommelin & Sons, and Bourne, to scour Holland for enough individual investors to fill out the loan.

Unfortunately, it was a very inauspicious moment for American speculators to be attempting to borrow big money in Holland. The difficulties that Bourne and his associates faced were threefold. First, they were competing in the marketplace with the agents of Russia's aging despot Catherine the Great, who was also attempting to raise a huge loan. Then there was the knotty problem of the Americans' creditworthiness. A decade earlier, Robert Morris's credit was virtually limitless. It wasn't anymore. Nicholson's credit was also overextended. Even as Bourne lobbied for the loan on which the federal city depended, Morris and Nicholson were bombarding European financial markets with hundreds of thousands of dollars' worth of their personal notes, in an untimely and ultimately futile effort to pay off past debts. There were few takers, and those who did so would accept the notes only at steep discounts. The third obstacle was a force that was beyond the power of any American to overcome: the French Revolution.

On February 1, 1793, ten days after Louis XVI was guillotined to a roll of drums in the Place de la Revolution, France's revolutionary regime had declared war on England and Holland. "They threaten you with kings!" the Montagnard leader Georges-Jacques Danton declaimed to the Convention. "You have thrown down your gauntlet to them, and this gauntlet is a king's head, the signal of their coming death." French armies swarmed north through the Austrian Netherlands, present-day Belgium, and into the southern provinces of the Dutch Republic, intending to overthrow its pro-British government and establish a regime friendly to France. Revolutionary fervor, however, was not enough. Though the lines of battle swayed back and forth, by July combined English and Austrian forces had routed the French. It was only a temporary respite.

Surrounded by the armies of her enemies, contending with royalist rebellion from within, betrayed by several of her most senior generals, France descended into the nine-month-long maelstrom of horror that came to be known, with good reason, as the Reign of Terror. On September 17, as George Washington and his Masonic friends were laying the Capitol's cornerstone, in Paris the governing Convention enacted the Comprehensive Law of Suspects, a draconian measure that mandated revolutionary committees to arrest anyone who "either by their conduct, their contacts, their words or their writings, showed themselves to be supporters of tyranny." Arrests began almost immediately. Between sixteen thousand and forty thousand people would be executed in the name of liberty, including not only royalists and reactionaries, but also liberals, revolutionaries caught on the losing side of factional strife, and countless men and women who were guilty of little more than making a remark that someone construed as subversive. "Still more heads and every day more heads fall!" exclaimed one delighted revolutionary.

Opinion in the United States was sharply divided over the events in France. Federalists, including Hamilton and Vice President Adams, regarded the bloody tumult with loathing. They were in a minority. Many more Americans saw it as a continuation of their own revolution, and remembered that barely a decade earlier generous French aid and military might had turned the tide against England to make victory possible. William Thornton, afire with revolutionary ardor, sent Washington a list of warlike inventions to use against the English, including barbed harpoons and glass cannonballs; Thornton had traveled far indeed from his Quaker roots. Thomas Jefferson, for one, memorably rationalized the bloodletting in France. "The liberty of the whole earth was depending on the issue of the contest, and was ever a prize won with so little innocent blood?" he wrote with chilling loftiness. "My own affections have been deeply wounded by some of the martyrs to this cause, but rather than it should have failed, I would have seen half the earth desolated." Pro-French political clubs sprang up overnight, providing forums for urban workmen and frontier farmers marginalized by the Federalist elite.

Turmoil in Europe posed a dire challenge for the United States. Public opinion might favor the French, but tariffs on British imports provided the lion's share of the government's revenues. President Washington steered a course of rigorous neutrality. It wasn't easy. France's ambassador Edmond Genet, usually called by his revolutionary title Citizen Genet, proclaimed that he intended to use the United States as a base for privateers to harry British shipping, tried to recruit

Kentuckians to seize New Orleans from Britain's ally Spain, and when thwarted in his schemes, publicly called upon Congress to repudiate the president's policy. England, meanwhile, nearly provoked the United States into war. The British Admiralty simply ignored Washington's protestations of neutrality, seizing 250 American ships carrying cargoes to the French West Indies, and wreaking havoc with trade. Britain's continued occupation of several key posts on the western frontier had been an irritant in Anglo-American relations since the end of the Revolutionary War. Now British agents were circulating through the Ohio Country, encouraging the Indians there to resist American settlement. There were rumors of British plans to annex Vermont, western Pennsylvania, and even Kentucky. British consul Phineas Bond reported to his masters in London, "In every direction in which this country is to be viewed, its situation must be deemed exceedingly critical—critical in respect to the powers of war—critical as to the continuation of peace—and immensely so as to its constitution and government."

When thousands of western Pennsylvania farmers began agitating against federal taxes in the summer of 1794, eastern elites feared they were the avatars of a foreign-inspired conspiracy to overthrow the government. What was really behind them: British subversion? Or the incendiary influence of revolutionary France?

In Europe, the tide of war had now turned in favor of the French, whose campaign of 1794 has been called "a triumph for ruthless makeshift action." Hundreds of thousands of barely trained conscripts were thrown into the field. That summer, the Austrians abandoned Belgium, which was swiftly reoccupied by French forces. When winter came, the French poured across the frozen River Scheldt into the Dutch Republic. Dutch liberals welcomed the arrival of the revolutionary tricolor, anticipating that they would be treated as brothers in spirit, and as political equals. Instead, the French imposed on them a bitter peace, imperiously renamed their country the Batavian Republic, and demanded a crushing indemnity of 100 million florins. To finance their ongoing wars, the French further compelled Dutch bankers to lend them an additional 100 million florins, at a favorable rate of interest. There wouldn't be much left over for loan-hungry Americans.

As the armies marched and countermarched across the lowlands, Sylvanus Bourne and his allies at Crommelin & Sons continued to dispatch their agents through Amsterdam's cobbled lanes, in their quixotic effort to winkle out florins for the anxious speculators back on the Potomac. By midsummer 1794 they had still raised only a fraction of the authorized loan. Greenleaf remained maddeningly unruffled, in public at least. He wrote to the commissioners, in his characteristic racing script, that it "would be unsafe for the Gentlemen Commissioners to place much dependence on the success of the loan negotiating in Amsterdam," unless they were willing to transfer title for one thousand lots to him as security for the bankers. He assured them that he was always ready and willing to furnish the commissioners with whatever he owed them, in spite of his own "immense engagements" and "the constant calls for money" against his account—a quaint way of saying that he was in debt over his head. He was "not without the apprehension should some of his resources fail, that his power may reasonably fall far short of his wishes." A born salesman, Greenleaf could always turn a phrase so that imminent catastrophe sounded like an act of grace.

"When we entered on the subject of the loan, it was our general expectation that it would be speedily concluded," the aggrieved commissioners wrote back to the once sainted Greenleaf. "The situation of our funds makes us hope that we shall not yet be disappointed." They reminded him that they had already gone further to accommodate him "than rigid caution would dictate." By mid-August they were essentially broke. "We suffer much from the delay of the payments," they informed Edmund Randolph, who earlier in the year had replaced Thomas Jefferson as secretary of state. It might have been possible to beg, cajole, or bully the State of Virginia into advancing some cash, but Governor Lee was off somewhere in western Pennsylvania, marching against the rebels. With no other source of funds in sight, the commissioners could no longer afford the inhibitions that had held them back: they gave in to the speculators once again. In lieu of cash, they now told Randolph, "We are much disposed to believe that much good might result from taking the bills of Morris, Nicholson, and Greenleaf." On the condition of punctual payment, they also grudgingly granted Greenleaf a deed for 854 lots, bluntly emphasizing that they were "deviating from the common mode respecting landed property." They would later provide him with title certificates for another fifteen hundred lots, secured by a bond issued against the speculators' personal estates. On the basis of these certificates, the Bank of Columbia advanced the speculators $60,000 toward paying the commissioners their first—now twelve months overdue—installment for the lots they had "purchased" in the autumn of 1793. Had the commissioners known the dizzying depth of the speculators' indebtedness, they might have recognized that their hopes were delusional.

As if this was not enough to aggravate the commissioners, Samuel Blodget continued to insinuate himself into the capital's increasingly tangled affairs. The winning ticket for his hotel had finally been drawn in January. But the ostentatious groundbreaking of the previous July proved to have been little more than theater. Six months later, the hotel was still a hole in the ground. Of the $207,000 in prizes that had originally been promised, Blodget admitted that only $103,750 had been paid out. He had spent another $13,500 toward the hotel's construction, leaving $89,750 still unaccounted for. When the commissioners appointed Treasury Department inspectors to audit the lottery, Blodget coyly told them that he could not actually show them any of the redeemed tickets, because their edges might become "fretted."

Meanwhile, the promoter was hawking tickets for his second lottery, this one purporting to offer a "magnificent dwelling house" plus $400,000 in cash prizes. The inspectors learned, however, that Blodget was actually paying off winners of the first lottery at only a fraction of their tickets' value, or in new tickets for the second lottery. This was a bit much even for the loose ethics of the eighteenth century. Adding insult to injury, Blodget asserted that the new lottery was officially sanctioned by the commissioners. Washington was disgusted, and blamed the commissioners for failing to rein Blodget in. "It was unfortunate that we ever had any connection with him in any way," Commissioner David Stuart fumed. Responding to a query from a member of the public, the commissioners declared, "We disdain entering into any further controversy with him. We had no connection, and would have none with Lottery No. 2." Greenleaf, who owed his own involvement in the federal city to Blodget, wrote superciliously to the commissioners, on behalf of his partners, that as Blodget "has in a great measure deprived him of the sufferages of the very few who thought well of him, and as he has really sunk to a degree of insignificance far beneath your notice, we have concluded to say nothing more to him."

Blodget was dismissed as superintendent of the federal city, a job for which he had shown no trace of interest or competence. "I was at a loss how to account for a conduct so distant from any of the ideas I had entertained of the duties of a Superintendent, but it appears evidently enough now, that speculation has been his primary object from the beginning," the president wrote, perhaps a little disingenuously. Once again, he had extended his trust to a young protégé and had been betrayed. Unrepentant as always, Blodget whined that he was guilty of nothing improper, and was simply the victim of a "compleat finesse" by Morris, Nicholson, and his former friend Greenleaf. The "superb hotel" was never completed; for some years, its shell would stand as a blighted midway landmark for citizens traveling between the President's House and the Capitol. The mansions that were to have been the grand prizes in the second lottery were never built. Eventually, irate ticket holders sued and succeeded in wresting from Blodget what little property remained to him in the Federal District. When the commissioners' investigators sought to interrogate him in person, they discovered that he had skipped town. Washington, who had once waxed so enthusiastic over the financier's talents, now claimed that he hardly knew him. Blodget would eventually die in poverty in Philadelphia, in 1814.

STRESS WAS TAKING a toll on the speculators. Although they remained superficially cordial, testiness began to creep into their letters to one another. Nicholson complained that Greenleaf was not putting enough hard money into the capital. Greenleaf retorted, "I am mortified beyond measure"; to pay "a presumptive balance due on an unexamined and unapproved account, and without previous notice, approbation or permission, is unquestionably *wrong*." For his part, the young Bostonian felt misused when he had to pay out nearly $60,000 to cover some of Nicholson's debts, and another $20,000 of his own money as downpayment for the partnership's purchase of tracts in New York. Greenleaf looked to Morris for support, but was treated instead to the older man's groans over his own indebtedness. "You call your disappointments cruel and so they may probably be, but remember, other people suffer cruelties in pecuniary matters also, and I feel mine as much at this time as you can," Morris grumbled. The triumvirate nevertheless remained unbowed by the mounting wave of debt that was looming over their heads. Paddling onward toward its towering shadow, they continued to buy still more land from the original property owners in the Federal District, including 220 lots from Daniel Carroll of Duddington, the landowner whose house L'Enfant had so high-handedly demolished back in 1791, more than 400 lots from Notley Young, another 200 from Uriah Forrest and Benjamin Stoddert. Naturally they bought them all on credit.

In late 1794 the Potomac capital more than ever seemed likely to become a symbol of collective failure, rather than heroic national purpose. "The year 1800 is approaching with hasty strides; equally so ought the public buildings to advance towards completion," cajoled the overworked president, who was personally expected to weigh in on questions ranging from the degree of polish that might be desirable for the capital's curbstones to a proposal to transplant the entire faculty of the University of Genoa to the Potomac. (A rough finish was acceptable, but nix to the Italians, Washington suggested.) However, the commissioners knew that the entire project rested on a quicksand of facile promises, rapidly dwindling funds, and unsecured credit, and they were worried once again about a complete collapse. To Washington, they confessed "this melancholy truth, that the remaining funds of the City must fall very short of accomplishing the great and necessary objects in view." They feared that the public buildings might never be completed, warning, "Such an event might ultimately shake the Dignity and Honor and peace of the Union." The city's landscape was littered with the wrecked dreams of idealists and opportunists alike. L'Enfant was long gone, and his grandiose plans unfulfilled. Ellicott had tired of quarreling with the commissioners and quit. (He would go on to survey the country's southern border with Spanish Florida, to train Meriwether Lewis in surveying in preparation for his departure on the Lewis and Clark expedition, and to finally end his days as a professor of mathematics at West Point, where he died in 1820.) Two of the commissioners, Thomas Johnson and David Stuart, were begging to be relieved. Blodget's reputation was ruined, and Greenleaf's was tottering. Morris and Nicholson were wounded. Landowners were growing corn in the rights of way that were supposed to have been the boulevards of the imperial city. Progress had been made on the President's House, but construction of the Capitol was at a near standstill. The Masonic fanfare of the previous September, the glorious cannonades, the sacred laying of the cornerstone all seemed like distant memories.

It was at this moment that James Greenleaf wrought what was arguably his only act of wizardry on behalf of the federal city. Trailing intriguing rumors like exotic plumage in his wake, yet another agent of salvation had appeared from a most unexpected quarter. It was said that Thomas Law had come all the way from faraway India, that he had married a fabulously wealthy Hindu, that he had personally saved the reputation of the famous colonialist Warren Hastings, that he was also a passionate republican, and had abandoned his native England to make a life in the new world. The truth was less romantic, but not by much. The thirty-seven-year-old Law—"bright in speech, elegant in manner, intellectually handsome, and a plethoric purse withal"—had indeed made a fortune in India. He did have two sons who his blood-conscious contemporaries considered to be biracial (though no Indian wife was in sight), and he spared no expense to have them educated as cultured young Americans. And he threw in his lot with the federal city with a depth of commitment that would put to shame the schemes of the man who lured him there. Law also had something else that the other speculators lacked: cash, a great deal of it.

Law was born in Cambridge, to an aristocratic family with connections in colonial India. He went to Bengal at the age of seventeen, to serve as a clerk in the offices of the East India Company, a typical starter job for an ambitious young man, and rose rapidly in the company's service to become a member of the powerful Revenue Board, then a judge and, at the age of twenty-seven, Collector for the district of Bahar, in effect a kind of proconsul with fiscal, judicial, and executive responsibilities for over two million people. He earned respect for reforming the tax system and increasing revenues, and an official commendation issued at the time of his departure from India, for health reasons in 1791, praised him for attending to "the welfare of all ranks of people, distinguishing the liberal and noble, rendering justice to the oppressed, and cherishing the afflicted." The fortune that he brought to the federal city, he asserted in an 1824 pamphlet that defended his land speculations, derived from a "moiety" of the increased tax revenues that his reforms had raised, as permitted by colonial law. It can reasonably be assumed that his position in India had also enabled him, as it did many other officials, who after all were representatives of a commercial enterprise rather than the British government, to profit from the colonial trade. By the standards of his day, Law was an enlightened liberal, who professed himself to be both a democrat and an emancipationist—despite the fact that he purchased slaves, with a view to setting them free when they came of age, he asserted—and was accused by his pious enemies of harboring "atheistical tenets."

Law came to the United States in the summer of 1794, prospecting for investment opportunities. He met Greenleaf in New York and, like so many others, was immediately taken with the genteel Bostonian, who impressed him as "a man of enlarged understanding," and "a most respectable man for abilities and integrity." Greenleaf assured Law that the metropolis-to-be was destined to become the epicenter of the nation, and that "if a few of us sit down in Washington City" more eager buyers would soon follow, and that investment there was virtually risk free, since "1,000 Dollars will soon rise to 1000 pounds." Law was sold. "I shall certainly go to Washington City & my heart & mind are full of it," he exclaimed. He was charmed by what he saw. The humid climate of the Potomac, no matter how much discomforted New Englanders complained about it, was no match for the steamy plains of India.

On Christmas Eve, Law agreed to buy 445 lots at $293 apiece—Greenleaf had bought them a year earlier for $80 per lot—for a total of $133,000 in cash, much of which (though by no means all) would be dispatched to the long-suffering commissioners, to pay off some of the partners' overdue debts. He selected lots along the Eastern Branch, then expected to become the commercial center. Next day, Greenleaf and his partners promised Law that if within eighteen months he was dissatisfied with his purchase, his payment would be returned with interest. Until the partners acquired clear title to these squares by paying the commissioners for them, as security they agreed to mortgage to Law other city properties that they already owned. Law fairly gushed with gratitude to Greenleaf for doing business with him: "I am fully satisfied with the whole transaction & am happy that it has made me acquainted with one whose Character stands so high." He was so excited by the city's prospects that he tried to recruit wealthy friends from England to join him, and fairly begged Greenleaf to sell him even more lots at the same price.

For the moment, everyone was reasonably content, except the president. He remained troubled that although more than half the city's land had been disposed of, less than a quarter of the money needed for completing the project had been raised. Instead of developing lots and building up the city, Greenleaf, Morris, and Nicholson were simply reselling their property to others, on credit no less, and (in Washington's opinion) reaping "an immense profit." The president warned, rather late in the game, "To part with the legal title to the lots (especially in large sales of them) on personal security, may be hazarding more than prudence will warrant."

But Law was a happy man. "You may say that I had rather sell my horses or books or anything rather than part with a foot at present of Washington City," he boasted. He had great plans. He intended to build a wharf and establish an agency for East India commissions; idealistically, he also dreamed of helping to bring about Washington's vision of a national university in the city, where "the young men from the North & South shall here meet & imbibe amicable dispositions &

general philanthropy." Thanks to Law, Greenleaf, Morris, and Nicholson had gained breathing space. The tide of debt paused miraculously, as it were, over their heads. The stonemasons, the carters, the owners of the slaves who were making bricks and digging trenches at the Capitol would all be paid, for at least the next few months. Once again, everyone could now step back from the edge of the precipice. The president could keep his attention focused where it needed to be, on stamping out the rebellion in the West, on steering the nation clear of foreign war, and on his final years in office, for he had made it clear to the dismay of countless Americans that he would not accept a third term. Of the federal city, he pronounced, "The business, I conceive, is now fairly on its legs."

Most of Law's property lay on the elevated promontory of land, still known as Greenleaf's Point, which lies between the Potomac and the Eastern Branch, today's Anacostia River, and which many believed was destined to become part of the city's commercial core. Apart from the site of the Capitol, nothing matched the expansive view that Law enjoyed from the crest of the low ridge. The landscape had changed since that time, three years before, when Benjamin Banneker had gazed northward from his observatory on Jones Point, on the Virginia shore. Across the plain where Banneker had seen plantations and forest, Law now saw a tracery of streets, the walls of the President's House rising a mile away, and perhaps, in his mind's eye, a teeming entrepôt, a London, or even a kind of Yankee Calcutta, surging with trade and travelers from every continent. Law could take justified pride in believing that his investment, more than any other to date, would make that vision a physical reality. One day, he took a British visitor to the site he had selected for his own home. His mind flirted with an unexpressed memory of languorous days in India, to which he would never return. Turning to his companion, he sighed, "Here I will make a terrace, and we will sit and smoke our hookahs."

Chapter 8

A Scene of
Distress

"If it is a city it is one in embrio, which will not come
to perfection for these two centuries, if it ever does at
all—So much for the Federal City of Washington."

—English immigrant, 1795

PHILADELPHIANS WOULD SCATHINGLY CALL it "Morris's
Folly": America's preeminent financier was erecting a mansion like no
other in the city, as grand as his outsize ambitions and his appetite for
reputation. Robert Morris already owned a famously luxurious retreat
on the Schuylkill River, just outside the city, replete with a private brew
house, rambling walks and drives, fish ponds stocked with goldfish, and
hothouses where he raised exotic tropical fruit. However, he had leased
his townhouse to George Washington for the presidential mansion,
while Morris's family rented quarters nearby. Now he was building
a home that would advertise to all that the orphaned immigrant of a
half-century earlier had ascended into the empyrean of the republican aristocracy. To design his palace, in 1793, Morris chose the most

famous architect in the United States, whose name was the cynosure of elegance and grandeur, and whose prestige in his sphere matched Morris's in his own—but a man who, Morris would quickly learn to his misery, could complete nothing at all: Peter Charles L'Enfant. All too soon, the project would vault beyond architectural sanity, and its spectacular failure would epitomize the crashing fortunes of the man whom President Washington and so many others counted on to save the federal city.

L'Enfant's contentious experience in the Federal District in 1791 had done little immediate damage to his reputation. He still had many supporters, and they tended to blame his fall from official grace on the district's commissioners, who were also causing Morris endless annoyance with their nattering demands that he pay his mounting debts on schedule. Since L'Enfant's departure from the Potomac in 1792 he had been quite busy indeed. That same year, Alexander Hamilton had hired him to design the waterworks for what a group of the secretary of the treasury's investor friends intended to be a model manufacturing center at Paterson, New Jersey. But the outcome, for L'Enfant, was a replay in a minor key of his operatic behavior in the Federal District. He once again proposed a visionary design that was far beyond his employers' budget, and when he was ordered to rein himself in, he abruptly quit, ostentatiously refusing once again to hand over his plans for the project. Nonetheless, in 1794 Secretary of War Knox handed him yet another plum: a commission to design fortifications for the harbors of Wilmington and Philadelphia. However, the state of Pennsylvania had the shocking affrontery—in L'Enfant's opinion—to investigate the project's financing. Treating this as a personal insult, he yet again defiantly walked off the job. Had Morris been paying close attention, he might have detected the ominous pattern. But his own grip on reality was also slipping.

For his new home, Morris had purchased an entire city block near the heart of Philadelphia, bounded by Chestnut, Walnut, Seventh, and Eighth Streets. With a cavalier disregard for contractual niceties that he would later have cause to regret, he offered L'Enfant a free hand. This was sheer catnip to a man for whom bricks and mortar were the equivalent of the oils with which his father had painted epic canvasses of France's continental wars. L'Enfant promised Morris an architectural pièce de résistance. The financier would get both much more than he bargained for, and harrowingly less.

I<small>N THE SPRING</small> of 1795 Morris tottered on the cliff's edge of debt, bad judgment, and unfulfillable promises, his eyes fixed on a beckoning vision of stupendous profits. President Washington complained that although half the public lots in the capital had been yielded to Morris, Nicholson, and other money men, only a fraction of the money promised had actually been delivered into the commissioners' depleted coffers. The partners' indebtedness was already so deep that Thomas Law's purchase of $133,000 worth of city lots offered only fleeting relief. The partners found themselves with a paper empire that included almost half the available lots in the federal city, but virtually no cash. They had added to their burden by contracting with the commissioners to undertake various public improvements, and to build at least twenty houses annually for the next seven years. In all, they owed the commissioners about $1.1 million, or $41,360,000 in present-day terms, not to mention additional promises they had smugly made to several local landowners. True, the Dutch government had approved a loan of $780,000 for Morris and his partners, but like so many overly optimistic plans whose tattered shreds now festooned the federal city, it proved another mirage. By March, investors had subscribed only $80,000: of that, they would ultimately pony up, months later, the paltry sum of $48,000. The commissioners, meanwhile, had less than $7,000 in their treasury. They had nothing to show for the tens of thousands of dollars spent on the Capitol, except muddy trenches and a shoddily built foundation, graphically reminding visitors of both the republic's feeble resources and its halfhearted commitment to the capital. An installment of $68,000 was due from the partners on May 1. To ensure that work was kept going through the summer, the commissioners invited them to pay early, betraying their ignorance of the bloodletting that was taking place on the unforgiving battlefield of high finance, where the partners feared for their own survival. They had borrowed heavily, pledging holdings elsewhere as collateral, certain that they could sell their city lots in Europe at a handsome profit and pay off their loans with the proceeds.

The capital's fate had become the prisoner of a speculative scheme so gargantuan and so tangled that it continues to defy attempts to fully unravel it. In February the partners combined their far-flung assets into the North American Land Company, with more than six million acres of holdings spread across New York, Pennsylvania, Virginia, the Carolinas, Kentucky, and Georgia. Morris was named chairman of its board. He and his partners were counting, in part, on profits from the land company's speculations to pay off their debts to the commissioners. The company's prospectus seductively asserted: "The proprietor of back lands gives himself no other trouble about them than to pay taxes, which are inconsiderable. As nature left them, so they lie till circumstances give them value. The proprietor is then sought out by the settler who has chanced to pitch upon them, or who has made any improvement thereon, and receives from him a price which fully repays his original advance with interest." Any fool can make a fortune in land speculation, it promised. It was a sucker's come-on.

The largest chunk of the company's holdings, more than 2.3 million acres, lay in Georgia, a state that, in an era that smiled benignly on buccaneering speculators, had already earned a national reputation for political corruption and fraud. Between 1789 and 1796 the Georgia legislature had approved the sale of more public land than actually existed in the state, as well as vast unmapped and overlapping tracts in the future states of Alabama and Mississippi, to which Georgia had only an uncertain claim. (The 1783 peace treaty with England had recognized the Mississippi River as the western boundary of the United States, but did not explicitly recognize Georgia's claim to the land; in its separate treaty with Spain, Britain recognized Spanish sovereignty over the same territory.) In a few years, much of this land would indeed become fabulously valuable, thanks to the newly invented cotton gin. By separating the seeds from raw cotton much faster than they could be by hand, the gin transformed an inefficient local industry into an exponentially expanding one that was based on mass slavery, and was always in search of new plantation land. All this would come too late to save Morris and his partners: for the present, the region remained an unfriendly, mosquito-infested wilderness of desolate pine barrens, boot-sucking bogs, and murky forests threaded with the meandering trails of Cherokee, Chickasaw, and Choctaw Indians, who were all but oblivious to the onslaught of settlement that white politicians and financiers were planning for them.

Georgia represented in exaggerated form the whole gamut of problems that plagued the frontier lands on which Morris and his partners had staked their fortune. Much of their land had never even been surveyed. Titles were often fatally clouded by competing claims, unpaid taxes, truculent squatters, and understandably hostile Indians. Moreover, much of the land the trio was hawking back East and in Europe was already known to be mortgaged as security for debt. Even where land was accessible and unencumbered, few people wanted it: in contrast to the glowing scenario presented in the land company's prospectus, roads had to be built, rivers cleared, and taxes paid off before settlers would come at all. The value of the company's shares plummeted when land could not be resold quickly enough to turn a profit. Much of what remained reverted to state ownership when they failed to pay overdue taxes.

The trio's reckless plunge into the Washington land market was fatal. Morris's once flawless commercial instincts had deserted him. The anticipated Dutch loan had fizzled. Although it had been approved in principle by both the American and Dutch governments, only a tiny fraction was ever raised from investors beleaguered by war and competing demands on their purses. Even had the Dutch loan succeeded, the glacial sale of city lots would probably have prevented the partners from repaying it in time to salvage their credit. Ironically, the same European wars that sucked away the European loans the partners so desperately sought had a dynamic effect on American shipping, which grew by leaps and bounds, carrying cargoes for both the embattled British and the French. Thus while Morris's wealth disappeared into the quicksand of land speculation, other Americans made fortunes in the very sphere in which he had once excelled. His addiction to real estate only grew as he eked out his ever-shrinking credit to acquire more and yet more land, with an irrationally exuberant faith that buyers would magically appear. "He borrows at a dreadful interest & sells disadvantageously like a desperate gambler to recover what he has lost—He has I know great resources, but no fortune can support his constant drains," Thomas Law confided in a letter to Greenleaf. Inevitably, as it became evident that Morris had mortgaged many tracts two and three times over, the doors of the world's capital markets began to close to him. His once unimpeachable notes, notes that had once kept the American Revolution alive and made his name the benchmark of commercial trustworthiness, commanded barely fifteen cents on the dollar. "Money grows Scarcer and the probability of obtaining it on almost any terms becomes daily more doubtful," Morris confessed.

Troubles came at the partners in battalions. In 1794 John Nicholson was blown from his seemingly impregnable redoubt in Philadelphia, when the state legislature impeached him for his manipulation of state loan certificates. Although acquitted, he was forced to resign from his base of power as the state's comptroller-general. Suits against him multiplied. Morris himself was wounded by a separate assault. For years, he had been the target of accusations that he misused public money during the Revolutionary War. In 1790 he finally asked Congress to audit his wartime accounts, certain that the outcome would vindicate him. To his consternation, when the report was released in 1795, it declared that Morris owed the government $93,312.63 in fees and damages for commercial transactions he had conducted during the war. In the face of such difficulties, the partners still somehow managed to borrow $20,000 from the Bank of Columbia, as a stopgap to fend off the commissioners. But time was running out. As the trio fired off promissory notes representing stratospheric sums of money, the ground was slipping away under their feet: below, the abyss of insolvency gaped.

Morris and Nicholson blamed Greenleaf for defaulting on notes that the two men had endorsed, allegedly ruining their credit. Greenleaf claimed that it was the others who were failing to pay their fair share, and that their liabilities were subjecting him to "the most humiliating & unjustifiable sacrifices." In truth, the self-righteous Bostonian never met his own share of the installments due on the partners' land acquisitions, and habitually used their money for his personal business. Greenleaf's own brother-in-law, the lexicographer Noah Webster, later wrote damningly of him, "I have known for years that James was in the path of ruin, converting with astonishing zeal and folly, good property into bad. I knew he was wantonly and deliberately feeding a long train of *whores* and *rogues*. But I could not believe till lately, that he would rob his innocent friends for that purpose."

Meanwhile, the trio was diddling its best client, the English immigrant and retired colonial official Thomas Law. Because the partners had failed to meet their installments, the commissioners were refusing to hand over the deeds to land that Law had already paid for. Law's contract required him to begin erecting houses on "his" land immediately, but how could he build on it without proof that it was actually his? Law was apoplectic. He "bounced around the room like a madman," according to Nicholson. He begged repeatedly for the deeds, a posture that did not sit at all well with a man who, in India, had governed an entire province and its millions of inhabitants. "Pardon me if I hurt your feelings—you must be conscious that mine are lacerated," Law wrote to Greenleaf, with barbed irony. "If not—like a hunted Boar I will seat myself at the end of New Jersey Avenue, relinquish all my plans of promotions & foam & goar till I fall under chagrine. In short an accumulation of mortifying circumstances will overwhelm me." Beneath the hyperbole, his meaning was unmistakable: *Give me what I have paid for—I am not a man to be trifled with!* Greenleaf cheerily assured him that his apprehensions were groundless. But sweat must have been soaking the Bostonian's exquisitely turned neckcloth.

In July the partnership finally collapsed. Greenleaf offered to buy out the Pennsylvanians. But Morris and Nicholson decided to buy him out instead, for $1.15 million in promissory notes drawn on each other, acidly reasoning that the lots were worth more than anything with Greenleaf's signature on it. "The unhappy engagements which I have been tempted to make with that man have proved source of vexation & misfortune to me beyond anything I could have conceived possible,"

Morris confessed to members of a bank in firm in Holland. This was a desperate maneuver. With Greenleaf gone, they still owed the commissioners $40,000. And they now found themselves contractually bound to erect scores more houses on all the empty lots that Greenleaf had purchased independently of the partnership. They were now like aerialists seemingly suspended in the air, legs churning, spinning impossibly high over their audience of creditors, public officials, family, and prospective investors, appearing for a brief moment as if they were about to pull off an impossible new trick that would bring them back safely to earth with a flourish. Instead, they came down in a tumbling heap, not to a roar of approval, or even for that matter a murmur of sympathy, but to shattered hopes, lost fortunes, ruined reputations, and eventually prison.

In public, Morris remained boastfully confident as he scrambled to raise funds, swearing that, against all evidence, by selling off one-half of the city lots that he and Nicholson had acquired, the remaining ones would inevitably double in value, transforming the prospect of bankruptcy into a financial coup that would more than wipe the slate clean. He continued to boast shamelessly of the prospects for the North American Land Company, predicting that within fifteen years dividends would multiply five times over—if not ten. Privately, he was deeply worried. He was tens of thousands of dollars in arrears in his payments to the commissioners. Did he really expect his creditors like Law to extend him unlimited trust? Perhaps not. But he had nothing to lose by pretending. To him, a man of commerce, trust was but another commodity, a bankable cargo like molasses or rum, which could be sold dear or cheap according to the oscillations of the market. Morris's notes were losing value literally by the day. He assured the commissioners that he would pay them as soon as he could convert the notes into cash. Privately, however, he was close to despair. "I am beating hard up against wind and tide," he wrote to a friend, adding ominously that it was now impossible to either sell property or to raise loans. "Our ready money [has] run out and not being able to pay as the notes fall due they have depreciated down to nothingness, and we are held in continual scenes of distress."

THE PRESIDENT WAS distraught. Washington feared that if construction now came to a halt it would "throw such a cloud over the public & private concerns of the City as to give it a vital wound." Workers would have to be discharged and might never be reassembled. Popular support for the project would continue to disintegrate. Moreover, costs were bound to rise as more expensive materials and more skilled labor were required for the later stages of the public buildings. The city needed money now, not more facile promises. If the wizardry of Robert Morris could not make the federal city a reality, what could? It must have pained the president to address his old friend thus, but he now instructed the secretary of state to warn Morris "in earnest and strong terms" that serious consequences would result if they failed to meet their commitments. The commissioners gave Morris and Nicholson until mid-October to remit $15,000. It was their last best offer. Washington pleaded with Morris to pay the commissioners, for his own sake, for friendship's sake, for the country's sake. But the partners' plight was hopeless.

THE WEIGHT OF age tugged at Washington's body and his mind. There were whispers that he was growing senile. He felt surrounded by enemies and beset by unending national crisis. True, Thomas Jefferson, the least supportive member of his cabinet, had retired from the government—defected, some might say—and ensconced himself at Monticello, but his allies in Philadelphia assiduously continued to undermine the administration. The Indian menace had receded in the Northwest after General Anthony Wayne's decisive victory at the Battle of Fallen Timbers, in June 1794. But the frontier was still a tinderbox: the Cherokees remained on the warpath in Tennessee, where settlers were still murdered, prisoners carried off, farms plundered. The United States had also drawn back from the brink of war with England, a foreign policy success that maddeningly translated into a domestic near disaster.

For years, the British Navy had boarded American ships with impunity, seizing sailors and cargoes bound for blockaded France, wreaking havoc on shipping, and driving Americans to a fever pitch of patriotic Anglophobia. In the spring of 1794 Washington dispatched Chief Justice John Jay to Europe to negotiate a treaty. Jay got his treaty, but it was not what proud Americans expected. The United States abandoned its claim to freedom of the seas, renounced the right to transport cargoes that Britain deemed to be contraband, promised to bar from American ports both French privateers and the sale of war prizes captured from the British, and—particularly galling to American merchants—restricted American trade in the Caribbean to small ships, which could not challenge the crown's commercial dominance there. So much for the vaunted rights of neutrality, which the United States had sworn to defend. The treaty was not entirely one-sided. Britain agreed to surrender the remaining posts on the Great Lakes south of the international boundary, to which it had defiantly clung since the end of the Revolutionary War, and to pay damages for its attacks on American commerce. The treaty even had elements of brilliance. It staved off a war that the United States could not have won, and it allowed American shippers to take advantage of opportunities created by the conflict in Europe. "Jay's Treaty was a shrewd bargain for the United States," historian Joseph J. Ellis has written. "It bet, in effect, on England rather than France as the hegemonic European power of the future, which proved prophetic. It recognized the massive dependence of the American economy on trade with England [and] it linked American security and economic development to the British fleet, which provided a protective shield of incalculable value throughout the nineteenth century."

The problem was that many Americans didn't see it that way: they saw it as abject surrender. The summer of 1795 presented Washington with the most difficult trial of his entire presidency: would he sign the treaty or not? Conflicting advice came at him from all sides. Alexander Hamilton and the Federalists strongly supported the treaty. James Madison and the coalescing factions that were becoming the Republican Party even more strongly opposed it. Republicans seethed with outrage at Jay's abandonment of faithful France, whose troops and money had made victory possible in the Revolutionary War, and which was now carrying out its own revolution inspired, in part, by American ideals. Reports that Jay had actually kissed the Queen of England's hand added to the popular fury. All over the country, mass meetings fiercely denounced the treaty. Flaming effigies of John Jay lit up the night sky. In Charleston, the public hangman burned a copy of the treaty. In New York, Alexander Hamilton was stoned when he spoke in the treaty's defense. Rioters stormed the British ambassador's home in Philadelphia. Within his own cabinet, the patrician Virginian Edmund Randolph, who had moved from the State Department to the office of attorney general, urged Washington to delay ratification. The president was caught on the horns of a dilemma: the ferocity of the opposition to it made him fear for the country's stability, but peace with Britain was imperative. For weeks he temporized. Then, in October, he was shocked to learn that Randolph had divulged the content of private government discussions to the French ambassador, allegedly in return for a bribe, seeming proof that a sinister French hand was at work. The attorney general resigned in disgrace literally on the spot, leaving the president feeling vulnerable and betrayed. The next day, somehow, the old soldier mustered the courage, which in wartime had led him to expose himself repeatedly to the enemy's bullets, and signed the treaty.

The intensity of popular opposition to the treaty seemed to Washington and the ruling Federalists just the latest phase in a rising tide of anarchy. In July 1794 violent agitation had flared through twenty western counties, with its epicenter in Pennsylvania. The frontiersmen had legitimate grievances, ranging from the difficulty of travel to the state courts in Philadelphia, to inadequate protection from Indian attacks, to the growing concentration of power in the hands of wealthy landowners. But the most pointed protests focused on the federal whiskey tax, which discriminated against small farmers, for whom the distillation of corn was their only way to convert their crop into a cash commodity. Only in liquid form could they carry it inexpensively, and thus profitably, through the mountains to markets in the East. Buckskin-clad mobs raised liberty poles, burned barns, and tarred and feathered tax collectors. In August six thousand irate frontiersmen massed at Braddock's

Field, where in 1755 British and colonial forces (young George Washington among them) had been ambushed during the French and Indian War. There they erected mock guillotines to proclaim their affinity for the French. The symbolism of the site, and of the guillotine, was not lost on the president. There was near panic in Philadelphia as exaggerated reports trickled eastward of "riots" and "outrages" perpetrated by the "insurgents." The rebellion climaxed when the frontiersmen assaulted the fortified home of a tax collector near Pittsburgh, and forced the surrender of soldiers sent to subdue them. John Jay worried that hordes of "white savages" would overrun the East, like the barbarians who sacked Rome. Although modern historians believe that the threat posed by the rebellion was exaggerated, at the time rebel leaders certainly fed the government's fear of a far-reaching conspiracy. "The question will not be whether you march to Pittsburgh, but whether [the insurgents] will march to Philadelphia, accumulating in their course, and swelling over the banks of the Susquehannah like a torrent, irresistible and devouring in its progress," one rebel menacingly wrote to Hamilton's assistant secretary of the treasury Tench Coxe. As far as Federalists were concerned, the frontiersmen's behavior amounted to nothing less than treason at a time of international crisis: the Federalist *Pennsylvania Gazette* declared that "laws opposed to force must be executed by force."

The Whiskey Rebellion seemed like the fulfillment of Washington's darkest anxieties: that settlers who migrated beyond the firm grip of the federal government would loosen their moorings to the East, and ultimately defect to the British or Spanish. Wasn't this precisely why he had always argued for the development of the Potomac, to anchor frontiersmen to the Atlantic Coast? Defiance of the government would not be tolerated. Washington called upon the neighboring states to contribute troops to an army that would eventually total nearly thirteen thousand men, the largest force to be assembled in North America since the Revolutionary War. He appointed Virginia Governor Henry "Light Horse Harry" Lee to lead the gathering army against the rebels, even as he carried out sham peace talks with their representatives. When the army reached Pittsburgh in November, guilty and innocent alike were dragged from their beds and driven barefoot at bayonet point along the frozen roads; at least one man, when he collapsed, was dragged along lashed to the tail of a horse. An unknown number died. Hundreds reportedly fled west beyond the frontier for safety. The backbone of the revolt was broken, but resentment against the federal government, against the Federalists, and against the once untouchable George Washington seethed.

Much of the organized agitation against both the whiskey tax and the Jay Treaty sprang from pro-French, self-described "Democratic Societies," which had sprouted around the country by the dozens in early 1790s. By present-day standards, these were for the most part little more than debating societies, exercising the elementary rights of speech and assembly that were guaranteed by the Constitution. Although the United States was a republic, it was not a democracy. To Federalists, such societies smacked of unseemly partisanship, disobedience to established institutions, and revolution. Significantly, many members of the Democratic Societies were smallholders or landless working men, who, in an era when property was a requirement for voting in most states, were barely even citizens, much less respectable in the eyes of the elite. Most Federalists regarded the white working class as little more than an irresponsible rabble that had to be kept in check. No one knew what horrors might result when the mob got out of hand. The bloodthirsty example of the French Revolution was plain for all to see. "Beheading Federalists is the present reigning fashion in France," one conservative newssheet meaningfully warned.

A SIMILAR DISDAIN FOR working men infected the commissioners' attitude toward free labor at the site of the capital on the Potomac. Slavery's fundamental role in the city's construction may not have been inevitable, at least not quite. The question of who would actually build the new capital had posed problems from the outset. Maryland and Virginia were both populous states. In theory, it should have been possible to hire a sufficient number of free men to undertake the jobs that needed to be done. However, local whites vehemently shunned what they harshly called "nigger work." As Duc Rochefoucauld-Liancourt, an acute French exile who visited the Federal District in the 1790s, observed, "In a country abounding in slaves, the whites do not apply much to labour. Their ambition consists in buying negroes; they buy them with the first sum of money they get, and when they have two of them they leave off working themselves." Those too poor to buy slaves tended to abandon the country altogether and migrate westward, mainly to Kentucky and Tennessee, selling their land to great proprietors who converted their farms into slave-worked plantations.

Skilled masons, carpenters, and quarrymen were difficult to attract at the wages that the commissioners were willing to pay. For years, the commissioners had sought to recruit such men from as far afield as Scotland, Ireland, and England, where promoters planted wildly propagandistic articles portraying the new American capital as already bustling with commerce and teeming with immigrants. "The magnificent city of WASHINGTON, in America, has already SEVEN THOUSAND HOUSES, built in a very *handsome style*, and they continue building in a very rapid manner," London's *Morning Chronicle* preposterously proclaimed. Another writer claimed that an astonishing "eleven thousand artificers, besides labourers" were already employed on the site. Agents for ships bound for the Potomac hovered like birds of prey along the Thames, lavishly promising immigrants well-paid work and free land in the Federal District.

With luck and fair winds, the voyage from Britain to the Chesapeake might be accomplished in under a month; for the unlucky, the trip could take more than twice as long and strain travelers to the breaking point. Passengers on one ship spent two excruciating months dodging Barbary pirates and French cruisers, battling fierce seas, short rations, and incessant bickering, buoyed only by glowing anticipation of life in the American metropolis. "You may conceive what kind of panygyric we bestowed *upon those who had been the occasion* of our peregrination to this mart of happiness," one passenger sarcastically wrote home, after laying eyes on the supposed metropolis of Washington. Another, a master carpenter, at his first sight of the federal city, wept "tears of repentance for my own folly, in suffering myself to be so miserably duped." Reported a young stonemason: "The five streets so pompously lain out in the map which we examined in London, are avenues cut through the woods, with not a solitary house standing in either of them. The hills are barren of everything but impenetrable woods, and the valleys are mere swamps, producing nothing except myriads of toads and frogs (of enormous size)." Newcomers found just forty houses, many of them apparently abandoned in midconstruction. Instead of free housing and land, immigrants discovered that they were expected to live either in barracks, or in unpainted shacks resembling plantation slave quarters or the booths erected at country fairs. For men accustomed to well-stocked English larders, the food was repulsive: salt pork for every meal, corn mush, oily butter, inedible cheese, bread floating "in a mestruum of oleagious matter," all of it washed down with prodigious quantities of cheap, potent corn whiskey. (Americans believed that water could be lethal, and they were not entirely wrong given the sanitary conditions of the time.) The heat was so intolerable that livestock was killed at night lest the meat instantly spoil. Brief spells of intense work rewarded with high wages were interspersed with long intervals of idleness and near penury. Troublemakers were flogged, or even branded. The wife of one of the carpenters at the President's House turned her hovel into a "riotous and disorderly house," and was accused by the commissioners of pulling men in off the street. Morale was abysmal, and lurid rumors rife: L'Enfant, it was said, had pocketed all the cash he could get his hands on and fled, abandoning his (nonexistent) foster child . . . the speculators had abandoned the city to its fate . . . the whole project was at a standstill because the commissioners had embezzled all the funds. Instead of thousands of industrious workmen, there were forty-six at work on the President's House, barely thirty at the Capitol, and a similar number at the quarries, many of them slaves—a fact that appalled many of the Englishmen, partly for moral reasons, and partly because they knew that slave labor undercut their own wages.

The commissioners of the federal city were deeply suspicious of independent white labor. Free men were liable to complain, agitate, disobey their superiors, and walk off the job when they were unhappy, as many did. In 1794 newly appointed Commissioner Gustavus Scott— a Virginia attorney who was deeply invested in both the Potomack

Company and the land schemes of Morris and Nicholson—grumbled that workers were abandoning their jobs to join the army that was raised to suppress the Whiskey Rebellion, rather a contradiction to fears that they were closet revolutionaries, but a telling commentary on working conditions in the Federal District, when a march across three hundred miles of near wilderness, harsh discipline, and the risk of death seemed a more appealing alternative. Worse yet, free workers might carry within themselves the subversive incubus of revolutionary French ideas, as the insurrection in Pennsylvania and the urban mob opposition to Jay's Treaty seemed to have amply proved. In America, sneered the aristocratic English traveler Richard Parkinson, the once docile workman "soon becomes the greatest puppy imaginable, and much unpleasanter even than the negro."

There was, of course, a solution to the commissioners' labor anxieties readily to hand: slaves—slaves in abundance. As the productivity of land in the Tidewater region declined, and farmers shifted away from tobacco to less labor-intensive crops like wheat, many hard-pressed masters liquidated their investment in human property by shipping it to the new lands being opened up in the West, where the demand for slaves was climbing: between 1780 and 1810 Tidewater planters would export 115,000 slaves to the trans-Appalachian West. Others preferred to lease their slaves' labor for a handsome profit, which might range as high as 23 percent of their market value for one year's work. As early as 1793 the federal commissioners had deliberately undercut white workers' demands for higher wages by making it clear that they could always be replaced by slaves, who "have proven a very useful check and kept our affairs cool." Slaves were docile and cheap. They couldn't quit, protest, or demand higher wages. They could generally be hired locally for about $55 per year, about three-fifths the cost of the cheapest unskilled free labor. By 1795 the use of slave labor was well established, with as many as three hundred slaves working in the District, half of them for the commissioners and the rest for private contractors and suppliers, and perhaps one hundred fifty whites. Although there were a few significant exceptions—James Hoban's private team of enslaved carpenters, for example—slaves for the most part were assigned to the roughest and least-skilled tasks. To the Southern-born, the district now presented the reassuringly familiar panorama of a plantation work site, with white overseers directing black workmen grubbing stumps, hauling timber, dragging sledges, digging foundations, toting baskets of stone, bushels of lime, and kegs of nails, chiseling stone, stirring mortar, and tending brick kilns. Wherever buildings were under construction, including the Capitol and the President's House, teams of enslaved sawyers in broad-brimmed hats could be seen sweating at their work in the sawpits beneath cascades of sawdust, slicing logs into boards, with the rhythmic, angled, back-breaking strokes of a six-foot-long blade.

Who were these men? Although slave sales regularly took place in and around the Federal District, the commissioners never purchased slaves outright. The commissioners' yellowing records usually speak delicately of "Negro hire," as if slaves were but the utilitarian rental equipment of the day, which in a sense they were. Their scribbled names stare out cryptically from the scraps of two-centuries-old paper. There are Commissioner Gustavus Scott's two slaves, Kitt and Bob; William Somerwell's Charles; Susannah Johnson's Peter, Nace, Basil, and Will; Hancock Eustace's Philip; George Fenwick's Auston; Middleton Belt's Peter; Charles Love's James and George. James Hoban, the architect at the President's House, earned $60 a month from the commissioners for the work of his five carpenters, one of whom was so skilled that he—or rather Hoban—was paid more than free white workers on the same job. Although hiring out slaves could be quite profitable—one owner earned £300 from the hire of his four slaves in 1795—in other instances, a slave's labor might be all that stood between his master and destitution. In February 1795 impecunious John Linton of Dumfries piteously begged his agent for the overdue wages of his slave Lark Fuller, who worked quarrying stone: "Sir, you'll not fail in paying the money as I am in the greatest distress."

No one was interested in what enslaved workers thought about their work, or about the grandiose enterprise into which they had willy-nilly been drafted. The only published memoir by a contemporary African American, Josiah Henson, who grew up on a farm ten miles from the city in Rockville, Maryland, makes virtually no mention of the capital at all, as if it lay a thousand rather than just five miles away from his home, as for him it might as well have. Yet, in the commissioners' spartan records there are occasional hints of something more, like shadowy images glimpsed for a split second at twilight. There is, for instance, the elusive figure of "Jerry." In December 1794 the surveyor's office asked the finance officer to "please pay Jerry the black man at rate of 8 dollars per month, for his last months services, he is justly entitled to the highest wages that is [due] to our hands—being promised it—and the best hand in the Department." Who was this exceptional worker? He was obviously a free black man, who received and kept his own wages, who was more skilled than all or most of the white men in his crew, and was sufficiently respected by his boss to warrant a special application to the commissioners on his behalf. Unfortunately, the outcome was not recorded. Nor did Jerry's name reappear after early 1795. Did he quit? Was he a man who knew the value of his work, and refused to accept less than it was worth? Or did white men refuse to work with a black man whose labor was worth more than their own? Where he went no one knows. Nor is anything more known about the man who is recorded only as "Caesar, Free," except that he *was* free, and was paid for nineteen days' work in August 1795 at the same rate as the white men with whom he worked.

In some ways, the most enigmatic figure of all was the vividly named Anise-Chloe Leclear (or LeClair), who served as nurse in the workers' hospital in 1795 at a salary of $10 a month. It is impossible to tell if she was white or black. She was clearly a free person, and evidently illiterate, since she signed for her wages with an "X." She would seem to have been French, given her name. However, it seems highly unlikely (though not impossible) that a white woman would be hired to tend male slaves, who comprised most of the infirmary's clientele. Leclear may very possibly have been a refugee from Sainte-Domingue, one of the thousands who poured into the United States helter-skelter in the early 1790s. She may have been an impoverished white colonial of course, but just as likely a free mulatto, some of whom fled with the whites, or even a former slave who managed somehow to acquire her freedom. If so, she was the first, and probably the only, salaried black woman to participate in the creation of the nation's capital.

Slaves, like most free laborers, worked six days a week, twelve hours each day, from dawn to dusk, with a one-hour midday break for a meal, usually, of salt pork or mutton, hoe cakes, and grease sandwiches. Slaves were not chained, although they must have been closely watched, since there is no record of escapes from the district's labor camps, even though ads for runaways in the local newspapers make clear that fugitive slaves from farms in the surrounding area posed a continuing headache for their owners. For most, flight was hopeless: there was really nowhere to go. The Underground Railroad lay years in the future. Apart from Philadelphia, there was no safe haven in a country where almost every state was to some degree still a slave state.

The irony of slave labor erecting the buildings that would house the political machinery of the republic was lost on the political luminaries whose wealth and prestige depended in differing degrees on the slave-labor economy. George Washington; Thomas Jefferson; his successor as secretary of state and (until 1795) cabinet-level point man for the project, Edmund Randolph; and James Madison were all slaveholders, as were the district's appointed commissioners. Most simply took the institution of slavery for granted. But some of the leading figures who played key roles in the project were Northern men, or immigrants, and in one way or another, slavery captured them, too. James Hoban, whose enslaved carpenters were at work on the President's House, was Irish, as was James Dermott, who in 1792 was teaching mathematics in Alexandria when the commissioners hired him to "handle the Negroes" on Andrew Ellicott's surveying crew; the commissioners initially feared that Dermott might not be up to the job, but he was so successful at it that by the end of the decade he would be trading in slaves. (Dermott was also the focus of bitter complaints by Andrew Ellicott, who alleged that he had stolen his papers, arbitrarily removed boundary stakes, and erased details in the city plan—and was a sot, to boot.) Of the three Yankee speculators who dominated investment in the district in the middle years of the decade, Robert Morris had always taken a businesslike attitude toward slavery; having once dealt commercially in slaves, he still owned slave-worked estates in Delaware and New Jersey. James Greenleaf never expressed himself on the subject of slavery, but he owned at least one slave, named Cudjo, and used slave labor to build his houses in the federal city. John Nicholson, an open opponent of slavery, also owned a personal slave, named Jim, but was philosophically opposed to slavery as an institution, and lent the money that had enabled Richard Allen and Absalom Jones to build the nation's first black church, in Philadelphia. After an initial reluctance, he too acquiesced to the use of slaves to develop his property in the federal city.

Of all the personalities who were struggling to bring the federal city into being, there was one among them who might have been expected to point out the hypocrisy of relying so heavily on slave labor: William Thornton. Appointed to the three-man Board of Commissioners in the autumn of 1794 at a salary of £600 per year, Thornton and his wife, Anna Maria, settled on Falls Street (now M Street), in George Town, where they soon became a magnet for local society and a stream of eminent visitors; they also acquired a farm just across the district line in Montgomery County, Maryland, as well as property in the city, adjacent to lots belonging to President Washington. The good doctor was immensely proud of his appointment: "The trust reposed in us is so great that I do not know a more extensive power in any offices of our government, except the President, or perhaps the Secretary of State, Treasury, and War," he boasted to his cousin John Coakley Lettsom. He was also happy just to have a paying job, having failed to make a go of it as a medical doctor in Philadelphia, where "the fees were in my estimation so low in comparison to the duties required that I was glad to abandon the practice."

Thornton fell in love with the Potomac landscape. "The site is the most beautiful I have ever seen," he enthused. "It is much like that of Constantinople, only we have on one side a river two miles wide, on the other one mile wide, containing a fine harbor for the largest ships. The country round rises in all the diversity of hill and dale that imagination can paint." He quickly immersed himself in the commissioners' daily flow of work orders, receipts, bills of procurement, regulations, disbursements, and slave hires, devoting himself with particular ardor to a meticulous reexamination of the Capitol's troublesome foundation: should the hill's crown be leveled so as not to overshadow the building, or the building be moved closer to the crown? In a stream of letters graced with his sweeping signature, he reported to the president about the nuances of street patterns, access to wharves, debates over the number of chimneys that should be allowed to each waterfront warehouse, and the knotty problem of trees, pointing out with annoyance that although L'Enfant had intended that the city's broad streets should be lined by trees, axemen had cut them all down, and that it would take half a century for new ones to grow. "Our country is extensive, our resources great, and our ideas ought to be exalted," he enthused. "I wish to see the American character outshine all others, and our public characters supported with the consideration due to their stations." There was no mention now of the grand colonization scheme over which he had rhapsodized just a few years earlier. New enthusiasms crowded in upon him. Perhaps he would establish a philosophical society, he opined, or maybe an agricultural society, or even a university.

Thornton never lost his driving ambition to achieve both greatness and moral vindication. "I cannot rest when I think what I might have done, and reflect on what I could have done," he wrote to Lettsom. "I sicken at the idea, and lament the loss of time—God grant grace to me, and direct me to be, if possible, a benefactor to man! I must do more than I have ever yet done, or my name too will die." In his restless anguish, he vividly incorporated the irreconcilable contradictions that lay half-concealed in the hearts of a great many professed antislavery men of his generation, Thomas Jefferson not least among them: personal guilt warring with a principled belief in emancipation, and a morally crippling insistence that freed slaves must be kept at a safe distance from their former masters, lest they mix with them or massacre them. In the free air of Philadelphia, such contradictions were not fatal. Had Thornton remained there, quite possibly he would have loosened his colonizationist moorings and evolved into a genuine abolitionist.

But the Potomac was another world, where even the mildest advocacy of emancipation was under siege, and could ruin the career of a man dependent for his advancement on Southern friends. In 1794 the Virginia General Assembly declared Alexandria's Quaker-based emancipation society a "menace." The campaign against emancipation continued two years later with accusations that the society was "infusing into the slaves a spirit of insurrection," a charge perilously close to treason. Before the decade was out, every emancipation society in Virginia would be defunct. In the Federal District, Thornton was surrounded by men he admired who believed that black slavery in no way compromised white men's freedom. Then, too, there was the income from his own estate on Tortola, which helped to pay for his stable of race horses and his farm on the Fredericktown Road, and helped to buy him access to the drawing rooms of the Madisons, Jeffersons, and others of their class—which, in short, helped make Thornton the gentleman that he was. Inexorably, he yielded to the gravitational pull of Southern slavery, and to an ethical paralysis that would haunt him to the end of his days.

Along with other slaveholders who regarded themselves as enlightened, Thornton felt paralyzed by irreconcilable contradictions. His mind caromed helplessly from sympathy with slaves to empathy with their owners, from the moral imperative of emancipation to fear of race war and bloodshed. He reasoned, however, that even gradual emancipation was ultimately only a "partial good" that would create new problems, which would, in turn, increase the "general evil," as slaves who saw fellow blacks at liberty and with money to spend became envious and discontented, and turned to gambling and thievery, or worse. "Evil thus rests on evil till a mountain rises whose summit is shadowed by a cloud of sin," he sighed. "It is a melancholy reflection that while the energies of white men directed to shake off impositions, merely on trade, in every part of the world, meet with applause, the struggle of the blacks for liberty should meet with death if unsuccessful. Yet there is while tyranny pervades our polity, a necessity for severe policies, if attempts are made to shake off the yoke," since a general slave rebellion "would involve in promiscuous ruin" the cruel and the "humane" alike. "The Negroes must be free, and yet I would not injure an individual."

In July 1795—he had just bought two slaves for his own use at home—Thornton made the radical suggestion to his fellow commissioners that they purchase slaves outright, rather than merely hire them, to speed along the construction work. "Since it is impossible to hire a sufficient number of stonecutters from Philadelphia on account of the high price of work it would perhaps be advisable to hire 50 intelligent negroes for six years, to be superintended and directed how to cut stone by two or three persons, who may even be paid, as an inducement from 15 to 30 shillings per day," he wrote. "At first these men may be employed in cutting the stone till it be nearly ready for rubbing: the last cutting to be done by more experienced men . . . If Negroes were to be purchased, to have their liberty at the expiration of 5 or 6 years, it would be perhaps still better, as no interference of the owners could then take place." The plan was a quintessentially Thorntonian attempt to square the circle, to reconcile his increasingly theoretical opposition to slavery with the practical problem of recruiting dependable, obedient labor to speed up the capital's lagging construction. As far as the other commissioners were concerned, the plan was a nonstarter. They had no interest in emancipation at all, and would do nothing to undermine the principle of slavery for life upon which both their Southern political support and the livelihood of their friends and neighbors depended.

All of Thornton's visions would go up in smoke, of course, unless there was money to pay for them. By autumn, it was clear that private enterprise had utterly failed to make the national capital a reality. Robert Morris and his fellow speculators were in financial freefall. The state of affairs in the Federal District was graphically illustrated in July, when the Capitol's foundation wall collapsed. What remained was so poorly constructed that much of it had to be demolished. The general impression of incompetence was all the more embarrassing because Washington himself had explicitly ordered the Capitol's construction to be pressed forward ahead of everything else, including the President's House: the president could live anywhere, but the Capitol was, in effect, the republic. Back in 1793—it seemed so long ago—the commissioners had proclaimed that the city "will express in the stile of our Architecture the sublime Sentiment of Liberty, a grandure of

conception, a Republican Simplicity, and that true Elegance of proportion." Such pompous pronouncements now seemed pathetic. Tens of
thousands of dollars had been spent, and thousands of man-hours of
labor, and all that was left to show were a heap of rubble and a hole
in the ground. In Congress, there was growing talk of building the
Capitol in stages rather than all at once, or abandoning it altogether
as a total loss, and assigning the President's House to Congress for its
meeting place instead. An atmosphere of fiasco gathered around the
whole project like miasma in the damp bottoms along the Potomac.
Common folk scoffed. When one newly arrived immigrant told people
in Norfolk that he was en route to Washington to look for work, they
laughed at him. So inconsequential did the site seem that one stranger
crossing the Potomac from Virginia failed to even find the "city," and
found himself stuck overnight on an island in the Potomac, trapped
there by the tide.

Problems continued to multiply. Hundreds of lots remained to be
marked off. Large sections that had been inaccurately surveyed had to
be redone. In many places, the commissioners had failed to divide the
public lots from the private ones, hobbling sales. Morris and Nicholson
couldn't pay their creditors. The agent who had contracted to supply
brick claimed that because of rain he could only supply 360,000 pieces
of the 500,000 that he had promised. Much of the quarried stone that
was delivered was of such poor quality that it couldn't be used. The
stonemasons threatened to quit unless they were housed closer to the
Capitol, claiming that walking three times a day to work from their
hotel in the heat injured their health. Then their supervisor absconded
with $2,000, and was never seen again.

In the end, work on the Capitol resumed in a desultory fashion. In
October, a British architect, George Hadfield, was appointed as superintendent of works at the Capitol. In his first letter to the commissioners, he delivered a scathing critique: "I find the building begun, but do
not find the necessary plans to carry on a work of this importance, and I
think there are defects that are not warrantable, in most of the branches
that constitute the profession of an architect, Stability—Economy—
Convenience—Beauty . . . deformity in the rooms, chimneys and win-

dows placed without symmetry." The foundations were still "in a state not to be depended on." After studying Thornton's plans, he discovered that the floor plan failed to match the outside of the building. Hadfield advised omitting the basement, changing the height of the House chamber, and replacing the arcades in both chambers with columns. If Hadfield's alterations were to be followed, the deeply offended Thornton retorted, "No progress can be made this season or perhaps the next. A small delay may be fatal."

Once again, the dream of the American metropolis seemed to recede further and further beyond reach the harder the dreamers strained to grasp it. "Season goes away after Season & the year 1800 will soon be upon us," sighed Thomas Law from his perch overlooking the Potomac.

IN PHILADELPHIA, ROBERT Morris waited apprehensively for the sword of debt to fall. Humiliation followed upon humiliation. The mansion that was to have celebrated his enshrinement at the pinnacle of American society instead had made him a laughingstock. He had become as much a captive of his architect's delusions of grandeur as the federal city was of Morris's own. L'Enfant had assured the financier that he would be able to move in by autumn. Taking him at his word, Morris sold his temporary home on Market Street and rented a house opposite the mansion, where he bore tortured witness to a slow-motion disaster that would bleed away his remaining fortune and mock his dreams. The opulence of L'Enfant's aspirations were there for all to see: the magnificent ornamental porticos, bas-reliefs, and pillars, the walls slathered with pale blue imported marble. Before the climax of this sorry tale, more than $1 million of Morris's shrinking fortune— $35 million in today's money—would disappear into this last apocalyptic expression of the architect's feverish imagination. Morris begged, cajoled, and demanded that L'Enfant at least put a roof over the house. L'Enfant coolly replied that he was waiting for more marble to arrive. (How L'Enfant loved marble—there couldn't be enough of it!) Morris waxed incandescent with frustration. "Although it was not my intention or desire to have the marble you have introduced into this building, yet an inclination to indulge your genius, induced me to permit so much of it (before I knew the extent to which you meant to carry it) as seemed to call for the remainder. Had you executed my intentions instead of your own, my family would now have inhabited the House instead of being liable to be turned out of Doors." Autumn came and went, but "Morris's Folly" remained a roofless shell, a tourist attraction that gawping visitors dismissed as "a huge mass," a monstrosity that "bids defiance to simplicity and elegance." The same might have been said of Morris's calamitous failure in the federal city.

Chapter 9

THE GENERAL'S
LAST CAMPAIGN

"It is essential that this work should be vigorously prosecuted—and I require it accordingly."

—GEORGE WASHINGTON

ON FEBRUARY 2, 1796, with less than five years remaining before the deadline set for the capital's completion, James Madison rose to face the four semicircular, seated rows of his fellow congressmen in Congress Hall in Philadelphia to propose a bailout of the foundering federal city. The initial grants provided by Virginia and Maryland were long gone, while the sale of lots had produced but a small fraction of the revenues that had been expected. The cascading failures of Morris and Nicholson had spread like a bacillus through the heart and the limbs of the capital, infecting everything they touched. It was in this grim climate that Congress undertook its first serious examination of the financing of the federal city, which for the past five years had been shielded from scrutiny by executive privilege, and further obscured by complacent official assurances of steady progress. The honeymoon was now over. Beneath the often sarcastic rhetoric that now resounded through the winter-chilled chamber profound issues percolated. The dream of a national city, the investment of years of labor, and national prestige all hung once again in the balance. The two colliding philosophies that shaped the debate would echo down through the ensuing two centuries, pitting the advocates of strong central government and public spending against those who regarded federal power as a form of despotism and public subsidies as a financial cancer. Madison, who was not usually found on the side of the spenders, had helped to give birth to the federal city on Thomas Jefferson's dinner table in 1790, and he was not going to abandon it now.

The debate quickly exposed a deep vein of resentment toward the federal city. A South Carolina newspaper captured the public mood in doggerel:

> O ye who sit at helm of state
> Your vast designs you broach too late
> Leave the ship of state on rocky ground
> And fools to pay for Federal Towns

Development of the capital had been carried on from its inception without congressional oversight, public accounting, or debate. Congressmen were just beginning to grasp that for half a decade huge sums of money had been disappearing into the muddy work site on the Potomac, with very little to show for it. The president somewhat disingenuously blamed the board of commissioners for "all the Faupaus which have been committed—all the neglects, inattentions, and want of the close & constant scrutiny of those to whom the business was intrusted." However, they had done nothing without Washington's personal approval. Secrecy had served him well enough. Had the full story of the project's spiraling costs, speculative intrigues, and, yes, bumbling management been revealed earlier, Congress might have sought to shut it down long ago, dealing a devastating defeat to the president, and refueling the regional rivalries that always steeped just below the nation's roiling political surface.

Thus far, Congress had not allocated a single dollar of public money for the construction of the Capitol or the President's House. As recently as January, Washington had blandly assured Congress that all the buildings required for the accommodation of the government could be completed on time without any federal aid at all. "The law of 1790 never would have passed if the most solemn assurances had not been given that no such application would ever be made to the government," Federalist Samuel Sitgreaves of Pennsylvania reminded his colleagues. The amount of money that had been spent for the construction of only two buildings was staggering by the standards of the time, and perhaps surpassed only by "Morris's Folly" in Philadelphia. Seventy-eight thousand dollars had already been spent on the Capitol, and another $75,000 was needed just to finish the North Wing. Newly appointed Commissioner Alexander White—yet another Potomack Company shareholder, and one of the Virginia congressmen who in 1790 had grudgingly traded his vote for the federal assumption of state debts in exchange for Hamilton's support for a Southern capital—was dispatched to represent the board's interests in Philadelphia. When pressed, White admitted that it might well take another $400,000 to finish the entire building. More than $97,000 had been spent on the President's House, and at least $90,000 more would be needed. Another $100,000 was needed to build offices for the executive departments. Forget the rest of the sprawling Federal District, which existed almost entirely in the imagination of its promoters. Without a giant federally guaranteed loan, the entire project would lurch to a halt by summer. Madison—always the voice of the president, for whom completion of the capital was nonnegotiable—was proposing $500,000.

As snow and rain pelted the hall, skeptical congressmen, some of them crowding around the chamber's four huge stoves for warmth, professed themselves shocked by the federal city's imperial pretensions. One speaker after another denounced the capital as a monument to pride and folly, a black hole into which hundreds of thousands of dollars had been poured, in the words of one irate congressman, "to what was worse than no purpose." Joshua Coit of Connecticut sneered, "Lots in the city were worth nothing more than garden plots, unless you built on them"—and no one wanted to build on them. Where was the tide of commerce that had been promised, the cargo ships of the world groaning with American exports? Was the government now to make good on the outlandish promises of speculators who had told gullible investors that *seven thousand* houses were already standing in the city, when in fact there were barely two hundred? John Williams of New York scornfully asserted that the public buildings were more magnificent than any palace in Europe, and warned—this would prove to be an understatement—that they could cost another $700,000 before they were done. One North Carolina member proclaimed himself so disgusted with the President's House that he would vote any sum just to pull it down. Connecticut's Zephaniah Swift urged Congress to leave the project to stew, acidly asserting, "the more money there is granted, the less will be the economy in spending it."

Supporters of the loan guarantee fought back aggressively, warning that the entire project could miscarry as a result of "ill-timed, illiberal, contracted" opposition. "If it was desirable to remove the government at the time appointed, it is essentially necessary to guarantee the loan, as the buildings are now at a stand for want of the necessary aid, or they must legislate under the canopy of Heaven," asserted Richard Brent of Virginia. The nation's integrity was at stake, he reminded his fellow congressmen: thousands of Americans had invested in Potomac real estate, trusting in the government's word. If the project failed, they would be ruined. "It is a city in speculation, and one false step may prostrate it," William Vans Murray of Maryland declared. "Yes, the scheme is a speculation—the whole of life and its concerns, perhaps, are no more." But, he added, it was a brilliant, worthy speculation, founded on a fair calculation of economic interest, and "bottomed for the security of its profits in the faith of the Union." Refusal of this "small parental aid," as Jeremiah Crabbe of Maryland put it, would send the unfortunate message that the government was not serious in its intentions.

Failure now would wreck the future sale of lots and betray the public interest. He cautioned, "Such a manifest, indecent, impolitic violation of public faith would shake the union to the center, if not burst asunder those political bands that so happily cement and bind this wide extended union."

Despite the heated rhetoric of the capital's critics, it became evident that its supporters were in the majority. Everyone knew that if the Potomac project were to be abandoned, the capital would revert indefinitely, and quite likely permanently, to Philadelphia. Support for Philadelphia had noticeably cooled since the horrific yellow fever epidemic of 1793: recurrence of the fever since then, though less virulent, fed fears that the city's climate would forever be dangerously pestilential. Congressmen, many of them at least, feared for more than their physical health. Philadelphia's pro-French mobs and its rabid Republican press rattled conservative Federalists, while the state's antislavery laws constantly reminded slaveholding Southerners why they wanted to leave for friendlier climes. Adding further insult, Pennsylvania's governor publicly disputed rank with the vice president, while city residents relentlessly nagged members of Congress for contracts, jobs, and special interest legislation on local projects, such as the construction of wharfs on the Delaware.

While members of Congress harangued each other over the proposed loan, Southerners were blocking the appropriation of funds to implement the hated Jay Treaty with Britain, a measure that Northerners argued was imperative to protect American commerce and the New England economy. Once again, the federal city was saved by a deal. Southerners agreed to hold their noses and vote for the treaty appropriation in exchange for equally grudging Federalist support for the loan. When the loan bill came to a vote on March 31, the result was lopsided. The supporters of the federal city prevailed decisively by seventy-two to twenty-one, approving up to $300,000 in loans from bankers who, it was assumed, would readily fork over to the federal commissioners the funds that they had denied to the speculators. The Senate concurred a month later by a vote of sixteen to seven. (By comparison, at about this same time, the United States was appropriating $1.25 million—about 20 percent of the federal budget—to ransom American captives from assorted Barbary pirates.)

The commissioners breathed a collective sigh of relief—they had only $1,300 on hand left to pay contractors. Since it would take months to negotiate the anticipated loans, as a stopgap measure the Bank of the United States agreed to lend the commissioners $10,000 a month for the next four months. The capital had a new lease on life. Work could now move forward for the summer season. But Congress's action had only bought time. It by no means guaranteed success. Indeed, even to speak of a "city" on the Potomac in any conventional sense was patently absurd. The grandiose promises of the early 1790s had grown very stale. An odor of failure and disappointment continued to hover over the federal city like fog in the frosty streets of Philadelphia.

No ONE WAS more grateful for the passage of the loan bill than the president. The lopsided vote vindicated his belief in the "great and arduous business" of inventing the federal city. He had selected its site, hired its designer, arbitrated between its landed proprietors, rebuked naysayers, appointed its commissioners, and bullied them like a general driving his troops to battle. After the slogging years of effort and disappointment, he wasn't about to give up on the Potomac now. He was sixty-four. Time was growing short, for both himself and for the city. He would not seek a third term, and would soon hand the reins of government over to his successor, most likely Vice President Adams, or the de facto leader of the opposition, Thomas Jefferson, who with feigned detachment keenly followed the hammering surge of national politics from his aerie at Monticello.

In the spring of 1796 Washington was like a wounded lion, scarred from the savage political battles of his second, difficult term. Increasingly he had become the target of cruel personal attacks from Republicans— some of them orchestrated by Jefferson—who distrusted the centralizing tendencies of his administration. Some called him a tyrant and monster, a closet monarchist. The *Aurora* of Philadelphia, in particular, served as an ideological battering ram for the Jeffersonians, relentlessly attacking Washington for his "apish mimickry of Kingship," and his addiction to "pompous carriages, splendid feasts, and tawdry gowns." Enemies hinted scurrilously that the president, who liked to portray himself as a reluctant and self-sacrificing public servant, had actually exploited the national treasury for his own expenses. They even assailed his patriotism, accusing him of having taken bribes from the British during the Revolutionary War. When he announced his retirement later in the year, the *Aurora* crowed: "If there ever was a period for rejoicing, this is the moment—every heart, in unison with the freedom and happiness of the people, ought to beat high with exultation that the name of WASHINGTON from this day ceases to give political currency to political iniquity and to legalize corruption." Washington endured all this with stoicism, rarely deigning to answer his critics directly.

Like the soldier that he was, he marshaled his resources for this one final campaign, the capstone of his career, and his final gift to his countrymen, the battle for the capital. National unity seemed more precarious than ever to the old man. Seven years of common struggle in the Revolutionary War had brought Americans together, but regional prejudices were reviving with a vehemence that worried him, and seemed harder than ever to repress. Partisan strife between Federalists and Republicans led some to predict the collapse of the government, secession, humiliation by foreign powers, even war. In his Farewell Address, Washington proclaimed that "The very idea of the power and right of the People to establish Government presupposes the duty of every Individual to obey the established government." That duty could only be assured by means of a strong government that was undergirded by a sense of common interest. This was, if not a novel idea, then still a deeply controversial one in the late 1790s.

Washington had consistently advocated measures that would promote both unity and central power: a national university, a national military academy, a national bank, a strong chief executive, federal support for agriculture and manufacturing, federal sovereignty over the states, and vigorous national government. In Washington's scheme, the Potomac capital was endowed with unique potency. It was to be not just the seat of government, although it was that above all. It was also to be the linchpin of a great commercial highway linking the Eastern seaboard to the interior of the continent. Greater still, it was to be a dynamic social engine that would inexorably draw together the disparate, mutually suspicious parts of the nation, and forge from them a common identity. Washington had been saying this for years, since before the first streets on L'Enfant's map had been drawn, and before survey lines were ever run, and from it he had never wavered. Although Washington did not mention the federal city in his Farewell Address, it was the concrete embodiment of everything that he had in mind. Yes, of course it was grandiose, as its central buildings must be, precisely because it enshrined the principle of federal sovereignty made manifest. For most of a generation, Washington the man had been the living symbol of a national unity that transcended local jealousies and selfish interests. When he was gone, a new symbol that transcended one man's personal charisma must knit together the disparate people who called themselves Americans: Washington the city.

During his last months in office, as Federalists and Republicans squared off against each other in a brutal election campaign, Washington worried that his ability to command the project would wane once he left office. His directives to the commissioners became increasingly peremptory: "The time is very short in which a great deal for the reception of Congress is to be done; and no means, or exertion should be wanting to accomplish it." He badgered them unrelentingly to abandon their cozy accommodations in George Town and move with their minions into the city itself, no matter how inconvenient for their families: there would be no accommodations for Congress if the commissioners didn't set an example. "Let me give it strongly as my opinion that *all* the offices, and *every matter*, and *thing*, that relates to the city ought to be transacted therein, and they to whose care they are committed residents." He reminded them that had they been paying closer attention, the Capitol's basement walls would never have collapsed, and immeasurable amounts of money, time, and labor could have been saved. The time for debate over the minutiae of design and the trivial interests of petty men was past. *Just obey orders and get on with it.*

Seen from a vantage point near present-day Canal Street, New York was little more than an overgrown town. Less than a mile north of the Battery, its streets petered out amid meadows and marshes. By Archibald Robertson. *(Courtesy of the Metropolitan Museum of Art)*

Though small by European standards, New York was already a bustling port where Yankee merchants, immigrants, slaves, and free blacks mingled in an increasingly cosmopolitan vortex. By Francis Guy. *(Collection of the New York Historical Society)*

Congress met in New York's Federal Hall, a workhorse of a building which Peter L'Enfant had remodeled into a masterpiece of contemporary taste. By Cornelius Tiebout. *(Metropolitan Museum of Art)*

Alexander Hamilton. The treasury secretary controlled enough votes in Congress to determine the site of the nation's capital. He first offered to back Pennsylvania in return for its support for his financial plan. When the Pennsylvanians failed to agree to his terms, he gave his support to the South instead. By James Sharples. *(National Portrait Gallery, Smithsonian Institution/Art Resource, NY)*

James Madison. As the administration's point man in Congress, he brokered the compromise that led to the capital's establishment on the Potomac. In 1814, as president, he would preside over the humiliating capture of Washington by British forces. By Gilbert Stuart. *(Courtesy of the Library of Congress)*

Thomas Jefferson. As secretary of state, he grudgingly lent his influence to the compromise with Hamilton and Madison. He later supervised the contest to design the Capitol. *(Courtesy of the Library of Congress)*

Congress on the Road to Philadelphia." The New York press attacked the financier and senator Robert Morris for allegedly attempting to bribe Congress to place the seat of government in Philadelphia. In this 1790 cartoon, while clutching a money bag, Morris drags Congress toward Philadelphia, while politicians crouch behind him on the "ladder of preferment." *(Courtesy of the Historical Society of Pennsylvania)*

Washington as hero. Even in his lifetime, he was often treated as a demigod above ordinary human concerns. He was in fact a land speculator on a massive scale, as well as principal in the Patowmack Company, whose members expected to reap fortunes if the seat of government was established on the Potomac. By Charles Balthazar Julien Fevret de Saint-Memin. *(Courtesy of the Library of Congress)*

L'Enfant's 1791 map endowed the undeveloped landscape with a semblance of urban reality that still existed only in his fertile imagination. *(Courtesy of the Library of Congress)*

Washington as a gentleman farmer. He longed to return to his beloved estate at Mount Vernon. Although he was one of the largest slave owners in Virginia, he struggled over the morality of slavery and its consequences for the United States. By Junius Brutus Stearns. *(Courtesy of the Library of Congress)*

Peter Charles L'Enfant, the planner of the federal city. His vision was breathtaking, but his inability to work with others ruined his career. By Bryan Leister. *(Courtesy of the artist and the Washington Historical Society)*

The bucolic setting of the federal city enchanted many early visitors. Others complained of its isolation, an appalling lack of fresh foodstuffs, and its giant toads. By T. Cartwright after George Beck of Philadelphia, 1801. *(Courtesy of the Library of Congress)*

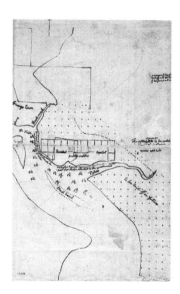

Thomas Jefferson's sketch map was a reproach to L'Enfant's imperial plan. In keeping with his professed republican values, he envisioned the capital as a modest country town nestled just south of Rock Creek. *(Courtesy of the Library of Congress)*

The Irish-born James Hoban won the competition to design the president's house. He arrived on the Potomac accompanied by his own team of enslaved craftsmen, and would eventually supervise much of the early construction work in the federal city. White House Historical Association. By John Christian Rauschn. *(White House Collection)*

Among the earliest known images of the White House was this one, which appeared on the cover of a travelers guide. White House Historical Association. *(White House Collection)*

Benjamin Banneker. A largely self-taught mathematician and amateur astronomer, he played a key role in the surveying of the Federal District. His almanacs later became popular in the rural households of early America.

William Thornton, the designer of the United States Capitol. He was a polymath who authored treatises on comets, steamboats, and linguistics, and dreamed of leading emancipated slaves back to Africa. By Robert Field. *(Courtesy of the Smithsonian American Art Museum, Washington D.C./Art Resources, New York)*

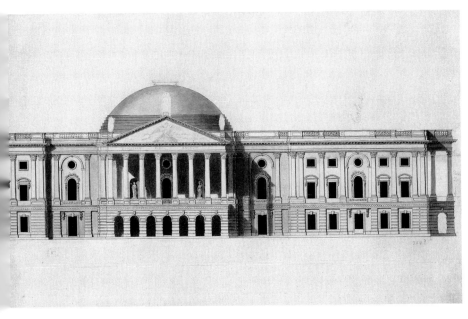

Capitol, east elevation. By William Thorton. *(Courtesy of the Library of Congress)*

The City & Port of *PHILADELPHIA*, on the River Delaware from Kensington.

Published as the Act Cited by W.Birch. Springland Cot, near Bristol. 1800.

Philadelphia's port was the largest in the United States. The "unwholesome effluvia" that fouled its streets bred disease, and would reach epidemic proportions during the horrific autumn of 1793. By William Birch. *(Courtesy of the Historical Society of Pennsylvania)*

CONGRESS HALL and NEW THEATRE, in Chesnut Street PHILADELPHIA.

Drawn, Engraved & Published by W.Birch & Son, Neshaminy Bucks 1800.

The city fairly hummed with political excitement during the 1790s. The sixty-five congressmen and thirty senators met in the county courthouse on Sixth Street (left). By William Birch. *(Courtesy of the Historical Society of Pennsylvania)*

In "Liberty Displaying the Arts & Sciences," (1792).
Samuel Jennings captured the mingled idealism and
paternalism of early Philadelphia abolitionists. Liberty
in the form of a benign white woman distributes
symbols of culture while breaking the chains of
grateful slaves. *(Courtesy of the Library Company of
Philadelphia)*

Absalom Jones and Richard Allen founded the first independent black church in America, and led the city's burgeoning African American community in the 1790s. They hoped that the heroic efforts of black Philadelphians to care for the victims of the 1793 Yellow Fever epidemic would win white support for black aspirations. *(Courtesy of the Historical Society of Pennsylvania)*

Richard Allen's Bethel Church was originally a blacksmith shop. It was hauled by teams of horses to its permanent location on Sixth Street in 1794. By William Birch. *(Courtesy of the Historical Society of Pennsylvania)*

Benjamin Rush was a tireless advocate of black self-empowerment. As one of Philadelphia's leading doctors, he also led the campaign against the Yellow Fever epidemic of 1793. His methods may have killed more victims than they saved. After Thomas Sully. *(Courtesy of the Historical Society of Pennsylvania)*

James Greenleaf. The young speculator initially charmed all who met him, including George Washington. He helped to convert the development of the federal city into a giant speculative pyramid scheme. By Gilbert Stuart. *(Courtesy of the Library of Congress)*

Robert Morris. He pledged his personal fortune to sustain the rebellious colonies during the Revolutionary War. He and his partners owned or controlled most of the property in the federal city. The collapse of his vast speculative empire almost brought federal city to ruin. By Robert Edge Pine. *(Courtesy of the Historical Society of Pennsylvania)*

Morris's Folly." Morris wasted extravagant sums of money on the grandiose mansion that L'Enfant designed for him on Chestnut Street. Never completed, the project graphically symbolized the increasingly hopeless state of Morris's financial affairs in the late 1790s. By William Birch. *(Courtesy of the Historical Society of Pennsylvania)*

Washington's funeral procession in Philadelphia. Washington never lived to see Congress govern in the capital that he had worked so hard to make a reality. However, his death in 1799 spurred others to complete the project on schedule. By William Birch. (*Courtesy of the Historical Society of Pennsylvania*)

The 1800 election was characterized by savage personal attacks by the supporters of both John Adams and Thomas Jefferson. In this Jeffersonian cartoon, a satanic Federalist with a bag of gold and the British lion egg on the conservative propagandist William Cobbett, who wrote under the pen name Peter Porcupine, while the Goddess of Liberty weeps. "I hate this country and will sow discord in it," Cobbett writes. (*Courtesy of the Historical Society of Pennsylvania*)

Washington in 1800: Pennsylvania Avenue from Capitol Hill. When Congress finally arrived in 1800, the national capital fell far short of the cosmopolitan grandeur that its promoters had promised. That the city existed in any form seemed like a miracle, however. By Conrad Malte-Brun. *(Courtesy of the Library of Congress)*

The Capitol was the largest building in North America at the time. It seemed startlingly out of place in its still-rural setting. By William Birch. *(Courtesy of the Library of Congress)*

"The Taking of Washington." Advocates for the Potomac as the nation's seat of government stressed its supposed invulnerability to attack. The British captured the city with ease in 1814. By G. Thompson. *(Courtesy of the Library of Congress)*

In the antebellum era, Washington grew into one of the nation's largest slave trading centers. Congressmen were frequently treated to the sight of chained slaves being marched past the windows of the Capitol. *(Courtesy of the Washington Historical Society)*

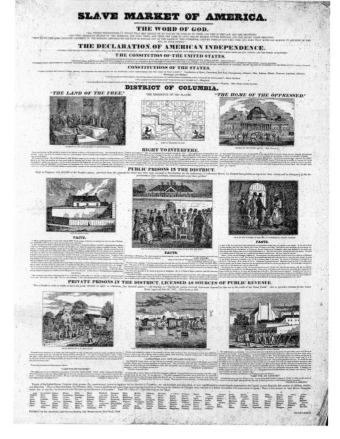

The Capitol was left a mere shell after being burned by British troops in 1814. By William Strickland. (*Courtesy of the Library of Congress.*)

Dolley Madison fled the British attack in such haste that she left behind a half cooked dinner, which the invaders enjoyed before they set fire to the president's house. By William Strickland. (*Courtesy of the Library of Congress*)

The Capitol's dome was finally completed in 1863, at the height of the Civil War. It brought to climax the vision of the capital as first delineated by William Thorton. It proclaimed the Union's determination to survive. *(Courtesy of the Library of Congress)*

In February 1797, with little more than a month left to his presidency, Washington ordered work on offices for the executive departments suspended and construction of the President's House slowed. All available workers were to be concentrated at the Capitol, like assault troops ready to storm an enemy position. "The public mind is in a state of doubt, if not in despair of having the principal building in readiness for Congress," he warned the commissioners. From now on, completing the Capitol on time must become the single-minded target of everyone's efforts. Only success in this paramount endeavor could restore the public's battered faith in the capital. Failure would mean failure for the entire project. But failure was not to be permitted. "It is essential that this work should be vigorously prosecuted—and I require it accordingly," he ordered. "It is not only of infinite importance to make all other measures yield, in *reality* to this, but in *appearance* also—especially under the present difficulty of obtaining loans and the uncertainty of your funds, which must depend on public opinion, and the confidence which is placed in the administration of them."

On MARCH 21, 1797, George Washington's presidency came to an end. In the republic's first peaceful transition of executive power, he was replaced by John Adams, a New Englander who had never suffered from "Potomac Fever," and whose tumultuous tenure would pose new challenges for the federal city. Traveling south from Philadelphia, Washington passed in a fizz of celebratory pomp through the Federal District, where he was greeted at the Capitol by a cannonade, and then by another sixteen rounds as he passed by the site of the President's House, followed all the while by cheering crowds. He was grateful after an absence of eight years, except for short visits, to at last reach his beloved Mount Vernon, even though he found things there "very much deranged" after years of neglect, with many buildings in such a state of disrepair that it would cost him as much to fix them as it would to build new ones from the ground up. His notion of retirement would soon have run a less energetic man into the ground. There were farms to visit, hundreds of slaves to be managed, crops to be planted and harvested, accounts to be untangled, rafts of letters to write, and a steady stream of curious and adulatory visitors to be greeted, most of them uninvited: the great man had become the nation's first tourist attraction. He rose before dawn every morning to visit his scattered farms, then returned to breakfast on corn cakes and honey, spent several hours writing in his library, dined early, and then after a social hour or two retired again to write, read, or sit with friends, finally going to bed at nine o'clock, usually without supper. It was the life of which he had long dreamed: Cincinnatus beneath his metaphorical vine and fig tree, the ancient Roman euphemism that he had deployed more and more often in these recent exhausting years to evoke his idyll of restful ease. But the federal city wasn't done with him yet.

In theory, responsibility for the city now fell to John Adams. The election campaign, from which Adams and his rival Thomas Jefferson largely held aloof in keeping with the custom of the time, spawned a degree of bitter partisanship and viperous rumor-mongering that left Americans reeling. Jefferson's partisans mocked the portly Adams as "his Rotundity," and accused him of outright insanity and a secret plan to reestablish monarchy, while the Virginian's enemies charged him with fanatical revolutionary tendencies, atheism, and even physical cowardice during the Revolutionary War. Adams was hurt by residual anger at the Jay Treaty, and might well have lost the election over it, had the vote been held a year earlier. He also enjoyed, at best, only tepid support from the most prominent Federalist of all after Washington, former Treasury Secretary Hamilton, who barely concealed his preference for Adams's running mate, Thomas Pinckney of South Carolina. The election would ultimately be determined in the Electoral College. Its members each cast two votes, but were not required to vote for any particular candidate. The Constitution at that time mandated that the candidates receiving the largest numbers of votes would be declared president and vice president respectively, regardless of their party. Adams narrowly emerged the winner, with seventy-three votes, five more than Jefferson, with sixty-eight votes, thus yoking the new president to a partner who would spend the next four years undermining him. On March 4, 1797, dressed in a plain gray suit and standing with Washington by his side in the House of Representatives' chamber at Congress Hall, the son of a Yankee farmer placed his hand on the Bible, and was sworn in as the second chief executive of the United States.

The new president—a "dumpy little man" with a good, honest face "touched nevertheless with a grain of malice," in the words of one contemporary—had no great interest in the federal city, and even less knowledge of what was going on there. "The whole of this business is so new to me," he confessed to the commissioners soon after taking office. They gave him a crash course: they explained the failure of land sales and lotteries, lost loans, fast-talking speculators, squabbling land-owners, and the vagaries of architects, contractors, and workmen. But it was—and would remain throughout his term in office—distressingly difficult to get his attention for anything relating to the city. Often the commissioners waited weeks for a reply to a simple query. On one occasion, when Alexander White pushed Adams for an answer to an urgent problem, the disconcerted commissioner reported to George Washington that the president "shewed an uncommon degree of Warmth, said he shouldn't make himself a Slave to the Federal City; that he would do what his official duty required of him *and no more.*"

To be fair, Adams had much to distract him. He took office with the political deck stacked against him, inheriting both Washington's cabinet, whose members were more loyal to Hamilton than to the new president, and an opposition vice president who was actively scheming against him. Like Harry Truman in a later age, Adams would from the start be measured unfavorably against his predecessor, the majestic Washington, and found dwarfed and crabbed by comparison. His thirty years of public service included none as an executive or a military man, at a time that cried out for a president with experience as both. Foreign crisis absorbed his energies from the start, and would continue to do so throughout of his presidency. Fear of revolutionary France had reached hysterical proportions that would rarely if ever be matched until the Red Scares of the twentieth century. Rumors of invasion metastasized.

French armies were said to be approaching Florida, then off the coast of Louisiana. Supposed spies were seen everywhere. Not all the threats were imaginary. Reacting to Jay's Treaty of cooperation with Britain, French warships had seized more than three hundred American ships in the Caribbean. One of the first prizes captured was an American cruiser named, with cruel irony, the *Mount Vernon*. The revelation that French officials had demanded bribes merely to confer with the envoys Adams had dispatched to negotiate with them sent Federalists into paroxysms of fury. Adams struggled manfully, with a degree of success for which he was given little credit, to maintain American neutrality while members of his cabinet vociferously urged him to declare war on France. Jefferson's pro-French Republicans, meanwhile, damned the president as a warmonger, and did their best to thwart his efforts to rebuild the nation's armed forces and shore defenses, in case war finally did come, as so many feared it would. Even the generally phlegmatic Washington, ensconced amid his placid wheat farms, was not immune to war fever, declaring that the French, "are endeavoring if not to make us afraid, yet to despoil us of our property, and are provoking us to acts of self-defence, which may lead to war."

Increasingly, the commissioners of the federal city circumvented Adams unless they had no choice, and brought their problems directly to Washington. This suited the ex-president quite well. Heaving what he wished to be taken as a dutiful sigh of aged weariness, he told friends that all he could offer the city at this late stage in life was his fervent good wishes. This was more than a bit deceptive. In the two and a half years left to him, Washington would continue to act as an unofficial and proprietary behind-the-scenes godfather to the city whose birth he had midwifed at the beginning of the decade. He would make it live if it was—and it virtually would be—the last thing he did. The devoted William Thornton and the wealthy British expatriate Thomas Law, who had recently married Martha Washington's granddaughter Eliza, would serve as his scouts, bringing news from the city directly to Mount Vernon on their frequent visits. In Philadelphia, Alexander White would be his discreet eyes and ears, keeping him apprised of backroom developments in Congress and shifts in public opinion. Washington would also visit the federal city in person at regular intervals, to gauge for himself the pace of construction, and to confer face-to-face with the commissioners and with the eternally disgruntled landowners. To prove that his commitment was in earnest, he personally bought four lots near George Town and four more near the Capitol, as encouragement to investors and settlers.

From his redoubt at Mount Vernon, Washington launched oracular opinions like mortar shells at the beleaguered commissioners. *Build a Marine hospital near the Eastern Branch. There should be a botanical garden at the national university. A navy yard? Absolutely!* After all, the region abounded with the best ships's timber, iron, tar, pitch, and oak, he reminded the secretary of the newly created Navy Department, a wealthy Potomac landowner named Benjamin Stoddert. Back in 1791 Washington had declared that only stone or brick houses would be permitted in the city. Now he reversed himself: let "mechanics" and other workmen build their little wooden houses and shacks if they wanted to now. *The city needs people!* He arbitrated the persistent controversy over the many odd pieces of land—triangles, circles, parallelograms—that remained where streets and avenues intersected. Thornton the aesthete begged for them to be embellished with "fountains, obelisks, statues, parks, temples, and academies." Property owners, who claimed these scraps had been chiseled off their property, rolled their eyes and demanded that the odd bits be developed commercially. (One of them testily complained, "What kind of *Temples* we are to have in this city, or to what *Gods* or *Goddesses* they are to be dedicated, I have not yet learned.") Washington solomonically ruled: tracts that resulted from street-building belonged to the commissioners, but if they were deliberately taken to enlarge the size of the squares and circles, the owners ought to be paid. He weighed in even on minute questions of design at the Capitol, proposing for instance that the columns in the Senate chamber be executed in the Ionic order, that large niches be left in the angles formed by the walls at the north entrance, and that railings on the private staircase to the upstairs rooms be made of mahogany. In the absence of any other guiding hand, Washington was as close to a field commander as the new capital could claim.

Not everyone considered the former president's actions either selfless or particularly competent. Indeed, among working men, many of whom shared the kind of radical sentiments that Federalists feared, his preoccupation with the new capital was regarded as gross egomania. "I think he has manifested a great portion of vanity in the ardent desire he has expressed in wishing to perpetuate his name, by building a metropolis under so many disadvantages, both in respect of climate and situation," one young stonemason wrote to friends back in England. "During his life, it may out of compliment to him be carried on in a slow manner, but I am apprehensive as soon as he is *defunct*, the city, which is to be the boasted monument of his greatness, will also be the *same*."

To at least one visitor, the future did not bode well for the ex-president's infant city. François-Alexandre-Frédéric, duc de la Rochefoucauld-Liancourt, had briefly been president of France's National Constituent Assembly before the hurricane of revolution swept liberal monarchists like himself from the political stage. More fortunate than many of his class, the duke escaped to England in 1792, and then in 1794 to the United States, where he lived as an exile for most of the remaining years of the decade, traveling widely through the Northern states and Canada. Like his later more famous compatriot, Alexis de Tocqueville, who toured the United States in the 1830s, Rochefoucauld-Liancourt was an unusually acute observer, who applied his friendly but skeptical eye and incisive intellect to the mores, institutions, and pretensions of his host country. In 1797, bored and depressed in Philadelphia, he set off southward on a tour through rural Maryland and the Federal District, "to seek tranquillity, or at least amusement." He admired the new capital's handsome setting amid the otherwise dismal and impoverished Maryland countryside. But the whole project seemed to him impractical, if not hopeless. To his great disappointment, he found none of the urban accoutrements—churches, pavements, lamps, fountains, gardens—that he had expected, and the President's House and the Capitol mere gaping shells surrounded by a hodgepodge of stone blocks, clay pits, and muddy paths. There was no sense of community. The few inhabitants seemed wholly occupied with their internecine rival-ries and speculations. Shops were miserably provided and exorbitantly expensive. In the course of six days, Rochefoucauld-Liancourt saw no beef at all, and even eggs were in short supply. "I have not been in any of the obscurest parts of America, where I found provisions so badly furnished," he grumbled in his diary.

Rochefoucauld-Liancourt had an unusually good grasp of the cap-ital's potent, even mythic, symbolism. "The plan of the city is both judicious and noble; but it is in fact the grandeur and magnificence of the plan which renders the conception no better than a dream," he rather brutally observed. "Exclusive of the inconvenience of the great distance between the place where Congress holds its sittings, and the president's home, which will every day be more felt, it will require more than three hundred houses to fill the interval, of which there is not even a single house built." Communication between these two key points would be impractical in winter, for it was scarcely to be supposed that the government would ever pave and light the streets at its own expense. Members of Congress could hardly be expected to do without the most simple conveniences of life, for "it would not be greatly exaggerating the idea of comfort to desire to be in safety from being plunged in the mud for want of pavements, or breaking one's neck for want of lamps." His prognosis was bleak. He was convinced that the United States was so fatally riven by competing interests that it could not long survive, and that the new capital was powerless to save it. The federal city, he wrote, "has no other base than the Union of the several states; and if this foundation is not already destroyed, it cannot be denied that it is at least shaken." He predicted that even if the government did suc-ceed in moving to the Potomac in 1800, the misery of life there would soon drive it away again. The consequences for the nation would be catastrophic and unpredictable, and certainly far worse than leaving the seat of government where it was, in Philadelphia.

Rochefoucauld-Liancourt visited the federal city at its lowest ebb. The financial slide that had begun with the failure of the speculators' Dutch loan had turned into an avalanche that was now hurtling down upon the frantic figures of Morris and Nicholson as they scrambled to erect a shelter for themselves against the storm. They owed money to the federal commissioners, bankers, insurance companies, savings funds, trading houses, architects, workmen, former agents, factories, stores, and hundreds of individuals. Maryland was suing them for land in the district that they had bought from the state but never paid for. Pennsylvania was suing them for nonpayment of debts. James Greenleaf's agent in Amsterdam was suing them on behalf of Dutch bankers. In Philadelphia, the sheriff was threatening to seize Morris's property. The Bank of North America was about to go to court against Nicholson, who alone was facing sixty-one suits by September 1796 and an *additional* sixty-four by the following spring.

The commissioners were demanding immediate payment for the more than seven thousand lots the partners had nominally bought, and for them to begin construction of the 370 houses their contract called for—a commitment that drifted laughably further beyond their reach by the month. The speculators, in turn, begged the commissioners to issue titles to the city lots they had not yet paid for, claiming hopefully that with the titles in hand they could use the lots as security for new loans with which to pay off their debts. The two tried everything to raise ready money. Nicholson even negotiated with a Philadelphia whoremaster to lease a hotel that he owned in the federal city for a brothel. Meanwhile, Morris offered to mortgage his lands to Alexander Hamilton as security for paying off some of his debts. Hamilton wisely declined.

Morris habitually bought blind, investing in property he had never seen, in keeping with his history as a merchant who never saw the ships he dispatched reach their destination. The federal city was no exception. Thus it was not until the middle of 1796 that Morris paid his first visit to the site of the capital-to-be, in an effort to obtain titles "and clear away difficulties and intricacies." He surprised himself by falling in love with its majestic rolling hills, the grandeur of L'Enfant's plan, and—he was always a sucker for Southern pretensions—the local society of "genteel families of easy manners." There was an element of tragedy to what a few years earlier would have been for Morris a pleasant enough journey. All the long haggling over lots, and squares, and interest rates finally came into focus for him as a real landscape inhabited by real people, no longer just an abstract speculation. That the city would someday grow and prosper, he had no doubt. But he knew that he would never be a part of it. "The property we now hold will hereafter be of a value beyond calculation, but alas we cannot continue to hold but must sell it," he wrote mournfully to his son Tom.

Publicly the two partners presented a rictus of forced optimism, acting as if their lack of money were a force of nature rather than the bitter fruit of their own bad investments and overreaching. To once trusting investors, they continued to offer promises and more promises. Morris reassured Thomas Law, "You may now rely on my exertions to promote the City of Washington by every means in my Power—I expect that we shall by and by get the Command of Money—when that is accomplished everything that you can wish from Mr. Nicholson & myself will follow." But no one wanted their paper, shares in anything they owned, or their ever more steeply discounted word of honor. When Nicholson offered a tract of encumbered land in payment for a debt, one creditor scoffed, "To be satisfied with such Security is Impossible, I can scarcely believe you can think of it yourself." By the summer of 1797 the value of the partners' notes would plummet to two cents on the dollar. Washington wanted to believe the best of the two men from whom he had expected so much, but it was no longer possible. "One would hope that their assurances were not calculated for delay, and yet they seem to admit of hardly any other interpretation."

When a sheriff arrested his fellow speculator U.S. Supreme Court Justice James Wilson for failure to pay his debts, Morris knew that he would likely be next. To banker friends in Holland, he wrote, "Our ready money [has] run out and not being able to pay as the notes fall due they have depreciated down to nothing, and we are held in continual scenes of distress." Nicholson, hunkered like "a stricken Lear" in the federal city's Eastern Branch Hotel, worked compulsively for days on end without sleep, in a doomed effort to bring order to their affairs. It was like trying to hold back the tide. When urged to return to home, Nicholson refused, for fear of arrest by his creditors, declaring, "I am safe yet and hope to continue so altho all Hell should turn loose." But he could stave off the inevitable only for so long: he could not escape Philadelphia forever. Morris, for his own part, was near the end of his rope. To Nicholson, he wrote, "I hardly know which way to turn myself. I shall fight hard to weather the storm, but God knows how it will end."

Compounding his problems, Morris remained a virtual prisoner of the runaway architect L'Enfant, whom he had so cheerfully hired to design his Philadelphia mansion. Folly though this monstrous project appeared to everyone else, Morris was fatalistically incapable of walking away from it, as if his very identity were embedded in the Frenchified bays, mansards, and fripperies, as in a sense it perhaps was. "It is with astonishment I see the work of last fall now pulling down in order to put up more marble on my House, on which there is already vastly too much," he wrote in numb astonishment when he discovered that L'Enfant had actually dismantled part of the building to put up more ornamentation. "The delay and accumulation of Expence becomes intolerable. The difficulty & Cost of getting Money is vastly greater than you can conceive, and if you persist in exposing yourself to Censure & me into ridicule by alterations and additions, you will force me to abandon all Expectations of getting into the House & to stop the Work." L'Enfant was utterly unmoved. He obeyed no voice but the aesthetic sirens in his own capacious imagination. His art simply would not be hurried, or tainted by reason. The house, never to be completed, would ultimately suck away $1 million of Morris's rapidly shrinking fortune, standing for years to come in forlorn mockery of his outsized ambitions and ruined fortunes.

To the end, Morris and Nicholson would blame the slippery James Greenleaf for all their woes. While Morris and Nicholson had acted irresponsibly, and in Nicholson's case sometimes illegally, Greenleaf's behavior was downright appalling. Even as relations grew ever more venomous between the two Pennsylvanians on one side and the debonair Bostonian on the other, their financial fates remained chained together. All three were principals in the ill-fated North American Land Company, with its many millions of acres of frontier lands, and its towering pyramid of debt. Their affairs in the federal city also remained maddeningly tangled, despite the fact that they no longer held their property in common. Hot words flew in both directions. Nicholson accused Greenleaf of outright fraud for attempting to sell lots that were already mortgaged, while the Bostonian in turn claimed that Nicholson owed him more than a million dollars for lots and for shares in the North American Land Company. It only got worse. When Greenleaf failed to pony up his share of the payment for tracts acquired by the land company, creditors descended on Morris and Nicholson because they had endorsed his notes. In May 1796 they had bought out Greenleaf's shares in the land company for $1.15 million in drafts payable from one to four years after the date, but Greenleaf would retain the shares until complete payment was made. When the two Pennsylvanians failed to meet their payments to the commissioners, thus compromising their title, Greenleaf sued them, and attached their property.

The partners had endorsed earlier notes for Greenleaf, trusting him to repay them after the Dutch loan had been achieved. When the loan failed, the two were stuck with his paper. A single Philadelphia broker alone now held over $194,000 in Greenleaf's defaulted notes, which he expected the partners to pay. Greenleaf had also used what money he did manage to get from the Dutch for his own benefit, along with additional sums that Morris and Nicholson had advanced to him to pay their collective debts to the commissioners of the federal city. In addition—there seemed no end to Greenleaf's finagling—he had deliberately hoodwinked Morris and Nicholson when he sold his personal property in the city to them, claiming that the eight hundred lots that he was handing over to them were near the President's House and the Capitol, when they were in fact "at the extreme parts of the city," and therefore worth just a fraction of the claimed value. On the principle that the best defense must be a good offense, Greenleaf defiantly rejected the accusations against him, retorting in one of many coruscating letters to his former partners that it was in fact they who had despoiled him of his rightful property and been the cause of all his misfortunes. "Though the lure of your arts and the contagion of your example have undoubtedly led me into great errors, I trust that I have never yet been so debased by prosperity or by misfortunes as to render it hazardous, on any point of reputation, or in any form of inquiry, to engage in a comparison with you," he savagely wrote. He concluded triumphantly with a cruel allusion to Nicholson's impeachment, and an even nastier one to the recent revelation that Nicholson, once famous for his philanthropy, had looted the Widows' Fund of the Presbyterian Church, of which he was trustee, for cash in an attempt to pay his debts: "My veracity is, at least, untainted by any abuse of public trust; my conscience will never be disquieted by the embezzlement of a widow's or an orphan's portion."

Wily as he was, Greenleaf too would eventually be swept off his feet by the surging collapse of the partners' fortunes. Like Morris, he also approached Alexander Hamilton, offering him a third of his estate, which he claimed was worth $5 million, to bail him out of debt. Hamilton replied with an iciness that perhaps made the onetime wonderboy cringe, "I think myself bound to decline the ouverture."

In March 1797 Morris retreated to his estate overlooking the Schuylkill River outside Philadelphia, naming it with mordant humor "Castle Defiance." Since Pennsylvania law barred law officers from entering a debtor's house by force, the debtor could legally defy arrest and the seizure of his personal property by literally barricading himself inside his own home. Morris gazed out for the next year through his locked windows upon the small army of creditors, lawyers, constables, and bailiffs who camped among his beloved fruit trees and greenhouses, and menaced him from the doorstep. His household possessions were taken away and sold at auction, leaving the Morrises with a few sticks of borrowed furniture, broken sets of old books, bottles of wine drained off from a leaky cask, parts of an experimental steam engine, and barely enough food to survive. Once a creditor actually dispatched six men armed with sledgehammers and pick axes to break into Morris's home to seize him. Morris's remaining servants rushed to block the windows and doors. Weapons were drawn, flintlocks cocked. Morris was still too sure of himself, too much the survivor, to cower in fear. But there was no escaping the fact that his own world had turned against him. Faced with the prospect of actual bloodshed, his enemies abandoned the assault at the last moment. "They would have had me in five minutes if every Pistol & gun in the house had not been manned and fixed at them," Morris wrote to Nicholson, who was holed up in his own Philadelphia home, which, in a deliberate echo of Morris's wit, he dubbed "Castle Defense."

The partners' combined debt was estimated at $12 million, roughly $350 million in present-day dollars. It was a mountain that they simply could not climb. In June, they agreed to place all their remaining holdings in an Aggregate Fund controlled by their creditors, who were authorized to sell off whatever they could to recoup their losses. The two, still incorrigible, fantasized that somehow a surplus would remain to enable them to rebuild their fortunes. But it was of course not to be. News from the frontier dashed their last hopes for recovery. Georgia's new reform-minded legislature ripped the curtain of secrecy from the fraudulent sale of the state's western lands, and revoked the purchases on which Morris and Nicholson had pinned their hopes, turning to vapor the value of millions of acres of the partners' lands. Elsewhere, vast tracts of their holdings were sold off by local sheriffs for failure to pay taxes. "You may as well piss against the wind as offer the trustees Georgia and South Carolina lands," Morris dismally wrote to Nicholson. The new year of 1798 did not augur well. Even the trustees were resigning.

In the course of a year, Morris had watched his empire whittled to nothing. Everywhere he looked he saw about him a vast wrecked landscape of broken contracts, foundered debts, squandered trust, hopeless loans, and shattered hopes strewn like the ruined contents of homes blown out by a hurricane. Reduced to begging mere pittances—$200 here, $60 there—from those who still owed him money, he howled, "By heaven, there is no bearing of these things. I believe I shall go mad. God help us, for men will not. We are abandoned by all but those who want to get from us all we yet hold." Finally, in a terse envoi to Nicholson, he wrote on February 5, "My money is gone, my furniture is to be sold, I am to go to prison and my family to starve, good night."

Ten days later, the great Robert Morris, whose word was once good enough to support the treasury of the Continental Congress, and who barely three years earlier had been the best hope of bringing George Washington's vision of the federal city to glorious fruition, surrendered to the sheriff, and was led behind the twenty-foot-high walls of Prune Street prison. Debtors actually enjoyed considerable freedom within the jail's confines, since friends or family were permitted to rent them better accommodations inside the walls. Unlike ordinary inmates, they could also wander the prison's grounds, conduct business, and receive visitors freely. George Washington himself would dine formally with Morris in the prison, during a November 1798 trip to Philadelphia. After a brief but humiliating stay in a crowded cell—"Having no particular place allotted to me, I feel myself an intruder in every place into which I go," he moaned—Morris's sons succeeded in arranging a private room for him, where for the next three and a half years he lived surrounded by his account books, worthless contracts, and melancholy fantasies of what might have been.

Among his neighbors in the debtors' wing was the man whom of all his hundreds of friends, acquaintances, and business associates he least wanted to see: James Greenleaf, whose own creditors had expedited his removal to Prune Street as well. The two men apparently shared rooms on the same corridor, and saw each other every day, passing each other in silence, all the while carrying on their legal barrage of lawsuits against each other through their lawyers, in the Philadelphia courts. To both, the enforced parody of intimacy must have been bitterly trying. To a common friend, Morris wrote, "I shall be glad to see you, if it is only knocking at my door as you go to or from Mr. Greenleaf's room." The Bostonian's catlike facility for landing on his feet would keep his sojourn at Prune Street comparatively brief. Of the three original partners, his self-serving machinations had probably done the most harm to the federal city, by promising far more than he could deliver, and ultimately crippling what slight chance Morris and Nicholson had of stabilizing their fortunes. And in the end, he would pay the least price of all, returning to the Potomac a few decades hence, long after the others were gone, to live out his last years in luxury as a mysterious, half-forgotten figure in the city that he almost destroyed.

For Morris, the years of fooling himself were over. He knew now that there would be no more clever new deals, no brilliant stroke that would sweep the board clean and restore his honor. "My expectation of getting hence on the terms wished is over," he wrote to his daughter Maria. "It is a great comfort to your fond father to believe his family are better off than himself. My feelings nowadays are all for them, being indifferent as to what regards only myself." A fellow prisoner during this period left a poignant picture of Morris as he day after day trod silently in circles around the prison grounds: "His person was neat, and his dress, although a little old fashioned adjusted with much care . . . dropping from his hand at a given spot a pebble on each round, until a certain number which he had in his hand was exhausted." In October 1798 Morris had only a dollar and a half to his name, and expressed pathetic gratitude for a visitor's gift to him of a French crown.

John Nicholson managed to hold out for a few more months. Then he too at last surrendered to the authorities, and entered Prune Street prison in August 1799. He would never leave. In an effort to pay his expenses, he published a newspaper, *The Supporter or Daily Repast*, which he wrote and edited, and sold at six cents a copy. Its subscribers included John Adams and the Pennsylvania Abolition Society. But his creditors allowed him no respite. He tried to satisfy one with a couple of volumes of Shakespeare, another with eleven barrels of soured cider, a third with a shirt. To a fourth, he was forced to sign over title to his only slave, Jim. With nowhere else to turn, he even begged for charity from the African American members of St. Thomas's church, who had once celebrated his generosity to them at the church's inaugural banquet, in 1794. Nicholson died in disgrace at Prune Street on December 5, 1800, aged forty-three, leaving a wife and eight children.

THE COLLAPSE OF the speculative bubble brought land sales and construction almost to a halt. Thousands of the best lots were encumbered by liens and tied up in litigation. Would-be investors already regarded the place as a failure. There was only one important question now: would anything be ready for Congress by November of 1800? Given the feeble rate of work on just two buildings upon which so much money had already been spent, the crippled real estate market, and the doubts that still lingered among many in Congress, it was an open question. George

Washington joked with forced levity to a visitor at Mount Vernon that if the Capitol wasn't finished on time, "Oh well, they can camp out. The Representatives in the first line, the Senate in the second, the President with all his suite in the middle." But it was hardly a laughing matter.

Despite the guarantees enacted by Congress in March 1796, money remained in frustratingly short supply. Workmen went without pay for months; shopkeepers were in arrears to their suppliers; contractors were restive. In December of that year, after a personal appeal from George Washington, the Maryland senate had voted by an unenthusiastic one-vote margin to lend the commissioners $100,000 in stock. After depreciation, the stock actually proved to be worth only about $84,000. This would pay off the commissioners' debts to contractors, and keep workmen on the job for a few months more. But it was far from enough to complete both the Capitol and the President's House, not to mention the infrastructure that would make the city a place where people might actually want to live. Without another, bigger infusion of money, more months would be lost, and much of what had already been built would rot. One obvious option, so it seemed anyway, was to sell off the lots that Morris and Nicholson had failed to pay for. But even at fire sale prices—lots for which the partners had demanded twenty-five cents per square foot a year earlier were now on offer for three cents a square foot—there were few buyers willing to face down the speculators' creditors: no one wanted land with such dizzyingly clouded title.

Once again Washington stepped into the breach. He more than anyone had maintained from the project's beginning that it must not depend on government support. That position was now as untenable as his lines in the Battle of New York, when the British army swarmed over his trenches on Long Island, and nearly drove his army into the sea. Washington now told the commissioners bluntly that they must go back to Congress. Support from Congress—this was becoming an old song—would once and for all erase all doubt about the government's intention to move to the Potomac, he assured them. "Confidence will take place in every mind." Congress was at last being asked to abandon the pretense that private enterprise, which had brought the entire project to a public epiphany of embarrassment and the brink of ruin, and self-interest could do the job better than government itself.

WASHINGTON KNEW THAT asking support from Congress was also an invitation to meddle. Indeed, a new controversy with potentially far-reaching consequences now erupted, which threatened to spoil the central axis of L'Enfant's city plan, if not the configuration of power in the United States government. Some congressmen, convinced that only the Capitol or the President's House would actually be completed, proposed in the name of "economy" that the troubled Capitol be abandoned, the President's House be converted to the seat of Congress, and the president assigned a modest dwelling somewhere else. Others wanted to complete the Capitol, but move the president and his executive departments to Capitol Hill, and house the Judiciary in the intended President's House. This was by no means an empty debate: relocating the president's home would symbolically but significantly imperil the balance of powers. The Republican opposition made no secret of its hostility to the "imperial" pretensions of the federal city. Many Republicans believed that a presidential "palace" located so far from what they regarded as the nation's true locus of authority, the Congress, aggrandized the executive branch at the expense of the legislative, and would enshrine "monarchical" Federalist ideology for all eternity. Conversely, Federalists feared that if the president were to be lodged in the shadow of Congress, he would become its political pawn. President Adams, who though a Federalist tended to regard the executive departments as agents of Congress, ineptly offered to split the difference. By all means, put the executive departments next to the Capitol, he volunteered. It was fine with him.

At this moment Washington, in his last decisive act as the nation's emeritus commander in chief, weighed in with what was as close to a command as he could still issue to his fellow countrymen. Rather than defend the President's House per se, which might be misinterpreted as advocating the regal style for which he and Adams had often been criticized, Washington instead focused on the offices of the executive departments, the effective arms of presidential power. Where the President's House, or any other offices, are put "is to me as an individual a matter of moonshine," he snorted in a letter to Commissioner Alexander White, who he knew would communicate his feelings directly to Congress. But "nothing short of insanity can remove Congress from the building intended for its sittings to any other part of the city." Characteristically, he couched his argument in practical rather than ideological terms. Placing the executive offices alongside the Capitol would indeed be convenient for congressmen, he reasoned, but it would wreak havoc with the work of the departments. In Philadelphia, as everyone knew, the executive officers were so besieged by congressmen badgering them for attention that they often fled to their homes to get their work done. In the end, Washington's wishes prevailed: there would be no change in the grand plan. Thanks to him, in ages to come the executive and legislative branches would continue to eye each other with Constitutionally ordained respect and suspicion from the opposite ends of Pennsylvania Avenue. A month later, in April, after intensive lobbying by Alexander White and the federal city's partisans, Congress voted to guarantee a new $300,000 loan for the beleaguered new capital. It was the last time the commissioners would worry about money.

WHILE CONGRESS WRANGLED, the federal city slumbered. Of the perhaps three hundred buildings that lay scattered between George Town and the Eastern Branch, half stood empty, waiting forlornly for settlers who never came. With a breeze-driven grace that belied their gritty industrial mission, the hired schooners *Columbia, Sincerity,* and *Ark* periodically crept up the Potomac with cargoes of stone from the quarries at Aquia. Oxcarts plodded from the Potomac wharves to the depots at Capitol Hill, and to the future site of Lafayette Square, hauling mortar, lime, stone, bricks, pine logs and planks, shingles, nails, rum, tea, and sugar. Draymen from George Town piloted wagons piled high with pigs' carcasses along the muddy tracks that might one day be city streets, traveling at night to avoid spoiling the meat in the heat of the day. Slaves continued to chop trees, bake bricks, dig clay, and grind down stones collected from Rock Creek to boil for plaster. Through forest glades the desultory smack of hammers and the chuff of saws dully echoed.

The feeling of paralysis affected everyone. Contractors grumbled that the surveyors had produced only "mutilated, unfinished, and discordant plans." The architects bickered incessantly. William Thornton denounced George Hadfield, who was superintending the work on the Capitol, as "extremely deficient in practical knowledge." One of James Hoban's men returned the insult by dismissing Thornton as "a fribbling quack." Theft was rampant. A contractor's slaves were spied lifting wood from the public supplies and taking it to their master's furniture workshop. A disgruntled supervisor accused James Hoban's "Irish vagabons" of looting construction materials to build houses for themselves. Among the workers, morale was at rock bottom. Masons and carpenters drifted away from the job to idle in the little dramshops that had sprung up around the worksites. "Every man in the yard took whatever liberty almost he pleased," one carpenter truculently reported to the commissioners. "If I am discharged for not doing a full day's work every day, every carpenter might be discharged for the same reason."

Almost five years after the much heralded laying of its cornerstone, after the Masonic parades, and the celebratory cannonades, and the bloviating oratory, the Capitol was still just a shell, its walls no higher than the Corinthian columns on its facade. Even now, after exhaustive debate and a congressional investigation, nothing seemed to go right. Recently it had been discovered that three floors had been so incompetently laid that they would have to be taken out again and replaced, and that a newly installed staircase was already in danger of collapse.

One of the visitors to the Capitol that spring was another exiled European, Julian Ursyn Niemcewicz, a Polish writer, and a close friend of George Washington's wartime comrade Tadeuz Kosciuszko. Niemcewicz came with high expectations. Like Rochefoucauld-Liancourt, he too looked beyond the mere architectural aspects of the project and recognized its tremendous symbolic importance to the United States. As an idealist whose own nation had just been ruthlessly dismembered and erased from the map by the empires of Eastern Europe, he looked to the new American nation as an inspiration to liberals and democrats everywhere.

Although the Capitol's setting "in the middle of superb woods" inspired him to flights of sylvan Latin poetry, he deemed the building itself too heavy and massy, and was shocked by its cost, commenting in his diary that, "In all other countries one would be able, with the same sum, to build four times more and four times better." At the invitation of the superintendent, he climbed up the scaffolding, past workers who were raising stone blocks with ropes and pulleys, for a spectacular view of the surrounding countryside. Perched at the top of the walls, Niemcewicz fell into an intense reverie, a vision of a remote and glorious future, which after all the disappointments of the past years would have seemed like a mocking chimera, a ridiculous improbability, to many who had once believed in the city, with the monumentally steadfast exception of George Washington. As he gazed along the angling route of Pennsylvania Avenue, Niemcewicz pictured a future traveler like himself a century hence, riding between rows of sumptuous buildings illuminated with lights enclosed in crystal, a crowd of pedestrians, and the noise of carriages passing each other at full tilt. Today, he wrote, "One sees and hears there only the silence of the trees, where one day great houses will be built. One sees there only robins, red or blue birds flitting from branch to branch or flying through the air where thousands and thousands of inhabitants will come one day to live. What a contrast between the stillness of these silent forests and the uproar and all the tumult of passions which will come one day to agitate the poor mortals." Suddenly the reverie was broken by an intense feeling of vertigo, whether from the height or the dizzying effect of his vision Niemcewicz did not say. With the future swimming in his eyes, he climbed back to earth.

Chapter 10

THE CAPITAL OF
A GREAT NATION

Thank heaven! Ten tedious years are past,
And here we've altogether met at last;
The Grecian States, ambitious to destroy,
Took the same time to level cloud capt Troy.

—FROM A THEATRICAL PERFORMANCE,
WASHINGTON, SEPTEMBER 1800

IN MAY 1798 A visitor to Mount Vernon found George Washington a "majestic figure," still hale at sixty-six, his hair still thick on his massive head, and his blue eyes and aquiline nose as commanding as ever they had been. With the same attention to detail that he had for so long lavished on the plans for the federal city as a whole, Washington was now micromanaging construction of his two brick houses on North Capitol Street as prospective residences for congressmen. He fired off letters almost daily to William Thornton, who adored the old man, and had undertaken to personally supervise the project for him. Orders flew from Washington's quill, advising Thornton on the minutiae of joists, purlins, rafters, cross ties and stooths, scantling and molding, the carting of sand, the need to exclude sappy and knotty wood from the flooring planks, and the placement of a parapet along the roofline—"something to relieve the view of a plain and dead surface." Be sure to remember, he admonished the accommodating Thornton, that "everything proper and useful may be had without superfluity or waste." He also urged Thornton to keep an eye on his contractor, Thomas Blagden. "I have no objections to Mr. Blagden's frequent calls for money," the ex-president warned, "but I fear the work which is not enumerated in the contract with him is pretty smartly whipped up in the price of it—I had no expectations (for instance) that a well little more than thirty feet deep was to cost me upwards of 70 pounds."

Washington regularly visited the Federal District to monitor prog-ress on the houses, often in Thornton's company. The doctor cherished the intimacy of what he called their "little excursions," rambling alone together around the federal city. In Thornton, Washington had not only an eager and intelligent audience, but also one who without reser-vation shared his glowing faith in the city's future. "I have many things confided to me that, could I consistently with my duties disclose, would make our prospect to thee truly grand," he wrote excitedly to his cousin John Coakley Lettsom. "We are approaching to a state which will, I doubt not, be truly grand." Thornton and his young wife, Anna Maria, also made frequent trips to Mount Vernon, where they were treated as members of the Washingtons' extended family. On one occasion, Thornton reciprocated the old man's kindnesses to him with a gift of a dozen bottles of Tortola rum, distilled twenty-eight years earlier on the family estate, which he promised "would be of no disservice to a Virginia planter in a dram fog."

The rambles grew fewer later in the year, as Washington's attention snapped back to urgent questions of national security. War with France threatened to draw him one last time from his lair at Mount Vernon and onto the political battlefield. After months of French provocation, in May President Adams accused France of trying to drive a wedge between the American people and their government, and promised to repel any attack "with a decision which shall convince France and the world that we are not a degraded people, humiliated under a colonial spirit of fear and sense of inferiority." Americans of almost all political persuasions were outraged when they learned, in June, that the French had demanded a bribe of £50,000 simply for the privilege of negotiating with the peace mission that Adams had dispatched to Paris. The scandal that ensued was labeled the XYZ Affair, after the coded initials that were assigned to the French officials involved. Public opinion, which until now had largely favored the French, abruptly made a 180-degree turn. Frenchmen were assaulted in the streets of Philadelphia, and the pro-French revolutionary tricolor cockades that had long been so popular disappeared overnight. Federalists who had been on the defensive benefited from a sudden surge of support. Abigail Adams fairly crowed with delight upon hearing of one particularly bloodcurdling toast to her husband: "John Adams—May he, like Samson, slay thousands of Frenchmen with the jawbone of Jefferson."

Nurtured by the climate of palpitating xenophobia that swept the land, with Adams's approval, Federalists enacted the most overtly repressive laws in American history, the Alien and Sedition Acts. The worst of the new laws provided for fines and prison time for anyone publishing or uttering "false, scandalous, and malicious" statements against the government or its officers. Others retarded citizenship for immigrants, whom Federalists claimed brought with them to America the insidious virus of revolution, and gave the president the power to deport aliens without a hearing. Opposition newspapers were shut down. Hostile editors and writers were arrested; others fled the country. Ordinary citizens, mostly in Federalist strongholds in the Northeast, were seized for erecting liberty poles, or just for making casual remarks disparaging of the president. Public debate chilled. Not even elected officials were immune. Vermont Congressman Matthew Lyon was arrested in the midst of his campaign for reelection, and accused of criminal disloyalty for writing in a local newspaper that "every consideration of the public welfare [is] swallowed up in a continual grasp for power, [and] in an unbounded thirst for ridiculous pomp, foolish adulation, or selfish avarice." Three days later, Lyon was hauled into court without legal representation and sentenced to four months' imprisonment—beginning the next day.

A greater degree of acrimony appeared among the members of Congress than even during the debate over the Jay Treaty. Republicans warned that the great American experiment had been betrayed, and that despotism was at hand. "We are compleatly under the saddle of Massachusetts & Connecticut, and they ride us very hard," Adams's own vice president, Thomas Jefferson, wrote in a private letter, scathingly alluding to Federalist rule as a "reign of witches." Jefferson's followers in the legislatures of Kentucky and Virginia enacted incendiary resolutions decrying the Alien and Sedition laws as unconstitutional, and appealing to other states to declare them void. Accusing Federalists of creating a "mixed monarchy," the resolutions established a platform for the Republican resurgence that was to come in 1800. Decades later, Jefferson would be revealed as the principal author of the resolutions. Although he strongly opposed secession, his defiant conception of states' rights provided intellectual fodder for the States Rights movement, which would haunt the nation through and beyond the Civil War.

Federalists remained in firm control of the government for the time being, however. To counter the alleged (and imaginary) threat of imminent French invasion, Congress voted to recruit a ten-thousand-man standing army, naming Washington as its titular commander-in-chief. The ex-president was essentially a figurehead: the real moving force behind this extravagant enterprise was Alexander Hamilton, who intended to use the army as an agent of Federalist power. Implausible as it sounds two centuries later, he fantasized leading the army through Jefferson's stronghold of Virginia, and then on a barely disguised imperialist adventure through Florida, Louisiana, Mexico, and on into Central America. Abigail Adams warned her husband that Hamilton had it in him to become "a second Bonaparte"—a military dictator. Washington, meanwhile, perched far outside the policy-making loop at Mount Vernon, took his appointment with his customary gravity, poring over lists of Revolutionary War veterans, nominating officers for commissions, and ordering a crisp new buff-and-blue copy of his Revolutionary War uniform from his favorite Philadelphia tailor. Before Hamilton's megalomaniac scheme became operational, however, President Adams cannily outflanked his Federalist rival by dispatching a second, and ultimately successful, peace mission to France, eventually defusing the crisis. Washington would never wear his new uniform to battle.

A FEW DAYS AFTER Julian Niemcewicz's visit to the Capitol, he crossed the Potomac to visit Mount Vernon. Washington was away inspecting his farms when Niemcewicz turned up, so he passed the time examining the interior of the house, particularly admiring a stone model of the Bastille ("It is a pity that the children have already damaged it a little"), a glass case containing a key to the actual Bastille, which had been sent to Washington by Lafayette, a harpsichord, and several paintings, including a portrait of the younger Washington in his pre-Revolution British uniform. The starstruck Pole had found himself literally speechless at meeting Washington for the first time some days earlier in George Town, and nearly died from embarrassment. Happily, when the great man returned from his rounds, he was reassuringly hospitable, and obligingly led his doting visitor on a tour of his estates, proudly pointing out gardens opulent with currants, raspberries, strawberries, peaches, and cherries, lilies, roses, pinks, and magnolias, as well as the several farms, grist mills, flocks of sheep, extensive stables, a whiskey distillery, and the slave quarters. As much as he admired Washington, Niemcewicz was frankly appalled at the living conditions of his slaves. Washington was reputed to treat his slaves more humanely than most masters, but Niemcewicz judged their huts to be more miserable than those of the poorest Polish peasants, and found every able soul working seven days a week under a seemingly pointless regime, which arbitrarily permitted them, for instance, to raise hens, but barred them from owning ducks, geese, or pigs.

In the waning of his life, Washington's entanglement with slavery had forced him into tortured contradictions that set his moral commitment to emancipation at odds with both his self-interest and his overweening concern for his reputation and legacy. His reaction to the escape of Ona Judge during the last year of his presidency had revealed those contradictions in an especially stark light. Judge, then twenty-three, ran away one night in May 1796 while the Washingtons were at dinner in their Philadelphia mansion. The escape was clearly well-planned. For several weeks, Judge was kept hidden in the city by local blacks, and then spirited aboard a ship sailing for the free North, with the cooperation of its white captain. What happened next showed Washington at his worst. Learning that Judge was in Portsmouth, New Hampshire, he told Oliver Wolcott, secretary of the treasury, to have the federal customs officer there, Joseph Whipple, surreptitiously seize her and put her aboard a southbound vessel. "The ingratitude of the girl, who was brought up and treated more like a child than a Servant ought not to escape with impunity if it can be avoided," Washington fumed. What he was asking was illegal, and he certainly knew it: federal law required that a slaveholder or his representative appear in person before a magistrate and prove evidence of ownership before transporting an alleged fugitive across state lines. This the president had not the slightest intention of doing.

When Whipple wrote back that Judge was willing to bargain for her freedom, Washington had snapped that the idea of compromise with a mere slave was intolerable, "for however well disposed I might be to a gradual abolition, or even to an entire emancipation of that description of People (if the latter was in itself practicable at this moment) it would neither be politic or just to reward *unfaithfulness* with a premature preference; and thereby discontent beforehand the minds of all her fellow-servants who by their steady attachments are far more deserving than herself of favor." Ona Judge would never return. Washington was ultimately more interested in protecting his name than in recovering his property; he feared being seen by the nation as just another ruthless slave master hunting down a runaway like prey, even if that was, in fact, just what he had in mind. Judge would leave the Father of his Country to wallow in his aggrievement. She would safely live out the remainder of her long life in a small New Hampshire town, dying in 1848, impoverished but free.

Judge was not the only presidential slave to "elope," as the idiom of the time rather quaintly put it. In March 1797, on the morning of the Washingtons' departure from Philadelphia for Virginia, their trusted chef Hercules abruptly decamped and was never heard from again. A visitor who later spoke with Hercules's small daughter at Mount Vernon remarked that she must feel sad that she would not see her father again. She replied, "Oh! Sir, I am very glad because he is now free."

Even now in this last year of Washington's life, he still did not understand how determined black Americans like Hercules and Ona Judge were to create their own freedom outside the paternal grip of well-intentioned whites like himself. Although a professed supporter of emancipation, during his years in Philadelphia he had never noticed, much less appreciated, the remarkable success of the churchmen Richard Allen and Absalom Jones in establishing churches, schools, and support networks among the city's free blacks. At the same time, he was quite well aware that the rhetoric of liberation had percolated from Quaker meeting rooms and the parlors of liberal intellectuals into the humble quarters of the still-enslaved, who almost daily became more "insolent" and difficult to control. "It is my opinion that these elopements will be MUCH MORE before they are LESS frequent: and that the persons making them should never be retained, if they are recovered, as they are sure to contaminate and discontent others," the former president wrote to a slaveholding friend.

As Henry Wiencek has amply shown, in contrast to many men of his class, most notably Thomas Jefferson, Washington did grapple seriously with the moral imperative of emancipation. He believed neither that blacks were biologically inferior to whites, nor ordained to eternal servitude by Biblical stricture. Nor did he feel, like the idealistic William Thornton, that emancipated blacks must be separated from whites and returned "home" to Africa. Rather, Washington believed that blacks could be uplifted by education, and that there was a place for them as free people in the new nation. As early as 1783 he had toyed with founding a community for freed slaves with the ardently abolitionist Marquis de Lafayette, and he had contemplated freeing his own bondsmen before becoming president in 1789. Even as he schemed to recapture the ungrateful Ona Judge, he was thinking about how to disencumber himself of unwanted farmland without risking the security of the slaves who worked it for him. He understood that slavery threatened the survival of the country he loved, and he genuinely believed that ending it would help to preserve the Union "by consolidating it in a common bond of principle." Two years before his death, he wrote, "I wish from my soul that the Legislature of this State could see the policy of a gradual Abolition of Slavery; it would prevt. much future mischief."

In the summer of 1799 Washington made a detailed inventory of the 317 slaves at Mount Vernon. He determined from a purely businesslike point of view that he had far more slaves than he could use. "To sell the surplus I cannot, because I am principled in this kind of traffic in the human species," he opined. "To hire them out is almost as bad, because they cannot be disposed of in families to any advantage, and to disperse the families I have an aversion. What then is to be done?" Self-interest commanded him to sell; ethics refused to permit it. Washington personally owned only 124 of the Mount Vernon slaves. Nearly all the rest were in Martha's name, and after her death would revert to the Custis estate, to be distributed among her grandchildren; over these, he had no control. In his will, which he formalized in July, he declared, "Upon the decease of my wife, it is my will and desire that all the slaves which I hold in my *own right*, shall receive their freedom." He thought through meticulously just how this would be done. The elderly and infirm who preferred to remain as slaves for their own security were to be kept clothed and fed by Washington's heirs. Orphans with no one to care for them would be indentured until the age of twenty-five, and prepared properly for life in freedom: "The Negroes thus bound are (by their Masters or Mistresses) to be taught to read & write; and to be brought up to some useful occupation," he ordered. A special fund was to be provided for their support. He also expressly forbade the sale or transportation out of Virginia of any of his slaves "under any pretence whatsoever." He bluntly added, "I do moreover most pointedly and most solemnly enjoin it upon my executors . . . to see that this clause respecting slaves be religiously fulfilled without evasion, neglect, or delay." It is a revealing commentary on the climate in which Washington lived on the Potomac that he could trust neither his lawyers nor his family to ensure that his slaves would actually be emancipated after his death unless commanded by law to do so. He knew that the provisions of his will would become public: it was a way of speaking his mind to the nation. But he took no stand for the nearly 1 million black Americans who were enslaved when he died. Nor did he ever speak up for the scores of slaves he saw toiling on the site of the new Capitol and the mansion where his successors would live. In the end, the best that he could do was to liberate *himself* from slavery.

O<small>N</small> N<small>OVEMBER</small> 9 Washington set out from Mount Vernon a little after eight o'clock in the morning, to check on his buildings on North Capitol Street. He probably traveled by his usual route up the west bank of the Potomac to Alexandria, and crossed the river from there to the Commissioners' Wharf, near the President's House. It was an unseasonably pleasant day for travel, clear and mild after a run of blustery weather. Most likely following Pennsylvania Avenue directly toward Capitol Hill, Washington proceeded to North Capitol Street, where he might have barked a few orders to the workmen at hand, to remind them who was in charge. He then rode southward a short distance to the home of Thomas Law, where he dined, perhaps discussing, as they ate, the lagging work on the Capitol and the ever frustrating paucity of settlers. After dinner, Washington most likely rode back past the Capitol, and turned northwest up Pennsylvania Avenue, passing the President's House, and eventually arriving at the Twenty-sixth and K Street home of Martha's granddaughter Patsy Peter, where he would spend the night. He returned home to Mount Vernon the next day. He would never see the federal city again.

Money, as always, was in short supply in the federal city. The beleaguered commissioners still depended for part of their budget on income from land sales, which proved maddeningly difficult to collect. Hundreds of properties once belonging to Morris and Nicholson were being liquidated for nonpayment of their debts. But even new purchasers were lackadaisical in meeting their obligations. "The funds are much more than sufficient, could the debts be collected, but the impossibility of enforcing the payment has induced us for some time past to suspend work on the President's House and confine work to the houses necessary for Congress and the exec offices," the commissioners wearily reminded President Adams. Nonetheless, stone by stone, and brick by brick, the walls of the Capitol continued to rise. By mid-November, the bricklayers were finishing the chimneys, gutters were being installed, the eighty-six-by-forty-eight-foot Senate chamber had been floored, and its doorways and windows trimmed. Doorways and window sashes had also been fitted in the smaller chamber of the House of Representatives, floors laid in several of the committee rooms, and plastering begun in the halls. At the President's House, the masons had completed the stone- and brickwork, window frames had been made, and the sashes and doors were ready to install. The walls of the Treasury building were up, as were the foundations and basement walls for the War Department. Here and there—signs of a thaw in the frozen real estate market, landowners hoped—a few elegant houses were rising near the Capitol.

As November sheered into December, the weather turned wet and heavy, converting roads to rivers, and low-lying fields to soggy bottoms. For a full week, it rained almost every day, sending cascades of water down the bluffs along the Potomac, fattening the river with muddy runoff. Temperatures hovered in the thirties, driving a frigid damp through ill-heated mansions and slaves' huts alike. Wet woolen clothing clung to already chilled bodies. Warmth was a luxury. The rain finally abated on the eighth, though the air remained bitingly cold. Bad news arrived at Mount Vernon that morning from William Thornton, complaining to Washington that Adams's attorney general had blocked the commissioners' most recent attempt to obtain a loan to tide them over, asserting that they lacked the authority to borrow money without congressional approval. "By the obstructions continually thrown in its way, by friends or enemies, this city has had to pass through a fiery trial," Washington memorably wrote back, with a passion that he reserved for few things besides his beloved new city. "Yet I trust [it] will, ultimately, escape the ordeal with éclat."

It began to rain again on the eleventh; the next day, the rain turned to snow, then to hail. Cold settled like a shroud over the valley. Washington stoically made his usual daily round of his farms, no more deterred by the wretched weather than he had been by redcoats. There was much planning to be done for the first year of the new century. He wanted wheat planted in Union Farm's field number one, the stubble plowed under, and rye sown there for a sheep pasture. Field number two was to be sown in corn. Another field was to remain enclosed and left fallow in preparation for planting wheat there in 1801. Still another was to be planted with peach trees spaced precisely sixteen and a half feet apart. After five hours in the saddle, Washington returned home for dinner. He didn't bother to change his wet clothes, so as not to delay dinner for his guests.

He woke up the morning of the thirteenth with a sore throat. Ignoring it, he went out in three inches of snow to mark trees for pruning. That night, the inflammation grew rapidly worse until his throat was so swollen that he could barely breathe. Doctors were called. They diagnosed his condition as "the croup," and prescribed an aggressive regimen of laxatives, blistering, and repeated bleeding. But the infection was untreatable by the medicine of Washington's day. Several slaves attended him to the end, as did the loyal Thomas Law, trying ineffectually to comfort him. But his throat inexorably continued to close up, as doctors milled helplessly around him, accomplishing nothing but to increase his pain. "Doctor, I die hard," he said, "but I am not afraid to go." The old man breathed his last on the evening of December 14.

Law had sent for William Thornton, but he arrived too late to do any good. Washington was already gone. Thornton then made a weird proposal: to bring Washington back from the dead. Thornton, who had trained as a medical doctor, had come intending to perform a tracheotomy. "When we arrived, to my unspeakable grief, we found him laid out a stiffened corpse," Thornton later wrote. "I was overwhelmed with the loss of the best friend I had on Earth. The weather was very cold, and he remained in a frozen state for several days. I proposed to attempt his restoration, in the following manner. First to thaw him in cold water, then to lay him in blankets, and by degrees and by friction to give him warmth, and to put into activity the minute blood vessels, at the same time to open a passage to the lungs by the trachaea, and to inflate them with air, to produce an artificial respiration, and to transfuse blood into him from a lamb. If these means had been resorted to and had failed all that could be done would have been done, but I was not seconded in this proposal; for it was deemed unavailing." Thornton was deterred from this bizarre experiment by the other doctors present. "It was doubted by some whether—if it were possible—it would be right to attempt to recall to life one who had departed full of honor and renown, free from the frailties of age, in the full enjoyment of every faculty, and prepared for eternity," he rather disappointedly remarked.

WASHINGTON WAS NO more. But the city that bore his name, his posthumous offspring, was on the eve of its birth about to be delivered to the nation, like the child who he never had. What greater gift could Americans give to the memory of its indispensable man than to nurture it, this cynosure of national unity, to which he had devoted both his heart and his leadership for the decade past? The city would become Washington's ultimate monument rendered for the ages, with the hopes, ideals, and political institutions of the nation enshrined in its freestone and brick. The city had begun as a dream—a dream within a dream, really—encased within Washington's grandiose vision of the Potomac as the great highway to the heart of the continent. The Potomac had sung to him its siren song, and he had done his utmost to give it the nation's capital. To the friend of his youth Sarah Fairfax he had confided, "A Century hence, if this country keep united (and it is surely its policy and Interest to do so) will produce a City—though not as large as London—yet of a magnitude inferior to few others in Europe."

For many Americans, Washington was already a kind of god, and beyond reach of death. In life, Washington was a supreme realist, a visionary blessed with an extraordinarily astute instinct for the ways in which power moved men, and devoid of illusions but for his obsessive and spectacularly wrong belief in the destiny of the Potomac River. In a country suddenly bereft of its most precious unifying symbol, this tough-minded, self-interested, and thoroughly human Washington was rapidly subsumed into the secular national religion. His image appeared on silverware, plates, music sheets, rings, engravings, and all sorts of patriotic tschotschkes. Americans saw him everywhere in popular artwork, in quite literally godlike guise, posed heroically among palm branches, banners, laurel wreaths, and sunbursts, suspended in clouds, alongside eagles and cornucopias, the centerpiece of innumerable allegories of freedom, prosperity, and federal union. Death merged his many roles—frontiersman, war hero, statesman, president—into a transcendental embodiment of national self-sacrifice and fortitude, of faith and probity, of common purpose. His accomplishments were no longer seen as the work of a mere human being, but as the nation's own destiny. Orators keened that the soul of the country had withered, that its energy had died, that its virtue had fled.

Without Washington, there would have been no Washington, D.C. Without his unflagging commitment, the city might never have been placed on the Potomac, and certainly not at its present location, which he personally selected. Without him, L'Enfant might never have been hired, and would not have been given a free hand to create the grand design that became the lasting plan for the city. Without his encouragement toward magnificence, the Capitol and the President's House would probably have been much more modest. Without his sometimes superhuman persistence, construction would never have survived the repeated financial failures and shattered hopes of the mid-1790s.

As the old century bled into the new, work on the government buildings moved forward at a slow but steady pace. At the President's House, the enslaved carpenters Oliver and Moses continued to saw joists. The commissioners' tally sheets lengthened: $40 to George Jacobs for cutting doorjambs, $497.38 to Thomas Munroe for shingles, $56.47 to Brian Duffe for digging the president's well. William Brent had to be paid for the labor of his "Negro Henry," and James Wallace for his slave Sam, and James Stone for his Salisbury and Big Jacob. Orders were placed for red Morocco leather for the senators' chairs, and goatskin for those of the House members. Congressmen who were disposed to finding fault with anything that involved spending more money on the federal city complained that not only were the chairs exorbitant at $20 apiece, but they had even been made in England.

Despite the progress that had been made on the public buildings, the city presented a panorama of abandonment more than it did a would-be capital. Stones marking nonexistent avenues poked up through briars and blackberries. Footpaths meandered among corn fields, muddy ponds, brickyards, workers' hovels, and ruinous houses abandoned by failed speculators. At high tide, the waters of Tiber Creek rose to flood Pennsylvania Avenue. Horses sometimes drowned trying to cross Rock Creek. Many deemed the President's House particularly appalling. "Would you not be ashamed to conduct the President to the house without there being an enclosure of any kind about it?" Secretary of the Navy Stoddert complained to the commissioners, urging them to at least plant some trees around the mansion, to conceal its ugliness. Secretary of the Treasury Wolcott was even more caustic. "I had no conception until I came here, of the folly and infatuation of the people who have directed the settlements," he wrote to his wife. "You may look in almost any direction over an extent of ground nearly as large as the city of New York, without seeing a fence or any object except brick kilns and temporary huts for laborers. Mr. Law and a few other gentlemen live in great splendor; but most of the inhabitants are low people, whose appearance indicates vice and intemperance, or negroes. Immense sums have been squandered in buildings which are but partly finished, in situations which are not, and never will be the scenes of business."

Then, with the coming of spring, something startling began to happen. Suddenly the city began to swarm with people. After a decade of disappointment and thwarted hopes, the government was actually beginning to move south. Congress met in Philadelphia for the last time on May 14, 1800. The next day, President Adams directed the executive departments to begin shipping their offices, clerks, and papers to the Potomac. The largest department by far was Treasury, which had sixty-nine employees. (Congress itself had only eight permanent staff members.) Wagons had to be hired, sloops chartered, carpenters found to build crates, archives and furniture packed, and then hauled to the Delaware River docks. For weeks, confusion reigned. Half of the Adamses' official tea set disappeared en route, never to be seen again.

The secretary of the navy was in Washington to open his office, but his files were missing; a week later the files turned up, but the clerk responsible for them was nowhere to be found. In all, the move cost the government $78,924.95, including $15,000 for moving the contents of the President's House, $1,000 for the clerk of the House of Representatives and his staff, and $114 for the slender archives of the Supreme Court.

One of the newcomers, Margaret Bayard Smith, the wife of the editor of the newly established *National Intelligencer*, eagerly explored the city from her lodgings on Capitol Hill. Unlike the dyspeptic secretary of the treasury, she loved the rural surroundings, and found a poignant moral drama in the contrast of splendid buildings set against uncultivated plains and woods. She imagined everywhere civilization replacing nature as "lofty oak trees" tumbled to make room for palaces. The landscape symbolized for her the innocence of the nation, an era of goodness that surely was about to end, she feared, shriveling in the grip of political man. The mind "contemplates the moral change that will soon take place," she told her diary. "Soon will honest industry and ignorant simplicity yield to designing ambition and polished dissimulation and all its train of evils will usurp the land." Smith would acclimate, however. In time, she would become one of early Washington's most sought after hostesses, and friend to a long line of the powerful, among them Thomas Jefferson, James and Dolley Madison, John Calhoun, and Henry Clay.

By June, more than one hundred federal workers had trickled into the city, scarcely the tide of immigrants whom the city's promoters bombastically predicted. But it was a start. In their wake came the kind of immigrants who until now had been so conspicuously missing: lawyers, doctors, tavern keepers, printers, shopkeepers, clergymen, and families. They came on sloops and brigs, on horseback, and on painfully hard-benched stagecoaches where congressmen and senators jostled and bounced alongside shoemakers and seamstresses, the epitome of democracy on wheels. Settlers in the capital could now order sofas, sideboards, and hardback chairs from John Duhy's new cabinet-making shop on New Jersey Avenue, fine boots from John Minchin, who had just opened a shop near Barry's Wharf, and any sort of fabric from Irish linen to "Negro cotton" from John Cox's dry goods store. At an emporium near the President's House, Samuel McIntyre sold such luxuries like French brandy, Dutch gin, mustard in bottles, shelled almonds, raisins, and Spanish "segars." John Barns was advertising fine Hyson, Souchang, and Bohea teas. At Richard Beck's, there was a new shipment of lute strings, just imported from India. At John Marsh's, one could find assorted pharmaceuticals, including "anodyne essence" for headaches, antispasmodic elixir for hysteria and epilepsy, and vermifluge lozenges for killing worms in children. One could buy people, too, such as the "good sawyer," with or without his wife and five children, who was on offer by Benjamin Oden, "cash or credit." Or one could pick and choose among the "thirty likely country-born slaves," including laborers handy in planting and farming, and a variety of "stout lads and girls," who were being sold off by the Charles County Orphans' Court.

New stage lines were bringing immigrants daily from Baltimore, Philadelphia, and New York, Richmond and Norfolk, and points farther south and west. A traveler from Philadelphia could now, with luck, make the trip to the federal city in a mere thirty-three hours, down from three days, although it remained a bone-jolting journey in a mail wagon or coach lurching over stones, potholes, and stumps. Those homesick for Philadelphia found on the Potomac at least the stirrings of culture. The Reverend Michael Arthur, recently come from England, had just opened an academy to teach mathematics, bookkeeping, Latin, Greek, navigation, and "the use of globes." A Mr. Francis, a dancing master from Philadelphia, was teaching the minuet, reels, and all the latest new steps in cotillion and country dances. There were even amateur theatricals, although William Thornton's sophisticated wife, Anna Maria, found them "intolerably stupid."

The Thorntons, who had lived in the Federal District less than five years, now counted as established pillars of local society. Politicians, generals, and cabinet officers flocked to their teas and dinners. Although Thornton still professed his belief in emancipation, he and Anna Maria had accommodated themselves, if somewhat uneasily, to the Tidewater way of life. "I am myself an oppressor, I feel the injustice of remaining so, but I inherit the misery of being a tyrant," he balefully acknowledged. Slaves worked the Thorntons' farm on the Frederick Road, and periodically trotted down to their house in the city with fresh butter, strawberries, and vegetables for their dinner table. Like other masters, they also coped with the perennial annoyance of runaways: when Nick ran off from the farm in September, an annoyed Thornton dispatched the more trustworthy Joe fifteen miles into Maryland to bring him back. While some fugitives, like Nick, fled from the federal city, others ran toward it, hoping to find work and anonymity in a place where almost everyone was still a stranger. Nearly every issue of the *The Centinel of Liberty and George-Town Advertiser* carried ads for runaways, such as the brothers Cato and Frank from Charles County, Maryland, who were thought to be passing as freemen, and pockmarked Jim Poplin and his fast-talking wife, Hannah, who were "lurking" somewhere near the city. Other blacks who may not have been runaways at all were swept up and jailed by local sheriffs. Sheriff Notley Maddox of Prince Georges County advertised Will, "who says he is free," and who would be sold for jail fees unless he was collected by his master. Will might really have been free, but he would be sold anyway. For masters too busy to chase their own slaves, there were professional services. James Dermott, the former schoolteacher who had been hired back in 1791 to oversee slaves on the first surveying crews in the city, now was in business hunting runaways on commission.

Among the new arrivals in the federal city was another "old timer," Peter Charles L'Enfant who, after George Washington himself, had left a greater personal imprint on the city than any other man in America. The engineer's return was a far cry from his flamboyant departure in 1792, when he cavalierly threw his job as the city's designer into the faces of the federal commissioners and withdrew to Philadelphia in high dudgeon. Washington's death had freed him from his principled refusal to claim payment for the services he had rendered then. L'Enfant appeared in the Federal District in September, no less proud, but now nearly friendless, half-forgotten, and dependent for emotional and financial support on his companion and probable sometime lover, Richard Soderstrom, a businessman of somewhat doubtful ethics, as well as the consul-general of Sweden. (The Swede, for his part, had during the 1790s borrowed more than $18,000 from Robert Morris, money that the jailed financier would never see again; Soderstrom "never had a guinea of his own," grumped Morris.) From their rooms at Stelly's tavern, L'Enfant immediately began firing off elephantine, baroquely worded petitions to the commissioners and to Congress, alternately begging and demanding exorbitant sums for his work at the beginning of the decade. In 1792 he had contemptuously dismissed an offer of $1,000 from the commissioners. Now he wanted a hundred times that much. Pleading "a concurrence of disastrous events rendering my position so difficult as to be no longer possible to withstand," L'Enfant called upon them to redress a long list of grievances that he claimed to have suffered at the hands of the first board of commissioners. He had been subjected to "unprecedented Indignities." His right to design the government buildings had been denied. His map for the city had been snatched away from him, and his name erased from it. His papers had been stolen. He had been abused by the commissioners. He had been insulted and tricked. He had been the hapless victim of spies and intrigues. His health and livelihood had suffered. It was he who had made the federal city possible, L'Enfant reiterated over and over. If the authorities had only listened to him, the disasters of the past decade could have been avoided. Hadn't he warned against trying to finance the city through land sales and speculation? "I conscious of no wrong at my hand done would simply reply but my endeavors were uniformly to the purpose of the enterprize, and the System of my Process likewise the best calculated (known of) to have within the appointed term raised the City a fit Capital for this vast growing Empire," he argued. But the querulous, often incoherent tone of the petitions virtually guaranteed that he would not be taken seriously. For L'Enfant, things would only get worse.

On APRIL 23 Vice President Thomas Jefferson wrote to William Thornton, proposing some alterations in the layout of the Senate chamber. "The preservation of order in a deliberative body depends more than is imagined on the arrangement of the room," he ventured.

With this in mind, he suggested that space be left for people to pass behind the presiding officer's chair, rather than having it permanently attached by its back to the wall, as it was in Philadelphia, so as to prevent senators from walking back and forth in front of him, and disrupting deliberations. He also advised erecting a balustrade close behind the last row of senators' desks, to discourage idle wandering there as well. This was hardly earthshaking. But it was Jefferson's first expression of interest in the Capitol since he had approved Thornton's design in 1792. Jefferson was now running for president, and he was thinking about the quarters that he expected his supporters to occupy when, if all went as he wished, they took office in March 1801.

The election of 1800 was unique in American history, the only instance of a sitting president running head-to-head against his own vice president. Battered though Adams's popularity was—by opposition to the treaty with England, unhappiness with his weak response to the perceived French threat, resentment at the sedition laws, and plain dislike for his cantankerous personality—he intended to run for reelection as the Federalist candidate. That Jefferson would lead the Republican opposition was taken for granted by everyone. The political atmosphere was even more vitriolic than it had been four years earlier. Federalists warned that if the opposition took power a reign of terror would commence in the United States and attacked the freethinking Jefferson once again, as they had in 1796, as a supposed atheist and "infidel," warning that Bibles would have to be hidden from his agents if he was elected. "Suppose such a man as Mr. Jefferson were to hold the reins of government," one partisan Federalist feverishly wrote in *The Centinel of Liberty*. "In a short time, licentiousness and immorality would meet with the most public approbation, every restraint would soon be thrown off, and men would soon bring themselves to be infamous debauchees, assassins, cheats, thieves, liars, hateful and hating one another, a curse upon the earth." They also accused him of fathering children by his slave Sally Hemings, a charge that would be proved true two centuries later by modern DNA analysis. Federal agents took advantage of the sedition law to arrest the strident Republican journalist James Callender, charging him "with intent to influence the coming election of president," for which crime he was sentenced to nine months in prison. Republicans, for their part, trashed Adams as a "repulsive pedant," a madman, a warmonger, a "hideous hermaphroditical character which has neither the force nor firmness of a man, nor the gentleness and sensibility of a woman." No less savage attacks came from some of Adams's putative Federalist friends, who mercilessly attacked their own party's candidate for his eccentricity, rageful personality, incompetence, and—these were Alexander Hamilton's words—"disgusting egotism." Extremists talked again of civil war.

In the middle of the campaign, the discovery of a slave conspiracy barely one hundred miles south of the federal city heightened the atmosphere of instability and danger. The rattled governor of Virginia, James Monroe, told Jefferson, "It is unquestionably the most serious and formidable conspiracy we have ever known of the kind." Led by an enslaved blacksmith named Gabriel, immense numbers of slaves armed with swords made from scythes and a handful of guns allegedly planned to seize the state capitol and armory, set fire to warehouses, and take Monroe hostage. After executing all white men—with the exception of Frenchmen, Methodists, and Quakers, who were considered to support the cause of emancipation—the rebels would escape west to Indian country. White panic probably exaggerated the extent of the conspiracy. But it seems that as many as one hundred rebels did plan to rendezvous on the night of August 31. They were prevented from doing so by a downpour that flooded rivers and roads. The next day, several of the conspirators confessed. The militia was quickly mustered, and swept the countryside, arresting scores of blacks. Rumors of French involvement lent an even more terrifying edge to white fears, linking the bloody specters of Sainte-Domingue and revolutionary France. In all, sixty-five slaves were tried, and twenty-seven hanged. Probably far more would have been executed, but for Jefferson. "There is a strong sentiment that there has been hanging enough," he wrote to Monroe. "The other states and world at large will forever condemn us if we indulge in a principle of revenge, or go one step beyond absolute necessity." Jefferson's moderating sentiments may well have been sincere. But he also understood that it was the wrong moment to alienate Northern voters whose support Jefferson needed in the upcoming election. His running mate, after all, was Aaron Burr, a founding member of the New York Manumission Society. Federalists and Republicans applied equal imagination to turn Gabriel's Rebellion to their advantage. Federalists claimed that the Jeffersonians' loose talk about liberty for all had undermined slaves' loyalty, and charged that the imprisoned James Callender had somehow planned the revolt from his jail cell. Callender retorted that the slaves' plan could only have sprung from the devious brain of Alexander Hamilton.

The Republicans also worked to turn voters against Adams by linking the federal city with popular suspicion of the central government. As the Republican poet Philip Freneau sarcastically put it:

An infant city grows apace,
Intended for a royal race,
Here capitols of an awful height,
Already boast upon the site,
And palaces for embryo kings,
Display their fruits and spread their wings.

Republicans took particular aim at George Washington's proposed mausoleum, a tempting target that for many seemed to encapsulate the imperial pretensions and spendthrift ways of the whole twelve-year-long Federalist reign. At the center of this controversy stood the hapless William Thornton. Upon Washington's death, Thornton had succeeded in having the great man's remains encased in lead, intending that they eventually be interred "in the center of that national temple," the Capitol, "the point from which we calculate our longitudes," as he grandiloquently put it. For the tomb itself, Thornton proposed his own design, a giant allegorical ensemble of figures symbolizing Independence, Victory, Liberty, Peace, Virtue, and Prosperity, with Eternity leading Washington toward a craggy pinnacle 150 feet high, and pointing him upward ready to take flight. Amid the onrush of grief following Washington's death, Congress had voted to place the tomb where Thornton wanted it. Had the mausoleum and monument been built, they would have created a pilgrimage site with unmistakably religious overtones as a focal point for the nation's secular faith in republican government. But it never happened. The first problem was a practical one: money was so short that construction of the rotunda had to be postponed indefinitely, and in the midst of the hard-fought election campaign there was no political will for appropriating new funds to erect a memorial that offended Republican sensibilities. Angry Republicans denounced the whole business as a "monument mania" unfit for the simple citizens of a republic. Callender scoffed that the money would be better spent on shorts and breeches for the impoverished veterans of the Revolutionary War, whom Federalist speculators had stripped to the skin. With both Robert Morris and now John Nicholson in debtors' prison, it was a charge that resonated.

PRESIDENT ADAMS ARRIVED unobtrusively in Washington on November 1. Anna Maria Thornton happened by chance to be looking out the window of a silversmith's shop in George Town, and saw him pass by in his carriage, traveling alone but for a secretary and a single servant, hardly an image of the "monarchical" pretensions for which he was so often unjustly accused. Abigail Adams followed on the sixteenth, after having gotten lost for hours in the dense woods between Baltimore and the capital, with her escort holding down and breaking the boughs of trees to enable them to pass. She found the President's House grand, but a monster of discomfort. Not a single room was finished, closet doors were missing, and a three-hole "necessary" had barely been finished in time for her arrival. The main stairs had not even been installed, and no fewer that thirteen fires had to be kept burning just to make the damp house habitable. "Bells [with which to call the servants] are wholly wanting, not one single one being hung through the whole house, and promises are all you can obtain," she complained in a letter to her sister. "This is so great an inconvenience that I know not what to do, or how to do." Firewood was maddeningly hard to find. (Secretary of the Treasury Wolcott imported his all the way from Philadelphia.) "Surrounded with forests," Abigail went on, "can you believe that wood is not to be had, because people cannot be found to cut and cart it!" Coal, on the other hand, was readily available, but there were no grates to protect the rooms from burning cinders. "We have not the least fence, yard, or other convenience without, and the great unfinished audience-room I make a drying-room of, to hang up the cloaths in." The Southern dependence on slaves also deeply offended her. "The effects of slavery are visible everywhere," she wrote. "The lower order of whites are a grade below the negroes in point of intelligence and ten below them in point of civility. They look like the refuse of human nature; the universal character of the inhabitants is want of punctuality, fair promises—but he who expects performance will rapidly be disappointed." From her window, she observed a crew of twelve slaves clearing construction rubble from the front of the house. She noted that whenever four went off with the carts to dump their loads, the other eight leaned on their shovels. "Two of our hardy N. England men would do as much work in a day as the whole twelve," she wrote in disgust.

The latest in the capital's long history of woeful mishaps occurred on November 8. That night, the family of a carpenter named Jonathan Jackson was mourning his death earlier that day, in his house adjoining the War Department building, at Twenty-first Street and Pennsylvania Avenue. Just what happened was never entirely clear. Possibly heat from too many candles burning around Jackson's coffin set fire to the party wall between the two buildings. The result was a calamity. Along with Jackson's house, most of the new War Department building burned to the ground, taking with it most of the department's records. Jackson's family lost in a single day not only their breadwinner, but also their home, and everything they owned. In any other city, this tragic event would have been recognized as the unfortunate accident that it was. In the federal city, coming as it did at the climax of the election, it took on darker coloration. Voting was still taking place in some districts, and sinister rumors hinted that the Federalists were destroying evidence of their corruption and malfeasance before turning the government over to the opposition.

Because federal elections took place not on a single day at that time, but over a span of weeks, confirmation of the results would not come until December. Further prolonging this already complicated process, in most states the state legislature named the presidential electors. In such states, the key vote thus might take place months in advance of the national canvass. In New York, for instance, a brilliant campaign led by Aaron Burr had, in April, reversed the Federalist majority in the Assembly, handing a pivotal state to the Republicans, and winning for Burr himself the nomination as vice presidential candidate on Jefferson's ticket. By November, a national Republican victory appeared increasingly likely. "The elections as far as I have learned are successful beyond expectation," Jefferson breathlessly reported to James Madison. It was obvious to all, as John Adams prepared to address the first session of Congress in its new home on the Potomac, that his presidency was at an end.

The Republican victory has generally been credited to Burr's New York strategy. However, it is equally true that the Republicans could not have won without the concentrated power of slavery behind them. Under the Constitution's federal ratio, each slave counted as three-fifths of a person for the purpose of establishing the number of seats a state had in the House, and thus also in the Electoral College, which combined the House and Senate numbers for each state. At least twelve of Jefferson's electoral votes reflected the effects of the federal ratio. Had the slave states received no extra votes in 1800, Adams would decisively have won reelection. Jefferson, one Boston newspaper cried, would ride "into the temple of liberty on the shoulders of slaves."

CONGRESS WAS SUPPOSED to convene on November 17, but the Senate could muster only 15 out of 32 members, and the House of Representatives only 42 members out of 106, well short of a quorum in either house. Over the next few days, congressmen and senators trickled into the city from around the country: the eminent Roger Griswold from Connecticut, Quaker abolitionist Robert Waln from Pennsylvania, former Governor Henry Lee from across the river in Virginia, Elmendorf from upstate New York, Spaight from North Carolina, Taliaferro from Georgia. Early arrivals found accommodations at the better taverns, where they might be charged as much as $15 a week for a private room, plus $5 for a temporary servant, and $3 for wood and candles. Latecomers, and the less well-heeled, packed as best they could into boardinghouses and private homes. "I do not perceive how the members of Congress can possibly secure lodgings, unless they will consent to live like scholars in a college, or monks in a monastery, crowded ten or twenty in one house, and utterly secluded from society," Wolcott acerbically commented. He was exaggerating, but not by much. Many congressmen wound up camping on cots, two each to a room so narrow that one member had to remain in bed while the other dressed, and grateful that they had a place to sleep at all.

Five days later, on the twenty-second, enough members had arrived to declare the session open. Only the north wing of the Capitol was complete, so both senators and representatives would have to pack into the Senate's lofty, half-elliptical chamber to hear the president's address. At 10:00 AM, contingents of civic leaders, public officials, soldiers, professional men, and "mechanics" mustered at the Little Hotel, just east of the President's House, and marched along with the president's carriage down Pennsylvania Avenue to the Capitol. There, Adams made his way past the detritus of brick kilns, lumber, and half-cut stones to the tall Georgian door in the building's southeast corner. The smell of fresh plaster, paint, and raw lumber assailed him as he passed through the vestibule, accompanied by the heads of his executive departments, and turned right into the Senate chamber. Bevies of brilliantly dressed ladies filled the columned visitors' gallery, and spilled onto the floor of the chamber, craning their heads as the president entered. Adams bowed to the "vast concourse" of citizens, who rose to greet him. He then made his way to the Speaker's dais, where he seated himself in the large chair that would normally be occupied by the vice president, the Senate's presiding officer. From behind him, high overhead, gazed down a pair of enormous portraits of Louis XVI and Marie Antoinette, gifts to the United States by pre-Revolutionary France, which had hung in Congress Hall in Philadelphia, lending an oddly regal touch to this most republican of moments.

Despite the universal excitement, Anna Maria Thornton reported, the atmosphere was intensely solemn. At noon, Adams lifted his portly bulk and prepared to speak. As he looked out over the crowded amphitheater, he well knew that he stood at a pivotal moment in the nation's short history. Although the election's ultimate outcome was not yet official, he knew that the Federalist ascendancy was over.

It was at this moment that Washington, D.C., became the nation's capital in fact, not merely in aspiration. It was the moment for which so many had labored over the past decade, and that had so often seemed beyond reach. The race against time that began ten years earlier in New York had been won. This wishful city that owed itself to this strange amalgam of regional self-interest, George Washington's idealism, proslavery politics, and greed had become a reality. The nation had its seat of government, and a Capitol far grander than any building that existed in the western hemisphere. The journey to this point had been a much more difficult one than George Washington had imagined when he rode with L'Enfant across the valleys and hills of what was to become the Federal District on that misty morning in 1791, conjuring marble palaces and broad boulevards from oak forests and cornfields. It had taken the labor of many men to make this moment possible: Washington more than anyone, certainly; the unfortunate L'Enfant, of course; the choleric surveyor Andrew Ellicott, and his erudite assistant Benjamin Banneker; the architects Thornton and Hoban; Salisbury, "Negro Henry," Big Jacob, and the other slaves and free white workers whose sweat had gone into the stonework, brickwork, and planking of the President's House and the Capitol. True, the federal city fell far short of the promises that were once blandished by the willing victims of Potomac Fever. Only a few years earlier the capital's prospects looked laughable: now the government was really here. By the end of the year, there would be 3,210 people in the city proper, and more than 14,000 if you counted George Town, Alexandria, and the rural parts of the Federal District. It was a beginning.

Most of Adams's brief speech was devoted to foreign policy and national security. After a decade in which the United States had endured catastrophic wars with the Indians of the Northwest, the near insurrection of the Whiskey Rebellion, and rumblings of war against the two most powerful nations in Europe, Adams could declare without stretching the truth too much that the country was now "prosperous, free, and happy," and safer from foreign foes than it had been for years. Talks were continuing with Great Britain to amicably iron out differences over the Jay Treaty. Negotiations with France would soon bear fruit, too, he hoped. (Although Adams had not yet received news of it, American negotiators had already succeeded in concluding a peace treaty with France, whose new dictator, Napoleon Bonaparte, had formally proclaimed that differences between the two countries were at an end.) Another treaty of friendship had also been inked with the mighty King of Prussia. The United States must strive to preserve harmonious relations with all nations, Adams told Congress, but it must also learn to protect itself with a strong navy, modern coastal defenses, and self-sufficiency in the manufacture of armaments. He also took particular pleasure in announcing the disbandment of the temporary army, and the "patriotic" speed with which soldiers had returned to the status of private citizens. So much for Alexander Hamilton's vaunting military ambitions.

The most eloquent part of the president's speech, however, was devoted to the federal city. Describing the Capitol as "this solemn temple," a choice of words that self-consciously invoked the secular religion that it was intended to embody, he went on to declare, "I congratulate you, gentlemen, on the prospect of a residence not to be changed. Although there is cause to apprehend that accommodations are not now so complete as might be wished"—that was an understatement!—"yet there is great reason to believe that this inconvenience will cease with the present session." His next words were a kind of prayer. Although he did not say so in so many words, he seemed to imply that regardless of where George Washington's tomb might eventually be built, the city itself was his true sepulcher, infused like a living body with his eternal spirit. "May this territory be the residence of virtue and happiness! In this city may that piety and virtue, that wisdom and magnanimity, that constancy and self-government, which adorned the great character whose name it bears be forever held in veneration! Here and throughout our country may simple manners, pure morals, and true religion flourish forever!" Look beyond your present discomfort, he was saying: a great thing has been created here, a city whose meaning for Americans would unfold over time as the country grew great. "You will consider it," he proclaimed, "as the capital of a great nation advancing with unexampled rapidity in arts, in commerce, in wealth, and in population, and possessing within itself those energies and resources which, if not thrown away or lamentably misdirected, will secure to it a long course of prosperity and self-government."

O<small>N</small> F<small>EBRUARY</small> 11 the ballots cast by members of the Electoral College were opened. The election should have ended at this point. But the result exposed an unrecognized flaw in the thinking of the Constitution's authors, and ignited a new political crisis. Thomas Jefferson and his running mate Aaron Burr received seventy-three votes each, a tie. (Adams and his running mate, Charles Pinckney of South Carolina, had received sixty-five and sixty-four votes respectively.) The Constitution, which never contemplated the rise of political parties, made no distinction between candidates for president and those for vice president. It simply stated that if two or more candidates received the same number of votes, the election was to be decided by the House of Representatives. In other words, the Federalist-controlled House would now decide which of the two Republicans was actually to become president. Members were free to make their own decision. Their only obligation was to select the man deemed most fit to govern. Popular will hardly came into it.

In the House, a whole new set of rules applied. Members would vote not as individuals, but collectively by state. Among the Federalists, a movement was afoot to throw the election to Burr, whom many considered more pragmatic, and thus the lesser evil. The atmosphere was tense. Some Federalists openly talked of turning the government over to Chief Justice John Jay or Secretary of State John Marshall, if there was no clear-cut winner. Rumors of a coup swept the city. "A legislative usurpation would be resisted by arms," Jefferson warned James Madison. It was not only Republicans who were worried. Lame duck

President Adams confided to a friend, "We shall be at any rate in the tempestuous sea of liberty for years to come & where the bark can land but in political convulsion I cannot see."

The Republicans initially could count on eight of the states voting for Jefferson, one state short of the needed majority. The first vote was eight states for Jefferson, six for Burr, and two divided. Vote after vote produced the same results. For six days and thirty-six ballots the House remained deadlocked. Finally, on the eighteenth, someone blinked. Swayed by the tide of public opinion in Jefferson's favor, Delaware's sole congressman, Federalist James A. Bayard, decided to abstain, and convinced the Federalist representatives from Maryland and Vermont to do the same, moving those divided states into Jefferson's column, and at last providing the nation with a new president.

On the morning of March 4, Jefferson left his lodgings on New Jersey Avenue and walked the short distance to the Capitol to be sworn in. It was a deliberately democratic gesture, this walk, to visibly contrast his party's proclaimed yeoman manners with the elaborate official carriages that Washington and Adams had favored for state ceremonies. His ascent to the presidency would not produce the disintegration of public morality that Federalists feared. But this Revolution of 1800, as many would later call it, would lead eventually to the weakening of the old entrenched elites, and to the first stirrings of true popular democracy. In his inaugural address to Congress later that day, Jefferson would call memorably for national reconciliation: "We are all Republicans, We are all Federalists," he would declare. The "tempestuous sea of liberty" would subside, for the time being. The first transfer of political power from one political party to another in American history would take place without violence.

Although Jefferson's supporters had often attacked the federal city as an extravagance, he would continue building the Capitol and other public buildings, though not much else. After all, he, too, had a stake in the city's success. But for the dinner with Hamilton and Madison at his New York home in 1790, the capital might never have come to the Potomac. And thanks to him, the country now had a capital that was safe for the men of the South. That long-ago afternoon in New

York, a single enslaved servant had hovered over the table, like a ghostly asterisk marking the equivocal place of slavery in the deal that played out over dinner. Now, as Jefferson walked to the Capitol on this spring morning in 1801, that silent presence had grown vast. Almost a million enslaved Americans walked with him.

O<small>N AUGUST 24, 1814</small>, forty-five hundred battle-hardened British regulars under General Robert Ross overran an outclassed force of Americans at Bladensburg, Maryland, and with the brisk discipline of veteran troops they swung off in an unstoppable red-coated column for the city of Washington, four miles away. Americans had brought this on themselves with an ill-advised declaration of war in 1812. It was true that the British had provocatively seized American ships trading with France, and impressed their sailors into the Royal Navy. However, imperialist jingoes had fanned war fever with dreams of invading Canada and acquiring it for the United States. The land war had been a standoff, at best. Detroit had surrendered to the British without even a fight, while invading American armies had failed dismally in their campaigns to conquer Canada. In 1813 the Americans had provoked outrage by sacking York (present-day Toronto), where they looted private homes and burned down the provincial legislature and governor's residence. Later that year, American raiders had wantonly burned the town of Newark, driving hundreds of helpless refugees including women and children into a blinding snowstorm. Reinforced by troops fresh from the Napoleonic wars, the

British had now brought the war to the gates of the capital, and they were bent on revenge. The American rout was so complete and hectic that those who witnessed it referred to it ever afterward as the "Bladensburg Races." Demoralized militiamen, public officials, and terrified civilians jammed the roads toward George Town and beyond. James Madison, who had succeeded Jefferson as president, fled with his staff into Virginia. Government clerks tried desperately to haul public papers to safety. At the Navy Yard, crews grimly scuttled half-built warships and destroyed precious stocks of provisions, equipment, and weapons, to deny them to the enemy. Although orders were issued to the remaining militia to stand and fight on Capitol Hill, almost no one showed up.

Although Washington's population had now reached eight thousand, it was still a city more in aspiration than in fact. For a few months each year, when Congress was in session, it flickered briefly into cosmopolitan life, and then lapsed once again into provincial lassitude. Fourteen years after the arrival of the government, there was still no *there* there. One local wag, in a satire entitled *The Freaks of Columbia, a Farce*, drily suggested turning the Capitol into a cattle barn and fruit stalls, so that the public would at least derive some benefit from what was now just "a drag horse on the treasury." While the president's whitewashed residence gleamed from its gentle hilltop with snowy brilliance—locals were already calling it the "White House"—the families of working men still occupied flimsy huts and half-finished, half-ruined houses scattered over patches of wasteland. Tradesmen and craftsmen who had purchased property in anticipation of the city's rapid growth had soured with disappointment. "Many of them brought hither have sunk the earnings of a laborious life, which in any other spot would have given to them ease and to their children education," the architect Benjamin H. Latrobe had noted, in 1806. "Distress and want of employment has made many of them sots. Few have saved their capital. Most of them hate, calumniate, or envy each other, for they are all fighting for the scanty means of support which the city affords." The reasons for the capital's stagnation were complex. Among them was the governing Republicans' ideological distaste for large cities (at least American ones), and preference for a capital scaled down to the supposed needs of their mostly rural constituency. However, Thomas Jefferson had during his presidency, from 1801 to 1809, appointed the talented Latrobe to carry on the construction of the public buildings in the magnificent style in which they had been begun. Latrobe, who professed himself a "bigot" on behalf of Grecian aesthetics, had supervised the construction of the Capitol's new South Wing, a splendid vaulted chamber for the Supreme Court, and extensive renovation of William Thornton's North Wing, which was already showing the strains of its shoddy construction, infusing his work with an elegance that surpassed anything wrought by his predecessors, including the jealous Thornton. In a city that had little to boast of, the Capitol was the nation's pride.

By the evening of the twenty-fourth, the redcoats were marching down Maryland Avenue, and approaching the east side of the Capitol. General Ross personally led forward an advance party carrying a flag of truce, intending to demand a ransom not to destroy the city. Then shots rang out from the residence of Albert Gallatin, the former secretary of the treasury, near Second Street—Gallatin, ironically enough, was in Belgium attempting to negotiate an end to the war—killing a British soldier and Ross's horse, which hurled the general to the ground as it collapsed. "All thoughts of accommodation were laid aside," a member of the general's party, George Gleig, later wrote. Soldiers torched Gallatin's house, and then swarmed into both wings of the Capitol. As an officer denounced "this harbour of Yankee democracy" from the House Speaker's chair, soldiers fired rockets through the new chamber's glass-domed roof and smeared gunpowder paste on the walls. Others hacked at window frames, doors, and paneling, tore down the visitors' galleries, and heaped the congressmen's mahogany desks, tables, and chairs into the center of the chamber, and then set everything alight. Nearly all of Latrobe's magnificent work went up in flames: the giant statue of Liberty behind the Speaker's chair, the carved eagle over the rostrum, the exquisite allegorical friezes of Art, Science, and Commerce. Stone cracked under the heat. Fluted columns burned to lime. Glass skylights melted. Roofs collapsed. The invaders' work was even easier in the North Wing, where the Senate chamber's older, dried-out wood ignited with a whooshing roar. Few Americans ventured onto the streets to witness the destruction of the building, which above all others symbolized the proud independence of the United States and the highest ideals of its Founders. It took just hours to turn to ruin the embodied hopes of Washington and L'Enfant, the grandiose designs of Thornton and Latrobe, the laborious work of immigrant masons and enslaved sawyers, all the fruit of a decade's feverish struggle to meet the deadline set by Congress. The redcoats were artists at their work. There would be little left to salvage.

From Capitol Hill, a party of 150 British sailors and marines hastened up Pennsylvania Avenue to the President's House. Dolley Madison had fled in such a panic—the British had threatened to put her on exhibit in London—that the invaders found the presidential table set for forty, with wine in cut glass decanters and joints still roasting on spits before the cookfire. They made short work of the Madisons' dinner, and then ran from room to room, snatching up souvenirs, including the president's hat and dress sword. "Having satisfied their appetites, and partaken freely of the wines, they finished by setting fire to the house which had so liberally entertained them," recalled Gleig. Fifty men surrounded the house with long poles, each with a bundle of oil-soaked rags tied to the end. Once lit, the poles were hurled through the broken windows, setting fire to piles of yellow damask curtains, bedclothes, and delicate furniture. The mahogany doors and windows, the holly and satinwood inlay, the imported windowpanes, the fine brassware crumpled and melted in the flames. Anna Maria Thornton, who witnessed the catastrophe, recalled, "The spectators stood in awful silence, and the heavens redden'd with the blaze."

Acrid smoke from stocks of tar and hemp burning at the Navy Yard filled the humid air, while the blazing public buildings cast a crimson glow over the faces of the soldiers and sailors as they went about their grim business. Along with the nation's proudest buildings and their valuable furnishings, the invaders destroyed records that could never be replaced. The entire Library of Congress with its three thousand books went up in smoke, along with months' worth of the House's accounts, the annals of the Ways and Means Committee, and untold numbers of manuscripts. Apart from the Gallatin house, the British were under orders to avoid destroying private property. In their wake, however, looters swarmed through the wreckage, and broke into private homes left by their fleeing owners, carrying off whatever they could. Among the intrepid Washingtonians who remained in the city that night was the socialite Margaret Bayard Smith, who lay awake with a pistol under her head, and a penknife clasped to her bosom, wondering if the end of the world had come.

She and the few other Washingtonians who remained woke the next morning to find themselves in an occupied city. One contingent of British troops was dispatched to the federal arsenal at Greenleaf Point, where they torched storehouses filled with military supplies and destroyed hundreds of cannon and tens of thousands of small arms. Vast stores of shells, cannonballs, and hand grenades were thrown into the Potomac. Another contingent marched to the building that housed the Departments of State and War. There they were confronted by the only person in any position of authority still in the capital: William Thornton. Thornton had hoped to be appointed overall superintendent of the Federal District by President Jefferson who, to his great disappointment, had instead named him the first director of the U.S. Patent Office, which was lodged in the upper floors of the War Department. But on the morning of August 25, history beckoned to him once again. He pleaded with the kind of idealistic passion that he was so skilled at mustering that there were hundreds of models of wonderful new inventions in the building—all of them private property—and that "to burn them would be like destroying the library of Alexandria, for which the Turks have ever since been condemned by enlightened nations." Amazingly, he succeeded. The troops left. For the next twenty-four hours, Thornton served as the de facto czar of the beleaguered city, dispatching guards to what was left of the Capitol and other smoldering public buildings to deter further looting, and personally accompanying the British occupiers in an effort to limit their ravages. Thornton could justly claim in later life that on the republic's worst day, he had done more than anyone else to protect what remained of his adopted country's patrimony.

The British departed on the evening of the twenty-fifth, bound for Baltimore, which they failed to capture before sailing away for their bloody rendezvous with Andrew Jackson at the Battle of New Orleans. As demoralized Washingtonians pondered the wreckage around them, they struggled to come to grips with what had happened. Most blamed the destruction on imaginary spies and traitors, rather than their incompetent generals, outclassed troops, or their city's indefensible location.

On September 19, the Thirteenth Congress returned to Washington, packing uncomfortably into Thornton's cramped Patent Office, the only significant public space left to the government of the United States. Many of them were old enough to remember the pompous boasts of the early 1790s, such as that of George Washington, that "no place, either north or south of this, can be more effectually secured against the attack of an Enemy."

Back in 1812 the jingoes had promised an easy victory. Two years later, the country was bankrupt, commerce was paralyzed, the army was humiliated, and the capital's shocking vulnerability had been exposed for all to see. Nevertheless the war hawks were still full of bombast, proclaiming lost battles to have been heroic victories, and the British withdrawal from Washington a panicked retreat. Forgetting the barbarities that Americans had perpetrated in Canada, they scathingly condemned the British as "Vandals" who had "trampled the usages of civilized warfare." Northerners who had opposed the war from the beginning were a lot less sanguine. Anger at the administration's inept prosecution of the war fused with long-simmering unhappiness over the half-built capital. Years of pent-up discontent boiled over. In the minds of many congressmen, possibly a majority, it was time to abandon the Potomac.

The debate that ensued foreshadowed the struggle for power that would soon take place between North and South, and that would dominate the nation's politics until the Civil War. The argument for removal was made mostly by a succession of New York congressmen, primarily Jonathan Fisk, who proposed the immediate removal of the government northward to a place of greater security. Both Philadelphia and Lancaster had offered immediate accommodation. The members of the government must not only be safe, Fisk argued, they must also be seen to be so by the nation at large, and by the centers of finance that were being asked to lend the government money. "Menace this safety, and public confidence is impaired, public credit is shaken," he declared. Were congressmen to wait supinely until the enemy returned, Thomas P. Grosvenor demanded, "and be dragged from our seats, the President stolen?" What was there to prevent the city from being sacked again? Nothing! What if the members of Congress and the president were to be captured? Moreover, Grosvenor added, it would cost untold sums to replace the buildings that had been destroyed, and to pay the tens of thousands of troops who would be required to defend the city—if it could be defended at all by militiamen who had already disgraced the nation by their cowardice at Bladensburg.

Southerners, always alert to any perceived attempt to weaken their disproportionate power, retorted that moving the seat of government would be an act of cowardice and an admission of defeat. The British wanted to drive the government from the Potomac: therefore the government must stay. North Carolina's Joseph Pearson, who presented the fullest expression of the South's position, proclaimed that he would rather sit under a tent in the city than move one mile out of it to live in a palace. To carp about the cost of defending the city was simply too unpatriotic to take seriously. Abandoning Washington would betray everyone who had ceded land to the government, bought property there, and invested in its development. Were a free people, Pearson demanded, choosing a decidedly inapt analogy, "thus to be sported with, thus to be bought and sold like the slaves of Jamaica?" (He might just as well have said the slaves of North Carolina, but never mind.) Gathering steam, he reminded his fellow congressmen of the "passions and jealousies" that had attended the debates over the site of the capital in 1789 and 1790, and that if again aroused might well "shake the Union to its centre." Altering their predecessors' intent was far too reckless even to contemplate. "Thus by a sort of legislative legerdemain we put the Government on wheels and push off at full gallop," he warned, deploying an exceptionally vivid metaphor that must have evoked to his mostly country-bred listeners the homely yet terrifying image of a farm wagon packed with one's belongings careening wildly along those famously potholed roads, its contents flying out in every direction. The capital was intended to be *permanent*: it must not be changed.

In the end it all came down to simple numbers, down to the formula that had been enshrined to placate slaveholders at the Constitutional Convention nearly forty years earlier. The opposing sides split sharply along regional lines, with almost every member from north of Maryland calling for removal, and nearly every Southerner just as adamant about remaining on the Potomac. President Madison also opposed the move. Back in 1790 he had helped to cut the deal with Jefferson and Hamilton that had established the capital on the Potomac. Despite the dismal sight of the ruined White House, easily visible from his cramped temporary quarters in the former home of the French minister, he hadn't changed his mind. On October 6, the Northerners won by a vote of seventy-two to seventy-one on a nonbinding resolution to abandon Washington. But when a vote was called on the decisive third reading of the bill, opponents of removal managed to round up enough supporters to defeat the measure by eighty-three to seventy-four. Just five votes decided the fate of the capital. The margin of victory hinged once again on the extra seats that had been bestowed on slaveholders by the Constitution, guaranteeing them extra representation for three-fifths of their enslaved population. (Overall the slave states enjoyed about one-third more seats in Congress than their free white population warranted, amounting to a bonus of fourteen seats in 1793 and seventeen in 1814.) Congress, usually so stingy when it came to appropriations for the national capital, would somehow find the money—an estimated $1.2 million—to rebuild. President Madison wrote upon the passage of a law for reconstruction that it would not "deviate from the models destroyed farther than material and manifest conveniency or general and known opinion." That is, everything was to be rebuilt exactly as it had been before. The seat of government had once again been captured by the Potomac thanks to the power of American slavery.

A s determined as they were to keep the capital on the Potomac, the Southern members of the Thirteenth Congress could not be encouraged by the desolation that they saw around them. The capital's population continued to creep upward, but it would be many years before any sane person dared to suggest that the aspirational "metropolis of America" could seriously rival the burgeoning entrepôts of nineteenth-century America, much less those of Europe. At the end of the 1820s, real estate in the district was selling for only one-half, or even one-quarter, of

what it had in 1794. A few years later, the aged Daniel Carroll of Duddington, the razing of whose house had initiated L'Enfant's downfall,
would write, "After nearly half a century the result is now fully known;
the unfortunate proprietors are generally brought to ruin, and some with
scarcely enough to buy daily food for their families. The subject is now so
truly frightful to me that I hate to think of it, much less write of it." As late
as 1841, when the Federal District's population was more than thirty-five
thousand (not counting Alexandria, which was soon to vote to reaffiliate
itself with Virginia, or "retrocede"), the visiting Charles Dickens would
describe a landscape of lingering desolation. It wasn't a pretty picture. "It
is sometimes called the City of Magnificent Distances, but it might with
greater propriety be termed the City of Magnificent Intentions: Spacious
avenues, that begin in nothing, and lead nowhere; streets, mile-long, that
only want houses, roads, and inhabitants; public buildings that need but
a public to be complete; and ornaments of great thoroughfares, which
only lack great thoroughfares to ornament are its leading features," he
wryly observed, adding: "Plough up all the roads; plant a great deal of
coarse turf in every place where it ought *not* to be; erect three handsome
buildings in stone and marble, anywhere, but the more entirely out of
everybody's way the better, make it scorching hot in the morning, and
freezing cold in the afternoon, with an occasional tornado of wind and
dust; leave a brick-field without the bricks, in all central places where a
street may naturally be expected: and that's Washington."

The Republican aversion to cities accounted for a portion of
the capital's doldrums. Geography was also partly responsible. The
Potomac River never became the nation's highway to the interior of the
continent. George Washington's rhetorical excesses couldn't change
physical reality: the route made no real sense, since at best the river was
navigable only in flood, about forty days each year. Despite decades of
dredging and canal-building, the Patowmack Company failed to turn a
profit. Then, in the 1820s, the Erie Canal created precisely the national
artery to the West that Washington and his cronies had dreamed of, but
it was New York City that benefited, rapidly becoming just the kind of
dynamic commercial metropolis that Washington would never be.

But nothing had done more to subvert the city's hopes than the swindling manipulations of the speculators. Their domination of the market and their cataclysmic collapse scared away trustworthy investors and immigrants for years, indeed for decades afterward. Litigation over Robert Morris's Washington holdings would still be underway in the 1840s, and it would be almost a century before his tangled estate was finally settled. In an age more skeptical of unregulated private enterprise, exposure of the speculators' activities would have rocked the government. For the speculators themselves, the results only vaguely approximated justice. John Nicholson had died a pauper, in 1800. Perhaps he remembered, in his last hours, the kindly words of one of the grateful African American picnickers at the founding of St. Thomas's church, which he had helped to finance, in 1793: "May you live long, sir, and when you die, may you not die eternally." Robert Morris, after his release from the Prune Street prison in 1801, lived on for another five years in Philadelphia, on a modest pension arranged for him by Gouverneur Morris. What was left of his tangled estate would remain in litigation for almost a century. James Greenleaf, the most shameless of all the speculators, alone escaped serious punishment. Following a brief stint in debtors' prison, he married the daughter of a well-connected Pennsylvanian and recouped his fortune developing land around Allentown.

Among the capital's principal founders, only L'Enfant consistently opposed speculation. He had warned George Washington that to exploit the city's real estate to pay for its development would "destroy the capital from the very beginning," and urged the government instead to borrow the money that was needed, and then sell the land later at a higher value. History would vindicate the engineer's skepticism. However, he was already a spent force before Morris and his partners arrived on the scene. Later, in its attempt to climb out of the wreckage left by the speculators, Congress partially followed his advice, in the form of federal loan guarantees. By then it was of course too late to save L'Enfant, whose prickly personality had long before destroyed his value to the project. In later years, his forlorn figure was a common sight stumping around the city, "the picture of famine," in the words of Latrobe, accompanied only by his dog. He was eventually taken up as a charity case by Thomas Digges, who provided the indigent major with a home on his estate just outside the district. L'Enfant died in 1825 at the age of seventy; he was buried in the Digges family graveyard, next to the family's slaves. His property at his death consisted of three watches, three compasses, some books, maps, and small collection of surveying instruments, worth about $45. L'Enfant deserved better. But he, too, was partly responsible for the depressing emptiness that almost every early visitor to Washington remarked on. The twentieth-century architectural critic Lewis Mumford observed that L'Enfant's plan was essentially "baroque," that is, a cityscape designed for absolutism, regularity, and display, epitomized by theatrically wide boulevards that might be splendid for military parades, but that made no allowance for the organic life of a city inhabited mostly by ordinary men and women whose daily work, shopping, and desire for community would have been better facilitated by the kind of homely urban grid, such as Philadelphia's, that L'Enfant despised. For almost a hundred years, Washington grew with virtually no thought to L'Enfant's original intentions. At the turn of the twentieth century, a new generation of planners would rediscover and celebrate his vision, at a time when the wealth, power, and global ambitions of the United States at last began to match the scale of the major's imperial dreams.

By contrast to the unfortunate L'Enfant, William Thornton enjoyed comfort and public respect as a member of the early capital's elite. In its own way, however, his life too was a study in failed promise. To the end of his days, he believed that too much of the credit for his work on the Capitol had unjustly been attributed to Benjamin Latrobe and other latecomers. Poor remittances from his estate in Tortola, speculations gone bad, and his unconquerable passion for fast horses gnawed at his fortune. His investment in John Fitch's steamboat came to naught. None of his inventions caught the popular fancy. He never rose to higher rank than director of the Patent Office. Despite disappointment, he always remained an idealist, in his wife's words, "a friend to the oppressed of all nations and colors." His evangelical enthusiasm for the deportation of freed slaves to Africa was finally redeemed, to his satisfaction if not to that of most African Americans, by the founding of the American Colonization Society in 1816 and the subsequent establishment of Liberia as a haven for the emancipated. On his deathbed, Thornton told a minister that he did not think that any person aiding that society needed to dread the hereafter. When he died, in 1828, he still owned a half-share in his family's Tortola plantation and its 120 slaves.

Thornton's compromise with slavery was a microcosm of the nation's. Slavery infused the capital from its inception, and continued to shape its daily life in a multitude of ways. Between 1800 and 1840 the number of slaves in the city proper rose from 623 to 1,713, and from 3,244 to 4,694 in the Federal District as a whole. (Because the total population grew at a faster rate, from 3,210 in 1800 to 23,364 in 1840, the proportion of slaves in the city declined from 19 percent of the total to about 7 percent in 1840 and eventually to 4 percent in 1860.) Especially in the early decades, slaves did most of the capital's hard labor, opened its doors, cooked its meals, drove its carriages and wagons, cleaned its chimneys, and tended its children; in the 1850s, an enslaved ironmonger would forge the statue of Freedom that stands atop the Capitol.

Yet Washington was not entirely like the rest of the South. The number of free blacks in the city proper grew from 123 in 1800 to 4,808 in 1840 and to more than 18,000 in 1860, as emancipated slaves and fugitives from the surrounding region migrated there in search of work. The presence of Northern legislators, judges, appointed officials, and other antislavery whites enabled local blacks to live marginally freer lives than outside the Federal District. Black schools and churches flourished. Free blacks were permitted to testify in court, own businesses and real estate, and mingle with whites at public events. Individuals who alleged that they had been illegally enslaved were also allowed to sue in court, although it was a right that was perhaps honored more frequently in the breach than in the observance. At the same time, discriminatory laws required each free African American to post a "peace bond" of $20 with a respectable white man as a guarantee of good behavior, and to carry a certificate of freedom signed by three whites, vouching for the bearer's unblemished character. Those lacking such documents were liable to be arrested and sold into slavery to pay their jail fees.

Nonetheless, wedged as it was between two slave states, Washington rapidly developed into a hub of the domestic slave trade, serving as a collection depot for surplus slaves to be shipped southward. As the marble halls of Congress rang with Southerners' stentorian defense of slavery, members could gaze from the Capitol's windows on heartrending processions of men, women, and children bound with ropes and chains, trudging to the pens of the thirty or more slave traders who did business in the nation's capital. On Thursdays, the auctioneer's cry resounded from the slave market that stood on Pennsylvania Avenue, on the future site of the National Archives. The country's largest slave trading company, Franklin and Armfield, based in Alexandria, kept two transports in constant service, shipping out an estimated one thousand slaves annually. Alexandria's "retrocession" to Virginia in 1846 was attributable, at least in part, to a desire to protect that city's lucrative slave trade from interference by increasingly assertive Yankee congressmen and the Underground Railroad. One of retrocession's advocates was George Washington Parke Custis, Martha Washington's grandson and heir, and the self-appointed custodian of George Washington's reputation and legend.

At the outbreak of the Civil War in 1861 there were still 3,185 enslaved men and women in the Federal District. Among them was a "well made," "chestnut colored," sixty-seven-year-old man named Charles Young, one of eighteen slaves belonging to Henry Naylor. One year later, after the South's secession and under abolitionist pressure, Congress at last voted to emancipate the district's remaining slaves, and to reimburse up to $300 per slave to politically loyal masters. (Before the war, healthy young slaves were worth five times that much in the marketplace.) The records of the federal commission that evaluated masters' claims are now in the National Archives, where they provide poignant, if tantalizingly hazy, insight into the lives of these men and women who embodied the capital's oldest and most shameful tradition. Charles Young, judging from his name, may have begun life as the property of Notley Young, or one of the other branches of the Young family, who were among the most prominent local landowners when the Federal District was laid out. Having been born in 1795 he may well have witnessed firsthand the city's emergence from plantations and groves. Perhaps someone had even pointed out to the small boy the larger-than-life figure of George Washington chasing his vision of the future over the forested hills. In 1862 Young was an old man, and used up—Naylor valued him at only $200—but this was his city, too. He had given his life to it, as had many thousands of enslaved men and women, beginning with Salisbury, Big Jacob, and their comrades in the 1790s. And he was, as much as anyone, an heir to its aspirations and its founding deceptions.

Only once was removal of the capital again seriously debated. After the Civil War, a rising tide of petitions from Midwesterners called upon Congress to uproot the capital—still a shabby, helter-skelter sprawl of undistinguished buildings and depressingly empty vistas—and to move it closer to the center of the growing country, for example to St. Louis, where a national convention for selecting a new site was held in 1869. Leave George Washington's ashes behind on the Potomac and follow those of Abraham Lincoln westward, urged former Union General John A. Logan, now a powerful and ambitious congressman from Illinois. As settlement spread ever more rapidly from coast to coast, such proposals made sense. President Ulysses S. Grant, elected in 1868, would have none of it, however. He made it clear that he would veto any law to abandon the city that the Union had spent so much blood defending, however unloved Washington might be, unless the bill was supported by a two-thirds vote in both houses of Congress. He held that the agreement that had established the seat of government on the Potomac in 1790 enjoyed virtually Constitutional stature, and ought not to be undone with anything less than the degree of support required for Constitutional amendments. Instead, throughout his two terms in office, Grant vigorously prodded Congress to appropriate funds to improve the city's infrastructure, and to ornament it with architecture that would, in his words, finally "merit the just pride of the American people." Republican administrations continued Grant's commitment through the Gilded Age and beyond, paving its famously muddy boulevards, and encouraging architects to beautify its forlorn avenues with solemn monuments, greenswards, and majestic new public buildings that reflected America's swelling power and international influence. Although the city that George Washington, Thomas Jefferson, and James Madison anchored to the slaveholding South in 1790 remained Southern in tone until well into the twentieth century, it was no longer a mere "seat of government" that might figuratively be put on wheels and rolled from place to place, as Joseph Pearson of North

Carolina had put it back in 1814. It had become a true national capital that both physically and symbolically reflected the supremacy of the federal government over the once fractious states.

The establishment of Washington, D.C., was, at least in part, rooted in fictions: that the Potomac was destined to become the high road to the West, that there was no better location for the seat of government, that land speculators could do for the nation what its elected officials would not, that executive privilege could shield Congress and the public from unpleasant truths, and that—the biggest illusion of all—slavery had little or nothing to do with putting the capital on the Potomac in the first place. Yet, in spite of everything—in spite of the tainting infection of slavery, the financial fakery, and all the unfulfilled promises—the capital was a success, even of epic proportions. Nothing even remotely like it had ever before been undertaken in North America. Lack of money, a plan beyond the nation's financial and engineering abilities, constricted vision, flagging political will, public weariness of a project that seemed never to end—anything might have brought the plan to a crashing halt long before 1800.

It would be an exaggeration to say that the creation of Washington, D.C., saved the United States from collapse, but perhaps not by much. When members of Congress debated the location of the seat of government in 1790 they repeatedly warned of the ever-present danger that regional rivalries would spin out of control and shatter the union into a pack of squabbling statelets. The building of the federal city was not only a determined, but also a *desperate* attempt to create a massive symbol that would embody the spirit of a nation that barely yet existed. At their best, the capital's founders saw the United States not merely as a new kind of government, but as Thomas Jefferson memorably put it, a "signal of arousing men to burst the chains under which monkish ignorance and superstition had persuaded them to bind themselves," bequeathing to Americans a sense of global mission that persists to the present day. The city of Washington was then, and still is, the most potent physical symbol of that national ideology. As Georgia Congressman James Jackson said of the seat of government during the debates of 1790, "It might be compared to the heart in the human body. It was a center from which the principles of life were carried to the extremities." The creation of the city, or at least its embryo, and its two most important and emblematic buildings, the Capitol and the White House, set the pattern for the great national engineering—and, if less obviously, political—projects of the future, such as the National Road in the early 1800s, the Transcontinental Railroad later in the century, the Tennessee Valley Authority, and other ambitious public projects in the twentieth century. Perhaps more important, the painful, decade-long birthing of the federal city fostered in rivalrous, shortsighted, and self-interested political men a dawning sense of common aspiration, a determination that their first great collective project, like the national enterprise as a whole, must be made to work.

What if the compromise of 1790 had gone another way, or if the project had simply failed? The seat of government probably would have remained in Philadelphia or its suburbs, giving the United States a Northern capital, instead of a Southern one. Philadelphia was not just any Yankee city either, but a hotbed of progressive thinking and of antislavery activity. Northerners rather than proslavery Southerners would have filled the ranks of government service, and Southern congressmen would have witnessed the success of Pennsylvania's policy of peaceful emancipation, and the enlarged capabilities of free African Americans like Absalom Jones and Richard Allen. Just months before George Washington's death, blacks led by Jones had petitioned Congress to grant them full citizenship, proclaiming, "We beseech that as we are *men*, we may be admitted to partake of the Liberties and unalienable Rights therein held forth" in the Constitution. It is hard to imagine that even a Southern-dominated Congress based in Philadelphia would have voted repeatedly through the first half of the nineteenth century to protect and extend slavery, and to ruthlessly suppress even the most hesitant debate over it. The freer air of a Northern capital might have reshaped the thinking of proslavery congressmen, and eased the nation toward a peaceful solution of its most divisive issue. That's one scenario. There is another. Southern congressmen might not have tolerated abolitionist assaults on their prerogatives any more willingly in Philadelphia than they did on the Potomac. Secession might have occurred long before 1861, when the disparities of wealth and population between the sections were much narrower, Northern industry was far less advanced, and Northern whites were much less willing to take up arms against slavery. Ironically, although he was an abolitionist at heart, George Washington did more than any other man to bestow upon the country he loved a capital that was shackled to slavery. But by doing so, he may have saved the United States from a civil war that the free North might well have lost.

T ODAY SOME 550,000 Washingtonians live at the core of a linear megalopolis with millions of inhabitants, extending deep into Maryland and Virginia. The tacit assumption that the capital would always be a white man's city—no one even remotely imagined otherwise in the 1790s—has also been overthrown by time: today 57 percent of the city's inhabitants, most of the leading members of its municipal government, and a significant portion of its business establishment are African American. The skeleton of L'Enfant's grand plan survives, adapted to the exigencies of modern life. His boulevards continue to shape (and confuse) the flow of traffic, nudging the eye toward the majestic symmetries that lie half-buried, like an elegant palimpsest, beneath the modern cityscape. The White House remains where L'Enfant put it, although a more fearful age has hemmed it in with fences, barriers, and rings of invisible security to a degree that would have profoundly dismayed Americans of the 1790s, who expected even their highest officials to be easy of access, and available to them at almost any time. The Capitol, too, remains what the Founders intended, much larger and grander than it was two centuries ago, of course, but still framed by the proportions sketched by William Thornton on the steamy island of Tortola, and more than ever a magnet to the eye, proof to all of the astonishing persistence of American democracy.

There have also been drastic transformations. Commuters to Washington today travel daily into the city from the vicinity of the Conococheague, a river so remote and wild-sounding to the Americans of the 1790s that it was said that maidens blushed at its very name. Americans no longer worry about losing their way, as Abigail Adams did, in the forests between Baltimore and the capital, while the corrugated post roads that rattled the bones of early America lie buried beneath the concrete of I–95 and the web of superhighways that link Washington with the rest of the country. Today's travelers may still share Abigail's frustration, however: where she was delayed by overgrown thickets, they suffer the modern agonies of traffic congestion. The Potomac River has diminished not only in the nation's dreams, but also in fact, having been narrowed by extensive landfills and largely obscured to the eye by the vertical sprawl of the modern city. Similarly, the city's picturesque hills have been paved over as completely as the human-sized political machinery of the late eighteenth century has disappeared into the behemoth of twenty-first-century government, with its legions of bureaucrats, lobbyists, consultants, analysts, advocates, lawyers private and public, courtiers of the media, and the attendant thousands who serve them. Were Peter L'Enfant to somehow return to life, he would doubtless find more than a few modern Americans ready to agree with his fear that the moral simplicity of the Revolutionary age might someday give way to political deceit, self-interest, and scheming ambition to betray the lofty ideals that he wished so much to embed in the nation's new capital. But then L'Enfant was a bit of an innocent even in the feral political jungle of the 1790s.

N O T E S

PROLOGUE

Page

1   With native industry in its infancy: *New-York Daily Gazette*, June 14, 1790; Jacques-Pierre Brissot de Warville, *New Travels in the United States of America*, 1788, trans. Mara Soceanu Vamos and Durand Echeverria, ed. Durand Echeverria (Cambridge: Harvard University Press, 1964), pp. 110–11, 121; James A. Bear Jr., and Lucia C. Stanton, eds., *Jefferson's Memorandum Books*, vol. 1 (Princeton: Princeton University Press, 1997), pp. 758–60.

2   For a decade: Forrest McDonald, *Alexander Hamilton: A Biography* (New York: W. W. Norton & Co., 1982), pp. 163–68; Richard Brookhiser, *Alexander Hamilton, American* (New York: Free Press, 1999), pp. 83–86; Elizabeth M. Nuxoll, "The Financier as Senator: Robert Morris of Pennsylvania, 1789–1795," in Kenneth R. Bowling and Donald R. Kennon, eds., *Neither Separate nor Equal: Congress in the 1790s* (Athens: Ohio University Press, 2000), pp. 96–99; *Pennsylvania Gazette*, October 10, 1787, and November 5, 1788; Brissot de Warville, *New Travels in the United States*, p. xxii.

2   No one really knew: William Maclay, *The Diary of William Maclay and Other Notes on Senate Debates*, ed. Kenneth R. Bowling and Helen E. Veit (Baltimore: Johns Hopkins University Press, 1988), pp. 27–29; Joseph J. Ellis, *His Excellency: George Washington* (New York: Knopf, 2004), p. 193; *Pennsylvania Gazette*, May 7, 1789.

2   "The people should have": Online at www.senate.gov/artandhistory/minute/State_ Houses_Elect_Senators.

2   James Jackson, a congressman: McDonald, *Alexander Hamilton*, p. 174.

2   During debates, many: Charlene Bangs Bickford, Kenneth R. Bowling, William Charles diGiacomantonio, and Helen E. Veit, eds., *Documentary History of the First Federal Congress of the United States of America*, vol. XII (Baltimore: Johns Hopkins University Press, 1992–1996), pp. xiii–xiv; United States Senate Web site www.senate.gov/artandhistory.

3   Only a small percentage: *Pennsylvania Gazette*, January 7, 1789; McDonald, *Alexander Hamilton*, pp. 118–20; Stephen L. Schechter and Richard B. Bernstein, *Well Begun: Chronicles of the Early National Period* (Albany: New York State Commission on the Bicentennial of the United States Constitution, 1989), p. 19.

3   Inside Congress and out: Brookhiser, *Alexander Hamilton*, pp. 75–76; Joseph J. Ellis, *American Sphinx: The Character of Thomas Jefferson* (New York: Vintage, 1998), pp. 143–44; *Pennsylvania Gazette*, October 10, 1787, and November 5, 1788; Lawrence Goldstone, *Dark Bargain: Slavery, Profits, and the Struggle for the Constitution* (New York: Walker & Co., 2005), pp. 36–37.

3   "these separate independencies": Thomas Jefferson, "The Anas," in *Writings* (New York: The Library of America, 1984), p. 663.

4   "To those Americans": Kenneth R. Bowling, *The Creation of Washington, D.C.: The Idea and Location of the Federal Capital* (Fairfax, Va.: George Mason University Press, 1991), p. 6.

5   no fewer than thirty: *Pennsylvania Gazette*, March 18, 1789; Kenneth R. Bowling, *Creating the Federal City, 1774–1800: Potomac Fever* (Washington: American Institute of Architects Press, 1988), pp. 23–37, 61–67; Bickford, et. al., *Documentary History*, vol. XI, pp. 1414, 1429–30; Garry Wills, *"Negro President": Jefferson and the Slave Power* (Boston: Houghton Mifflin, 2003), pp. 205–7.

5   "deficiency of accommodation": "Notes on the Permanent Seat of Congress," in Saul K. Padover, ed., *Thomas Jefferson and the National Capital* (Washington: United States Government Printing Office, 1946), pp. 6–9.

5   "a set of strolling players": *New-York Daily Gazette*, June 14, 1790.

6   "It might be compared": Bickford, et. al., *Documentary History*, vol. XI, p. 1338.

6   "mistress of the western world": Quoted in Bowling, *Creating the Federal City*, p. 11.

6   The city's founders intended: Bowling, *The Creation of Washington, D.C.*, p. 11; François-Alexandre-Frédéric, duc de la Rochefoucauld-Liancourt, *Travels through the United States of North America, the Country of the Iroquois and Upper Canada, in the Years 1795, 1796, and 1797*, vol. 2 (London: R. Phillips, 1799), p. 312.

7   "radicals and rye coffee": Thomas Law, *A Reply to Certain Insinuations* (Washington: n.p., 1824).

7   "While we had": *Pennsylvania Gazette*, September 9, 1789.

 CHAPTER 1: THE NEW MACHINE OF GOVERNMENT

Page

12   Few men were more in demand: Digges-L'Enfant-Morgan Papers, LOC; Kenneth R. Bowling, *Peter Charles L'Enfant: Vision, Honor and Male Friendship in the Early American Republic* (Washington: The Friends of the George Washington University Libraries, 2002), pp. ix, 4–5, 11–14; Elizabeth S. Kite, *L'Enfant and Washington, 1791–1792* (Baltimore: The Johns Hopkins Press, 1929), pp. 2–5, 14; Scott W. Berg, *Grand Avenues: The Story of the French Visionary Who Designed Washington, D.C.* (New York: Pantheon, 2007), pp. 17ff; Iris Miller, *Washington in Maps, 1606–2000* (New York: Rizzoli International Publications, 2002), p. 15.

13   However, it was L'Enfant's transformation: William Maclay, *The Diary of William Maclay and Other Notes on Senate Debates*, ed. Kenneth R. Bowling and Helen E. Veit (Baltimore: Johns Hopkins University Press, 1988), pp. 3–4; *Pennsylvania Gazette*, June 6, 1790; Charlene Bangs Bickford, Kenneth R. Bowling, William Charles diGiacomantonio, and Helen E. Veit, eds., *Documentary History of the First Federal Congress of the United States of America*, vol. XII (Baltimore: Johns Hopkins University Press, 1992–1996), pp. xiii–xiv; Kite, *L'Enfant and Washington*, pp. 9–12; Bowling, *Peter Charles L'Enfant*, p. 18; John A. Kouwenhoven, *The Columbia Historical Portrait of New York* (New York: Harper & Row, 1972), pp. 82–85; James Duane to Peter Charles L'Enfant, October 13, 1789, Digges-L'Enfant-Morgan Papers, LOC; *New York Morning Post and Daily Advertiser*, March 14, 1789.

13   "vamped up Jimcrackery": Quoted in Bowling, *Peter Charles L'Enfant*, p. 14.

14   By European standards: Maclay, *Diary of William Maclay*, p. 270; *New-York Daily Gazette*, February 19, 1790, and June 9, 1790; Jacques-Pierre Brissot de Warville, *New Travels in the United States of America, 1788*, trans. Mara Soceanu Vamos and Durand Echeverria, ed. Durand Echeverria (Cambridge: Harvard University Press, 1964), pp. 80–90; Thomas Janvier, *In Old New York* (New York: Harper & Brothers, 1894), pp. 50, 202–3; Bayrd Still, *Mirror for Gotham: New York as Seen by Contemporaries from Dutch Days to the Present* (New York: Fordham University Press, 1994), pp. 68–78; Kouwenhoven, *Columbia Historical Portrait*, pp. 76, 87, 94–97; Elizabeth Blackmar, *Manhattan for Rent, 1785–1850* (Ithaca, N.Y.: Cornell University Press, 1989), pp. 38–45, 86; Edwin G. Burrows and Mike Wallace, *Gotham: A History of New York City to 1898* (New York: Oxford University Press, 1999), p. 301; Shane White, *Somewhat More Independent: The End of Slavery in New York City, 1770–1810* (Athens: University of Georgia Press, 1991), pp. 26–29, 165, 197–200.

14   "vortex of folly": Maclay, *Diary of William Maclay*, p. 284.

14   "the new machine of government": *New-York Daily Gazette*, June 1, 1790.

14   President Washington was suffering: *New-York Daily Gazette*, June 9, 1790; Burrows and Wallace, *Gotham*, pp. 299–300; Kenneth R. Bowling, letter to author, August 20, 2006.

15   Failure "will lay a foundation": *Pennsylvania Gazette*, March 18, 1789.

15   Congress had voted: *Pennsylvania Gazette*, September 9, 1789, and September 16, 1789.

15   The opening shots: *Pennsylvania Gazette*, September 9, 1789; Bickford, et. al., *Documentary History*, vol. XI, p. 1400, and vol. XII, pp. xiii–xiv; Willis L. Shirk Jr., "Wright's Ferry: A Glimpse into the Susquehannah Backcountry," *The Pennsylvania Magazine of History and Biography* 120 (January/April 1996); Kenneth R. Bowling, *The Creation of Washington, D.C.: The Idea and Location of the American Capital* (Fairfax, Va.: George Mason University Press, 1991), pp. 134–38; Bowling, *Creating the Federal City, 1774–1800: Potomac Fever* (Washington: American Institute of Architects Press, 1988), pp. 32–34; William V. Cox, *Celebration of the One Hundredth Anniversary of the Establishment of the Seat of Government in the District of Columbia* (Washington: U.S. Government Printing Office, 1901), p. 102.

16   The idea of a Susquehanna capital: *New-York Daily Gazette*, June 10, 11, 28, 29, and 30, 1790, and September 2, 1790; *Pennsylvania Gazette*, September 9 and 21, 1790; Robert Morris to Molly Morris, 28 August 1789, 6 September 1789, 9 September 1789, 11 September 1789, and 20 September 1789. Robert Morris Collection, Huntington Library, San Marino, CA.

16   Congressman Richard Bland Lee: Bickford, et. al., *Documentary History*, vol. XI, pp. 1400–1402, 1412–16; Bowling, *Creating the Federal City*, pp. 138–40.

16   Of the 3,929,827 Americans: Peter Kolchin, *American Slavery, 1619–1877* (New York: Hill & Wang, 1993), pp. 25–27, 242.

17   Slaves had helped: Gary B. Nash, *The Forgotten Fifth: African Americans in the Age of Revolution* (Cambridge: Harvard University Press, 2006), pp. 7–15, 23, 26–36; Henry Wiencek, *An Imperfect God: George Washington, His Slaves, and the Creation of America* (New York: Farrar, Straus and Giroux, 2003), pp. 190, 200–202, 220, 243–46; David Brion Davis, *Inhuman Bondage: The Rise and Fall of Slavery in the New World* (New York: Oxford University Press, 2006), pp. 146–48; Kolchin, *American Slavery*, pp. 72–73; Oscar Reiss, *Blacks in Colonial America* (Jefferson, N.C.: McFarland & Co., 1997), pp. 242–53; Fritz Hirschfeld, *George Washington and Slavery: A Documentary Portrayal* (Columbia: University of Missouri Press, 1997), pp. 100–101; James Oliver Horton and Lois E. Horton, *In Hope of Liberty: Culture, Community and Protest Among Northern Free Blacks, 1700–1860* (New York: Oxford University Press, 1997), pp. 60–61.

17   "Blush ye pretended": Quoted in Bernard Bailyn, *The Ideological Origins of the American Revolution* (Cambridge: Harvard University Press, 1967) p. 240.

18   There was widespread optimism: John C. Miller, *The Wolf by the Ears: Thomas Jefferson and Slavery* (Charlottesville: University Press of Virginia, 1991), p. 30; Joseph J. Ellis, *Founding Brothers: The Revolutionary Generation* (New York: Vintage, 2002), pp. 89–96, 102; Nash, *The Forgotten Fifth*, pp. 17–22; Kolchin, *American Slavery*, p. 81.

18   "the abolition of slavery": Quoted in Daniel P. Mannix and Malcolm Cowley, *Black Cargoes: A History of the Atlantic Slave Trade* (New York: Viking Press, 1962), p. 175.

18   The knottiest problem: Paul Finkelman, *Slavery and the Founders: Race and Liberty in the Age of Jefferson* (Armonk, N.Y.: M. E. Sharpe, Inc., 2001), pp. 12ff, 31–36; Lawrence Goldstone, *Dark Bargain: Slavery, Profits, and the Struggle for the Constitution* (New York: Walker & Co., 2005), p. 104.

19   "it was pretty well understood": Goldstone, *Dark Bargain*, p. 110.

19   "However, most Americans believed": ibid., pp. 104, 113–15, 141.

19   Some delegates to the convention: Finkelman, *Slavery and the Founders*, pp. 7–10, 17ff; Goldstone, *Dark Bargain*, pp. 132–33, 161ff; John D. Gordon III, "Egbert Benson: A Nationalist in Congress, 1789–1793," in Kenneth R. Bowling and Donald R. Kennon, eds., *Neither Separate nor Equal: Congress in the 1790s* (Athens: Ohio University Press, 2000), pp. 87–89; Wiencek, *An Imperfect God*, pp. 266–68; Garry Wills, *"Negro President": Jefferson and the Slave Power* (Boston: Houghton Mifflin, 2003), pp. 1–9; Joseph J. Ellis, *His Excellency: George Washington* (New York: Knopf, 2004), pp. 173–79.

19   "If the Convention": quoted in Goldstone, *Dark Bargain*, p. 169.

20   "Religion & humanity had": ibid., p. 165.

20   "The admission of slaves": Quoted in Wills, *"Negro President,"* p. 50.

21   He would curse: Quoted in Henry Mayer, *All on Fire: William Lloyd Garrison and the Abolition of Slavery* (New York: St. Martin's Press, 1998), p. 313.

21   "We know full well": Ellis, *Founding Brothers*, p. 88.

21   The shadow of slavery: Bickford, et. al., *Documentary History*, vol. XI, pp. 1399, 1409, 1414, and vol. XII, pp. xiii–xiv; *Pennsylvania Gazette*, September 21, 1790; William C. diGiacomantonio, "'For the Gratification of a Volunteering Society': Antislavery and Pressure Group Politics in the First Federal Congress," *Journal of the Early Republic* 15 (Summer 1995); Bowling, *The Creation of Washington, D.C.*, pp. 141–44.

22   "By *delaying* the removal": Alyn Brodsky, *Benjamin Rush: Patriot and Physician* (New York: St. Martin's Press, 2004), pp. 313–14.

22   In defense of the Potomac: *New-York Journal*, September 20, 1790; Ron Chernow, *Alexander Hamilton* (New York: The Penguin Press, 2004), pp. 174–75; Ellis, *Founding Brothers*, pp. 52–59; Bowling, *The Creation of Washington, D.C.*, p. 199; Thomas Jefferson to James Madison, 20 February 1784, in Saul K. Padover, *Thomas Jefferson and the National Capital* (Washington: U.S. Government Printing Office, 1946), p. 4; "Notes on the Permanent Seat of Government," April 13, 1784, in ibid., pp. 6–9.

22   a "cloistered pedant": *New-York Journal*, June 20, 1790.

23   But against those who objected: Bickford, et. al., *Documentary History*, vol. XI, pp. 1426, 1437ff; Bowling, *The Creation of Washington, D.C.*, pp. 143–44, 151.

23   the leading advocate: Maclay, *Diary of William Maclay*, p. 301.

24   Pennsylvania senator, Robert Morris: Maclay, *Diary of William Maclay*, p. 159; Frank Gaylord Cook, "Robert Morris," *The Atlantic Monthly* 66 (November 1890); Elizabeth M. Nuxoll, "The Financier as Senator: Robert Morris of Pennsylvania, 1789–1795," in Bowling and Kennon, *Neither Separate nor Equal*, pp. 92–101, 116–17, 122; Robert E. Wright and David J. Cowen, *Financial Founding Fathers: The Men Who Made America Rich* (Chicago: University of Chicago Press, 2006), pp. 119–20; Barbara Ann Chernow, Robert Morris, *Land Speculator 1790–1801* (New York: Arno Press, 1978), p. 9.

24   He invested in: *Pennsylvania Gazette*, June 23, 1763 and June 30, 1763; May 11, 1758; September 4, 1760; May 6, 1765, June 3, 1765, and June 27, 1765; Elizabeth M. Nuxoll, e-mails to author August 7, 2006, and August 8, 2006; Anna Coxe Toogood, e-mail to author, August 8, 2006.

24   "Pray cannot they": Elizabeth M. Nuxoll, "Robert Morris and the Shaping of the Post-Revolutionary American Economy" (paper presented at the Omohundro Institute of Early American History and Culture Conference, Austin, Texas, June 1999).

25   the archtypal money man: Wright and Cowen, *Financial Founding Fathers*, pp. 123–32; Chernow, *Robert Morris*, pp. 19–21.

25   Morris's primary goal: Nuxoll, "The Financier as Senator," p. 97; Bob Arnebeck, *Through a Fiery Trial: Building Washington, 1790–1800* (Lanham, Md.: Madison Books, 1991), pp. 15–17; Bowling, *Creating the Federal City*, pp. 30, 69.

25   Morris even promised: Maclay, *Diary of William Maclay*, pp. 157ff.

25   "He now came": ibid., p. 163.

25   The legislative ballet: Bickford, et. al., *Documentary History*, vol. XI, pp. 1481–1512; Bowling, *The Creation of Washington, D.C.*, pp. 138–40, 153–57; Maclay, *Diary of William Maclay*, pp. 163ff.

26   Measured by temperament: David McCullough, *John Adams* (New York: Simon & Schuster, 2001), pp. 19, 31–32, 133, 544–45.

27   "I cannot help": Maclay, *Diary of William Maclay*, p. 33.

27   A brief entry: ibid., pp. 162–64.

28   an influential essay: *Maryland Journal, and the Baltimore Advertiser,* January 23, 1789.

28   George Town was "without parallel": John O'Connor, *Political Opinions Particularly Respecting the Seat of the Federal Empire,* quoted in Bowling, *The Creation of Washington, D.C.*, pp. 163–64.

29   "groan under the pressure": *Federal Gazette,* February 23, 1790.

29   "It is in fact": Maclay, *Diary of William Maclay*, p. 308.

29   "a Federal City": L'Enfant to George Washington, 11 September 1789, in Kite, *L'Enfant and Washington*, p. 34.

 CHAPTER 2: DINNER AT JEFFERSON'S

Page

31   curiosity drew streams: William Maclay, *The Diary of William Maclay and Other Notes on Senate Debates*, ed. Kenneth R. Bowling and Helen E. Veit (Baltimore: Johns Hopkins University Press, 1988), pp. 297–98.

31   Palladian residence nearby: Damie Stillman, "Six Houses for the President," *The Pennsylvania Magazine of History and Biography* 129 (October 2005); Bayrd Still, *Mirror for Gotham: New York as Seen by Contemporaries from Dutch Days to the Present* (New York: Fordham University Press, 1994), pp. 57–60.

32   painted "a pathetic picture": Thomas Jefferson, "The Anas," in *Writings* (New York: The Library of America, 1984), p. 669; Maclay, *Diary of William Maclay*, p. 306.

32   a financial crisis: Forrest McDonald, *Alexander Hamilton: A Biography* (New York: W. W. Norton & Co., 1982), pp. 147ff; Ron Chernow, *Alexander Hamilton* (New York: The Penguin Press, 2004), p. 287ff.

33   "We are in the dark": Charlene Bangs Bickford, Kenneth R. Bowling, William Charles diGiacomantonio, and Helen E. Veit, eds., *Documentary History of the First Federal Congress of the United States of America*, vol. XII (Baltimore: Johns Hopkins University Press, 1992–1996), p. 214.

34   Raised in near poverty: McDonald, *Alexander Hamilton,* pp. 10ff; Chernow, *Alexander Hamilton,* pp. 23ff, 200–202; Joseph J. Ellis, *Founding Brothers: The Revolutionary Generation* (New York: Vintage, 2002), pp. 60–65.

35   The plan that: McDonald, *Alexander Hamilton*, pp. 157ff, 170–74; Chernow, *Alexander Hamilton*, p. 299.

35   "The science of finance": Bickford, et. al., *Documentary History*, p. 220.

35   Revaluing the tens: Bickford, et. al., *Documentary History*, pp. 113, 597–99; Chernow, *Alexander Hamilton*, pp. 297–98; Ellis, *Founding Brothers*, pp. 52–59; Richard Brookhiser, *Alexander Hamilton, American* (New York: Free Press, 1999), pp. 83–86.

36   "Immense sums were": Jefferson, "The Anas," in *Writings*, pp. 665–68.

36   The debate began: Maclay, *Diary of William Maclay*, p. 306; Chernow, *Alexander Hamilton*, pp. 304, 324; McDonald, *Alexander Hamilton*, p. 150.

36   "was no more able": John C. Meleney, *The Public Life of Aedanus Burke: Revolutionary Republican in Post-Revolutionary South Carolina* (Columbia: University of South Carolina Press, 1989), pp. 182–86.

37   They were a bloc: Bickford, et. al., *Documentary History*, pp. 101–13, 199ff; Jefferson, "The Anas," in *Writings*, 665–68; Chernow, *Alexander Hamilton*, pp. 296–97.

37   Slavery had rarely: *New-York Journal*, March 18, 1790; Tench Coxe to James Madison, 31 March 1790, copy FFCP; William Ellery to Benjamin Huntington, 5 April 1790, copy FFCP; William C. diGiacomantonio, "'For the Gratification of a Volunteering Society': Antislavery and Pressure Group Politics in the First Federal Congress," *Journal of the Early Republic* 15 (Summer 1995); Shane White, *Somewhat More Independent: The End of Slavery in New York City, 1770–1810* (Athens: University of Georgia Press, 1991), pp. 1–10, 26–29; Meleney, *Public Life of Aedanus Burke*, pp. 187–88; *Pennsylvania Gazette*, September 9, 1790; Ellis, *Founding Brothers*, pp. 81–87.

37   "They had even": Bickford, et. al., *Documentary History*, pp. 809–10.

38   Vice President Adams: John Adams to George Churchman and Jacob Lindley, 24 January 1801, in Charles Francis Adams, *The Works of John Adams* (Boston: Little, Brown & Co., 1850–1856), vol. 1, chapter 15, doc. 57.

38   "rather with a sneer": Maclay, *Diary of William Maclay*, p. 202.

38   dominated by proslavery speakers: Bickford, et. al., *Documentary History*, pp. 285–311, 719–25, 730–34, 751–61, 774–78; Meleney, *Public Life of Aedanus Burke*, pp. 188–90.

39   "Sidi Mehemet Ibrahim": Benjamin Franklin, *The Portable Benjamin Franklin*, ed. Larzer Ziff (New York: Penguin, 2005), pp. 434–37.

40   a stinging repudiation: William Thornton to John Coakley Lettsom, 15 June 1790, in C. M. Harris, ed., *Papers of William Thornton*, vol. 1, *1781–1802* (Char-

lottesville: University Press of Virginia, 1995), p. 115; Richard S. Newman, *The Transformation of American Abolitionism: Fighting Slavery in the Early Republic* (Chapel Hill: University of North Carolina Press, 2002), pp. 48–49.

40   "the slave business": George Washington to David Stuart, 28 March 1790, in John C. Fitzpatrick, ed., *The Writings of George Washington*, vol. 31 (Washington: U.S. Government Printing Office, 1940), pp. 28–30.

41   Hamilton's immense chagrin: Chernow, *Alexander Hamilton*, pp. 297ff, 325–29; McDonald, *Alexander Hamilton*, pp. 179–83.

41   a Gordian knot: Bickford, et. al., *Documentary History*, pp. 199ff, 278–82, 292–94, 313–15, 597–620; *New-York Daily Gazette*, June 12 and 14, 1790; *Pennsylvania Gazette*, September 9, 1790; Maclay, *Diary of William Maclay*, pp. 274ff; Bob Arnebeck, *Through a Fiery Trial: Building Washington, 1790–1800* (Lanham, Md.: Madison Books, 1991), pp. 21–22.

41   The financier Robert Morris: Robert Morris to Mary Morris, 25 April 1790, 23 May 1790, and 2 June 1790, Robert Morris Collection, Huntington Library, San Marino, CA; Elizabeth M. Nuxoll, "The Financier as Senator: Robert Morris of Pennsylvania, 1789–1795," in Kenneth R. Bowling and Donald R. Kennon, eds., *Neither Separate nor Equal: Congress in the 1790s* (Athens: Ohio University Press, 2000), pp. 105–8.

42   On May 30: Thomas Jefferson to Thomas Mann Randolph, 30 May 1790, in Saul K. Padover, ed., *Thomas Jefferson and the National Capital* (Washington: U.S. Government Printing Office, 1946), p. 13; Jefferson to William Short, 6 June 1790, in ibid., p. 13.

42   "This was not": Jefferson to George Mason, 13 June 1790, in ibid., p. 14.

42   "[I]f we are to bring": *Pennsylvania Gazette*, June 9, 1790.

42   Rumors of secret deals: ibid.

42   "It was nothing but": Maclay, *Diary of William Maclay*, p. 284.

42   On June 8: *Pennsylvania Gazette*, June 16, 1790.

42   The mere suggestion: *New-York Daily Gazette*, June 9, 1790; diGiacomantonio, "'For the Gratification of a Volunteering Society.'"

43   "where it has been proved": *New-York Daily Gazette*, June 1, 1790.

43   Morris remained confident: Robert Morris to Molly Morris, 2 June 1790, and 19 June 1790, Robert Morris Collection, Huntington Library; Maclay, *Diary of William Maclay*, pp. 291–97; Kenneth R. Bowling, *The Creation of Washington, D.C.: The Idea and Location of the American Capital* (Fairfax, Va.: George Mason University Press, 1991), pp. 178–80.

43   "I considered assumption": Maclay, *Diary of William Maclay*, p. 300.

43   Pennsylvania's last chance: Robert Morris to Molly Morris, 19 June 1790, and 21 June 1790, Robert Morris Collection, Huntington Library.

43   Jefferson portrayed himself: Ellis, *Founding Brothers*, p. 68.

43   "Congress are much": Jefferson to Thomas Mann Randolph, 20 June 1790, in Padover, *Thomas Jefferson and the National Capital*, pp. 14–16.

44   small "indifferent" dwelling: James A. Bear and Lucia C. Stanton, eds., *Jefferson's Memorandum Books*, vol. 1 (Princeton: Princeton University Press, 1997), pp. 754–60.

44   A Georgian named Telfair: Maclay, *Diary of William Maclay*, pp. 297–98.

45   the republic's power elite: Jacques-Pierre Brissot de Warville, *New Travels in the United States of America, 1788*, trans. Mara Soceanu Vamos and Durand Echeverria, ed. Durand Echeverria (Cambridge: Harvard University Press, 1964), pp. 91–92; Maclay, *Diary of William Maclay*, p. 275; Jefferson, "The Anas," in *Writings*, pp. 665, 669–70; Chernow, *Alexander Hamilton*, pp. 23, 174–75, 231–32; Ellis, *Founding Brothers*, pp. 41, 69–72; Kenneth R. Bowling, letter to author, August 20, 2006.

45   half-visible presence: Bear and Stanton, *Jefferson's Memorandum Books*, vol. 1, pp. 684, 758ff; Lucia Stanton, *Free Some Day: The African-American Families of Monticello* (Charlottesville, Va.: Thomas Jefferson Foundation, 2000), pp. 17–18, 103–6, 110–12, 125–29.

46   indeed condemned slavery: Jefferson, "Notes on the State of Virginia," in *Writings*, pp. 288–89.

46   "strong and disagreeable odor": ibid., pp. 264–70.

47   Hamilton was something: James Oliver Horton, "Alexander Hamilton: Slavery and Race in a Revolutionary Generation," *New-York Journal of American History* 65, no. 3 (Spring 2004); Brookhiser, *Alexander Hamilton*, pp. 14–16, 175–78; Chernow, *Alexander Hamilton*, pp. 210ff; Graham Russell Hodges, *Root and Branch: African Americans in New York and East Jersey, 1613–1863* (Chapel Hill: University of North Carolina Press, 1999), pp. 166–67.

47   "Their natural faculties": Alexander Hamilton, *Writings* (New York: The Library of America, 2001), pp. 56–58.

47   a driving force: *Minutes of the Manumission Society of New-York*. N-YHS.

47   Hamilton had it: McDonald, *Alexander Hamilton*, pp. 181–82; Chernow, *Alexander Hamilton*, pp. 327–29; Kenneth R. Bowling, *Creating the Federal City, 1774–1800: Potomac Fever* (Washington: American Institute of Architects Press, 1988), pp. 73–75; Ellis, *Founding Brothers*, pp. 69–74.

48   "It was observed": Jefferson, "The Anas," in *Writings*, pp. 668–69.

48   The sweetener was: ibid., pp. 665–68.

48   In return, Hamilton: Garry Wills, *"Negro President": Jefferson and the Slave Power* (Boston: Houghton Mifflin, 2003), pp. 205–7; McDonald, *Alexander Hamilton*, pp. 184–87.

48   To assuage the Pennsylvanians: Robert Morris to Molly Morris, 2 July 1790, Robert Morris Collection, Huntington Library.

48   "The influence [Hamilton]": Jefferson, "The Anas," in *Writings*, p. 669.

49   "the funding system": Quoted in Bowling, *The Creation of Washington D.C.*, p. 187.

49   In Congress, debate: Maclay, *Diary of William Maclay*, pp. 301–8.

49   "We have it now": *Pennsylvania Gazette*, July 21, 1790.

49   Henry "Lighthorse Harry" Lee: Henry Lee to James Madison, 3 April 1790, copy courtesy of FFCP.

50   assumption bill became law: McDonald, *Alexander Hamilton*, pp. 184–87.

50   A flood of invective: *New-York Journal*, June 2 1790, June 29, 1790, and September 20, 1790; *Federal Gazette*, June 12, 1790; *New-York Morning Post*, August 4, 1790, September 2, 1790, and September 21, 1790; *Connecticut Journal*, September 8, 1790; *Connecticut Courant*, September 12, 1790; *New-York Daily Advertiser*, October 23, 1790; Bowling, *Creating the Federal City*, pp. 76–78.

50   *Canst thou with patience: Weekly Museum*, July 30, 1790.

51   "Joy! Joy to myself!": Quoted in Bowling, *The Creation of Washington D.C.*, p. 189.

51   "I cannot even": Maclay, *Diary of William Maclay*, p. 323.

51   "Fixed as Congress": ibid., p. 331.

51   "sink of political vice": Quoted in Rufus Wilmot Griswold, *The Republican Court; or, American Society in the Days of Washington* (New York: D. Appleton and Co., 1867), p. 232.

51   Throughout the autumn: Griswold, *The Republican Court*, pp. 237–38, 251–52; Kenneth R. Bowling, "The Federal Government and the Republican Court Move to Philadelphia, November 1790–March 1791," in Bowling and Kennon, eds., *Neither Separate nor Equal*, pp. 4, 10–17, 28.

52   "The capital was placed": Wills, *"Negro President,"* pp. 212–13.

53   The president arrived: George Washington to Daniel Carroll, 16 March 1791, and 17 March 1791, Records of the Commissioners of the City of Washington, LOC; entries for March 21–31, 1791, in Donald Jackson and Dorothy Twohig, eds., *The Diaries of George Washington*, vol. 6 (Charlottesville: University Press of Virginia, 1979), pp. 99–106; *Pennsylvania Gazette*, April 13, 1791.

54   Tobacco cultivation was: François-Alexandre-Frédéric, duc de la Rochefoucauld-Liancourt, *Travels through the United States of North America, the Country of the Iroquois and Upper Canada, in the Years 1795, 1796, and 1797*, vol. 2 (London: R. Phillips, 1799), pp. 288–89; Frederick Gutheim, *The Potomac* (New York: Holt, Rinehart and Winston, 1974), pp. 71–81, 85–86.

54   "Their method of": Quoted in Paul Metcalf, *Waters of Potowmack* (Charlottesville: University of Virginia Press, 2002), pp. 56–57.

54   Congress gave Washington: Thomas Jefferson to Charles Carroll, 17 September 1790, in Saul K. Padover, ed., *Thomas Jefferson and the National Capital* (Washington: U.S. Government Printing Office, 1946), pp. 29–30.

55   "The pain which": Washington to the Federal Commissioners, May 7, 1791, Records of the Commissioners, LOC.

55   Washington's vision of: C. M. Harris, "Washington's Gamble, L'Enfant's Dream: Politics, Design, and the Founding of the National Capital," *The William and Mary Quarterly* 56, no. 3 (July 1999).

55   Congress had mandated: *Pennsylvania Gazette*, July 9 and 21, 1790; *Connecticut Journal*, September 8, 1790; William Maclay, *The Diary of William Maclay and Other Notes on Senate Debates*, ed. Kenneth R. Bowling and Helen E. Veit (Baltimore: Johns Hopkins University Press, 1988), pp. 309–10; Joel Achenbach, *The Grand Idea: George Washington's Potomac, and the Race to the West* (New York: Simon & Schuster, 2004), pp. 181–82; Kenneth R. Bowling, *The Creation of Washington, D.C.: The Idea and Location of the American Capital* (Fairfax, Va.: George Mason University Press, 1991), pp. 190ff; Joseph J. Ellis, *His Excellency: George Washington* (New York: Knopf, 2004), pp. 206–7.

56   a kind of secular deity: Wendy C. Wick, *George Washington an American Icon: The Eighteenth-Century Graphic Portraits* (Washington: The Barra Foundation, 1982), p. xv.

56   "His mind dwells": William Thornton to John Coakley Lettsom, 26 November 1796, in C. M. Harris, ed., *Papers of William Thornton*, vol. 1, *1781–1802* (Charlottesville: University Press of Virginia, 1995), p. 341.

56   "He stood in": Quoted in Rufus Wilmot Griswold, *The Republican Court; or, American Society in the Days of Washington* (New York: D. Appleton and Co., 1867), p. 368.

57   "No Virginian can": Maclay, *Diary of William Maclay*, p. 258.

57   "strain of Shakespearean excellence": Ellis, *Founding Brothers: The Revolutionary Generation* (New York: Vintage, 2002), p. 217.

57   a truly inspired leader: Ellis, *His Excellency*, pp. 73–74; Ellis, *Founding Brothers*, pp. 125–27; Henry Wiencek, *An Imperfect God: George Washington, His Slaves, and the Creation of America* (New York: Farrar, Straus and Giroux, 2003), pp. 65–66.

57   as naturally as he sat: Jefferson to Walter Jones, 2 January 1814, in Andrew Lipscomb and Albert E. Bergh, eds., *The Writings of Thomas Jefferson*, vol. 14 (Washington: Thomas Jefferson Memorial Foundation, 1903), p. 49.

57   "You are wrong": Wiencek, *An Imperfect God*, p. 38.

58   nearly three hundred: Ellis, *His Excellency*, pp. 161–66; Wiencek, *An Imperfect God*, pp. 81–82, 179–80, 220ff, 262–63; Rosemarie Zagarri, ed., *David Humphreys' "Life of General Washington"* (Athens: University of Georgia Press, 1991), p. 24.

58   "Their work is worth": Julian Ursyn Niemcewicz, *Under Their Vine and Fig Tree: Travels through America in 1797–1799, 1805, and with Some Further Account of Life in New Jersey*, trans. and ed. Metchie J. E. Budka (Elizabeth, N.J.: Grassmann Publishing Co., 1965), p. 104.

59   After the war: Washington to Marquis de Lafayette, 5 April 1783, in John C. Fitzpatrick, ed., *The Writings of George Washington*, vol. 26 (Washington: U.S. Government Printing Office, 1940), p. 297; Fritz Hirschfeld, *George Washington and Slavery: A Documentary Portrayal* (Columbia: University of Missouri Press, 1997), pp. 123–25.

59   "To make the adults": Zagarri, *"Life of General Washington,"* p. 78.

59   "In the last": Wiencek, *An Imperfect God*, p. 278.

59   "We were agreeably": Washington, diary entry for March 23, 1748, in Metcalf, *Waters of Potowmack*, p. 34.

60   named him "Caunotaucarius": Zagarri, *"Life of General Washington,"* p. 10.

60   Years afterward, he: Wiencek, *An Imperfect God*, pp. 59–62; A. M. Sakolski, *The Great American Land Bubble: The Amazing Story of Land-Grabbing, Speculations, and Booms from Colonial Days to the Present Time* (New York: Harper & Brothers, 1932), pp. 5–10; Thomas P. Slaughter, *The Whiskey Rebellion: Frontier Epilogue to the American Revolution* (New York: Oxford University Press, 1986), pp. 75ff.

60 "Potomac Fever": Tobias Lear, *Observations on the River Potomack, The Country Adjacent, and the City of Washington* (New York: Samuel Loudon and Sons, 1793), MHS; Achenbach, *The Grand Idea*, pp. 121ff; Ellis, *His Excellency*, pp. 154ff; William C. diGiacomantonio, "All the President's Men: George Washington's Federal City Commissioners," *Washington History* 3 no. 1 (Spring/Summer 1991).

60 "It is the River": Quoted in Metcalf, *Waters of Potowmack*, pp. 83–84.

60 "the whole produce": ibid., p. 112.

60 an elaborate zigzag: Washington to Benjamin Harrison, 10 October 1784, in W. W. Abbott and Dorothy Twohig, eds., *The Papers of George Washington*, Confederation Series, vol. 2 (Charlottesville: University Press of Virginia, 1992–), p. 86.

61 "would in a few": Washington to Jacob Read, 3 November 1784, in Abbott and Twohig, *Papers of George Washington*, p. 118.

61 Separatists in Tennessee: Slaughter, *Whiskey Rebellion*, pp. 48ff.

61 "dissolve into the horrors": *Maryland Journal*, January 22, 1790.

61 "No well informed": Washington to Benjamin Harrison, 10 October 1784, in Abbott and Twohig, *Papers of George Washington*, p. 86.

61 a less elevated interest: Garry Wills, *"Negro President": Jefferson and the Slave Power* (Boston: Houghton Mifflin, 2003), pp. 205–8; Achenbach, *The Grand Idea*, pp. 129ff; Sakolski, *Great American Land Bubble*, pp. 8–10; Ellis, *Founding Brothers*, pp. 69–72; Kenneth R. Bowling, *Creating the Federal City, 1774–1800: Potomac Fever* (Washington: American Institute of Architects Press, 1988), pp. 47–49; Forrest McDonald, *Alexander Hamilton: A Biography* (New York: W. W. Norton & Co., 1982), p. 175; *Pennsylvania Gazette*, June 1, 1785.

62 "the greatest retuns": Washington to Marquis de Lafayette, February 15, 1785, in Abbott and Twohig, *Papers of George Washington*, p. 363.

62 hair and eyebrows: *Maryland Chronicle*, February 22, 1786.

62 quickly became intertwined: Washington to David Stuart, April 8, 1792, in *Records of the Columbia Historical Society* (RCHS), vol. 17 (Washington: Columbia Historical Society, 1917), p. 54.

63 three commissioners whom: Washington, "Commission," RCHS 17, p. 3; diGiacomantonio, "All the President's Men"; *Pennsylvania Gazette*, July 21, 1790; Bowling, *The Creation of Washington, D.C.*, pp. 44ff, 79–84; Bob Arnebeck, *Through a Fiery Trial: Building Washington, 1790–1800* (Lanham, Md.: Madison Books, 1991), pp. 34–35; Achenbach, *The Grand Idea*, pp. 168–71.

63 "I have a mind": Washington to Benjamin Stoddert, 14 November 1792, RCHS 17, p. 60.

63   Everyone knew that: *Pennsylvania Gazette*, October 5, 1791; Washington, "Message to Congress," January 24, 1791, RCHS 17, p. 6; Washington to William Deakins Jr. and Benjamin Stoddert, February 3, 1791, RCHS 17, p. 8.

63   "No place, either": Washington to Benjamin Stoddert, September 26, 1798, in Abbott and Twohig, *Papers of George Washington*, p. 45.

64   "the Patowmack Navigation": *Pennsylvania Gazette*, April 13, 1791.

64   He now wanted Congress: Bowling, *The Creation of Washington, D.C.*, p. 209; Arnebeck, *Through a Fiery Trial*, p. 33; Constance K. Ring and Wesley E. Pippenger, *Alexandria, Virginia: Town Lots 1749–1801* (Westminster: Family Line Publications, 1995).

64   Hamilton had proposed: McDonald, *Alexander Hamilton*, pp. 192–95, 205–10; Reginald Horsman, *The New Republic: The United States of America 1789–1815* (Harlow: Longman, 2000), pp. 30–31; James Thomas Flexner, *Washington: The Indispensible Man* (Boston: Little, Brown and Co., 1969), pp. 239–40; Bowling, *The Creation of Washington, D.C.*, pp. 217–18; Washington, "Proclamation," RCHS 17, p. 17.

65   John Adams acerbically declared: Bowling, *The Creation of Washington, D.C.*, p. 213.

65   Andrew Ellicott, one of: Catharine Van Cortlandt Mathews, *Andrew Ellicott: His Life and Letters* (New York: The Grafton Press, 1908), pp. 1–13, 91; Sally Kennedy Alexander, "A Sketch of the Life of Major Andrew Ellicott," RCHS 2, 1899.

65   "Danger had been": Mathews, *Andrew Ellicott*, p. 213.

66   amateur astronomer Benjamin Banneker: John H. B. Latrobe, *Memoir of Benjamin Banneker*, pamphlet (Baltimore: John D. Toy, 1845); Martha E. Tyson, "A Sketch of the Life of Benjamin Banneker, from Notes Taken in 1836," read by Saurin Morris before the Maryland Historical Society, October 5, 1854, MHS; Tyson, *Banneker: The Afric-American Astronomer* (Philadelphia: Friends Book Association, 1884); Silvio A. Bedini, *The Life of Benjamin Banneker* (New York: Scribner, 1972), pp. 17ff, 109–12, 118–19.

67   more uninhibited mixture: David Brion Davis, *Inhuman Bondage: The Rise and Fall of Slavery in the New World* (New York: Oxford University Press, 2006), pp. 131–32; Oscar Reiss, *Blacks in Colonial America* (Jefferson, N.C.: McFarland & Co., 1997), pp. 182–83.

67   Tidewater slavery was "mild": Kenneth M. Stampp, *The Peculiar Institution: Slavery in the Ante-Bellum South* (New York: Vintage, 1956), pp. 208–9; Mary Tremain, *Slavery in the District of Columbia* (New York: G. P. Putnam's Sons, 1892), pp. 33–40; Metcalf, *Waters of Potowmack*, p. 54; Josiah Henson, *Uncle Tom's Story of his Life from 1789 to 1879* (Boston: B. B. Russell & Co., 1879), pp. 2–7; Lucia Stanton, *Free Some Day: The African-American Families of Mon-*

ticello (Charlottesville, Va.: Thomas Jefferson Foundation, 2000), p. 43; Lucia Stanton, *Slavery at Monticello* (Charlottesville, Va.: Thomas Jefferson Foundation, 1996), pp. 27–28.

68   George Washington expected: Niemcewicz, *Under Their Vine and Fig Tree*, pp. 100–101; Wiencek, *An Imperfect God*, pp. 95–96.

68   farm of Isaac Riley: Henson, *Uncle Tom's Story*, pp. 17–18.

68   "The whole commerce": Thomas Jefferson, "Notes on the State of Virginia," in *Writings* (New York: The Library of America, 1984), p. 288.

69   As a child: Latrobe, *Memoir of Benjamin Banneker*; Tyson, "Sketch" Tyson, *Banneker*, pp. 13–22; Bedini, *Life of Benjamin Banneker*, pp. 46–47, 121–22, 150.

69   Banneker's isolation was: Tyson, "Sketch" Bedini, *Life of Benjamin Banneker*, pp. 50–54, 58, 77–80.

70   "It is a hard matter": Benjamin Banneker to George Ellicott, October 13, 1789, MHS.

71   "an Ethiopian, whose": *George Town Weekly Ledger*, March 12, 1791.

70   "a very civil set": Latrobe, *Memoir of Benjamin Banneker*.

70   he would spend: Tyson, *Banneker*, pp. 36ff.

71   First he met: Washington to William Deakins Jr. and Benjamin Stoddert, 2 March 1791, and 17 March 1791, RCHS 17, pp. 11, 15; Washington to the Federal Commissioners, RCHS 17, p. 21; *Pennsylvania Gazette*, April 13, 1791.

72   the courtly immigrant: *Pennsylvania Gazette*, April 13, 1791; *George Town Weekly Ledger*, March 12, 1791; Wilhelmus B. Bryan, *History of the National Capital* (New York: Macmillan, 1916), p. 127; Andrew Ellicott to Sally Ellicott, August 9, 1791, in Elizabeth S. Kite, *L'Enfant and Washington, 1791–1792* (Baltimore: The John-Hopkins Press, 1929), p. 175.

72   "L'Enfant's personality was": Kenneth R. Bowling, *Peter Charles L'Enfant: Vision, Honor, and Male Friendship in the Early American Republic* (Washington: The Friends of the George Washington University Libraries, 2002), p. ix.

72   one of the most prominent: Bob Arnebeck, "To Tease and Torment: Two Presidents Confront Suspicions of Sodomy," online at www.geocities.com/bobarnebeck/LEnfant.htm.

72   "the whole immensity": Peter Charles L'Enfant to the Proprietors of land in the Federal District, March 10, 1792, in Kite, *L'Enfant and Washinton*, p. 163.

72   "proceed from thence": Jefferson to L'Enfant, March 1791, in Padover, *Thomas Jefferson and the National Capital*, pp. 42–43.

73   "having travelled part of the way": L'Enfant to Jefferson, March 11, 1791, in Padover, *Thomas Jefferson and the National Capital*, pp. 44–47.

73   Jefferson did not: Iris Miller, *Washington in Maps, 1606–2000* (New York: Rizzoli International Publications, 2002), pp. 42–43; Jefferson, "Proceedings to be had under the Residence act," note, November 29, 1790, in Padover, *Thomas Jefferson and the National Capital*, pp. 30–36; Kite, *L'Enfant and Washington*, p. 72.

73   L'Enfant considered: Jefferson to the Federal Commissioners, January 29, 1791, MLD, LOC; Jefferson to L'Enfant, (undated) March 1791, MLD; Jefferson to L'Enfant, March 17, 1791, MLD; Washington to L'Enfant, April 4, 1791, MLD; Jefferson to L'Enfant, April 10, 1791, MLD; L'Enfant to Washington, undated (probably March 1791), in Kite, *L'Enfant and Washington*, pp. 43–48; L'Enfant to Washington, "Report," June 22, 1791, in ibid., pp. 52–58; L'Enfant to Jefferson, April 4, 1791, in ibid., pp. 41–42; Wilhelmus B. Bryan, "Something about L'Enfant and His Personal Affairs," RCHS 2.

74   Washington too wanted: Metcalf, *Waters of Potowmack*, pp. 82–83.

74   they set off: Washington, diary entry for March 29, 1791, in Jackson and Twohig, *Diaries of George Washington*, vol. 6, pp. 104–5.

74   "such sort of places": L'Enfant to Washington, 22 June 1791, in Kite, *L'Enfant and Washington*, p. 57.

74   "Some were so wild": Daniel Carroll to Robert Brent, July 24, 1837, in ibid., p. 165.

74   these were his own neighbors: Washington to Jefferson, March 3, 1791, RCHS 17, p. 19; Washington to L'Enfant, April 4, 1791, in ibid, p. 22; Washington to the Federal Commissioners, April 3 and 13, and May 7, 1791, in Letters of the Presidents to the Commissioners of the City of Washington, LOC.

75   The president explained: Kenneth R. Bowling, "The Other G. W.: George Walker and the Creation of the National Capital," *Washington History* 3, no. 2 (Fall/Winter 1991–92); Washington to Jefferson, April 5, 1791, in Kite, *L'Enfant and Washington*, pp. 21–22; Jefferson, "Proceedings," in Padover, *Thomas Jefferson and the National Capital*, p. 30ff; Washington to Jefferson, March 31, 1791, in ibid., pp. 54–55; Washington, diary entry for March 30, 1791, in Jackson and Twohig, *Diaries of George Washington*, vol. 6, p. 105; *Pennsylvania Gazette*, July 21, 1790.

76   Washington remained anxious: Washington to the Federal Commissioners, April 3 and 13, and May 7, 1791, LOC.

76   surveyor Andrew Ellicott: Mathews, *Andrew Ellicott*, pp. 97–98; Bedini, *Life of Benjamin Banneker*, pp. 116ff.

76   "I have met": Andrew Ellicott to Sally Ellicott, March 20, 1791, quoted in Alexander, "A Sketch," RCHS 2, p. 173.

77   First Ellicott laid out: Miller, *Washington in Maps*, pp. 48–49; Andrew Ellicott to Jefferson, February 14, 1791, in Padover, *Thomas Jefferson and the National Capital*, pp. 41–42; Washington, "Proclamation," March 30, 1791, in ibid., pp. 52–53.

77   crews of woodsmen: Chris Cole, author interview, Stone Ridge, NY, April 8, 2006; Bedini, *Life of Benjamin Banneker*, pp. 112ff.

78   Benjamin Banneker spent: Bedini, *Life of Benjamin Banneker*, pp. 118ff.

79   "in reason much inferior": Jefferson, "Notes on the State of Virginia," in *Writings*, p. 266.

80   "He arrived on horseback": Tyson, *Banneker*, pp. 37–38.

CHAPTER 4: A CLOUDY BUSINESS

Page

81   "the most desirable position": Peter Charles L'Enfant to George Washington, March 1791 (undated), in Elizabeth S. Kite, *L'Enfant and Washington, 1791–1792* (Baltimore: The Johns Hopkins Press, 1929), pp. 45–46, 52–58.

82   "exhibits such striking proofs": Quoted in Kenneth R. Bowling, *Peter Charles L'Enfant: Vision, Honor, and Male Friendship in the Early American Republic* (Washington: The Friends of the George Washington University Libraries, 2002), p. 29.

82   there was a problem: C. M. Harris, "Washington's Gamble, L'Enfant's Dream: Politics, Design, and the Founding of the National Capital," *The William and Mary Quarterly* 56, no. 3 (1999), pp. 537ff; Kite, *L'Enfant and Washington*, p. 22.

82   "the genius of": Harris, "Washington's Gamble," p. 548.

82   "For near seven miles": Andrew Ellicott to Sally Ellicott, June 26, 1791, in Sally Kelly Alexander, "A Sketch of the Life of Major Andrew Ellicott," *Records of the Columbia Historical Society* (RCHS) 2, 1899, p. 174.

83   A chaos of felled timbers: Bob Arnebeck, *Through a Fiery Trial: Building Washington, 1790–1800* (Lanham, Md.: Madison Books, 1991), pp. 56–57, 62–64.

83   "Do not my dear": Andrew Ellicott to Sally Ellicott, August 9, 1791, in Catharine Van Cortlandt Mathews, *Andrew Ellicott: His Life and Letters* (New York: The Grafton Press, 1908), p. 90.

83   Feverish excitement filled: *Pennsylvania Gazette*, October 5, 1791; "The Journal of William Loughton Smith," *Proceedings of the Massachusetts Historical Society*, vol. LI, October 1917, N-YHS.

83   "grow up with a degree": Quoted in Arnebeck, *Through a Fiery Trial*, pp. 64ff.

83 decided to name the city "Washington": Federal Commissioners to L'Enfant, September 9, 1791, in Saul K. Padover, ed., *Thomas Jefferson and the National Capital* (Washington: U.S. Government Printing Office, 1946), p. 74.

83 time of the sale: "Public Sales of Lots in the City of Washington," October 12, 1791, broadside, Records of the Commissioners of the City of Washington, LOC; Arnebeck, *Through a Fiery Trial*, pp. 66ff.

83 the total value of this land: Daniel Carroll to James Madison, April 23, 1791, in Kite, *L'Enfant and Washington*, p. 51.

84 "For to look upon": L'Enfant to Washington, August 19, 1791, in Kite, *L'Enfant and Washington*, pp. 67ff.

84 provide a published version: Daniel Carroll to James Madison, April 23, 1791, in Kite, *L'Enfant and Washington*, p. 51; Federal Commissioners to L'Enfant, September 9, 1791, in Padover, *Thomas Jefferson and the National Capital*, p. 75; Washington to David Stuart, November 20, 1791, RCHS 17, p. 30.

84 taken care "to prevent": Kite, *L'Enfant and Washington*, p. 22.

84 The sale was scheduled: *Pennsylvania Gazette*, July 13, 1791; Arnebeck, *Through a Fiery Trial*, pp. 66–69; Kenneth R. Bowling, *The Creation of Washington, D.C.: The Idea and Location of the American Capital* (Fairfax, Va.: George Mason University Press, 1991), p. 227; Washington, October 25, 1791, speech to Congress, RCHS 17, p. 30; L'Enfant to Tobias Lear, October 19, 1791, in Kite, *L'Enfant and Washington*, p. 76; David Stuart to Washington, October 19, 1791, in ibid., p. 78.

85 "Men who possess talents": Washington to David Stuart, November 20, 1791, RCHS 17, p. 30.

85 essentially an abstraction: Stanley Elkins and Eric McKittrick, *The Age of Federalism: The Early American Republic, 1788–1800* (New York: Oxford University Press, 1993), pp. 174–75.

86 What happened next: Washington to Carroll of Duddington, November 28, 1791, RCHS 17, p. 34; Washington to L'Enfant, November 28, 1791, ibid., p. 36; Washington to Thomas Jefferson, November 30, 1791, ibid., p. 37; Washington to the Federal Commissioners, December 1, 1791, ibid., p. 38; Washington to Carroll of Duddington, December 2, 1791, ibid., p. 38; Washington to L'Enfant, December 2 and 13, 1791, ibid., p. 39–40; Washington to the Federal Commissioners, December 18 and 27, 1791, ibid., pp. 41–44.

86 "Having the beauty": Washington to L'Enfant, December 2, 1791, ibid., p. 39.

87 L'Enfant characteristically blamed: L'Enfant to the Federal Commissioners, December 6, 1791, in Kite, *L'Enfant and Washington*, pp. 85–88.

87 wanted everyone to believe: Washington to the Federal Commissioners, December 27, 1791, RCHS 17, p. 38.

87 "It would be unfortunate": Washington to Carroll of Duddington, December 2, 1791, ibid., p. 38.

87 "I hope the maj.": Washington to the Federal Commissioners, December 27, 1791, ibid., p. 38.

87 L'Enfant ignored the chill: L'Enfant to Washington, December 7, 1791, in Kite, *L'Enfant and Washington*, pp. 89–91; L'Enfant to Isaac Roberdeau, December 16 and 25, 1791, in ibid., pp. 97–99; L'Enfant to Washington, January 17, 1792, "Report," in ibid., pp. 111–25; L'Enfant to Washington, February 6, 1792, in ibid, p. 133.

87 "What his motives were": Wilhelmus B. Bryan, "Something about L'Enfant and His Personal Affairs," RCHS 2, 1899, p. 55.

87 Working from L'Enfant's drawings: Alexander, "A Sketch," pp. 177ff; Miller, *Washington in Maps*, pp. 35, 45.

88 "unmercifully spoiled and altered": L'Enfant to Tobias Lear, February 17, 1792, in Kite, *L'Enfant and Washington*, pp. 142–43.

88 "Every mode had been tried": Washington to L'Enfant, February 28, 1792, RCHS 17, p. 45; Washington to the Federal Commissioners, January 17, 1792, ibid., p. 45.

88 "ignorant and unfit": L'Enfant to Jefferson, February 26, 1791, in Kite, *L'Enfant and Washington*, pp. 146–50; L'Enfant to the Proprietors of property in the Federal City, March 10, 1792, in ibid., pp. 161ff; note, in ibid., p. 172.

88 the commissioners, for their part: Washington to L'Enfant, December 13, 1791, in ibid., p. 92; Federal Commissioners to Washington, January 9, 1792, in ibid., pp. 104–5; Jefferson to L'Enfant, February 22, 1792, in ibid., p. 145; Arnebeck, *Through a Fiery Trial*, pp. 87–88; Bowling, *Peter Charles L'Enfant*, pp. 30–33; Harris, "Washington's Gamble," pp. 546–50.

88 "rather than be any longer": Quoted in Kite, *L'Enfant and Washington*, p. 137.

88 "chicane and raise opposition": Jefferson, "Observations on Major L'Enfant's letter of December 7th," December 11, 1791, in Padover, *Thomas Jefferson and the National Capital*, pp. 82–86.

89 "Every mode has been tried": Washington to L'Enfant, February 28, 1792, RCHS 17, p. 45.

89 "Fearing that by my continuance": L'Enfant to Washington, in Kite, *L'Enfant and Washington*, p. 152.

89   "No farther overtures": Washington to Jefferson, March 14, 1792, in Padover, *Thomas Jefferson and the National Capital*, p. 121; Jefferson to George Walker, March 14, 1792, in ibid., p. 120; Kite, *L'Enfant and Washington*, p. 24.

89   Ellicott was placed: Washington to the Federal Commissioners, March 6, 1792, RCHS 17, p. 46; Silvio A. Bedini, *Life of Benjamin Banneker* (New York: Scribner, 1972), pp. 132–33.

89   "The enemies of the project": Jefferson to the Federal Commissioners, March 6, 1792, ibid., pp. 103–6.

89   Bruised and bitter: L'Enfant to the Federal Commissioners, March 18, 1792, in Kite, *L'Enfant and Washington*, pp. 174–75; George Walker to Jefferson, March 9, 1792, in ibid., p. 168; Walker to Washington, March 9, 1792, in ibid., p. 169; Washington to David Stuart, April 8, 1792, RCHS 17, p. 54; Bowling, *Peter Charles L'Enfant*, p. 34; Benjamin Henry Latrobe, *The Journal of Latrobe* (New York: D. Appleton & Co., 1905), p. 133.

89   problems with the commissioners: Mathews, *Andrew Ellicott*, p. 92.

90   an emotional toll: Andrew Ellicott to Sally Ellicott, October 10 and December 14, 1792, quoted in Mathews, ibid., pp. 95ff.

90   Adding insult to injury: Washington to Uriah Forrest, 20 January 1793, in W. W. Abbott and Dorothy Twohig, eds., *The Papers of George Washington*, Presidential Series, vol. 12 (Charlottesville: University Press of Virginia, 2002), p. 28; Stuart to Washington, February 1793, in ibid., pp. 177ff, note 80; Federal Commissioners to Washington, 11 March 1793, in ibid., p. 296; Federal Commissioners to Washington, 13 March 1793, in ibid., p. 311; Washington to the Federal Commissioners, 3 April 1793, RCHS 17, p. 79; Arnebeck, *Through a Fiery Trial*, pp. 147–50, 156–57; Bedini, *Life of Benjamin Banneker*, pp. 133–34.

90   he never forgave them: Andrew Ellicott to Sally Ellicott, January 15, 1793, and April 10, 1793, Mathews, *Andrew Ellicott*, pp. 98–100; Abbott and Twohig, *Papers of George Washington*, p. 401, note.

90   "a melancholy languor": Quoted in Bowling, "The Other G.W."

90   Time to organize: Jefferson to L'Enfant, February 22, 1792, in Kite, *L'Enfant and Washington*, p. 144; L'Enfant to Jefferson, February 26, 1792, in ibid., p. 144; Federal Commissioners to Washington, January 9, 1792, in ibid., pp. 104–5; Isaac Roberdeau to L'Enfant, January 9, 1792, in ibid., p. 109; L'Enfant to Washington, "Report," January 17, 1792, in ibid., pp. 111–25; *Pennsylvania Gazette*, June 13, 1792; Arnebeck, *Through a Fiery Trial*, pp. 120–21, 134–35.

91   the rumor mill: Ann Brodeau to William Thornton, 25 September 1791, in C. M. Harris, ed., *Papers of William Thornton*, vol. 1, *1781–1802* (Charlottesville: University Press of Virginia, 1995), pp. 153–54.

91   "a Congress of fiends": Quoted in Arnebeck, *Through a Fiery Trial*, p. 65.

91   "There is a current": Washington to David Stuart, 8 March 1792, RCHS 17, pp. 49–53.

91   the cornerstone was laid: *Pennsylvania Gazette*, May 16, 1792.

92   All along the frontier: Thomas P. Slaughter, *The Whiskey Rebellion: Frontier Epilogue to the American Revolution* (New York: Oxford University Press, 1986), pp. 114–16; *Pennsylvania Gazette*, November 2, 1791; Jack D. Warren Jr., "'The Line of My Official Conduct': George Washington and Congress, 1789–1797," in Kenneth R. Bowling and Donald R. Kennon, eds., *Neither Separate nor Equal: Congress in the 1790s* (Athens: Ohio University Press, 2000), pp. 258–62.

92   "whose enterprize, intrepidity and": *Pennsylvania Gazette*, November 2, 1791.

92   St. Clair's force was ambushed: *Pennsylvania Gazette*, January 11, 1792, and May 9 and 16, 1792; John C. Miller, *The Federalist Era, 1789–1801* (New York: Harper Torchbooks, 1960), pp. 146–47; Allan W. Eckert, *The Dark and Bloody River: Chronicles of the Ohio River Valley* (New York: Bantam, 1995), pp. 564–71.

93   On the high seas: Frank Lambert, *The Barbary Wars* (New York: Hill and Wang, 2005), pp. 37–40, 118–21; Walter Stahr, *John Jay* (New York: Hambledon and London, 2005), pp. 218–21; Samuel Eliot Morison, *The Oxford History of the American People*, vol. 2 (New York: Mentor, 1972), pp. 53–54; George Washington, "Prisoners at Algiers," Message to Congress, December 30, 1790, online at www.lectlaw.com/files/his03; Benjamin Franklin, "Sidi Mehemet Ibrahim on the Slave Trade," in Larzer Ziff, ed., *The Portable Benjamin Franklin* (New York: Penguin, 2005), pp. 434–37.

94   Another threatening sequence: *Pennsylvania Gazette*, November 2, 1791, and May 9, 1792; *Philadelphia General Advertiser*, November 11, 1791; C. L. R. James, *The Black Jacobins: Toussaint L'Ouverture and the San Domingo Revolution* (New York: Vintage, 1989), pp. 85–96; Elkins and McKittrick, *The Age of Federalism*, pp. 649–50; Gary B. Nash, *First City: Philadelphia and the Forging of Historical Memory* (Philadelphia: University of Pennsylvania Press, 2002), pp. 140–41.

95   Washington needed a miracle: Washington to David Stuart, 8 April 1792, RCHS 17, p. 55; Washington to Benjamin Stoddert, 14 November 1792, ibid., p. 60; Washington to David Stuart, 30 November 1792, ibid., p. 63; Washington to the Federal Commissioners, 13 November 1792, Records of the Commissioners of the City of Washington, LOC; Jefferson to the Federal Commissioners, 21 March 1792, in Padover, *Thomas Jefferson and the National Capital*, p. 125; Samuel Blodget to Jefferson, 20 April 1792, in ibid., p. 139; A. M. Sakolski, *The Great American Land Bubble: The Amazing Story of Land-Grabbing, Speculations, and Booms from Colonial Days to the Present Times* (New York: Harper & Brothers, 1932), pp. 153–54; Ron Chernow, *Alexander Hamilton* (New York: The Penguin Press, 2004), pp. 379–84; Arnebeck, *Through a Fiery Trial*, pp. 69–70, 104ff, 127ff; Miller, *Federalist Era*, pp. 44, 67.

96 "The extraordinary crush": Jefferson to the Federal Commissioners, 20 April 1792, in Padover, *Thomas Jefferson and the National Capital*, pp. 137–38.

96 Jefferson, who was helpless: Jefferson to the Federal Commissioners, 11 May 1792, in ibid., pp. 140–41.

97 "Not having heard": Jefferson to Samuel Blodget, 22 June 1792, in ibid., p. 146.

97 "I have found everyone": Samuel Blodget to Jefferson, 25 June 1792, in ibid., pp. 146–47.

97 he reassured Jefferson: Samuel Blodget to Jefferson, 5 July 1792, in ibid., p. 151; Jefferson to the Federal Commissioners, 11 July 1792, in ibid., pp. 152–53.

97 second land sale: "Announcement," June 2, 1792, Records of the Commissioners of the City of Washington, LOC; Washington to the Federal Commissioners, July 29, 1792, Letters of Presidents to the Commissioners of the City of Washington, LOC.

97 "a great want": Federal Commissioners to Jefferson, December 5, 1792, ibid., pp. 161–62.

97 The only real winner: Washington to Federal Commissioners, November 13, 1792, Letters of Presidents to the Commissioners of the City of Washington, LOC; Washington to the Federal Commissioners, November 17, 1792, RCHS 17, p. 61–62; Arnebeck, *Through a Fiery Trial*, pp. 134–36.

98 "He thinks it best": Jefferson to the Federal Commissioners, April 20, 1792, in Padover, *Thomas Jefferson and the National Capital*, p. 138; Federal Commissioners to Jefferson, April 11, 1792, in ibid., p. 135.

98 "everything was going": *Pennsylvania Gazette*, June 13, 1792.

98 Skilled workers were: Washington to David Stuart, March 8, 1792, in Padover, *Thomas Jefferson and the National Capital*, p. 112; Federal Commissioners to Jefferson, March 14, 1792, in ibid., p. 118; Jefferson to the Federal Commissioners, March 21, 1792, in ibid., p. 124; Federal Commissioners to Jefferson, April 11 and April 14, 1792, in ibid., p. 135; Jefferson to Herman Hend Damen, July 4, 1792, in ibid., p. 150; Jefferson to the Federal Commissioners, December 17 and December 23, 1792, in ibid., p. 164.

98 "fills me with": Washington to the Federal Commissioners, December 18, 1792, RCHS 17, p. 65.

98 Slaves would be: Bob Arnebeck, "The Use of Slaves to Build the Capitol and White House," online at www.geocities.com/bobarnebeck/slaves.html; Federal Commissioners to Jefferson, 5 January 1793, in Padover, *Thomas Jefferson and the National Capital*, pp. 165–66.

99 "the most unremitting": Thomas Jefferson, "Notes on the State of Virginia," in *Writings* (New York: The Library of America, 1984), p. 288.

99   His antislavery posture: Lucia Stanton, *Slavery at Monticello* (Charlottesville, Va.: Thomas Jefferson Foundation, 1996), pp. 16–17, 28–35; Lucia Stanton, *Free Some Day: The African-American Families of Monticello* (Charlottesville, Va.: Thomas Jefferson Foundation, 2000), pp. 81–82.

100   mantle of the Roman Republic: Carl J. Richard, *The Founders and the Classics: Greece, Rome, and the American Enlightenment* (Cambridge: Harvard University Press, 1994), pp. 12ff, 53ff.; Damie Stillman, "From the Ancient Roman Republic to the New American One," in Donald R. Kennon, ed., *A Republic for the Ages: The United States Capitol and the Political Culture of the Early Republic* (Charlottesville: University Press of Virginia, 1999), pp. 271ff; Elkins and McKittrick, *The Age of Federalism*, pp. 169–71; Jefferson to Thomas Johnson, March 8, 1792, in Padover, *Thomas Jefferson and the National Capital*, p. 112.

100   Americans of Jefferson's: Peter Kolchin, *American Slavery, 1619–1877* (New York: Hill & Wang, 1993), p. 45; Stanton, *Free Some Day*, p. 19; Ira Berlin, *Generations of Captivity: A History of African-American Slaves* (Cambridge: Harvard University Press, 2003), p. 73; David Lowenthal, *The Past Is a Foreign Country* (Cambridge: Cambridge University Press, 1986), pp. 40ff; Wendy C. Wick, *George Washington an American Icon: The Eighteenth Century Graphic Portraits* (Washington: The Barra Foundation, 1982), p. xviii; Eric Hobsbawm, "Inventing Traditions," in Hobsbawm and Terence Ranger, eds., *The Invention of Tradition* (Cambridge: Cambridge University Press, 1986), pp. 1–14.

100   consumption of alcohol: William J. Rorabaugh, *The Alcoholic Republic: An American Tradition* (New York: Oxford University Press, 1981), pp. 232–33.

101   designs were solicited: Harris, "Washington's Gamble," pp. 551–55; Harris, *Papers of William Thornton*, pp. 193–94; Washington to David Stuart, 8 March 1792, RCHS 17, p. 51; Washington to the Federal Commissioners, 23 July 1792, ibid., p. 57; Federal Commissioners to Washington, 11 March 1793, in Abbott and Twohig, *Papers of George Washington*, p. 296; "Draft of Competition for Plan of a Capitol," in Padover, *Thomas Jefferson and the National Capital*, p. 119.

101   James Hoban: Harris, *Papers of William Thornton*, p. 215n; William Seale, *The President's House*, vol. 1 (Washington: White House Historical Association, 1986), pp. 19, 39–44; Seale, *The White House: The History of an American Idea* (Washington: American Institute of Architects Press, 1992), pp. 6–14; Damie Stillman, "Six Houses for the President," *The Pennsylvania Magazine of History and Biography* 129 (October 2005); Martin I. J. Griffin, "James Hoban Architect and Builder of the White House," *The American Catholic Historical Researches*, vol. III, January 1907.

102   "I should prefer": Jefferson to L'Enfant, April 10, 1791, Digges-L'Enfant-Morgan Papers, LOC.

102   Designs began to arrive: William C, Allen, *History of the United States Capitol: A Chronicle of Design, Construction, and Politics* (Washington: U.S. Government Print-

ing Office, 2001), pp. 14–17; Federal Commissioners to Jefferson, July 5, 1792, in Padover, *Thomas Jefferson and the National Capital*, p. 152; Jefferson to the Federal Commissioners, ibid., p. 152–53.

102   "rude, misshapen piles": Quoted in Richard, *The Founders and the Classics*, p. 51.

102   "If none more elegant": Quoted in Allen, *History of the United States Capital*, p. 17.

102   yet another submission: Harris, *Papers of William Thornton*, p. xlvii; Federal Commissioners to Jefferson, 5 December 1792, in Padover, *Thomas Jefferson and the National Capital*, p. 162; William Thornton to the Federal Commissioners, July 12, 1792, Thornton Papers, LOC; Daniel Carroll to Thornton, November 15, 1792, Thornton Papers, LOC; Federal Commissioners to Thornton, December 4, 1792, Thornton Papers, LOC.

 CHAPTER 5: THE METROPOLIS OF AMERICA

Page

103   one of the most celebrated: Jacques-Pierre Brissot de Warville, *New Travels in the United States of America, 1788*, trans. Mara Soceanu Vamos and Durand Echeverria, ed. Durand Echeverria (Cambridge: Harvard University Press, 1964), pp. 91, 149, 301; diary, 1798, Anna Maria Thornton Papers, LOC; Elinor Stearns and David N. Yerkes, *William Thornton: A Renaissance Man in the Federal City* (Washington: American Institute of Architects Foundation, 1976), p. 9; Vernon W. Pickering, *A Concise History of the British Virgin Islands* (New York: Falcon Publications, 1987), pp. 37ff; James Johnston Abraham, *Lettsom: His Life, Times, Friends, and Descendants* (London: Heinemann Medical Books Ltd., 1933), p. 51.

103   "virtue and talents": William Thornton to Robert Batty, 16 November 1792, in C. M. Harris, ed., *Papers of William Thornton*, vol. 1, *1781–1802* (Charlottesville: University Press of Virginia, 1995), pp. 217–19.

104   a passionate radical: Thornton to George Washington, 2 June 1794, William Thornton Papers, LOC; Thornton to Benjamin Stoddert, 28 June 1798, in Harris, *Papers of William Thornton*, pp. 464–69.

104   There seemed no end: Brissot de Warville, *New Travels in the United States*, pp. 194–95; John Fitch to Thornton, 27 April 1791, in Harris, *Papers of William Thornton*, pp. 134–38; Thornton to Fitch, 21 June 1791, in ibid. pp. 141–47; Thornton to H. W. Mortimer, 13 August 1792, in ibid., pp. 198–202; Thornton to Herschel, 19 August 1792, in ibid., pp. 203–6; Thornton, *Short Account of the Origin of Steamboats* (Washington: Eliot's Patent Press, 1814); Stearns and Yerkes, *William Thornton*, p. 3–9, 13ff.

104   "when explaining to": "Life of William Thornton," William Thornton Papers, LOC.

104   "If I can't": diary, 1793, Anna Maria Thornton Papers, LOC; "Cadmus," William Thornton Papers, LOC.

105   plan for the United States Capitol: Thomas Jefferson to Daniel Carroll, 1 February 1793, in Saul K. Padover, ed., *Thomas Jefferson and the National Capital* (Washington: U.S. Government Printing Office, 1946), p. 171; Washington to the Federal Commissioners, 31 January 1793, Records of the Commissioners of the City of Washington, LOC; Washington to the Federal Commissioners, 3 March 1793, Letters of the Presidents to the Commissioners of the City of Washington, LOC; Washington to David Stuart, *Records of the Columbia Historical Society* (RCHS) 17, p. 72; Thornton to the Federal Commissioners, 10 April 1793, in Harris, *Papers of William Thornton*, pp. 242–47; editorial notes, in ibid., pp. 211–14, 239–42; Carl J. Richard, *The Founders and the Classics: Greece, Rome, and the American Enlightenment* (Cambridge: Harvard University Press, 1994), pp. 44–45; William C, Allen, *History of the United States Capitol: A Chronicle of Design, Construction, and Politics* (Washington: U.S. Government Printing Office, 2001), pp. 16–20.

106   "sa[l]ved and soothed": Washington to the Federal Commissioners, January 31, 1793, Records of the Commissioners, LOC.

106   when he stepped ashore: "Life of William Thornton," William Thornton Papers, LOC; "Address to the Heart, On the Subject of African Slavery," in Harris, *Papers of William Thornton*, pp. 49–53.

107   a rough, wild place: Ermin Penn, Tortola, author interview, December 12, 2006; Charles F. Jenkins, *Tortola: A Quaker Experiment Long Ago in the Tropics* (London: Friends Bookshop, 1923), pp. 2, 51–52; Abraham, *Lettsom*, pp. 51–53.

107   he came to believe: "Life of William Thornton," William Thornton Papers, LOC; Thornton to John Coakley Lettsom, 26 July 1788, in Harris, *Papers of William Thornton*, pp. 70–72; William Thornton, *Political Economy Founded in Justice and Humanity* (Washington: Samuel Harrison Smith, 1804), pp. 1–4, William Thornton Papers, LOC.

108   "A total and immediate": Thornton to Etienne Clavier, 7 November 1789, in Harris, *Papers of William Thornton*, pp. 103–7.

108   "I am induced": Thornton to John Coakley Lettsom, 18 November 1786, in ibid., pp. 30–35.

108   "If the taste": Thornton, *Political Economy*, p. 21.

108   With more reason: François-Alexandre-Frédéric, duc de la Rochefoucauld-Liancourt, *Travels through the United States of North America, the Country of the Iroquois and Upper Canada, in the Years 1795, 1796, and 1797*, vol. 2 (London: R. Phillips, 1799), pp. 281, 291; David Brion Davis, *Inhuman Bondage: The Rise and Fall of Slavery in the New World* (New York: Oxford University Press, 2006), p. 153.

109   New York slaves: Jill Lepore, *New York Burning: Liberty, Slavery, and Conspiracy in Eighteenth-Century Manhattan* (New York: Knopf, 2005), pp. 5–14, 248–59, et.al.

109   "If we persevere": Quoted in Arthur Zilversmit, *The First Emancipation: The Abolition of Slavery in the North* (Chicago: University of Chicago Press, 1967), p. 170.

109   "The experience of all": Adam Smith, *The Wealth of Nations* (New York: Modern Library, 1994), pp. 417–18.

109   By the 1780s: Zilversmit, *The First Emancipation*, pp. 109ff.

109   A Virginian: St. George Tucker to John Page, March 29, 1790, Pennsylvania Abolition Society Papers, PHS, copy courtesy of FFCP; letter to "Mr. Davis," *Virginia Independent Chronicle*, March 17, 1790, courtesy of FFCP.

110   envisioned a model colony: Thornton to John Coakley Lettsom, 18 November 1786, in Harris, *Papers of William Thornton*, pp. 30–35; Thornton to Lettsom, 20 May 1787, in ibid., pp. 55–57; Thornton to Jacques-Pierre Brissot de Warville, 29 November 1788, in ibid., pp. 80–81; Thornton to Samuel Hopkins, 29 September 1790, in ibid., pp. 117–19; Brissot de Warville, *New Travels in the United States*, pp. 250–52.

110   "Thus by proper encouragement": Thornton, "General Outlines of a Settlement on the Tooth or Ivory Coast of Africa," ibid., pp. 38–41.

111   "Few may be better fitted": Thornton to John Coakley Lettsom, July 26, 1788, ibid., p. 71.

111   "It is vain": Thornton to John Coakley Lettsom, November 13, 1789, ibid., p. 109.

112   Nowhere was that: Zilversmit, *The First Emancipation*, pp. 126ff.

112   Philadelphia was the real thing: Rufus Wilmot Griswold, *The Republican Court; or, American Society in the Days of Washington* (New York: D. Appleton and Co., 1867), pp. 238, 253–56, 324; Julian Ursyn Neimcewicz, *Under Their Vine and Fig Tree: Frauds through America in 1797–1799, 1805, and with Some Further Account of Life in New Jersey* (Elizabeth, N.J.: Grassman Publishing Co., 1965), pp. 35–38; Brissot de Warville, *New Travels in the United States*, pp. 253ff; Clement Biddle, *The Philadelphia Directory* (Philadelphia: Johnson, 1791); *Pennsylvania Gazette*, July 7, 1790, and April 25, 1792; Kenneth R. Bowling, "The Federal Government and the Republican Court Move to Philadelphia," in *Neither Separate nor Equal: Congress in the 1790s*, Kenneth R. Bowling and Donald R. Kennon, eds. (Athens: Ohio University Press, 2000), pp. 5ff, 19ff; Anna Coxe Toogood, "Philadelphia as the Nation's Capital," in Bowling and Kennon, ibid., pp. 48–49; Gary B. Nash, *First City: Philadelphia and the Forging of Historical Memory* (Philadelphia: University of Pennsylvania Press, 2002), pp. 122ff; Law-

rence Goldstone, *Dark Bargain: Slavery, Profits, and the Struggle for the Constitution* (New York: Walker & Co., 2005), pp. 94f; Simon P. Newman, *Embodied History: The Lives of the Poor in Early Philadelphia* (Philadelphia: University of Pennsylvania Press, 2003), p. 98.

113 "Philadelphia may be": Brissot de Warville, *New Travels in the United States*, p. 253.

113 "The inhabitants indulged": Anonymous, *An Account of the Rice, Progress and Termination of the Malignant Fever Lately Prevalent in Philadephia* (Philadelphia: Benjamin Johnson, 1793), p. 2.

113 "You cannot turn": Quoted in Griswold, *The Republican Court*, p. 252.

113 "Everywhere there is": Brissot de Warville, *New Travels in the United States*, p. 260.

114 a darker side: Gary B. Nash, *Forging Freedom: The Formation of Philadelphia's Black Community 1720–1840* (Cambridge: Harvard University Press, 1988), pp. 165–67; Billy G. Smith, *Life in Early Philadelphia* (University Park: Pennsylvania State University Press, 1995), pp. 3–11; Newman, *Embodied History*, p. 30.

115 "lawless and wandering": *Pennsylvania Gazette*, November 5, 1788.

115 "going into the river": Quoted in Julie Winch, *A Gentleman of Color: The Life of James Forten* (New York: Oxford University Press, 2002), p. 138.

115 Sanitation was primitive: *Pennsylvania Gazette*, September 1, 1790; Rochefoucauld-Liancourt, *Travels*, p. 245; Alyn Brodsky, *Benjamin Rush: Patriot and Physician* (New York: St. Martin's Press, 2004), pp. 13, 83.

115 "the receptacle of": *Pennsylvania Gazette*, February 29, 1792.

115 "a remarkable revolution": Biddle, *The Philadelphia Directory*.

115 "The citizens of Philada.": William Maclay, *The Diary of William Maclay and Other Notes on Senate Debates*, ed. Kenneth R. Bowling and Helen E. Veit (Baltimore: Johns Hopkins University Press, 1988), p. 331.

116 "laugh at the idea": *Pennsylvania Gazette*, July 9, 1790.

116 see George Washington: Griswold, *The Republican Court*, p. 365; Damie Stillman, "Six Houses for the President," *The Pennsylvania Magazine of History and Biography* 129 (October 2005).

116 government carried on its business: Toogood, "Philadelphia as the Nation's Capital," pp. 38ff.

116 "There is a current": quoted in Kenneth R. Bowling, *The Creation of Washington, D.C.* (Fairfax: George Mason University Press, 1991), p. 226.

117   the rented townhouse: Griswold, *The Republican Court*, pp. 240ff; Stillman, "Six Houses for the President," Edward J. Lawlor Jr., "The President's House Revisited," *The Pennsylvania Magazine of History and Biography* 129 (October 2005).

117   the presidential household included: Online at www.ushistory.org/presidents house, Web site of the Independence Hall Association.

117   the president's "negroes": ibid.

117   "The idea of freedom": Washington to Tobias Lear, April 12, 1791, ibid.

117   "I wish to have it": Quoted in Joseph J. Ellis, *His Excellency: George Washington* (New York: Knopf, 2004), p. 203.

118   more hospitable to blacks: Winch, *A Gentleman of Color*, pp. 128–30; John Woolman, "Some Considerations on the Keeping of Negroes," in Phillips P. Moulton, ed., *The Journal and Major Essays of John Woolman* (Richmond: Friends United Press, 1971), pp. 198ff; John M. Moore, *Friends in the Delaware Valley: Philadelphia Yearly Meeting 1681–1981* (Haverford: Friends Historical Association, 1981), pp. 30–32; Nash, *Forging Freedom*, pp. 27, 137, 143; Smith, *Life in Early Philadelphia*, pp. 77, 88; Carol Wilson, *Freedom at Risk: The Kidnapping of Free Blacks in America 1780–1865* (Lexington: University Press of Kentucky, 1994), p. 85; Lydia Maria Child, *Isaac T. Hopper: A True Life* (Boston: John P. Jewett & Co., 1853), pp. 263–64; *Pennsylvania Gazette*, July 13, 1791.

118   "Tho' they are black": Katherine Gerbner, "'We are Against the Traffik of Men-body'": The Germantonwn Quaker Protest of 1688 and the Origins of American Abolitionism, *Pennsylvania History*, Spring 2007.

118   "There exists, then": Brissot de Warville, *New Travels in the United States*, p. 217.

118   the Pennsylvania Abolition Society: Richard S. Newman, *The Transformation of American Abolitionism: Fighting Slavery in the Early Republic* (Chapel Hill: University of North Carolina Press, 2002), pp. 34–35, 44–46; William C. diGiacomantonio, "'For the Gratification of a Volunteering Society': Antislavery and Pressure Group Politics in the First Federal Congress," *Journal of the Early Republic* 15 (Summer 1995), pp. 171ff; Brissot de Warville, *New Travels in the United States*, pp. 240ff.; *Pennsylvania Gazette*, November 25, 1789.

118   "to use such means": *Pennsylvania Gazette*, May 23, 1787.

119   "his coat was": Brissot de Warville, *New Travels in the United States*, p. 300.

119   "But death were too mild": *Pennsylvania Gazette*, July 13, 1791.

119   also turned Benjamin Banneker: Silvio A. Bedini, *The Life of Benjamin Banneker* (New York: Scribner, 1972), pp. 85ff., 133ff; Martha E. Tyson, *Banneker: The Afric-American Astronomer* (Philadelphia: Friends Book Association, 1884), pp. 46–51.

119   illiterate "African Calculator": Brissot de Warville, *New Travels in the United States*, p. 234–35.

120   Banneker sent a copy: Benjamin Banneker to Jefferson, August 19, 1791, Bedini, *Life of Benjamin Banneker*, pp. 152–56.

120   "I shall be delighted": Jefferson to Banneker, August 30, 1791, ibid., pp. 157–60.

120   Meanwhile, Banneker's health: Tyson, *Banneker*, pp. 31ff, 56–58.

120   "I have a constant pain": Banneker to Susanna Mason, August 26, 1797, MHS.

121   Abolition Society fought: Richard S. Newman, *Transformation of American Abolitionism*, pp. 61–62, 69ff; Richard S. Newman, "The Pennsylvania Abolition Society: Restoring a Group to Glory," *Pennsylvania Legacies* 6, no. 2 (2005); Christopher Densmore, "Seeking Freedom in the Courts," *Pennsylvania Legacies* 6, no. 2 (2005).

121   "In Pennsylvania at least": Quoted in Newman, *Transformation of American Abolitionism*, p. 81.

121   "there were not wanting": Online at www.ushistory.org/presidentshouse.

121   Newspapers bulged with ads: Smith, *Life in Early Philadelphia*, pp. 94ff; Simon P. Newman, *Embodied History*, pp. 82ff; *Pennsylvania Gazette*, January 1, 1795, September 2, 1795, and October 21, 1795.

122   Kidnappers flourished, too: Wilson, *Freedom at Risk*, p. 10–11, 84–86, 49, 63; *Pennsylvania Gazette*, December 9, 1795.

122   "Says he is free": *Pennsylvania Gazette*, March 16, 1796.

122   Quaker influence had faded: Jenkins, *A Quaker Experiment*, pp. 54, 91; Pickering, *A Concise History*, pp. 45–46; Abraham, *Lettsom*, pp. 324ff.

122   Thornton shocked: William Thornton, "To the President and Members of the Council of the Virgin Islands," in Harris, *Papers of William Thornton*, pp. 129–30.

122   "hint me to be": Thornton to Granville Sharp, May 5, 1792, William Thornton Papers, LOC.

123   received the unwelcome news: Granville Sharp to Thornton, 5 October 1791, in Harris, *Papers of William Thornton*, pp. 158–61.

123   "have any effect in staying": Thornton to Granville Sharp, May 5, 1792, William Thornton Papers, LOC.

123   day and night, he worked: Thornton to John Fell, 5 October 1797, in Harris, *Papers of William Thornton*, pp. 418–20.

123   "First I thought": Thornton to Anthony Fothergill, 10 January 1797, in ibid.,
        pp. 424–26.

 CHAPTER 6: AN ALARMING AND SERIOUS TIME
Page

125   four black men entered: Gary B. Nash, *Forging Freedom: The Formation of Philadel-
        phia's Black Community 1720–1840* (Cambridge: Harvard University Press, 1988),
        pp. 108ff; W. E. B. DuBois, *The Philadelphia Negro* (Philadelphia: University of
        Pennsylvania Press, 1996), pp. 18–20; Julie Winch, *A Gentleman of Color: The Life
        of James Forten* (New York: Oxford University Press, 2002), pp. 139–42.

126   "We expected to take": Quoted in Nash, *Forging Freedom*, p. 118.

127   Thornton had arrived: William Thornton to John Coakley Lettsom, February
        15, 1787, in C. M. Harris, ed., *Papers of William Thornton*, vol. 1, *1781–1802*
        (Charlottesville: University Press of Virginia, 1995), p. 43.

127   who were creating a free world: Nash, *Forging Freedom*, pp. 4–6, 65–66; Winch,
        A Gentleman of Color, pp. 125ff.

127   first fugitive slave law: Marion Gleason McDougall, *Fugitive Slaves (1619–1865)*
        (New York: Ginn & Co., 1891), pp. 105–6; Paul Finkelman, *Slavery and the
        Founders: Race and Liberty in the Age of Jefferson* (Armonk, N.Y.: M. E. Sharpe
        Inc., 2002), pp. 86–87; Richard S. Newman, *The Transformation of American
        Abolitionism: Fighting Slavery in the Early Republic* (Chapel Hill: University of
        North Carolina Press, 2002), pp. 65, 78–80.

128   ads for runaway slaves: *Pennsylvania Gazette*, September 2, 1795, and October
        7, 1795; Richard Wojtowicz and Billy G. Smith, "Fugitives: Newspaper Adver-
        tisements for Runaway Slaves, Indentured Servants, and Apprentices," in Billy
        G. Smith, ed., *Life in Early Philadelphia* (University Park: Pennsylvania State
        University Press, 1995), pp. 87ff.

128   A new kind of man: Winch, *A Gentleman of Color*, pp. 38ff, 65ff.

128   "The American and the African": Quoted in Newman, *Transformation of Ameri-
        can Abolitionism*, p. 92.

130   "getting our liberty": Jupiter Hammon, *An Address to the Negroes in the State of
        New York*, pamphlet (Philadelphia: Daniel Humphreys, 1787).

130   Jones and Allen were its copresidents: Nash, *Forging Freedom*, pp. 67–68, 95–98,
        192–95; DuBois, *The Philadelphia Negro*, p. 19–21.

131   "leapt and swayed": Nash, *Forging Freedom*, pp. 194.

131   Although Methodists would: Donald G. Mathews, *Slavery and Methodism: A
        Chapter in American Morality 1780–1845* (Princeton: Princeton University Press,
        1965), pp. 3–25.

132 "the first wavering step": DuBois, *The Philadelphia Negro*, p. 19.

132 the "irreligious and uncivilized": "Preamble of the Free African Society," in William Douglass, *Annals of the First African Church in the United States* (Philadelphia: King & Baird, 1862), excerpted online at pbs/org/wgbh/aia, "Africans in America," Part 3.

132 "Remember, that you have enemies": ibid.

133 "so general as to embrace": ibid.

133 an utterly unforseen catastrophe: *Pennsylvania Gazette*, September 24, 1793; Nash, *Forging Freedom*, pp. 140–42; J. M. Powell, *Bring Out Your Dead: The Great Plague of Yellow Fever in Philadelphia in 1793* (Philadelphia: University of Pennsylvania Press, 1993), pp. 4–5.

133 philanthropist John Nicholson: Robert D. Arbuckle, *Pennsylvania Speculator and Patriot: The Entrepreneurial John Nicholson 1757–1800* (University Park: Pennsylvania State University Press, 1975), p. 206; Benjamin Rush to John Nicholson, August 12, 1793, in Allen C. Clark, *Greenleaf and Law in the Federal City* (Washington: W. F. Roberts, 1901), p. 43; Nash, *Forging Freedom*, pp. 119–20.

134 "The dinner was plentiful": Benjamin Rush to Julia Rush, August 22, 1793, HSP.

134 "A Fever prevails": Elaine Forman Crane, ed., *The Diary of Elizabeth Drinker: The Life Cycle of an Eighteenth-Century Woman*, vol. 1 (Boston: Northeastern University Press, 1991), pp. 494ff.

134 Some speculated that: Mathew Carey, *A Short Account of the Malignant Fever Lately Prevalent in Philadelphia* (Philadelphia: Mathew Carey, 1793), pp. 15ff; Anonymous, *An Account of the Rise, Progress and Termination of the Malignant Fever Lately Prevalent in Philadelphia* (Philadelphia: Benjamin Johnson, 1793), pp. 4–7; Anonymous, *An Earnest Call Occasioned by the Alarming Pestilential Contagion, pamphlet* (Philadelphia: Jones, Hoff, and Derrick, 1793).

134 The president had other things: George Washington to Henry Knox, et. al., 9 September 1793, in John C. Fitzpatrick, ed., *The Writings of George Washington*, vol. 35 (Washington: U.S. Government Printing Office, 1940), pp. 80–81, 86.

135 Irish architect James Hoban: Martin I. J. Griffin, "James Hoban Architect and Builder of the White House," *The American Catholic Historical Researches*, vol. III, January 1907; William Seale, *The President's House*, vol. 1 (Washington: White House Historical Association, 1986), pp. 47–48; Seale, *The White House: The History of an American Idea* (Washington: American Institute of Architects Press, 1992), p. 21.

135 "I had no idea": Washington to the Federal Commissioners, March 3, 1793, *Records of the Columbia Historical Society* (RCHS) 17, p. 76.

135   other upsetting reports: Federal Commissioners to Thornton, 5 April 1793, Letterbooks of the Commissioners of Washington, D.C., 1791–1798, Record Group 42, NA; Washington to James Hoban, 1 July 1793, RCHS 17, p. 83; Tobias Lear to Thornton, 13 July 1793, William Thornton Papers, LOC; Thomas Jefferson to Washington, 17 July 1793, Letterbooks, NA; Washington to the Federal Commissioners, 25 July 1793, in Fitzpatrick, *Writings of George Washington*, vol. 35, p. 29; Washington to the Federal Commissioners, 29 August 1793, in ibid., p. 74; "Editorial Note: Thornton's Capitol Modified: The Philadelphia Conference," in Harris, *Papers of William Thornton*, pp. 255–59; Washington to Jefferson, 8 July 1793, in ibid., p. 260; Thornton to Jefferson, 8 July 1793, in ibid.

135   "I was governed": Washington to Jefferson, 30 June 1793, William Thornton Papers, LOC.

135   Washington's thoughts turned: Washington to William Pearce, 25 August 1793, in Fitzpatrick, *The Writings of George Washington*, vol. 35, p. 61; Washington to Pearce, in ibid., p. 68.

136   The summer had been hot: Powell, *Bring Out Your Dead*, pp. 1–3.

136   The first to die: Anonymous, *An Account of the Rise*, pp. 4–5; Carey, *A Short Account*, pp. 14, 19.

136   Drinker recorded: Crane, *Diary of Elizabeth Drinker*, pp. 497–98.

136   "Some lost their reason": Absalom Jones and Richard Allen, *A Narrative of the Proceedings of the Black People, During the Late Awful Calamity in Philadelphia, in the Year 1793* (Philadelphia: William W. Woodward, 1794), p. 16.

137   Panic spread: Joshua Cresson, "Meditations written during visitation of sickness & mortality in Philadelphia," personal album, FHL; Anonymous, *An Earnest Call*; Anonymous, *An Account of the Rise*, pp. 10–20; *Minutes of the Proceedings of the Committee Appointed on 14 September 1793 to Attend and Alleviate the Sufferings of the Afflicted with the Malignant Fever* (Philadelphia: Crissy & Markey, 1848), entry for September 24, 1793; Journal of John Hunt, entries for September and October 1793, FHL, Robert Morris to Thomas Morris, November 24, 1793, Letterbooks of Robert Morris, LOC; Carey, *A Short Account*, pp. 22–33; Crane, *Diary of Elizabeth Drinker*, p. 497ff; Powell, *Bring Out Your Dead*, pp. 23–24, 45–59.

137   Rural vigilantes ordered: Anonymous, *An Account of the Rise*, pp. 26–27; Carey, *A Short Account*, pp. 60–61.

137   At distant ports: Powell, *Bring Out Your Dead*, pp. 220–25; Carey, *A Short Account*, pp. 68–69.

138   Desperate officials unceremoniously: *Minutes of the Proceedings*, September 14 to October 10, 1793; Anonymous, *An Account of the Rise*, pp. 19–20; Powell, *Bring Out Your Dead*, pp. 61–62.

138   "Tis very afflicting": Crane, *Diary of Elizabeth Drinker*, p. 517.

138   Benjamin Rush: Alyn Brodsky, *Benjamin Rush: Patriot and Physician* (New York: St. Martin's Press, 2004), pp. 323ff.

138   he "moved through": Ibid., p. 12.

138   "I love even the name": Quoted in Nash, *Forging Freedom*, p. 105.

139   "All the vices which": Benjamin Rush, *An Address on the Slavery of the Negroes in America*, pamphlet (New York: Arno Press, 1969).

140   He believed in bloodletting: Powell, *Bring Out Your Dead*, pp. 78ff, 122–27; Brodsky, *Benjamin Rush*, pp. 267–69.

140   Thornton, who also witnessed: Thornton to Lettsom, 11 December 1793, in Harris, *Papers of William Thornton*, pp. 273–75; Thornton to Anthony Fothergill, 10 January 1797, in ibid., pp. 424–26; Thornton to Jefferson, 7 May 1800, in ibid., pp. 543–45.

140   *"Streams of miasmata"*: Powell, *Bring Out Your Dead*. p. 117.

140   the plague rarely struck blacks: Jones and Allen, *Narrative of the Proceedings*, pp. 3ff; Powell, *Bring Out Your Dead*, pp. 94ff.

141   "a noble opportunity": Quoted in Winch, *A Gentleman of Color*, pp. 137.

141   "Much depends upon us": Jones and Allen, *Narrative of the Proceedings*, p. 27.

142   "We visited upwards": ibid., pp. 3–6.

142   In pairs, their teams: ibid., pp. 14ff.

142   scenes of heartrending tragedy: Carey, *A Short Account*, pp. 33–34; Anonymous, *An Account of the Rise*, pp. 13ff, 24–27.

142   "and none but little": Jones and Allen, *Narrative of the Proceedings*, p. 18.

143   "Our distress hath been": ibid., p. 15.

143   Lawyers, magistrates, and public officials: Powell, *Bring Out Your Dead*, pp. 46–47, 55–59, 260ff; Washington to Alexander Hamilton, 6 September 1793, in Fitzpatrick, *The Writings of George Washington*, vol. 35, p. 83; Washington to Henry Knox, 9 September 1793, in ibid., p. 86; Washington to Tobias Lear, 25 September 1793, RCHS 17, p. 91.

144   "I think we must": Jefferson to Washington, October 17, 1793, in Saul K. Padover, ed., *Thomas Jefferson and the National Capital* (Washington: U.S. Government Printing Office, 1946), pp. 187–88.

144   deaths continued to climb: Powell, *Bring Out Your Dead*, pp. 103ff, 197, 235; Winch, *A Gentleman of Color*, p. 136.

144   "This has been a long night": Thornton to John Coakley Lettsom, December 11, 1793, in Harris, *Papers of William Thornton*, pp. 273–75.

144   the weather turned cold: Powell, *Bring Out Your Dead*, pp. 266ff; Crane, *Diary of Elizabeth Drinker*, pp. 518–20;

145   The epidemic probably killed: Powell, *Bring Out Your Dead*, pp. 258, 281.

145   his monstrous treatment: ibid., pp. 122–25.

146   "diligency, attention and decency": duBois, *The Philadelphia Negro*, p. 18.

146   "appointed two illiterate Negro men": Quoted in Brodsky, *Benjamin Rush*, p. 341.

146   Mathew Carey, a journalist: Carey, *A Short Account*, p. 78; Anonymous, *An Account of the Rise*, pp. 28ff.

146   "that a black man": Jones and Allen, *Narrative of the Proceedings*, p. 24.

146   a detailed accounting: ibid., pp. 6–9.

147   "Thus were *our services*": ibid., p. 15.

147   the months after the epidemic: duBois, *The Philadelphia Negro*, pp. 20–24.

148   the dire speeches: Charlene Bangs Bickford, Kenneth R. Bowling, William Charles diGiacomantonio, and Helen E. Veit, eds., *Documentary History of the First Federal Congress of the United States of America*, vol. XI (Baltimore: Johns Hopkins University Press, 1992–1996), pp. 1409–14.

 CHAPTER 7: IRRESISTABLE TEMPTATIONS

Page

149   Washington and his fellow Masons: F. L. Brockett, *The Lodge of Washington: A History of the Alexandria-Washington Lodge, No.22* (Westminster: Willow Bend Books, 2001), pp. 46–48; John J. Lanier, *Washington: The Great American Mason* (New York: Macoy Publishing, undated), pp. 42ff, 170–72; Anonymous, *A Memorial to Washington the Mason* (Alexandria: Alexandria-Washington Lodge, No.22, A.F. & A.M., 1910); William C. Allen, *History of the United States Capitol: A Chronicle of Design, Construction, and Politics* (Washington: U.S. Government Printing Office, 2001), pp. 24ff.

150   Masonry claimed descent: Steven C. Bullock, *Revolutionary Brotherhood: Freemasonry and the Transformation of the American Social Order, 1730–1840* (Chapel Hill: University of North Carolina Press, 1996), pp. 9–13, 109–10, 129ff.

152   "a great want of punctuality": Federal Commissioners to Thomas Jefferson, December 5, 1792, in Saul K. Padover, ed., *Thomas Jefferson and the National Capital* (Washington: U.S. Government Printing Office, 1946), pp. 161–62;

C. M. Harris, "Washington's 'Federal City,' Jefferson's 'federal town,'" *Washington History* 12, no. 1 (Spring/Summer 2000).

153   the ingratiating person of Samuel Blodget: A. M. Sakolski, *The Great American Land Bubble: The Amazing Story of Land-Grabbing, Speculations, and Booms from Colonial Days to the Present Time* (New York: Harper & Brothers, 1932), pp. 154ff.

153   "it would be best": George Washington to the Federal Commissioners, 13 November 1792, Records of the Commissioners of the City of Washington, LOC.

153   "You are retained": Federal Commissioners to Samuel Blodget, 5 January 1793, Records of the Commissioners, LOC.

153   "He has great confidence": Federal Commissioners to Jefferson, January 5, 1793, in Padover, *Thomas Jefferson and the National Capital*, pp. 165–67.

153   Tobias Lear, was pressed: Tobias Lear, *Observations on the River Potomack, the Country Adjacent, and the City of Washington*, pamphlet (New York: Samuel Loudon and Sons, 1793).

153   Lotteries had been used: *Pennsylvania Gazette*, February 9, 1791, March 9, 1791, and October 12, 1791; Washington to the Federal Commissioners, November 13, 1792, Records of the Commissioners, LOC; John M. Findlay, *People of Chance: Gambling in American Society from Jamestown to Las Vegas* (New York: Oxford University Press, 1986), pp. 31–34; Herbert Asbury, *Sucker's Progress: An Informal History of Gambling in America* (New York: Dodd, Meade, and Co., 1938), pp. 72ff; Willis L. Shirk Jr., "Wright's Ferry: A Glimpse into the Susquehannah Backcountry," *The Pennsylvania Magazine of History and Biography* 120 (January/April 1996).

154   "we shall obtain": Samuel Blodget to Jefferson, June 25, 1792, in Padover, *Thomas Jefferson and the National Capital*, pp. 146–47.

154   He proposed to offer: Bob Arnebeck, *Through a Fiery Trial: Building Washington, 1790–1800* (Lanham, Md.: Madison Books, 1991), pp. 149–50.

154   Fifteen hundred people attended: *Pennsylvania Gazette*, July 17, 1793.

154   "We entreat, Sir": Federal Commissioners to Henry Lee, September 1793, Records of the Commissioners, LOC.

154   even his consummate salesmanship: Arnebeck, *Through a Fiery Trial*, p. 171–75; Barbara Ann Chernow, *Robert Morris: Land Speculator, 1790–1801* (New York: Arno Press, 1978), pp. 136–37; Sakolski, *Great American Land Bubble*, pp. 154–55; Blodget to the Federal Commissioners, 1794, otherwise undated letter, Records of the Commissioners, LOC.

155   "In a short time": Quoted in Arnebeck, *Through a Fiery Trial*, p. 188.

155　"wants judgment and steadiness": ibid., p. 201.

156　"Speculation has been": Washington to Thomas Johnson, January 23, 1794, *Records of the Columbia Historical Society* (RCHS) 17, p. 94–96.

156　"to forbear the publication": Federal Commissioners to Samuel Blodget, December 15, 1793, Records of the Commissioners, LOC.

156　"Altho' you may": Samuel Blodget to William Thornton, January 1, 1794, William Thornton Papers, LOC.

156　"[We] beg you sir": Federal Commissioners to Samuel Blodget, December 16, 1793, Letterbooks of the Commissioners of Washington, Record Group 42, NA.

156　"no further steps": Federal Commissioners to Samuel Blodget, December 21, 1793, Letterbooks, NA; Daniel Carrol to Blodget, December 22, 1793, Letterbooks of the Commissioners, NA.

156　a new savior: Washington to the Federal Commissioners, August 20, 1793, RCHS 17, p. 87; Washington to Tobias Lear, September 25, 1793, RCHS 17, p. 91; Kenneth R. Bowling, e-mail to the author, September 27, 2007.

157　he dazzled everyone: Allen C. Clark, *Greenleaf and Law in the Federal City* (Washington: W. F. Roberts, 1901), pp. 9, 81–83, 210; Robert D. Arbuckle, *Pennsylvania Speculator and Patriot: The Entrepreneurial John Nicholson 1757–1800* (University Park: Pennsylvania State University, 1975), pp. 114–15; Sakolski, *Great American Land Bubble*, p. 37.

157　Greenleaf contracted to buy: Chernow, *Robert Morris*, pp. 139–42.

157　he had lined up as partners: Federal Commissioners to Washington, December 23, 1793, Records of the Commissioners, LOC; "Articles," December 24, 1793, Records of the Commissioners, LOC; Sakolski, *Great American Land Bubble*, pp. 156–59; Clark, *Greenleaf and Law*, p. 68.

158　"the greatest land-grabbing"; Sakolski, *Great American Land Bubble*, p. 156.

158　"Be fully assured": Federal Commissioners to James Greenleaf, December 15, 1793, Records of the Commissioners, LOC.

158　"We have no fears": Federal Commissioners to Samuel Blodget, December 21, 1793, Letterbooks of the Commissioners, NA.

158　The president thought: Washington to Tobias Lear, September 25, 1793, RCHS 17, p. 91; Washington to Daniel Carroll, January 7, 1795, RCHS 17, p. 113.

159　"In America, where": François-Alexandre-Frédéric, duc de la Rochefoucauld-Liancourt, *Travels through the United States of North America, the Country of the Iroquois and Upper Canada, in the Years 1795, 1796, and 1797*, vol. 2 (London: R. Phillips, 1799), pp. 316–18.

159   the "Hannibal" of finance: Arbuckle, *Pennsylvania Speculator and Patriot*, p. 203.

159   John Nicholson was: ibid., pp. 6ff.

159   "All other places": ibid., p. 115.

160   Robert Morris's presence: Federal Commissioners to Washington, December 23, 1793, Records of the Commissioners, LOC; Chernow, *Robert Morris*, pp. 7–9, 19ff, 129ff; Elizabeth M. Nuxoll, "Robert Morris and the Shaping of the Post-Revolutionary American Economy" (paper presented at the Omohundro Institute of Early American History and Culture Conference, Austin, Texas, June 1999); Elizabeth M. Nuxoll, "The Financier as Senator: Robert Morris of Pennsylvania, 1789–1795," in Kenneth R. Bowling and Donald R. Kennon, eds., *Neither Separate nor Equal: Congress in the 1790s* (Athens: Ohio University Press, 2000), p. 91ff; Robert E. Wright and David J. Cowen, *Financial Founding Fathers: The Men Who Made America Rich* (Chicago: University of Chicago Press, 2006), pp. 119ff; Rufus Wilmot Griswold, *The Republican Court; or, American Society in the Days of Washington* (New York: D. Appleton and Co., 1867), pp. 309–11; Anna Coxe Toogood, e-mail to the author, August 8, 2006.

160   "No badly cooked": Samuel Breck, quoted in Clark, *Greenleaf and Law*, p. 25.

160   "I can never do things": ibid., p. 27.

161   "Were I to characterize": Quoted in Sakolski, *Great American Land Bubble*, p. 30.

161   Tens of millions of acres: Thomas P. Slaughter, *The Whiskey Rebellion: Frontier Epilogue to the American Revolution* (New York: Oxford University Press, 1986), pp. 78ff.; Sakolski, *Great American Land Bubble*, pp. 4ff, 29ff, 103–6; Chernow, *Robert Morris*, pp. 31–35, 179–80; Joel Achenbach, *The Grand Idea: George Washington's Potomac, and the Race to the West* (New York: Simon & Schuster, 2004), p. 207; Henry Wiencek, *An Imperfect God: George Washington, His Slaves, and the Creation of America* (New York: Farrar, Straus and Giroux, 2003), pp. 27–28; Richard Parkinson, *A Tour in America: 1798, 1799, and 1800* (London: J. Harding, 1805), pp. 10–16; Anonymous, *Look Before You Leap; or, A Few Hints to Such Artizans, Mechanics, Labourers, Farmers and Husbandmen, as Are Desireous of Emigrating to America* (London: W. Row, 1796), pp. 44–45.

161   "The men that say": Parkinson, *A Tour in America*, p. 21.

162   John Nicholson, for instance: Arbuckle, *Pennsylvania Speculator and Patriot*, pp. 6ff., 76–77; Sakolski, *Great American Land Bubble*, pp. 58–62; Chernow, *Robert Morris*, pp. 37–55; Clark, *Greenleaf and Law*, p. 26; Wright and Cowen, *Financial Founding Fathers*, p. 138.

162   "If I had contented": Quoted in Sakolski, *Great American Land Bubble*, p. 63.

162   Morris and Nicholson teamed up: Robert Morris to John Nicholson, November 30, 1793, et al., Robert Morris Collection, Huntington Library, San Marino,

CA; Arbuckle, *Pennsylvania Speculator and Patriot*, pp. 94ff, 167–68; Frank Gaylord Cook, "Robert Morris," *The Atlantic Monthly* 66 (November 1890); Chernow, *Robert Morris*, pp. 170–72; Clark, *Greenleaf and Law*, pp. 85–86.

163   "we know that their credit": Quoted in Arnebeck, *Through a Fiery Trial*, p. 235.

163   Everyone waited eagerly: Washington to Daniel Carroll, January 7, 1795, RCHS 17, p. 113; Federal Commissioners to John Randolph, undated, Records of the Commissioners, LOC; Chernow, *Robert Morris*, pp. 144–46; Arnebeck, *Through a Fiery Trial*, pp. 183–84, 234.

164   a very inauspicious moment: William Doyle, *The Oxford History of the French Revolution* (New York: Oxford University Press, 2002), pp. 196–203, 251–59; Simon Schama, *Citizens: A Chronicle of the French Revolution* (New York: Vintage, 1989), pp. 248ff, 684ff, 780–91; Stanley Elkins and Eric McKittrick, *The Age of Federalism: The Early American Republic 1788–1800* (New York: Oxford University Press, 1993), pp. 37ff.

165   "Still more heads": Quoted in Schama, *Citizens*, pp. 783.

165   Opinion in the United States: Joseph J. Ellis, *American Sphinx: The Character of Thomas Jefferson* (New York: Vintage, 1998), pp. 127ff; David McCullough, *John Adams* (New York: Simon & Schuster, 2001), pp. 442–47; Forrest McDonald, *Alexander Hamilton: A Biography* (New York: W. W. Norton & Co., 1982), pp. 270ff.

165   William Thornton, afire: Thornton to Washington, June 2, 1794, William Thornton Papers, LOC.

165   "The liberty of": Jefferson to William Short, January 3, 1793, in Thomas Jefferson, *Writings* (New York: The Library of America, 1984), p. 1004.

165   posed a dire challenge: Reginald Horsman, *The New Republic: The United States of America 1789–1815* (Harlow: Longman, 2000), pp. 39–43; Elkins and McKittrick, *The Age of Federalism*, p. 389; Joseph J. Ellis, *His Excellency: George Washington* (New York: Knopf, 2004), pp. 222ff; *Pennsylvania Gazette*, December 17, 1794.

166   "In every direction": Quoted in Slaughter, *Whiskey Rebellion*, p. 159.

166   In Europe, the tide: Doyle, *Oxford History*, pp. 206–9.

167   it "would be unsafe": James Greenleaf to the Federal Commissioners, July 18, 1794, Records of the Commissioners, LOC.

167   "When we entered on": Federal Commissioners to James Greenleaf, July 31, 1794, Records of the Commissioners, LOC.

167   "We suffer much": Daniel Carroll to Edmund Randolph, August 15, 1794, Records of the Commissioners, LOC; Federal Commissioners to James Greenleaf, September 19, 1794, Letterbooks of the Commissioners, NA.

167   the commissioners could no longer afford: Federal Commissioners to Edmund Randolph, September 19 and October 18, 1794, Records of the Commissioners, LOC; Chernow, *Robert Morris*, pp. 145–47.

168   Blodget continued to insinuate himself: Samuel Blodget to Thornton, January 1794, William Thornton papers, LOC; "Account" of Samuel Blodget, Federal Commissioners to George Washington, July 31, 1794, Letterbooks of the Commissioners, NA; *City of Washington: Scheme of the Lottery, No.II*, and *United States Lottery by Permission of the Commissioners*, broadsides, both January 1, 1794, Records of the Commissioners, LOC; Arnebeck, *Through a Fiery Trial*, pp. 215–16; Sakolski, *Great American Land Bubble*, pp. 155–56.

168   "It was unfortunate": Quoted in Arnebeck, *Through a Fiery Trial*, p. 202.

169   "We disdain entering into": Federal Commissioners to Mr. Fermo, July 30, 1794, Letterbooks of the Commissioners, NA.

169   "has in a great measure deprived": "Account" of Samuel Blodget, Federal Commissioners to Washington, July 31, 1794, Letterbooks of the Commissioners, NA.

169   "I was at a loss": Washington to Thomas Johnson, January 23, 1794, RCHS 17, p. 94.

169   Blodget whined that: Samuel Blodget to the Federal Commissioners, 1794 letter otherwise undated, Records of the Commissioners, LOC.

169   discovered that he had skipped town: Clark, *Greenleaf and Law*, p. 92; Sakolski, *Great American Land Bubble*, pp. 155–56; Benjamin H. Latrobe, *The Journal of Latrobe* (New York: D. Appleton & Co., 1905), p. 132.

170   "I am mortified": Quoted in Arnebeck, *Through a Fiery Trial*, p. 256.

170   "You call your disappointments": Robert Morris to James Greenleaf, December 23, 1794, Letterbooks of Robert Morris, LOC.

170   "The year 1800 is approaching": Washington to Thomas Lee, 25 July 1794, RCHS 17, p. 106; Washington to the Federal Commissioners, 23 July 1794, RCHS 17, p. 105; Washington to John Adams, 15 November 1794, RCHS 17, p. 109.

170   "this melancholy truth": Federal Commissioners to Washington, 29 January 1795, Letterbooks of the Commissioners, NA.

171   The city's landscape was littered: Sally Kennedy Alexander, "A Sketch of the Life of Major Andrew Ellicott," *Records of the Columbia Historical Society*, vol. 2, 1899; Gregory C. Spies, "Major Andrew Ellicott, Esq.: Colonial American Astronomical Surveyor, Patriot, Cartographer, Legislator, Scientific Instrument Maker, Boundary Commissioner & Professor of Mathematics," unpublished paper; Ashley Kline, "Andrew Ellicott," *Lancaster Heritage Outlook*, winter 2005;

W. W. Abbott and Dorothy Twohig, eds., *The Papers of George Washington*, vol. 12 (Charlottesville: University Press of Virginia, 2002), p. 401, note; Washington to Daniel Carroll, January 7, 1795, RCHS 17, p. 113.

171   Thomas Law had come all the way: Thomas Law, *A Reply to Certain Insinuations* (Washington: n.p., 1824); Arbuckle, *Pennsylvania Speculator and Patriot*, pp. 120–22; Arnebeck, *Through a Fiery Trial*, pp. 251–52; Clark, *Greenleaf and Law*, pp. 223ff.; Law to William Blane, December 5, 1794, in ibid., p. 94; Law to William Cranch, February 17, 1795, in ibid., p. 102.

173   On Christmas Eve, Law agreed: James Greenleaf to William Cranch, December 20, 1794, in Clark, *Greenleaf and Law*, p. 100; Thomas Law to Greenleaf, December 6, 1794, in ibid., p. 94; Law to Greenleaf, December 14, 1794, in ibid., p. 94.

173   "To part with the legal title": Washington to Daniel Carroll, January 7, 1795, in Clark, *Greenleaf and Law*, p. 92.

173   "You may say that": quoted in Sakolski, *Great American Land Bubble*, p. 161.

173   "the young men from the North": Thomas Law to James Greenleaf, December 31, 1794, in Clark, *Greenleaf and Law*, p. 100.

174   "The business, I conceive": Quoted in Arnebeck, *Through a Fiery Trial*, p. 261.

174   "Here I will make": Quoted in Clark, *Greenleaf and Law*, p. 238.

CHAPTER 8: A SCENE OF DISTRESS

Page

175   "Morris's Folly": Frank Gaylord Cook, "Robert Morris," *The Atlantic Monthly*, 66 (November 1890); Barbara Ann Chernow, *Robert Morris: Land Speculator, 1790–1801* (New York: Arno Press, 1978), pp. 101–102; Kenneth R. Bowling, *Peter Charles L'Enfant: Vision, Honor, and Male Friendship in the Early American Republic* (Washington: The Friends of George Washington University Libraries, 2002), pp. 38–42; Scott W. Berg, *Grand Avenues: The Story of the French Visionary Who Designed Washington, D.C.* (New York: Pantheon, 2007), pp. 208–10; Rufus W. Griswold, *The Republican Court; or, American Society in the Days of Washington* (New York: D. Appleton and Co., 1867), p. 264; Damie Stillman, "Six Houses for the President," *Pennsylvania Magazine of History and Biography*, October 2005.

177   Morris tottered on the cliff's edge: George Washington to Daniel Carroll, January 7, 1795, *Records of the Columbia Historical Society* (RCHS) 17, p. 113; William Thornton to the Federal Commissioners, March 13 and March 25, 1795, C. M. Harris, ed., *Papers of William Thornton*, vol. 1, *1781–1802* (Charlottesville: University Press of Virginia, 1995), pp. 313–16; Chernow, *Robert Morris*, pp. 144–46; Allen C. Clark, *Greenleaf and Law in the Federal City* (Washington: W. F. Roberts, 1901), p. 106.

178   a speculative scheme so gargantuan: Robert Morris to Josiah Watson, April 22, 1795, Letterbooks of Robert Morris, LOC; Morris to James Dunlop, April 22, 1795, Morris Letterbook, LOC; A. M. Sakolski, *The Great American Land Bubble: The Amazing Story of Land-Grabbing, Speculations, and Booms from Colonial Days to the Present Time* (New York: Harper & Brothers, 1932), pp. 47–53, 125ff, 142–43; Chernow, *Robert Morris*, pp. 170–72, 186–87, 197; Robert D. Arbuckle, *Pennsylvania Speculator and Patriot: The Entrepreneurial John Nicholson 1757–1800* (University Park: Pennsylvania State University Press, 1975), pp. 165–68; Robert E. Wright and David J. Cowen, *Financial Founding Fathers: The Men Who Made America Rich* (Chicago: University of Chicago Press, 2006), pp. 138–39; Federal Commissioners to James Greenleaf, July 31, 1794, Records of the Commissioners of the City of Washington, LOC; David Stuart and Daniel Carroll to Edmund Randolph, July 31, 1794, Records of the Commissioners, LOC; Carroll to Randolph, August 15, 1794, Records of the Commissioners, LOC.

180   "He borrows at a dreadful interest": Thomas Law to James Greenleaf, January 8, 1795, in Clark, *Greenleaf and Law*, p. 101.

180   "Money grows Scarcer": Quoted in Arbuckle, *Pennsylvania Speculator and Patriot*, p. 123.

180   when the report was released: Federal Commissioners to James Greenleaf, May 18, 1795, Records of the Commissioners, LOC; Elizabeth M. Nuxoll, "The Financier as Senator," in Kenneth R. Bowling and Donald R. Kennon, eds., *Neither Separate nor Equal: Congress in the 1790s* (Athens: Ohio University Press, 2000), pp. 122–26.

180   Morris and Nicholson blamed: Washington to the Federal Commissioners, April 24, 1794, Letters of the Presidents to the Commissioners of the City of Washington, LOC; Robert Morris to William Constable, in Clark, *Greenleaf and Law*, pp. 112–13; Arbuckle, *Pennsylvania Speculator and Patriot*, pp. 121–23; Chernow, *Robert Morris*, pp. 118–19.

181   "I have known for years": quoted in Bob Arnebeck, *Through a Fiery Trial: Building Washington, 1790–1800* (Lanham, Md.: Madison Books, 1991), p. 422.

181   "Pardon me if I hurt": Thomas Law to James Greenleaf, July 12, 1795, in Clark, *Greenleaf and Law*, pp. 108–9.

181   Greenleaf cheerily assured him: James Greenleaf to Thomas Law, July 15, 1795, in ibid., 110.

181   "The unhappy engagements": Robert Morris to Wilhelm and Jan Willink, April 19, 1797, in Clark, *Greenleaf and Law*, 113.

182   they now found themselves: Federal Commissioners to James Greenleaf, May 18, 1795, Records of the Commissioners, LOC; Chernow, *Robert Morris*, pp. 151, 160; Sakolski, *Great American Land Bubble*, 165.

182   he scrambled to raise funds: Robert Morris to Josiah Watson, April 22, 1795, Morris letterbook, LOC; Morris to William Constable, September 22, 1795, Morris letterbook, LOC; Morris to Henry Chercot, December 7, 1795, Morris letterbook, LOC; Morris to James Carey, December 7, 1795, Morris letterbook, LOC.

182   "Our ready money": Robert Morris to Wilhelm and Jan Willink, April 19, 1797, in Clark, *Greenleaf and Law*, 113.

182   The president was distraught: Washington to Edmund Randolph, July 22, 1795, RCHS 17, p. 137; Washington to the Federal Commissioners, July 29, 1795, RCHS 17, p. 137; Washington to Robert Morris, September 14, 1795, RCHS 17, p. 141.

183   beset by unending national crisis: Reginald Horsman, *The New Republic: The United States of America 1789–1815* (Harlow: Longman, 2000), pp. 47–62; Thomas P. Slaughter, *The Whiskey Rebellion: Frontier Epilogue to the American Revolution* (New York: Oxford University Press, 1986), pp. 176, 183; *Pennsylvania Gazette*, December 17, 1794.

184   "Jay's Treaty was": Joseph J. Ellis, *Founding Brothers: The Revolutionary Generation* (New York: Vintage, 2002), pp. 136–37.

184   most difficult trial of his entire presidency: Stanley Elkins and Eric McKittrick, *The Age of Federalism: The Early American Republic, 1788–1800* (New York: Oxford University Press, 1993), pp. 408–21; James Thomas Flexner, *Washington: The Indispensible Man* (Boston: Little, Brown and Co., 1969), pp. 326–36.

185   violent agitation had flared: *Pennsylvania Gazette*, August 27, September 3, and December 17, 1794; Slaughter, *Whiskey Rebellion*, pp. 179–88, 216–18; Elkins and McKittrick, *The Age of Federalism*, pp. 462–88; John C. Miller, *The Federalist Era, 1789–1801* (New York: Harper Torchbooks, 1960), pp. 155–62; Joseph J. Ellis, *His Excellency: George Washington* (New York: Knopf, 2004), pp. 224–25.

186   "The question will not be": Hugh Brackenridge to Tench Coxe, August 8, 1794, quoted in Elkins and McKittrick, *The Age of Federalism*, p. 475.

187   Hundreds reportedly fled: Slaughter, *Whiskey Rebellion*, p. 218.

187   Much of the organized agitation: Elkins and McKittrick, *The Age of Federalism*, pp. 451–61; Slaughter, *Whiskey Rebellion*, p. 164.

187   "Beheading Federalists": Quoted in Miller, *Federalist Era*, p. 160.

188   "In a country abounding": François-Alexandre-Frédéric, duc de la Rochefoucauld-Liancourt, *Travels through the United States of North America, the Country of the Iroquois and Upper Canada, in the Years 1795, 1796, and 1797*, vol. 2 (London: R. Phillips, 1799), p. 290.

188   Skilled masons, carpenters: Federal Commissioners to Thomas Jefferson, January 5, 1793, Letterbooks of the Commissioners of Washington, Record Group 42, NA; William Seale, *The White House: The History of an American Idea* (Washington: American Institute of Architects Press, 1992), pp. 20ff.

188   "The magnificent city": *Morning Chronicle,* January 28, 1796, quoted in Anonymous, *Look before You Leap; or, A Few Hints to Such Artizans, Mechanics, Labourers, Farmers and Husbandmen, As Are Desireous of Emigrating to America* (London: W. Row, 1796), p. 55.

188   "eleven thousand artificers": ibid., p. 57.

188   "You may conceive": ibid., pp. 63–64.

188   "tears of repentance": ibid., p. 92.

189   "The hills are barren": ibid., p. 85.

189   Immigrants discovered that: William Seale, *The President's House,* vol.1 (Washington: White House Historical Association, 1986), pp. 38–39; Anonymous, *Look before You Leap,* pp. 53–57, 63–64, 92–93; Richard Parkinson, *A Tour in America: 1798, 1799, and 1800* (London: J. Harding, 1805), pp. 12, 17; W. J. Rorabaugh, *The Alcoholic Republic: An American Tradition* (New York: Oxford University Press, 1979), pp. 113–19; Benjamin Henry Latrobe, *The Journal of Latrobe* (New York: D. Appleton & Co., 1905), p. 132.

189   "a mestruum of oleagious matter": Quoted in Rorabaugh, *The Alcoholic Republic,* p. 117.

189   commissioners of the federal city were deeply suspicious: William C. diGiacomantonio, "All the President's Men: George Washington's Federal City Commissioners," *Washington History* 3, no. 1 (Spring/Summer 1991); Seale, *The President's House,* pp. 66–67; Parkinson, *A Tour in America,* pp. 18–20; Bob Arnebeck, *Through a Fiery Trial: Building Washington, 1790–1800* (Lanham, Md.: Madison Books, 1991), pp. 265, 328, 479ff; Bob Arnebeck, e-mail to author, 7 September 2006; Gustavus Scott to Edmund Randolph, October 7, 1794, Records of the Commissioners, LOC; Accounts of the Commissioners of the City of Washington 1794–1802, NA, Record Group 217, box 44, item 65.

190   slaves—slaves in abundance: Receipts for slave hire, Accounts of the Commissioners, NA, boxes 43 and 44; Federal Commissioners to Jefferson, January 5, 1793, in Saul K. Padover, *Thomas Jefferson and The National Capital* (Washington: U.S. Government Printing Office, 1946), pp. 165–66; Henry Wiencek, *An Imperfect God: George Washington, His Slaves, and the Creation of America* (New York: Farrar, Straus, and Giroux, 2003), pp. 88–91; Bob Arnebeck, "The Use of Slaves to Build the Capitol and White House," online at www.geocities.com/bobarnebeck/slaves; Arnebeck, e-mails to author, September 3, 2006, and September 7, 2006; Rochefoucauld-Liancourt, *Travels through the United States,*

p. 287; John Joseph Zaborney, *Slaves for Rent: Slave Hiring in Virginia*, PhD thesis, University of Maine, 1997, pp. 20–24.

191   slave sales regularly took place: *The Centinel of Liberty*, June 10 and December 20, 1796; Arnebeck, *Through a Fiery Trial*, pp. 229, 407.

192   Anise-Chloe Leclear: Accounts of the Commissioners, NA, box 43, item 160, and box 44, items 76 and 161.

193   Slaves, like most free laborers: Anonymous, *Look before You Leap*, pp. 44–45, 63–64.

193   ads for runaways: *Virginia Gazette and Alexandria Advertiser*, September 1, 1791, June 19, August 1, and October 28, 1794.

193   James Dermott, who: Arnebeck, *Through a Fiery Trial*, pp. 123–24, 150ff; Andrew Ellicott to Thornton, February 23, 1795, in Harris, *Papers of William Thornton*, p. 296.

193   the three Yankee speculators: Elizabeth M. Nuxoll, "Robert Morris and the Shaping of the Post-Revolutionary American Economy" (paper presented at the Omohundro Institute of Early American History and Culture Conference, Austin, Texas, June 1999); Elizabeth M. Nuxoll, "Illegitimacy, Family Status and Property in the Early Republic: The Morris-Croxall Family of New Jersey," *New Jersey History*, 113 (Fall/Winter 1995): 3–21; Elizabeth M. Nuxoll, e-mail to the author, August 7, 2006; Arbuckle, *Pennsylvania Speculator and Patriot*, pp. 194, 199; Benjamin Rush to John Nicholson, August 12, 1793, in Clark, *Greenleaf and Law*, pp. 43; Arnebeck, "The Use of Slaves"; Bob Arnebeck, e-mail to author, September 3, 2006.

194   Of all the personalities: Washington to Thornton, 8 August 1794, RCHS 17, p. 108; Thornton to John Coakley Lettsom, 22 December 1794, in Harris, *Papers of William Thornton*, p. 286; Thornton to Lettsom, 26 November 1795, in ibid., p. 340; William to John Fell, 5 October 1797, in ibid., p. 418; Visiting Book for 1794, William Thornton Papers, LOC; diGiacomantonio, "All the President's Men"; Elinor Stearns and David N. Yerkes, *William Thornton: A Renaissance Man in the Federal City* (Washington: American Institute of Architects Foundation, 1976), p. 27.

194   "The site is the most beautiful": Thornton to John Fell, 5 October 1797, in Harris, *Papers of William Thornton*, p. 418.

194   He quickly immersed himself: Thornton to Washington, 12 March 1795, in ibid., p. 304; Thornton to Washington, 26 July 1795, in ibid., pp. 322–23, note p. 324.

195   "Our country is extensive": Thornton to Benjamin Stoddert, 30 January 1800, in ibid., pp. 533–34.

195   New enthusiasms crowded: Thornton to John Coakley Lettsom, 8 January 1795, in ibid., p. 295; Thornton to Washington, 13 September 1796, in ibid., p. 396; Thornton, "On National Education," in ibid., p. 353.

195   "I cannot rest": Thornton to Lettsom, January 8, 1795, in ibid., p. 295.

196   the Potomac was another world: Richard S. Newman, *The Transformation of American Abolitionism: Fighting Slavery in the Early Republic* (Chapel Hill: University of North Carolina Press), pp. 34–36.

196   Thornton felt paralyzed: William Thornton, *Political Economy Founded in Justice and Humanity,* (Washington: Samuel Harrison Smith, 1804), William Thornton Papers, LOC; "Life of William Thornton," Thornton Papers, LOC.

197   "Since it is impossible": Thornton to the Federal Commissioners, July 18, 1795, in Harris, *Papers of William Thornton,* p. 320.

197   The state of affairs: William C. Allen, *History of the United States Capitol: A Chronicle of Design, Construction, and Politics* (Washington: U.S. Government Printing Office, 2001), pp. 29–31; Bob Arnebeck, "Finding a Place in Early Washington" (paper presented at the District of Columbia Historical Studies Conference, 2005); Washington to Daniel Carroll, 4 January 1793, in Clark, *Greenleaf and Law,* p. 92.

197   "will express in the stile": January 4, 1793, Letterbooks of the Commissioners, NA.

198   An atmosphere of fiasco: Sakolski, *Great American Land Bubble,* pp. 162–63; Clark, *Greenleaf and Law,* p. 255; Isaac Weld, *Travels through the States of North America* (London: John Stockdale, 1799), p. 286; Anonymous, *Look before You Leap,* pp. 69, 78, 96; Arbuckle, *Pennsylvania Speculator and Patriot,* p. 120.

198   work on the Capitol resumed: Washington to Thornton, 9 November 1795, RCHS 17, p. 147; Washington to the Federal Commissioners, 9 November 1795, RCHS 17, p. 147; Thornton to Washington, 2 November 1795, in Harris, *Papers of William Thornton,* pp. 331, 332n.

199   "Season goes away": Thomas Law to James Greenleaf, July 4, 1795, in Clark, *Greenleaf and Law,* pp. 107–8.

199   Morris waited apprehensively: Chernow, *Robert Morris,* pp. 101–2; Wright and Cowen, *Financial Founding Fathers,* pp. 137–39.

199   "Although it was not my intention": Robert Morris to Peter Charles L'Enfant, September 24, 1795, in Clark, *Greenleaf and Law,* pp. 28–29.

200   Autumn came and went: Kenneth R. Bowling, *Peter Charles L'Enfant: Vision, Honor, and Male Friendship in the Early American Republic* (Washington: The Friends of the George Washington University Libraries, 2002), pp. 39–41; Cook, "Robert Morris."

200   "a huge mass": quoted in Clark, *Greenleaf and Law,* p. 28.

202   The two colliding philosophies that shaped the debate: *Annals of the Congress of the United States: Fourth Congress* (Washington: Gales & Seaton, 1854), pp. 266, 290–96, 826–39.

202   *O ye who sit:* Columbian Herald, Rubil Morales-Vazques, "Monuments and Nation Building in the Early Capital," *Washington History*, Spring/Summer 2000.

202   "all the Faupaus": George Washington to William Deakins, June 6, 1796, *Records of the Columbia Historical Society* (RCHS) 17, p. 158.

203   Washington had blandly assured: Washington, "Message to Congress," January 8, 1796, RCHS 17, p. 149; Washington to Alexander White, April 28, 1795, RCHS 17, p. 126; Washington to Daniel Carroll, RCHS 17, p. 129; Washington to White, May 17, 1795, RCHS 17, p. 130; Barbara Ann Chernow, *Robert Morris: Land Speculator, 1790–1801* (New York: Arno Press, 1978), pp. 153–54; William C. diGiacomantonio, "All the President's Men: George Washington's Federal City Commissioners," *Washington History* 3, no. 1 (Spring/Summer 1991); William C. Allen, *History of the United States Capitol: A Chronicle of Design, Construction, and Politics* (Washington: U.S. Government Printing Office, 2001), pp. 32–34; C. M. Harris, ed. *Papers of William Thornton*, vol. 1, *1781–1802* (Charlottesville: University Press of Virginia, 1995), p. 345–46, note.

203   As snow and rain pelted: Washington to Gustavus Scott, May 25, 1796, in John C. Fitzpatrick., ed., *The Writings of George Washington*, vol. 35 (Washington: U.S. Government Printing Office, 1940), p. 68; entries for February 1796 in Dorothy Twohig and Donald Jackson, eds., *The Diaries of George Washington*, vol. 6 (Charlottesville: University Press of Virginia, 1979), pp. 217–19; Julian Ursyn Niemcewicz, *Under Their Vine and Fig Tree: Travels through America in 1797–1799, 1805, and with Some Further Account of Life in New Jersey*, trans. and ed. Metchie J. E. Budka (Elizabeth, N.J.: Grassmann Publishing Co., 1965), pp. 42–43.

205   Adding further insult: Kenneth R. Bowling, "The Federal Government and the Republican Court Move to Philadelphia," in *Neither Separate nor Equal: Congress in the 1790s*, Kenneth R. Bowling and Donald R. Kennon, eds. (Athens: Ohio University Press, 2000), pp. 33–34.

205   When the loan bill came: C. M. Harris, "Washington's Gamble, L'Enfant's Dream: Politics, Design, and the Founding of the National Capital," *The William and Mary Quarterly* 56, no. 3 (1999), p. 559; Bob Arnebeck, *Through a Fiery Trial: Building Washington, 1790–1800* (Lanham, Md.: Madison Books, 1991), pp. 366–68; Harris, *Papers of William Thornton*, p. 392, note.

206   appropriating $1.25 million: Frank Lambert, *The Barbary Wars* (New York: Hill and Wang, 2005), pp. 90–93.

206   The commissioners breathed: Federal Commissioners to Alexander White, April 19, 1796, Records of the Commissioners of the City of Washington, LOC; Arnebeck, *Through a Fiery Trial*, pp. 364, 387.

206   No one was more grateful: Washington to Alexander White, 17 May 1795, RCHS 17, p. 130; diGiacomantonio, "All the President's Men."

206   Washington was like a wounded lion: Richard N. Rosenfeld, *American Aurora* (New York: St. Martin's Press, 1997), pp. 29–31, 238; Joseph J. Ellis, *His Excellency: George Washington* (New York: Knopf, 2004), pp. 228–31, 245–47; Washington to Alexander Hamilton, 1 September 1796, in Fitzpatrick, *The Writings of George Washington*, vol. 35, p. 198; Alexander White to William Thornton, 20 April 1796, in Harris, *Papers of William Thornton*, pp. 390–92.

207   "The very idea of": Washington, "Farewell Address," Online at www.yale.edu/ lawweb/ avalon/washington.htm.

207   Washington had consistently advocated: Washington to John Adams, 15 November 1794, RCHS 17, p. 109; Washington to Thomas Jefferson, 15 March 1795, ibid., p. 118; Washington to Robert Brooke, 16 March 1795, ibid., p. 121; Washington to Hamilton, 1 September 1796, in Fitzpatrick, *The Writings of George Washington*, vol. 35, p. 198; Washington to the Federal Commissioners, November 27, 1796, Letters of the Presidents to the Commissioners of the City of Washington, LOC; diGiacomantonio, "All the President's Men."

208   Washington worried that his ability: Washington to Alexander White, 5 June 1796, RCHS 17, p. 156; Washington to Gustavus Scott, 25 May 1796, in Fitzpatrick, *The Writings of George Washington*, vol. 35, p. 68.

208   He badgered them unrelentingly: Washington to the Federal Commissioners, 22 May 1796, RCHS 17, p. 149; Washington to Gustavus Scott, 25 May 1796, ibid., p. 154; Washington to Alexander White, ibid., p. 156; Washington to William Deakins, 6 June 1796, ibid., p. 158; Washington to the Federal Commissioners; 26 June 1796, ibid., p. 161; Washington to Scott, 4 July 1796, ibid., 164; Washington to the Federal Commissioners, 26 December 1796, ibid., 180.

208   "Let me give it": Washington to Thornton, 26 December 1796, in Harris, *Papers of William Thornton*, pp. 406–7.

209   Washington ordered work: Washington to the Federal Commissioners, 15 February 1797, in Fitzpatrick, *The Writings of George Washington*, vol. 35, pp. 388–92.

209   "It is not only of": Washington to the Federal Commissioners, 29 January 1797, in ibid., p. 378.

209   Washington passed in a fizz: Jackson and Twohig, *Diaries of George Washington*, vol. 6, p. 239; Washington to Thomas Law, 2 October 1797, RCHS 17, p. 197.

209   "very much deranged": Washington to David Humphreys, 26 June 1797, in Fitzpatrick, *The Writings of George Washington*, vol. 35, p. 480.

209   His notion of retirement: George Washington to William Augustine Washington, 27 February 1798, in ibid, vol. 36, p. 150; Thornton to John Coakley Lettsom, 9 October 1797, in Harris, *Papers of William Thornton*, p. 422; Washington to Sarah Fairfax, 16 May 1798, in W. W. Abbott and Dorothy Twohig, eds., *The Papers of George Washington*, Retirement Series, vol. 2 (Charlottesville: University Press of Virginia, 1998), p. 272.

210   In theory, responsibility for the city: Rosenfeld, *American Aurora*, p. 237; Stanley Elkins and Eric McKittrick, *The Age of Federalism: The Early American Republic, 1788–1800* (New York: Oxford University Press, 1993), pp. 513ff; David McCullough, *John Adams* (New York: Simon & Schuster, 2001), pp. 462–68; Reginald Horsman, *The New Republic: The United States of America, 1789–1815* (Harlow: Longman, 2000), pp. 64–66.

211   a "dumpy little man": Niemcewicz, *Under Their Vine and Fig Tree*, p. 29.

211   "The whole of this business": John Adams to the Federal Commissioners, 17 April 1797, Letterbook of the Commissioners of the City of Washington, LOC; Federal Commissioners to John Adams, 11 April 1797, 7 May 1797, and 8 June 1797, in ibid.

211   "shewed an uncommon degree": Alexander White to Washington, 20 February 1798, in Abbott and Twohig, *Papers of George Washington*, p. 96.

211   Adams had much to distract him: Horsman, *The New Republic*, pp. 68ff; McCullough, *John Adams*, pp. 483–99; Elkins and McKittrick, *The Age of Federalism*, pp. 539–86; Ellis, *His Excellency*, pp. 228–31; Niemcewicz, *Under Their Vine and Fig Tree*, p. 88; Jefferson to John Taylor, June 4, 1798, in Thomas Jefferson, *Writings* (New York: The Library of America, 1984), pp. 1048–51.

212   the French "are endeavoring": Washington to Sarah Fairfax, May 16, 1798, in Abbott and Twohig, *Papers of George Washington*, p. 272.

212   Washington would continue to act: Washington to Alexander White, March 1, 1798, in Abbott and Twohig, *Papers of George Washington*, vol. 2, p. 113; Washington to Alexander White, March 25, 1798, RCHS 17, p. 199.

212   Washington would also visit: entries for March 15, July 17, August 7, and October 12, 1797; February 8, May 19, and December 18, 1798; May 31, August 5, and November 9, 1799 in Jackson and Twohig, *Diaries of George Washington*, vol. 6; Washington to Thomas Law, 7 May 1798, RCHS 17, p. 201.

213   launched oracular opinions: Washington to the Federal Commissioners, October 21, 1796, RCHS 17, p. 167; Washington to Benjamin Stoddert, September 26, 1798, in Abbott and Twohig, *Papers of George Washington*, vol. 3, p. 45; Washington to the Federal Commissioners, June 26, 1796, RCHS 17, p. 161.

213   Thornton the aesthete: Thornton to Washington, in Harris, *Papers of William Thornton*, p. 407; Thornton to Washington, in ibid., pp. 493–94.

213   "What kind of *Temples*": George Walker to Washington, August 5, 1799, in Abbott and Twohig, *Papers of George Washington*, vol. 4, p. 226.

213   Washington solomonically ruled: Washington to the Federal Commissioners, February 27, 1797, RCHS 17, p. 188; Washington to the Federal Commissioners, April 17, 1799, in Harris, *Papers of William Thornton*, p. 489.

214   "I think he has manifested": Anonymous, *Look before You Leap; or, A Few Hints to Such Artizans, Mechanics, Labourers, Farmers and Husbandmen, As Are Desireous of Emigrating to America* (London: W. Row, 1796), pp. 56–57.

214   To at least one visitor: François-Alexandre-Frédéric, duc de la Rochefoucauld-Liancourt, *Travels through the United States of North America, the Country of the Iroquois and Upper Canada, in the Years 1795, 1796, and 1797*, vol. 2 (London: R. Phillips, 1799), pp. 245, 312–28.

215   at its lowest ebb: Alexander White to Thornton, 17 March 1798, in Harris, *Papers of William Thornton*, p. 450; Robert D. Arbuckle, *Pennsylvania Speculator and Patriot: The Entrepreneurial John Nicholson 1757–1800* (University Park: The Pennsylvania State University Press, 1975), pp. 124–33, 187–93; Chernow, *Robert Morris*, pp. 161–62; Arnebeck, *Through a Fiery Trial*, pp. 407–12, 511–12; Robert Morris to Thomas Law, 12 April 1796, Letterbooks of Robert Morris LOC; Morris and James Nicholson to the Federal Commissioners, 8 November 1796, Letterbooks of the Commissioners, LOC; Morris to William Cranch, 10 February 1796, and 12 February 1796, Morris letterbook, LOC; Morris to Charles Byrd, 17 March 1796, Morris letterbook, LOC; Morris to Hamilton, 14 March 1796, Morris letterbook, LOC.

216   Morris paid his first visit: Robert Morris to Molly Morris, October 2, October 5, October 10, and October 12, 1796, Robert Morris Collection, Huntington Library, San Marino, CA; Robert Morris to Thomas Morris, September 7 and October 29, 1796, Morris Collection, Huntington; Chernow, *Robert Morris*, pp. 156–59, 211.

217   To once trusting investors: Robert Morris to James Marshall, January 16, 1796, Morris letterbook, LOC; Morris to James Ringgold, February 5, 1796, Morris letterbook, LOC; Morris to William Constable, April 5, 1796, Morris letterbook, LOC; Morris to Thomas Law, July 4, 1796, Clark, *Greenleaf and Law*, p. 254.

217   no one wanted their paper: Susan Woodrow to John Nicholson, May 29, 1797, quoted in Arbuckle, *Pennsylvania Speculator and Patriot*, p. 187; Robert Morris to William Deakins, April 11, 1796, Morris letterbook, LOC; Morris to Thomas Morris, July 31, 1796, Morris Collection, Huntington; Morris to John Hopkins, January 18, 1796, Morris letterbook, LOC; Morris to Rawleigh Colston, January 28, 1796, Morris letterbook, LOC; Arbuckle, *Pennsylvania Speculator and Patriot*, pp. 190–91.

217 "One would hope": Washington to the Federal Commissioners, July 1, 1796, RCHS 17, p. 162.

217 Morris knew that he would likely: Chernow, *Robert Morris*, pp. 157–58; Arbuckle, *Pennsylvania Speculator and Patriot*, pp. 127–28; Robert Morris to Wilhelm Van Willink, April 19, 1797, Morris Collection, Huntington; Morris to John Nicholson, January 5 and January 6, 1797, Morris Collection, Huntington.

218 "I hardly know which way": Robert Morris to John Nicholson, quoted in Chernow, *Robert Morris*, p. 214.

218 the runaway architect L'Enfant: Robert Morris to Peter Charles L'Enfant, August 15, 1796, in Clark, *Greenleaf and Law*, p. 29; Kenneth R. Bowling, *Peter Charles L'Enfant: Vision, Honor, and Male Friendship in the Early American Republic* (Washington: The Friends of the George Washington University Libraries, 2002), pp. 39–41; Chernow, *Robert Morris*, p. 102; Robert E. Wright and David J. Cowen, *Financial Founding Fathers: The Men Who Made America Rich* (Chicago: University of Chicago Press, 2006), p. 139.

218 Morris and Nicholson would blame: Arbuckle, *Pennsylvania Speculator and Patriot*, pp. 183–88; Clark, *Greenleaf and Law*, p. 72; Arnebeck, *Through a Fiery Trial*, pp. 397, 437–39.

219 "Though the lure": James Greenleaf to Robert Morris and John Nicholson, April 22, 1797, in Clark, *Greeleaf and Law*, pp. 165–66.

220 Wily as he was, Greenleaf: James Greenleaf to Hamilton, July 27, 1796, in Clark, *Greenleaf and Law*, p. 111; Hamilton to Greenleaf, July 30, 1796, in ibid., p. 112.

220 Morris retreated to his estate: Robert Morris to John Nicholson, September 22 and November 15, 1797, January 1, March 31, and April 29, 1798, Morris Collection, Huntington; Morris to Thomas Morris, January 6, 1798, Morris Collection, Huntington; Frank Gaylord Cook, "Robert Morris," *The Atlantic Monthly* 66 (November 1890); Roger H. Brown, review of Republic of Debtors, by Bruce H. Mann, in *The William and Mary Quarterly*, vol. X, 2003; Arbuckle, *Pennsylvania Speculator and Patriot*, pp. 195–97; Clark, *Greenleaf and Law*, pp. 41–42; Chernow, *Robert Morris*, pp. 103, 211–12; Robert Morris, *In the Account of Property*, Pennsylvania State Land Office, 1831, HSP, p. 23.

221 "They would have had": quoted in Arbuckle, *Pennsylvania Speculator and Patriot*, p. 195.

221 The partners' combined debt: Chernow, *Robert Morris*, p. 165; Arbuckle, *Pennsylvania Speculator and Patriot*, pp. 135, 178–88; Clark, *Greenleaf and Law*, p. 74; Robert Morris to John Nicholson, January 1, 1798, Morris letterbook, LOC; Morris to Nicholson, March 31, 1798, Morris letterbook, LOC; Morris to Nicholson, April 29, 1798, Morris letterbook, LOC; Morris, *In the Account of Property*, pp. 8ff.

221   "You may as well": Robert Morris to John Nicholson, November 23, 1797, quoted in Arbuckle, *Pennsylvania Speculator and Patriot*, p. 136.

221   "By heaven, there is": Quoted in A. M. Sakolski, *The Great American Land Bubble: The Amazing Story of Land-Grabbing, Speculations, and Booms from Colonial Days to the Present Time* (New York: Harper & Brothers, 1932), p. 166.

221   "My money is gone": Quoted in Arbuckle, *Pennsylvania Speculator and Patriot*, p. 197.

221   surrendered to the sheriff: Cook, "Robert Morris"; Arbuckle, *Pennsylvania Speculator and Patriot*, p. 217; entry for November 27, 1798, in Jackson and Twohig, *Diaries of George Washington*, vol. 6, p. 324; Scott Christianson, *With Liberty for Some: 500 Years of Imprisonment in America* (Boston: Northeastern University Press, 1998), p. 102; Brown, *Free Negroes*.

222   "I shall be glad to see you": Robert Morris to William Constable, February 26, 1798, in Clark, *Greenleaf and Law*, p. 171.

222   "My expectation of": Robert Morris to Maria Morris, probably April 1798, Morris Collection, Huntington.

223   "His person was neat": Quoted in Chernow, *Robert Morris*, p. 217.

223   expressed pathetic gratitude: Robert Morris to John Nicholson, October 19 and November 20, 1798, Morris Collection, Huntington; Morris to Maria Morris, October 20, 1798, Morris Collection, Huntington.

223   John Nicholson managed: Arbuckle, *Pennsylvania Speculator and Patriot*, pp. 194, 202; Sakolski, *Great American Land Bubble*, p. 37; Chernow, *Robert Morris*, p. 218.

223   Would-be investors already regarded: Rochefoucauld-Liancourt, *Travels through the United States*, pp. 322–25.

224   "Oh well, they can camp": Niemcewicz, *Under Their Vine and Fig Tree*, p. 86.

224   Despite the guarantees enacted: Wilhelm Van Willink to the Federal Commissioners, July 27, 1797, Records of the Commissioners, LOC; Federal Commissioners to John Adams, April 11, April 17, July 27, September 5, November 3, and November 25, 1797, January 3, January 8, April 18, and April 20, 1798, Records of the Commissioners, LOC; Adams to the Federal Commissioners, December 5, 1797, Records of the Commissioners, LOC; Washington to the Federal Commissioners, October 30 and November 4, 1795, Letters of the Presidents to the Commissioners, LOC; Washington to Gustavus Scott, December 7, 1796, RCHS 17, p. 176; Charles Lee to J. H. Stone, December 7, 1796, RCHS 17, p. 176; Washington to Gustavus Scott, January 8, 1798, RCHS 17, p. 197; Scott to Washington, December 21, 1797, in Abbott and Twohig, *Papers of George Washington*, vol. 1, p. 528; Alexander White to Wash-

ington, January 8, 1798, in Abott and Twohig, *Papers of George Washington*, vol. 2, pp. 7–8; Arnebeck, *Through a Fiery Trial*, pp. 454–63; diGiacomantonio, "All the President's Men."

224 Washington now told the commissioners: Washington to Alexander White, January 11, 1798, RCHS 17, p. 198; Washington to the Federal Commissioners, RCHS 17, p. 199; White to Washington, March 10 and March 17, 1798, in Abbott and Twohig, *Papers of George Washington*, vol. 2, pp. 134, 146.

225 a new controversy: Alexander White to the Federal Commissioners, March 8, March 11, and March 12, 1798, Records of the Commissioners, LOC; Federal Commissioners to Adams, April 18 and May 7, 1798, Records of the Commissioners, LOC; Rosenfeld, *American Aurora*, p. 237.

226 "is to me as an individual": Washington to Alexander White, March 25, 1798, RCHS 17, p. 199.

226 Washington's wishes prevailed: Federal Commissioners to Alexander White, 16 March 1798, in Harris, *Papers of William Thornton*, pp. 448–49; White to Washington, 8 April 1798, in Abbott and Twohig, *Papers of George Washington*, vol. 2, p. 231; Kenneth R. Bowling, *The Creation of Washington, D.C.* (Fairfax, Va.: George Mason University Press, 1991), p. 233; Chernow, *Robert Morris*, pp. 153–54.

226 While Congress wrangled: Receipts for work performed, various, Accounts of the Commissioners of the City of Washington 1794–1802, Record Group 217, boxes 43 and 44, NA.

227 The feeling of paralysis: Collen Williamson to the Federal Commissioners, November 27, 1797, Records of the Commissioners, LOC; Williamson to Washington, February 20, 1798, Records of the Commissioners, LOC; Alexander White to Jefferson, July 13, 1802, in Saul K. Padover, ed., *Thomas Jefferson and the National Capital* (Washington: U.S. Government Printing Office, 1946), pp. 276–77; *Commercial Advertiser* (NY), February 21, 1798; Martin I. J. Griffin, "James Hoban Architect and Builder of the White House," *The American Catholic Historical Researches*, vol. III, January 1907; William Seale, *The President's House*, vol.1 (Washington: White House Historical Association, 1986), p. 75; Arnebeck, *Through a Fiery Trial*, pp. 486, 500, 515–19.

228 "In all other countries": Niemcewicz, *Under Their Vine and Fig Tree*, pp. 77–81, 109.

 CHAPTER 10: THE CAPITAL OF A GREAT NATION
Page

229 a visitor to Mount Vernon: Julian Ursyn Niemcewicz, *Under Their Vine and Fig Tree: Travels through America in 1797–1799, 1805, and with Some Further Account of Life in New Jersey* (Elizabeth, N.J.: Grassmann Publishing Co., 1965), pp. 84–85.

229   Washington was now micromanaging: George Washington to William Thornton, 18 October 1798, and 28 October 1798, et.al., in C. M. Harris, ed. *Papers of William Thornton*, vol. 1, *1781–1802* (Charlottesville: University Press of Virginia, 1995), pp. 473–78; Thornton to Washington, 25 October 1798, in ibid., pp. 475–76; Thornton to Washington, 6 October 1799, in ibid. p. 512; Washington to Thornton, 28 August 1798, *Records of the Columbia Historical Society* (RCHS) 17, p. 212; Washington to Thornton, 15 February 1799, in ibid., p. 220; ibid., p. 203, note; Washington to Thornton, 18 November 1799, William Thornton Papers, LOC; Washington to the Federal Commissioners, 28 September 1798, in W. W. Abbott and Dorothy Twohig, eds., *The Papers of George Washington*, Retirement Series, vol. 3 (Charlottesville: University Press of Virginia, 1997), p. 52; Washington to the Federal Commissioners, 27 October 1798, in ibid., p. 144.

230   The doctor cherished: Anna Maria Thornton, diary, Anna Maria Thornton Papers, LOC; Thornton to John Coakley Lettsom, 9 October 1797, in Harris, *Papers of William Thornton*, p. 422; James Johnston Abraham, *Lettsom: His Life, Times, Friends, and Descendants* (London: Heinemann Medical Books, Ltd., 1933), p. 381; Washington to Sarah Fairfax, 16 May 1798, in Abbott and Twohig, *Papers of George Washington*, vol. 2, p. 272.

230   On one occasion: Thornton to Washington, 6 October 1797, in Harris, *Papers of William Thornton*, p. 421.

230   War with France threatened: Alexander White to Washington, 18 April 1798, in Abbott and Twohig, *Papers of George Washington*, vol. 2, p. 244; Thornton to Benjamin Stoddert, 28 June 1798, in Harris, *Papers of William Thornton*, p. 464; Richard N. Rosenfeld, *American Aurora* (New York: St. Martin's Press, 1997), p. 197.

230   repel any attack "with a decision": Quoted in Harris, *Papers of William Thornton*, p. 415, note.

231   "John Adams—May he": Quoted in Joseph J. Ellis, "Intimate Enemies," *American Heritage* 51, no. 5 (September 2000): 80–88.

231   the climate of palpitating xenophobia: Stanley Elkins and Eric McKittrick, *The Age of Federalism: The Early American Republic, 1788–1800* (New York: Oxford University Press, 1993), pp. 706–10; Reginald Horsman, *The New Republic: The United States of America 1789–1815* (Harlow: Longman, 2000), pp. 73–77; Rosenfeld, *American Aurora*, pp. 13, 184, 193, 200, 527, 541, 551, 590, 618; *Pennsylvania Gazette*, February 7, 1798.

232   A greater degree of acrimony: Elkins and McKittrick, *The Age of Federalism*, pp. 719–26; Alexander White to Washington, March 10, 1798, in Abbott and Twohig, *Papers of George Washington*, vol. 2, p. 134.

232   "We are compleatly under": Jefferson to John Taylor, June, 4, 1798, in Thomas Jefferson, *Writings* (New York: The Library of America, 1984), p. 1048.

232 Federalists remained in firm control: Elkins and McKittrick, *The Age of Federalism*, pp. 714–17; Horsman, *The New Republic*, pp. 72–73; David McCullough, *John Adams* (New York: Simon & Schuster, 2001), pp. 507–12, 517–18; Joseph J. Ellis, *His Excellency: George Washington* (New York: Knopf, 2004), pp. 248–55; Washington to James McHenry, October 15, 1798, in Abbott and Twohig, *Papers of George Washington*, vol. 3, pp. 97ff; McHenry to Washington, in Abbott and Twohig, *Papers of George Washington*, vol. 4, pp. 82ff.

233 Washington was away inspecting: Niemcewicz, *Under Their Vine and Fig Tree*, pp. 84–85, 95–101.

233 Washington's entanglement with slavery: Advertisement, 1 February 1796, in John C. Fitzpatrick, ed., *The Writings of George Washington*, vol. 33 (Washington: U.S. Government Printing Office, 1940), p. 433; Washington to William Pearce, 20 March 1796, in ibid., vol. 34, p. 21; Washington to Benjamin Dulany, 15 July 1799, in ibid., vol. 37, p. 307.

233 the escape of Ona Judge: Henry Wiencek, *An Imperfect God: George Washington, His Slaves, and the Creation of America* (New York: Farrar, Straus, and Giroux, 2003), pp. 321–38; Edward J. Lawlor Jr., "The President's House Revisited," *The Pennsylvania Magazine of History and Biography*, October 2005; Fritz Hirschfeld, *George Washington and Slavery: A Documentary Portrayal* (Columbia: University of Missouri Press, 1997), pp. 112–17; Gary B. Nash, *The Forgotten Fifth: African Americans in the Age of Revolution* (Cambridge: Harvard University Press, 2006), pp. 61–67; Anna Coxe Toogood, oral presentation, February 24, 2007, Capital Region Underground Railroad Conference, Albany, NY.

234 "The ingratitude of the girl": Washington to Oliver Wolcott, September 1796, in Fitzpatrick, *The Writings of George Washington*, vol. 35, p. 201.

234 "for however well disposed": Washington to Joseph Whipple, 28 November 1796, in ibid., p. 296.

234 She would safely live: *The Granite Freeman*, May 22, 1845; *The Liberator*, January 1, 1847.

235 "Oh! Sir, I am very glad": Quoted in Lawlor, "The President's House Revisited."

235 he was quite well aware: Washington to Alexander Spotswood, 14 September 1798, in Fitzpatrick, *The Writings of George Washington*, vol. 36, p. 444.

235 "It is my opinion": Washington to Lawrence Lewis, August 4, 1797, in ibid, vol. 37, p. 338.

235 Washington did grapple seriously: Wiencek, *An Imperfect God*, pp. 352–58; Hirschfeld, *George Washington and Slavery*, pp. 121ff; Washington to Tobias Lear, 6 May 1794, in Fitzpatrick, *The Writings of George Washington*, vol. 33, p. 385; Advertisement, February 1, 1796, in ibid., p. 175; Washington to William Pearce, 20 March 1796, in ibid., vol. 34, p. 501.

236   "I wish from my soul": Washington to Lawrence Lewis, 4 August 1797, in ibid., vol. 37, p. 338.

236   Washington made a detailed inventory: Washington to Robert Lewis, 18 August 1799, in ibid., p. 338; Hirschfeld, *George Washington and Slavery*, p. 81.

236   "Upon the decease of my wife": "Last Will and Testament," July 9, 1799, in Abbott and Twohig, *Papers of George Washington*, vol. 4, pp. 447ff; Wiencek, *An Imperfect God*, pp. 359–60.

237   He probably traveled: entries for November 9 and 10, 1799, in Donald Jackson and Dorothy Twohig, eds., *The Diaries of George Washington*, vol. 6 (Charlottesville: University Press of Virginia, 1979), p. 375.

237   Money, as always: Thornton and Alexander White to John Adams, November 17, 1799, Records of the Commissioners of the City of Washington, LOC.

238   At the President's House: Report of James Hoban, November 18, 1799, Records of the Commissioners, LOC.

238   signs of a thaw: *The Centinel of Liberty*, August 8 and 20, September 3 and 6, 1799; Thornton to Washington, September 1, 1799, in Harris, *Papers of William Thornton*, p. 507.

238   As November sheered into December: entries for December 1–13, 1799, in Jackson and Twohig, *Diaries of George Washington*, vol. 6, pp. 377–79.

238   "By the obstructions": Washington to Thornton, 8 December 1799, in Harris, *Papers of William Thornton*, p. 521.

238   Washington stoically made his usual daily round: Washington, plan for crops and farm operations, December 10, 1799, in Abbott and Twohig, *Papers of George Washington*, pp. 467ff; Wiencek, *An Imperfect God*, p. 357.

239   "Doctor, I die hard": Quoted in Ellis, *His Excellency*, pp. 269.

239   Thornton then made a weird proposal: Thornton, draft account, in Harris, *Papers of William Thornton*, p. 528.

240   "A Century hence": Washington to Sarah Fairfax, May 16, 1798, in Abbott and Twohig, *Papers of George Washington*, vol. 2, p. 272.

240   Washington was rapidly subsumed: Wendy C. Wick, *George Washington an American Icon: The Eighteenth-Century Graphic Portraits* (Washington: The Barra Foundation, 1982), pp. 53–57; Thornton to Samuel Blodget, 21 February 1800, in Harris, *Papers of William Thornton*, pp. 535–38.

241   work on the government buildings moved forward: Accounts of the Commissioners of the City of Washington, Record Group 217, box 50, various items, NA; Kenneth R. Bowling, "A Foreboding Shadow: Newspaper Celebration of

the Federal Government's Arrival," *Washington History*, Spring/Summer 2000; *The Centinel of Liberty*, August 9, 1800; Margaret Bayard Smith, diary entries for October 5 to 10, 1800, Margaret Bayard Smith Papers, LOC; Anna Maria Thornton Papers, LOC; Bob Arnebeck, *Through a Fiery Trial: Building Washington, 1790–1800* (Lanham, Md.: Madison Books, 1991), pp. 573, 582–85.

242   "Would you not be ashamed": Benjamin Stoddert to Thornton, 20 January 1800, in Harris, *Papers of William Thornton*, p. 532; Thornton to Stoddert, 30 January 1800, in ibid., p. 534.

242   "I had no conception": Quoted in John Ball Osborne, "The Removal of the Government to Washington," RCHS 3, 1900.

242   Suddenly the city began to swarm: Records of the Commissioners, May 15, 1800; Osborne, "Removal of the Government"; Pamela Scott, "Moving the Seat of Government," *Washington History* (Spring/Summer 2000); Arnebeck, *Through a Fiery Trial*, p. 572.

243   One of the newcomers: diary entries for October 6 to 23, 1800, Margaret Bayard Smith Papers, LOC.

243   By June, more than one hundred: Constance M. Green, *Washington: Village and Capital, 1800–1878* (Princeton: Princeton University Press, 1967), pp. 17–19; *The Centinel of Liberty*, August 8 and 20, 1799, July 1, August 15, September 2, October 3, November 4, 11, and 14, 1800; diary entries for August 9, 12, and 21, 1800, Anna Maria Thornton Papers, LOC; Osborne, "Removal of the Government."

244   One could buy people: *The Centinel of Liberty*, May 2 and November 11, 1800.

244   The Thorntons, who had lived: diary entries for May 21 and 24, June 11, September 10, October 22 and 25, December 12 and 15, 1800, Anna Maria Thornton Papers, LOC; William Thornton, *Political Economy Founded in Justice and Humanity*, pamphlet (Washington: Samuel Harrison Smith, 1804), William Thornton Papers, LOC.

245   Nearly every issue: *The Centinel of Liberty*, July 1, August 15, September 2, November 4 and 11, 1800; *Museum and George Town Daily Advertiser*, November 11 and 24, December 2 and 4, 1800.

245   James Dermott: Arnebeck, *Through a Fiery Trial*, pp. 123–24; Silvio A. Bedini, *The Life of Benjamin Banneker* (New York: Scribner's, 1972), pp. 133–34.

245   another "old timer": "Richard Soderstrom in Account with P. Charles L'Enfant," 1804; Robert Morris, *In the Account of Property*, Pennsylvania State Land Office, 1831, HSP, p. 43; Digges-L'Enfant-Morgan Papers, LOC; "Report of the Committee on Claims," December 17, 1800, Digges-L'Enfant-Morgan Papers; L'Enfant memorial to the Senate and House of Representatives, February 7, 1801, Digges-L'Enfant-Morgan Papers; "Memorial of Peter Charles L'Enfant," February 19, 1801, Digges-L'Enfant-Morgan Papers; L'Enfant "Deposition,"

February 8, 1803; Kenneth R. Bowling, *Peter Charles L'Enfant: Vision, Honor, and Male Friendship in the Early American Republic* (Washington: The Friends of the George Washington University Libraries, 2002), pp. 42ff; Scott W. Berg, *Grand Avenues: The Story of the French Visionary Who Designed Washington, D.C.* (New York: Pantheon, 2007), pp. 214–16, 226–27; Wilhelmus B. Bryan, "Something about L'Enfant and His Personal Affairs," RCHS 2, 1899, pp. 73–99; J. Workman, Secretary of the Land Office, "In the Account of Property" (inventory of the property of Robert Morris), 1831, Robert Morris Papers, QC.

246   "The preservation of order": Jefferson to Thornton, 23 April 1800, in Harris, *Papers of William Thornton*, p. 540.

247   The election of 1800: McCullough, *John Adams*, pp. 536–37; *Gazette of the United States*, November 29, 1800; Annette Gordon-Reed, *Thomas Jefferson and Sally Hemings: An American Controversy* (Charlottesville: University Press of Virginia, 2000), pp. 62ff, 210ff; Lucia Stanton, *Free Some Day: The African-American Families of Monticello* (Charlottesville, Va.: Thomas Jefferson Foundation, 2000), pp. 107ff.

247   "Suppose such a man": *The Centinel of Liberty*, September 2, 1800.

248   Alexander Hamilton's words: Quoted in McCullough, *John Adams*, p. 549.

248   the discovery of a slave conspiracy: Douglas R. Egerton, *Gabriel's Rebellion: The Virginia Slave Conspiracies of 1800 and 1802* (Chapel Hill: University of North Carolina Press, 1993), pp. 36–37, 60–94, 102, 112–14; "Confession of Solomon," and "Confession of Ben," in Robert S. Starobin, *Blacks in Bondage: Letters of American Slaves* (New York: Marcus Weiner, 1988), pp. 126–36; Scott French, *The Rebellious Slave: Nat Turner in American Memory* (Boston: Houghton Mifflin, 2004), pp. 15–19.

249   *An infant city:* In Rubil Morales-Vazquez, "Monuments and Nation Building in the Early Capital," *Washington History*, Spring/Summer 2000.

249   At the center of this controversy: Thornton, draft account, in Harris, *Papers of William Thornton*, p. 528; in ibid., pp. 522–25, note; Thornton to Samuel Blodget, February 21, 1800, in ibid., p. 535; Thornton to John Marshall, January 2, 1800, William Thornton Papers, LOC; C. M. Harris, "Washington's Gamble, L'Enfant's Dream: Politics, Design, and the Founding of the National Capital," *The William and Mary Quarterly* 56, no. 3 (1999), pp. 559–64; Morales-Vazquez, "Monuments and Nation Building."

250   President Adams arrived unobtrusively: diary entry for November 1, 1800, Anna Maria Thornton Papers, LOC; *The Centinel of Liberty*, November 4, 1800.

250   Abigail Adams followed: Abigail Adams to Mary Cranch, 21 November 1800, in Stewart Mitchell, *New Letters of Abigail Adams* (Boston: Houghton Mifflin, 1947), pp. 256–60; Abigail Adams to Abigail Smith, in Kenneth W. Leish, *The White House: A History of the Presidents* (New York: Newsweek, 1972), pp. 136–

38; William Seale, *The President's House*, vol. 1 (Washington: White House Historical Association, 1986), pp. 78–81; Seale, *The White House: The History of an American Idea* (Washington: American Institute of Architects Press, 1992), p. 35; Martin I. J. Griffin, "James Hoban Architect and Builder of the White House," *The American Catholic Historical Researches*, vol. III, January 1907; McCullough, *John Adams*, p. 551; Arnebeck, *Through a Fiery Trial*, pp. 594–97.

251   woeful mishaps occurred: *The Centinel of Liberty*, November 11 and 14, 1800; diary entry for November 10, 1800, Anna Maria Thornton Papers, LOC; Kenneth R. Bowling, "A Foreboding hadow: Newspaper Celebration of the Federal Government's Arrival," *Washington History* (Spring/Summer 2000).

252   prolonging this already complicated process: Elkins and McKittrick, *The Age of Federalism*, pp. 745–50; Horsman, *The New Republic*, p. 84.

252   "The elections as far as": Jefferson to James Madison, November 11, 1800, in James Morton Smith, *The Republic of Letters: The Correspondence between Thomas Jefferson and James Madison 1776–1826*, vol. 2 (New York: W. W. Norton Co., 1995), p. 1153.

252   would ride "into the temple": Quoted in Garry Wills, *"Negro President": Jefferson and the Slave Power* (Boston: Houghton Mifflin, 2003), p. 2.

252   Congress was supposed to convene: Osborne, "Removal of the Government"; *The Centinel of Liberty*, June 3, September 2, and October 3, 1800; *Museum and George-Town Daily Advertiser*, November 18 and 19, 1800; Arnebeck, *Through a Fiery Trial*, p. 596.

253   "I do not perceive how": Quoted in Osborne, "Removal of the Government."

253   enough members had arrived: *Museum and George Town Daily Advertiser*, November 24, 1800; diary entry for November 22, 1800, Anna Maria Thornton Papers, LOC; *Providence Journal*, December 10, 1800, in Bowling, "A Foreboding Shadow" Arnebeck, *Through a Fiery Trial*, p. 600; William C. Allen, interview with the author, April 26, 2007.

254   By the end of the year: Green, *Washington*, p. 21.

254   Adams's brief speech: Fourth Annual Message to Congress, online at www.yale.edu/lawweb/avalon.

256   The election should have ended: Horsman, *The New Republic*, p. 84; Wills, *"Negro President,"* p. 75.

256   The atmosphere was tense: *Gazette of the United States*, November 28, 1800; Jefferson to James Madison, December 19 and 26, 1800, January 10, February 1 and 18, 1801, in Smith, *The Republic of Letters*, pp. 1154–60.

257   "We shall be at any rate": Quoted in Arnebeck, *Through a Fiery Trial*, p. 616.

257   The Republicans initially could count: Elkins and McKittrick, *The Age of Federalism*, pp. 746–50; Horsman, *The New Republic*, p. 85.

257   Jefferson would call memorably: Jefferson, *Writings*, pp. 492ff.

EPILOGUE

259   On August 24, 1814: *Annals of the Congress of the United States: Thirteenth Congress* (Washington: Gales & Seaton, 1854), p. 16, 306–7; George Robert Gleig, *A History of the Campaigns of the British at Washington and New Orleans* (Charleston: Bibliobazar, 2007), pp. 77–85; Anthony S. Pitch, *The Burning of Washington: The British Invasion of 1814* (Annapolis: Naval Institute Press, 1998), pp. 90ff; Walter R. Borneman, *1812: The War That Forged a Nation* (New York: Harper Perennial, 2004), pp. 101–6, 170–71.

260   One local wag: "Timothy Taste," *The Freaks of Columbia; or, The Removal of the Seat of Government; A Farce* (Washington: n.p., 1808).

260   the president's whitewashed residence: Martin I. J. Griffin, "James Hoban Architect and Builder of the White House," *The American Catholic Historical Researches*, vol. 3, January 1907; William Seale, *The President's House*, vol. 1 (Washington: White House Historical Association, 1986), p. 77; Seale, *The White House: The History of an American Idea* (Washington: American Institute of Architects Press, 1992), p. 35.

260   "Many of them brought hither": Benjamin Henry Latrobe, *The Journal of Latrobe* (New York: D. Appleton & Co., 1905), p. 132.

261   to carry on the construction: Thomas Jefferson to Benjamin Latrobe, March 6, 1803, in Saul Padover, ed., *Thomas Jefferson and the National Capital* (Washington: U.S. Government Printing Office, 1946), p. 296; Latrobe to Jefferson, November 25, 1806, in ibid., p. 373; Latrobe to Jefferson, August 13, 1807, in ibid., p. 394; Latrobe to Jefferson, March 23, 1808, in ibid., p. 399; Latrobe, *The Journal of Latrobe*, pp. 115–51; William C. Allen, *History of the United States Capitol: A Chronicle of Design, Construction, and Politics* (Washington: U.S. Government Printing Office, 2001), pp. 49ff, 80–81; Pamela Scott, *Temple of Liberty: Building the Capitol for a New Nation* (New York: Oxford University Press, 1995), pp. 73ff; C. M. Harris, "Washington's 'Federal City,' Jefferson's 'federal town,'" *Washington History* 12, no. 1 (Spring/Summer, 2000); Rubil Morales-Vazquez, "Monuments and Nation Building in the Early Capital," *Washington History* 12, no. 1 (Spring/Summer 2000); Scott W. Berg, *Grand Avenues: The Story of the French Visionary Who Designed Washington, D.C.* (New York: Pantheon, 2007), pp. 219–20.

261   By the evening of the twenty-fourth: Gleig, *A History of the Campaigns*, pp. 85–93; Pitch, *The Burning of Washington*, pp. 99–121; Allen, *History of the United States Capitol*, pp. 97–98; Benjamin Latrobe to Jefferson, July 12, 1815, in Padover, *Thomas Jefferson and the National Capital*, p. 473.

262   From Capitol Hill: Seale, *The President's House*, pp. 133–36; Seale, *The White House*, p. 35; Griffin, "James Hoban."

262   the invaders destroyed: *Annals* 13, p. 307; Margaret Bayard Smith to Samuel H. Smith, undated letter, probably 1815, Margaret Bayard Smith Papers, LOC; Borneman, *1812*, pp. 226–33; Pitch, *The Burning of Washington*, pp. 71ff, 130–33.

263   history beckoned to him: "Life of William Thornton," William Thornton Papers, LOC; *National Intelligencer*, August 31 and September 2, 1814.

264   the Thirteenth Congress returned: *Annals* 13, p. 354.

264   "no place, either north or south": George Washington to Benjamin Stoddert, September 26, 1798, in W. W. Abbott and Dorothy Twohig, eds., *The Papers of George Washington*, Retirement Series, vol. 3 (Charlottesville: University Press of Virginia, 1997), p. 45.

264   the jingoes had promised: Borneman, *1812*, pp. 26–29, 47–53; Reginald Horsman, *The New Republic: The United States of America 1789–1815* (Harlow: Longman, 2000), pp. 248–50.

264   the war hawks were still full of bombast: *Annals* 13, pp. 12–16, 19.

264   The debate that ensued: ibid., pp. 311–22, 354–66, 370–72, 390; *National Intelligencer*, September 2, 1814.

265   In the end it all came down: *Annals* 13, pp. 388–96; Borneman, *1812*, pp. 250–52; Pitch, *The Burning of Washington*, pp. 223–25; Morales-Vazquez, "Monuments and Nation Building."

266   would not "deviate from the models": James Madison to the Federal Commissioners, May 28, 1815, Letters of the Presidents to the Commissioners of the City of Washington, LOC.

266   real estate in the district: "Life of William Thornton," William Thornton Papers, LOC.

267   "After nearly half a century": Daniel Carroll to Robert Brent, July 24, 1837, in Elizabeth S. Kite, *L'Enfant and Washington, 1791–1792* (Baltimore: The Johns Hopkins Press, 1929), p. 165.

267   "It is someimes called": Charles Dickens, *American Notes* (New York: Penguin, 2000), pp. 127–37.

267   the route made no real sense: Joel Achenbach, *The Grand Idea: George Washington's Potomac, and the Race to the West* (New York: Simon & Schuster, 2004), pp. 214–15; Paul Metcalf, *Waters of Potowmack* (Charlottesville: University Press of Virginia, 2002), p. 118.

268   Litigation over Robert Morris's: Barbara Ann Chernow, *Robert Morris: Land Speculator, 1790–1801* (New York: Arno Press, 1978), pp. 168, 222–28; A. M. Sakolski, *The Great American Land Bubble: The Amazing Story of Land-Grabbing, Speculations, and Booms from Colonial Days to the Present Time* (New York: Harper & Brothers, 1932), p. 145; Allen C. Clark, *Greenleaf and Law in the Federal City* (Washington: W. F. Roberts, 1901), pp. 26–27.

268   John Nicholson had died: Robert D. Arbuckle, *Pennsylvania Speculator and Patriot: The Entrepreneurial John Nicholson 1757–1800* (University Park: Pennsylvania State University, 1975), pp. 202–4.

268   "May you live long": Benjamin Rush to Julia Rush, August 22, 1793, HSP.

268   James Greenleaf, the most shameless: Clark, *Greenleaf and Law*, pp. 170–72, 202ff; Sakolski, *Great American Land Bubble*, p. 167.

268   L'Enfant consistently opposed: Kite, *L'Enfant and Washington*, pp. 27, 68, 71; Kenneth R. Bowling, *Peter Charles L'Enfant: Vision, Honor, and Male Friendship in the Early American Republic* (Washington: The Friends of the George Washington University Libraries, 2002), p. 20.

268   "the picture of famine": Latrobe, *The Journal of Latrobe*, p. 133.

268   taken up as a charity case: Berg, *Grand Avenues*, pp. 226ff, 243; Kite, *L'Enfant and Washington*, pp. 26–27.

269   Lewis Mumford observed: Stanley Elkins and Eric McKittrick, *The Age of Federalism: The Early American Republic, 1788–1800* (New York: Oxford University Press, 1993), pp. 180–81.

269   a new generation of planners: Berg, *Grand Avenues*, pp. 263ff; Iris Miller, *Washington in Maps, 1606–2000* (New York: Rizzoli International Publications, 2002), pp. 106–22.

269   William Thornton enjoyed comfort: "Life of William Thornton," William Thornton Papers, LOC; Charles F. Jenkins, *Tortola: A Quaker Experiment Long Ago in the Tropics* (London: Friends Bookshop, 1923), p. 61.

270   Between 1800 and 1840: Constance McLaughlin Green, *Washington: Village and Capital, 1800–1878* (Princeton: Princeton University Press, 1962), p. 21; Green, *The Secret City: A History of Race Relations in the Nation's Capital* (Princeton: Princeton University Press, 1967), p. 33; Felicia Bell, "The Negroes Work Alone," lecture delivered at U.S. Capitol Historical Society conference on Congress and slavery in the District of Columbia, April 27, 2007.

270   Washington was not entirely like: Green, *The Secret City*, pp. 16–17, 54; Mary Tremain, *Slavery in the District of Columbia* (New York: G. P. Putnam's Sons, 1892), pp. 45–47; Stanley Harrold, *Subversives: Antislavery Community in Washington, D.C., 1828–1865* (Baton Rouge: Louisiana State University Press, 2003),

pp. 40–41; Solomon Northrup, *Twelve Years a Slave* (New York: Dover, 1970), pp. 42ff.

270   hub of the domestic slave trade: *Alexandria Expositor*, undated article by "Uniformity," probably 1803, Records of the Commissioners of the City of Washington, LOC; Joseph Sturge, *A Visit to the United States in 1841* (New York: Augustus M. Kelley, 1969), pp. 73–78; Harrold, *Subversives*, pp. 20, 30; Tremain, *Slavery*, p. 50; John Michael Vlach, "From Slavery to Tenancy," lecture delivered at U.S. Capitol Historical Society conference on Congress and slavery in the District of Columbia, April 27, 2007.

271   Alexandria's "retrocession" to Virginia: Dean C. Allard, "When Arlington Was Part of the District of Columbia," *The Arlington Historical Magazine*, October 1978; A. Glenn Crothers, "The 1846 Retrocession of Alexandria," lecture delivered at U.S. Capitol Historical Society conference on Congress and slavery in the District of Columbia, April 27, 2007.

271   Congress at last voted to emancipate: Tremain, *Slavery*, pp. 94–95; Records of the Board of Commissioners for the Emancipation of Slaves in the District of Columbia, 1862–1863, petitions, Record Group 217, boxes 507, 514, and 896, NA.

272   Only once was removal: Kenneth R. Bowling, "From 'Federal Town' to 'National Capital': Ulysses S. Grant and the Reconstruction of Washington, D.C.," *Washington History*, Spring/Summer 2002.

273   "It might be compared": Charlene Bangs Bickford, Kenneth R. Bowling, William Charles diGiacomantonio, and Helen E. Veit, eds., *Documentary History of the First Federal Congress of the United States of America*, vol. XI (Baltimore: Johns Hopkins University Press, 1992–1996), p. 1338.

274   "We beseech that as we are *men*": Gary B. Nash, *Forging Freedom: The Formation of Philadelphia's Black Community 1720–1840* (Cambridge: Harvard University Press, 1988), p. 188.

SELECTED BIBLIOGRAPHY

Abbott, W. W., and Dorothy Twohig, et. al., eds. *The Papers of George Washington: January-May 1793*. The Papers of George Washington: The Presidential Series, vol 12. Charlottesville: University Press of Virginia, 2005.

Abraham, James Johnston. *Lettsom: His Life, Times, Friends, and Descendants*. London: Heinemann Medical Books, Ltd., 1933.

Achenbach, Joel. *The Grand Idea: George Washington's Potomac, and the Race to the West*. New York: Simon & Schuster, 2004.

Adams, Charles Francis, ed. *The Works of John Adams. Vol. 1*. Boston: Little, Brown & Co., 1850–1856.

Adams, Alice Dana. *The Neglected Period of Anti-Slavery in America, 1803–1831*. Gloucester, Mass.: Peter Smith, 1964.

Alexander, Sally Kennedy. "A Sketch of the Life of Major Andrew Ellicott," *Columbia Historical Society Records* 2 (1899): 158–202.

Allard, Dean C. "When Arlington Was Part of the District of Columbia," *The Arlington Historical Magazine* 6, no. 2 (1978): 36–47.

Allgor, Catherine. "'Queen Dolley' Saves Washington City," *Washington History* 12, no. 1 (2000): 54–69.

Allen, William C. *History of the United States Capitol: A Chronicle of Design, Construction, and Politics*. Washington: U.S. Government Printing Office, 2001.

An Account of the Rise, Progress and Termination of the Malignant Fever Lately Preva-

lent in Philadelphia. Anonymous pamphlet. Philadelphia: Benjamin Johnson, 1793. FHL.

An Earnest Call Occasioned by the Alarming Pestilential Contagion. Anonymous pamphlet. Philadelphia: Jones, Hoff and Derrick, 1793. FHL.

Annals of the Congress of the United States: Fourth Congress. Washington: Gales & Seaton, 1849.

———. *Thirteenth Congress.* Washington: Gales & Seaton, 1854.

Arbuckle, Robert D. *Pennsylvania Speculator and Patriot: The Entrepreneurial John Nicholson 1757–1800.* University Park: Pennsylvania State University Press, 1975.

Arnebeck, Bob. *Through a Fiery Trial: Building Washington, 1790–1800.* Lanham, Md.: Madison Books, 1991.

———. "To Tease and Torment: Two Presidents Confront Suspicions of Sodomy." Online at www.geocities.com/bobarnebeck/LEnfant.htm.

———. "The Use of Slaves to Build the Capitol and White House." Online at www.geocities.com/bobarnebeck/slaves.html.

Asbury, Herbert. *Sucker's Progress: An Informal History of Gambling in America.* New York: Dodd, Meade & Co., Inc., 1938.

Bailyn, Bernard. *The Ideological Origins of the American Revolution.* Cambridge: Harvard University Press, 1967.

Basker, James G., ed. *Early American Abolitionists: A Collection of Anti-Slavery Writings, 1760–1820.* New York: The Gilder Lehrman Institute of American History, 2005.

Bedini, Silvio A. *The Life of Benjamin Banneker.* New York: Scribner, 1972.

Benezet, Anthony. *Caution to Great Britain and Her Colonie, in a Short Representation of the Calamitous State of the Enslaves Negroes in the British Dominions.* Philadelphia: 1767.

Benjamin, Charles F. *A History of Federal Lodge No.1.* Washington: Gibson Bros., 1901.

Berg, Scott W. *Grand Avenues: The Story of the French Visionary Who Designed Washington, D.C.* New York: Pantheon, 2007.

Berlin, Ira. *Generations of Captivity: A History of African-American Slaves.* Cambridge: Belknap Press, 2003.

———. *Many Thousands Gone: The First Two Centuries of Slavery in North America.* Cambridge: Belknap Press, 1998.

Bickford, Charlene Bangs, Kenneth R. Bowling, William Charles diGiacomantonio, and Helen E. Veit, eds. *Debates in the House of Representatives.* 5 vols. *Documentary History of the First Federal Congress of the United States of America, March 4,*

1789–March 3, 1791, vols. 10–14. Baltimore: Johns Hopkins University Press, 1992–1996.

Biddle, Clement. *The Philadelphia Directory*. Philadelphia: James & Johnson, 1791.

Blackburn, Robin. *The Making of New World Slavery: From the Baroque to the Modern, 1492–1800*. New York: Verso, 1998.

Blackmar, Elizabeth. *Manhattan for Rent, 1785–1850*. Ithaca, N.Y.: Cornell University Press, 1989.

Borneman, Walter R. *1812: The War that Forged a Nation*. New York: HarperCollins, 2004.

Bowling, Kenneth R. *Creating the Federal City, 1774–1800: Potomac Fever*. Washington: American Institute of Architects Press: 1988.

———. *The Creation of Washington, D.C.: The Idea and Location of the American Capital*. Fairfax, Va.: George Mason University Press, 1991.

———. "A Foreboding Shadow: Newspaper Celebration of the Federal Government's Arrival," *Washington History* 12, no. 1 (2000): 4–7.

———. "From 'Federal Town' to 'National Capital': Ulysses S. Grant and the Reconstruction of Washington, D.C.," *Washington History* 14, no. 1 (2002): 8–25.

———. "The Other G. W.: George Walker and the Creation of the National Capital," *Washington History* 3, no. 2 (Fall/Winter 1991–1992): 4–21.

———. *Peter Charles L'Enfant: Vision, Honor, and Male Friendship in the Early American Republic*. Washington: The Friends of the George Washington University Libraries, 2002.

Bowling, Kenneth R., and Donald R. Kennon, eds. *Neither Separate nor Equal: Congress in the 1790s*. Athens: Ohio University Press, 2000.

Brissot de Warville, Jacques-Pierre. *New Travels in the United States of America, 1788*. Edited by Durand Echeverria. Translated by Mara Soceanu Vamos and Durand Echeverria. Cambridge: Harvard University Press, 1964.

Brodsky, Alyn. *Benjamin Rush: Patriot and Physician*. New York: St. Martin's Press, 2004.

Brookhiser, Richard. *Alexander Hamilton, American*. New York: Free Press, 1999.

Brown, Letitia Woods. *Free Negroes in the District of Columbia 1790–1846*. New York: Oxford University Press, 1972.

Bryan, Wilhelmus B., "Something about L'Enfant and His Personal Affairs," *Columbia Historical Society Records* 2 (1899): 111–17.

Brockett, F. L. *The Lodge of Washington: A History of the Alexandria Washington Lodge, No. 22.* Westminster, Md.: Willow Bend Books, 2001

Bullock, Steven C. *Revolutionary Brotherhood: Freemasonry and the Transformation of the American Social Order, 1730–1840.* Chapel Hill: University of North Carolina Press, 1996.

Burrows, Edwin G., and Mike Wallace. *Gotham: A History of New York City to 1898.* New York: Oxford University Press, 1999.

Carey, Mathew. *A Short Account of the Malignant Fever, Lately Prevalent in Philadelphia.* Philadelphia: Mathew Carey, 1793.

Cerami, Charles A. *Benjamin Banneker: Surveyor, Astronomer, Publisher, Patriot.* New York: John Wiley & Sons., 2002.

Chase, Philander D., ed. *The Papers of George Washington.* Charlottesville: University Press of Virginia, 2002.

Chernow, Barbara Ann. *Robert Morris: Land Speculator, 1790–1801.* New York: Arno Press, 1978.

Chernow, Ron. *Alexander Hamilton.* New York: The Penguin Press, 2004.

Child, Lydia Maria. *Isaac T. Hopper: A True Life.* Boston: John P. Jewett & Co., 1853.

Christianson, Scott. *With Liberty for Some: 500 Years of Imprisonment in America.* Boston: Northeastern University Press, 1998.

Clark, Allen C. *Greenleaf and Law in the Federal City.* Washington: W. F. Roberts, 1901.

Cobban, Alfred. *A History of Modern France, Vol. 1: 1715–1799.* Baltimore: Penguin, 1963.

Coghlan, Francis. "Pierce Butler, 1744–1822, First Senator from South Carolina," *South Carolina Historical Magazine* 78 (April 1977): 104–10.

Cook, Frank Gaylord. "Robert Morris," *The Atlantic Monthly* 66 (November 1890): 607–18.

Cox, William V. *Celebration of the One Hundredth Anniversary of the Establishment of the Seat of Government in the District of Columbia.* Washington: U.S. Government Printing Office, 1901.

Crane, Elaine Forman, ed. *The Diary of Elizabeth Drinker.* 3 vols. Boston: Northeastern University Press, 1991.

Cresson, Joshua. "Meditations written during sickeness & mortality in Philadelphia, 1793." Album. FHL.

Davis, David Brion. *Inhuman Bondage: The Rise and Fall of Slavery in the New World.* New York: Oxford University Press, 2006.

Densmore, Christopher. "Seeking Freedom in the Courts," *Pennsylvania Legacies* 6, no. 2 (2005): 16–19.

Dickens, Charles. *American Notes.* New York: Penguin Books, 2000.

diGiacomantonio, William C. "All the President's Men: George Washington's Federal City Commissioners," *Washington History* 3, no. 1 (Spring/Summer 1991): 52–75.

———. "'For the Gratification of a Volunteering Society': Antislavery and Pressure Group Politics in the First Federal Congress," *Journal of the Early Republic* 15 (Summer 1995): 169–97.

Douglass, William. *Annals of the First African Church, in the United States of America.* Philadelphia: King & Baird, 1862.

Doyle, William. *The Oxford History of the French Revolution.* 2nd ed. New York. Oxford University Press, 2002.

DuBois, Laurent, and John D. Garrigus. *Slave Revolution in the Caribbean 1789–1804: A Brief History with Documents.* Boston: Bedford/St.Martin's, 2006.

DuBois, W. E. B. *The Philadelphia Negro: A Social Study.* Philadelphia: University of Pennsylvania Press, 1899.

Eckert, Allan W. *That Dark and Bloody River: Chronicles of the Ohio River Valley.* New York: Bantam Books, 1995.

Egerton, Douglas R. *Gabriel's Rebellion: The Virginia Slave Conspiracies of 1800 and 1802.* Chapel Hill: University of North Carolina Press, 1993.

Elkins, Stanley, and Eric McKitrick. *The Age of Federalism: The Early American Republic, 1788–1800.* New York: Oxford University Press, 1993.

Ellis, Joseph J. *American Sphinx: The Character of Thomas Jefferson.* New York: Vintage, 1998.

———. Founding Brothers: *The Revolutionary Generation.* New York: Vintage, 2002.

———. *His Excellency: George Washington.* New York: Knopf, 2004.

Fehrenbacher, Don E. *The Slaveholding Republic: An Account of the United States Government's Relations to Slavery.* New York: Oxford University Press, 2001.

Ferling, John. "Cliffhanger: The Election of 1800," *Smithsonian Magazine*, November 2004.

Findlay, John M. *People of Chance: Gambling in American Society from Jamestown to Las Vegas.* New York: Oxford University Press, 1986.

Finkelman, Paul. *Slavery and the Founders: Race and Liberty in the Age of Jefferson.* Armonk, N.Y.: M. E. Sharpe, Inc., 2001.

Fitzpatrick, John C., ed. *The Writings of George Washington*. 39 vols. Washington: U.S. Government Printing Office, 1940.

Flexner, James Thomas. *Washington: The Indispensable Man*. Boston: Little, Brown and Co., 1969.

Franklin, Benjamin. *The Portable Benjamin Franklin*. Edited by Larzer Ziff. New York: Penguin, 2005.

French, Scot. *The Rebellious Slave: Nat Turner in American Memory*. Boston: Houghton Mifflin, 2004.

Gleig, George Robert. *The Campaigns of the British Army at Washington and New Orleans*. Charleston, S.C.: BiblioBazaar, 2007.

Goldstone, Lawrence. *Dark Bargain: Slavery, Profits, and the Struggle for the Constitution*. New York: Walker & Co., 2005.

Gordon-Reed, Annette. *Thomas Jefferson and Sally Hemings: An American Controversy*. Charlottesville: University Press of Virginia, 1998.

Green, Constance McLaughlin. *The Secret City: A History of Race Relations in the Nation's Capital*. Princeton: Princeton University Press, 1967.

———. *Washington: Village and Capital, 1800–1878*. Princeton: Princeton University Press, 1962.

Griffin, Martin I. J. "James Hoban Architect and Builder of the White House." *The American Catholic Historical Researches* (January 1907).

Griswold, Rufus Wilmot. *The Republican Court; or, American Society in the Days of Washington*. New York: D. Appleton and Co., 1867.

Guild, June Purcell. *Black Laws of Virginia: A Summary of the Legislative Acts of Virginia Concerning Negroes from Earliest Times to the Present*. New York: Negro Universities Press, 1969.

Gutheim, Frederick. *The Potomac*. New York: Holt, Rinehart and Winston, 1974.

Hamilton, Alexander. *Writings*. New York: The Library of America, 2001.

Hammon, Jupiter. *An Address to the Negroes in the State of New-York*. Pamphlet. Philadelphia: Daniel Humphreys, 1787.

Harris, C. M. "'The Best Friend I Had on Earth': William Thornton's 'Great Patron,' George Washington," *White House History*, no. 6 (Fall 1999): 360–69.

———. "The Politics of Public Building: William Thornton and President's Square," *White House History*, no. 3 (Spring 1998): 46–59.

———. "Specimens of Genius and Nicknacks: The Early Patent Office and Its Museum," *Prologue* 23, no. 4 (Winter 1991): 406–17.

———. "Washington's 'Federal City,' Jefferson's 'federal town.'" *Washington History* 12, no. 1 (Spring/Summer 2000): 49–53.

———. "Washington's Gamble, L'Enfant's Dream: Politics, Design, and the Founding of the National Capital," *The William and Mary Quarterly* 56, no. 3 (1999): 527–64.

———, ed. *Papers of William Thornton*, vol. 1, *1781–1802.* Charlottesville: University Press of Virginia, 1995.

Harrold, Stanley. *Subversives: Antislavery Community in Washington, D.C., 1828–1865.* Baton Rouge: Louisiana State University Press, 2003.

Henson, Josiah. *Uncle Tom's Story of his Life from 1789 to 1879.* Boston: B. B. Russell & Co., 1879.

Hirschfeld, Fritz. *George Washington and Slavery: A Documentary Portrayal.* Columbia: University of Missouri Press, 1997.

Hobsbawm, Eric, and Terence Ranger, eds. *The Invention of Tradition.* New York: Cambridge University Press, 1984.

Hodges, Graham Russell. *Root and Branch: African Americans in New York and East Jersey, 1613–1863.* Chapel Hill: University of North Carolina Press, 1999.

Horn, James, Lewis, Jan Ellen, and Onuf, Peter S., eds. *The Revolution of 1800: Democracy, Race, and the New Republic.* Charlottesville: University Press of Virginia, 2002.

Horsman, Reginald. *The New Republic: The United States of America 1789–1815.* New York: Longman, 2000.

Horton, James Oliver. "Alexander Hamilton: Slavery and Race in a Revolutionary Generation," *New-York Journal of American History* 65, no. 3 (Spring 2004): 16–24.

Horton, James Oliver, and Lois E. Horton. *In Hope of Liberty: Culture, Community and Protest Among Northern Free Blacks, 1700–1860.* New York: Oxford University Press, 1997.

Hunt, Gaillard, ed. *The First Forty Years of Washington Society in the Family Letters of Margaret Bayard Smith.* New York: Frederick Ungar, 1965.

Hunt, John. Journal. Part of John Hunt Papers. RG5/240 Friends Historical Library, Swarthmore College.

Jackson, Donald, and Dorothy Twohig, eds. *The Diaries of George Washington*, 6 vols. Vol. 6, January 1790–December 1799. Charlottesville: University Press of Virginia, 1979.

James, C. L. R. *The Black Jacobins: Toussaint L'Ouverture and the San Domingo Revolution.* 2nd ed. New York: Vintage, 1989.

Janvier, Thomas. *In Old New York*. New York: Harper & Brothers, 1894.

Jefferson, Thomas. *Writings*. New York: The Library of America, 1984.

———. *Jefferson's Memorandum Books*. 2 vols. Edited by James A. Bear Jr., and Lucia C. Stanton. Princeton: Princeton University Press, 1997.

Jenkins, Charles F. *Tortola: A Quaker Experiment of Long Ago in the Tropics*. London: Friends Bookshop, 1923.

Jones, Absalom, and Richard Allen. *A Narrative of the Proceedings of the Black People, During the Late Awful Calamity in Philadelphia, in the Year 1793*. Philadelphia: William W. Woodward, 1794.

Kaplan, Sidney, and Emma Nogrady Kaplan. *The Black Presence in the Era of the American Revolution*. Rev. ed. Amherst: University of Massachusetts Press, 1989.

Kite, Elizabeth S. *L'Enfant and Washington, 1791–1792*. Baltimore: The Johns Hopkins Press, 1929.

Kline, Ashley. "Andrew Ellicott," *Lancaster Heritage Outlook* 4, no. 4 (Winter 2005).

Kolchin, Peter. *American Slavery, 1619–1877*. New York: Hill & Wang, 1993.

Kouwenhoven, John A. *The Columbia Historical Portrait of New York*. New York: Harper & Row, 1972.

Lambert, Frank. *The Barbary Wars: American Independence in the Atlantic World*. New York: Hill & Wang, 2005.

Lanier, John J. *Washington: The Great American Mason*. New York: Macoy Publishing & Masonic Supply Co., 1922.

Latrobe, Benjamin Henry. *The Journal of Latrobe: Being the Notes and Sketches of an Architect, Naturalist and Traveler in the United States from 1796 to 1820*. New York: D. Appleton & Co., 1905.

Latrobe, John H. B. *Memoir of Benjamin Banneker*. Pamphlet. Baltimore: John D. Toy, 1845.

Law, Thomas. *A Reply to Certain Insinuations*. Pamphlet. Washington: n.p., 1824.

Lawler, Edward Jr., "The President's House Revisited," *The Pennsylvania Magazine of History and Biography* 129 (October 2005): 371–410.

Lear, Tobias. *Observations on the River Potomack, the Country Adjacent, and the City of Washington*. Pamphlet. New York: Samuel Loudon and Son, 1793.

Leish, Kenneth W. *The White House: A History of the Presidents*. New York: Newsweek, 1972.

Lepore, Jill. *New York Burning: Liberty, Slavery, and Conspiracy in Eighteenth-Century Manhattan.* New York: Knopf, 2005.

Loftin, T. L. *Contest for a Capital: George Washington, Robert Morris, and Congress, 1783–1791, Contenders.* Washington: Tee Loftin Publishers, 1989.

Look Before You Leap; or, A Few Hints to Such Artizans, Mechanics, Labourers, Farmers and Husbandmen, as Are Desirous of Emigrating to America. London: W. Row, 1796.

Lowance, Mason, ed. *Against Slavery: An Abolitionist Reader.* New York: Penguin Books, 2000.

Maclay, William. *The Diary of William Maclay and Other Notes on Senate Debates.* Edited by Kenneth R. Bowling and Helen E. Veit. Baltimore: Johns Hopkins University Press, 1988.

Mann-Kenney, Louise. *Rosedale: The Eighteenth-Century Country Estate of General Uriah Forrest, Cleveland Park, Washington, D.C.* Washington: (private printing), 1989.

Mannix, Daniel P., and Malcolm Cowley. *Black Cargoes: A History of the Atlantic Slave Trade, 1518–1865.* New York: Viking Press, 1962.

Mathews, Catharine Van Cortlandt. *Andrew Ellicott: His Life and Letters.* New York: The Grafton Press, 1908.

Mathews, Donald G. *Slavery and Methodism: A Chapter in American Morality, 1780–1845.* Princeton: Princeton University Press, 1965.

McCullough, David. *John Adams.* New York: Simon & Schuster, 2001.

McDonald, Forrest. *Alexander Hamilton: A Biography.* New York: W. W. Norton & Co., 1982.

McDougall, Marion Gleason. *Fugitive Slaves (1619–1865).* Fay House Monographs No. 3. Boston: Ginn & Co., 1891.

Meleney, John C. *The Public Life of Aedanus Burke: Revolutionary Republican in Post-Revolutionary South Carolina.* Columbia: University of South Carolina Press, 1989.

A Memorial to Washington the Mason. Alexandria: Alexandria-Washington Lodge, No. 22, A.F.&A.M, 1910.

Metcalf, Paul. *Waters of Potowmack.* Charlottesville: University Press of Virginia, 2002.

Miller, Iris. *Washington in Maps, 1606–2000.* New York: Rizzoli International Publications, 2002.

Miller, John C. *The Federalist Era, 1789–1801.* New York: Harper Torchbooks, 1960.

———. *The Wolf by the Ears: Thomas Jefferson and Slavery.* Charlottesville: University Press of Virginia, 1991.

Minutes of the Manumission Society of New York. Bound volumes. New-York Historical Society.

Minutes of the Proceedings of the Committee Appointed on 14 September 1793 to Attend to and Alleviate the Sufferings of the Afflicted with the Malignant Fever. Philadelphia: Crissy and Markley, 1848.

Mitchell, Stewart. *New Letters of Abigail Adams, 1788–1801.* Boston: Houghton Mifflin, 1947.

Moore, John M., ed. *Friends in the Delaware Valley: Philadelphia Yearly Meeting 1681–1981.* Haverford: Friends Historical Association, 1981.

Morales-Vazquez, Rubil. "Imagining Washington: Monuments and Nation Building in the Early Capital," *Washington History* 12, no. 1 (Spring/Summer 2000): 12–29.

Morison, Samuel Eliot. *The Oxford History of the American People,* vol. 2. *1789 Through Reconstruction.* New York: Mentor, 1972.

Moulton, Phillips P., ed. *The Journal and Major Essays of John Woolman.* New York: Oxford University Press, 1971.

Nash, Gary B. *First City: Philadelphia and the Forging of Historical Memory.* Philadelphia, University of Pennsylvania Press, 2002.

———. Forging Freedom: *The Formation of Philadelphia's Black Community 1720–1840.* Cambridge: Harvard University Press, 1988.

———. *The Forgotten Fifth: African Americans in the Age of Revolution.* Cambridge: Harvard University Press, 2006.

Newman, Richard S. "The Pennsylvania Abolition Society: Restoring a Group to Glory." *Pennsylvania Legacies* 6, no. 2 (2005).

———. *The Transformation of American Abolitionism: Fighting Slavery in the Early Republic.* Chapel Hill: University of North Carolina Press, 2002.

Newman, Simon P. *Embodied History: The Lives of the Poor in Early Philadelphia.* Philadelphia: University of Pennsylvania Press, 2003.

Niemcewicz, Julian Ursyn. *Under Their Vine and Fig Tree: Travels through America in 1797–1799, 1805, and with Some Further Account of Life in New Jersey.* Translated and edited by Metchie J. E. Budka. Elizabeth, N.J.: Grassmann Publishing Co., 1965.

Northrup, Solomon. *Twelve Years a Slave.* New York: Dover, 1970.

Nuxoll, Elizabeth M. "Illegitimacy, Family Status and Property in the Early Republic: The Morris-Croxall Family of New Jersey." *New Jersey History* 113 (Fall/Winter 1995): 3–21.

———. "Robert Morris and the Shaping of the Post-Revolutionary American Economy." Paper presented at the Omohundro Institute of Early American History and Culture Conference, Austin, Texas, June 1999.

Oberholtzer, Ellis P. *Robert Morris: Patriot and Financier.* New York: Macmillan, 1903.

Osborne, John Ball. "The Removal of the Government to Washington." *Columbia Historical Society Records* 3 (1900): 136–60.

Padover, Saul K., ed. *Thomas Jefferson and the National Capital.* Washington: U.S. Government Printing Office, 1946.

Parkinson, Richard. *A Tour in America in 1798, 1799, and 1800.* London: J. Harding, 1805.

Pickering, Vernon W. *A Concise History of the British Virgin Islands: From the Amerindians to 1986.* New York: Falcon Publications, 1987.

Pitch, Anthony. *The Burning of Washington: The British Invasion of 1814.* Annapolis, Md.: Naval Institute Press, 1998.

Pogue, Dennis J. "Interpreting the Dimensions of Daily Life for the Slaves Living at the President's House and at Mount Vernon," *The Pennsylvania Magazine of History and Biography* 129, no. 4 (2005): 433–44.

Powell, J. M. *Bring Out Your Dead: The Great Plague of Yellow Fever in Philadelphia in 1793.* Philadelphia: University of Pennsylvania Press, 1993.

Reiss, Oscar. *Blacks in Colonial America.* Jefferson, N.C.: McFarland & Co., 1997.

Richard, Carl J. *The Founders and the Classics: Greece, Rome, and the American Enlightenment.* Cambridge: Harvard University Press, 1994.

Ring, Constance, and Wesley E. Pippenger. *Alexandria, Virginia, Town Lots, 1749–1801.* Westminster, Md.: Family Line Publications, 1995.

Rochefoucauld-Liancourt, François-Alexandre-Frédéric. *Travels through the United States of North America, the Country of the Iroquois and Upper Canada, in the Years 1795, 1796, and 1797.* 2 vols. London: R. Phillips, 1799.

Rock, Howard B. *Artisans of the New Republic: The Tradesmen of New York City in the Age of Jefferson.* New York: New York University Press, 1979.

Rosenfeld, Richard N. *American Aurora: A Democratic-Republican Returns.* New York: St. Martin's Press, 1997.

Rush, Benjamin. *An Address on the Slavery of the Negroes in America.* New York: Arno Press, 1969.

Sakolski, A. M. *The Great American Land Bubble: The Amazing Story of Land-Grabbing, Speculations, and Booms from Colonial Days to the Present Time.* New York: Harper & Brothers, 1932.

Schama, Simon. *Citizens: A Chronicle of the French Revolution.* New York: Vintage, 1990.

———. *Patriots and Liberators: Revolution in the Netherlands, 1780–1813.* New York: Harper Perennial, 2005.

Schechter, Stephen L., and Bernstein, Richard B. *Well Begun: Chronicles of the Early National Period.* Albany: New York State Commission on the Bicentennial of the United States Constitution, 1989.

Scott, Pamela. "Moving to the Seat of Government: Temporary Inconveniences and Privations," *Washington History* 12. no. 1 (Spring/Summer 2000): 70–73.

———. *Temple of Liberty: Building the Capitol for a New Nation.* New York: Oxford University Press, 1995.

Seale, William. *The President's House.* 2 vols. Washington: White House Historical Association, 1986.

———. *The White House: The History of an American Idea.* Washington: American Institute of Architects Press, 1992.

Shirk, Willis L. Jr. "Wright's Ferry: A Glimpse into the Susquehannah Backcountry," *The Pennsylvania Magazine of History and Biography* 120 (January/April 1996): 61–87.

Shomette, Donald G. *Maritime Alexandria: The Rise and Fall of an American Entrepôt.* Bowie, Md.: Heritage Books, 2003.

Slaughter, Thomas P. *The Whiskey Rebellion: Frontier Epilogue to the American Revolution.* New York: Oxford University Press, 1986.

Smith, Adam. *The Wealth of Nations.* New York: Modern Library, 1994.

Smith, Billy G., ed. *Life in Early Philadelphia: Documents from the Revolutionary and Early National Periods.* University Park: Pennsylvania State University Press, 1995.

Smith, James Morton. *The Republic of Letters: The Correspondence between Thomas Jefferson and James Madison 1776–1826.* 3 vols. New York: Norton, 1995.

Smith, William Loughton. *The Journal of William Loughton Smith.* Proceedings of the Massachusetts Historical Society 51. Cambridge, Mass.: The University Press, 1917.

Spies, Gregory C. "Major Andrew Ellicott, Esq.: Colonial American Astronomical Surveyor, Patriot, Cartographer, Legislator, Scientific Instrument Maker, Boundary

Commissioner & Professor of Mathematics." Unpublished paper. Available at: http://www.fig.net/pub/fig_2002/HS2/HS2_spies.pdf.

Stahr, Walter. *John Jay: Founding Father.* New York: Hambledon and London, 2005.

Stampp, Kenneth M. *The Peculiar Institution: Slavery in the Ante-Bellum South.* New York: Knopf, 1956.

Stanton, Lucia. *Free Some Day: The African-American Families of Monticello.* Charlottesville, Va.: Thomas Jefferson Foundation, 2000.

———. *Slavery at Monticello.* Charlottesville, Va.: Thomas Jefferson Foundation, 1996.

Starobin, Robert S., ed. *Blacks in Bondage: Letters of American Slaves.* New York: Marcus Wiener, 1988.

Stearns, Elinor, and David N. Yerkes. *William Thornton: A Renaissance Man in the Federal City.* Washington: American Institute of Architects Foundation, 1976.

Still, Bayrd. *Mirror for Gotham: New York as Seen by Contemporaries from Dutch Days to the Present.* New York: Fordham University Press, 1994.

Stillman, Damie. "Six Houses for the President," *The Pennsylvania Magazine of History and Biography* 129 (October 2005): 411–31.

Sturge, Joseph. *A Visit to the United States in 1841.* New York: Augustus M. Kelley, 1969.

Sweig, Donald Mitchell. "Northern Virginia Slavery: A Statistical and Demographic Investigation." PhD diss., The College of William and Mary, 1982.

Taggart, Hugh T. "The Presidential Journey, in 1800, from the Old to the New Seat of Government," *Columbia Historical Society Records* 3 (1900): 180–209.

Taste, Timothy [pseud.]. *The Freaks of Columbia; or, The Removal of the Seat of Government: A Farce.* Washington: n.p., 1808.

Thomas, Hugh. *The Slave Trade: The Story of the Atlantic Slave Trade, 1440–1870.* New York: Touchstone, 1997.

Tremain, Mary. *Slavery in the District of Columbia.* New York: G. P. Putnam's Sons, 1892.

Tyson, Martha E. *Banneker, the Afric-American Astronomer.* Philadelphia: Friends' Book Association, 1884.

———. *A Sketch of the Life of Benjamin Banneker, from Notes Taken in 1836. Read by J. Saurin Morris before the Maryland Historical Society, October 5th, 1854.* Baltimore: J. D. Toy, 1854.

Wagner, Frederick. *Robert Morris: Audacious Patriot*. New York: Dodd, Mead & Co., 1976.

Waldstreicher, David. *Runaway America: Benjamin Franklin, Slavery, and the American Revolution*. New York: Hill & Wang, 2004.

Walker, George. *A Description of the Situation and Plan of the City of Washington*. Pamphlet. London: George Walker, 1792.

Weld, Isaac, Jr. *Travels through the States of North America and the Provinces of Upper and Lower Canada, During the Years 1795, 1796, and 1797*. London: John Stockdale, 1799.

White, Shane. *Somewhat More Independent: The End of Slavery in New York City, 1770–1810*. Athens: University of Georgia Press, 1991.

Whitman, T. Stephen. *The Price of Freedom: Slavery and Manumission in Baltimore and Early National Maryland*. New York: Routledge, 2000.

Wick, Wendy C. *George Washington, an American Icon: The Eighteenth-Century Graphic Portraits*. Washington: The Barra Foundation, 1982.

Wilson, Carol. *Freedom at Risk: The Kidnapping of Free Blacks in America 1780–1865*. Lexington: University Press of Kentucky, 1994.

Winch, Julie. *A Gentleman of Color: The Life of James Forten*. New York: Oxford University Press, 2002.

———. "Philadelphia and the Other Underground Railroad," *The Pennsylvania Magazine of History and Biography* 111 (January 1987): 3–25.

Wiencek, Henry. *An Imperfect God: George Washington, His Slaves, and the Creation of America*. New York: Farrar, Straus and Giroux, 2003.

Wills, Garry. *"Negro President": Jefferson and the Slave Power*. Boston, Houghton Mifflin, 2003.

Wright, Robert E., and David J. Cowen. *Financial Founding Fathers: The Men Who Made America Rich*. Chicago: University of Chicago Press, 2006.

Zaborney, John Joseph. "Slaves for Rent: Slave Hiring in Virginia." PhD diss., University of Maine, 1997.

Zagarri, Rosemarie, ed. *David Humphreys' "Life of General Washington."* Athens: University of Georgia Press, 1991.

Zilversmit, Arthur. *The First Emancipation: The Abolition of Slavery in the North*. Chicago: University of Chicago Press, 1967.

NEWSPAPERS

Alexandria Expositor (VA)

The Centinel of Liberty, George-Town and Washington Observer (MD)

Commercial Advertiser (NY)

Connecticut Courant

Connecticut Journal

Federal Gazette (MD)

Gazette of the United States (PA)

Maryland Journal, and the Baltimore Advertiser

Museum and Washington and George-Town Daily Advertiser (DC)

National Intelligencer (DC)

New-York Daily Advertiser

New-York Daily Gazette

New-York Journal

New-York Morning Post

Pennsylvania Gazette

The Virginia Gazette and Alexandria Advertiser

Weekly Museum (NY)

ARCHIVES AND COLLECTIONS

Alexandria Public Library, Alexandria, VA

First Federal Congress Project (FFCP), George Washington University, Washington, DC

Friends Historical Library (FHL), Swarthmore College, Swarthmore, PA

Historical Society of Pennsylvania (HSP), Philadelphia, PA

Library Company of Philadelphia (LCP), Philadelphia, PA

Library of Congress (LOC), Washington, DC

  Records of the Commissioners of the City of Washington

  Letters of Presidents to the Commissioners of the City of Washington

  Morgan-L'Enfant-Digges Papers (MLD)

Margaret Bayard Smith Papers

Anna Maria Brodeau Thornton Papers

William Thornton Papers

Maryland Historical Society (MHS), Baltimore, MD

National Archives (NA), Washington, DC

> Accounts of the Commissioners of the City of Washington, Manning Collection. Record Group 217.

> Letterbooks of the Commissioners of Washington, DC, 1791–1798. Records of the Office of Public Buildings and Public Parks of the National Capital. Record Group 42.

> Records of the Board of Commissioners for the Emancipation of Slaves in the District of Columbia, 1862–1863. Treasury Accounts. Record Group 217.

New-York Historical Society (N-YHS)

New York Public Library (NYPL)

Pennsylvania Historical Society (PHS)

Queens College, Robert Morris Papers, microfilm.

> Letterbooks of Robert Morris, LOC

> Robert Morris Collection, Henry E. Huntington Library, San Marino, CA

Washington Public Library, Martin Luther King Branch, Washingtonia Collection

INDEX

Anacostia River, *see* Potomac River, Eastern Branch of

Arlington National Cemetery, 64

Arnold, Benedict, 45

Articles of Confederation (1781), 18

Aurora, 206–7

Austria, 164, 166

Baltimore, Md., 5, 15, 16, 41, 42, 49, 69, 263

Bank of Columbia, 168, 180

Bank of the United States, 64–65

Banneker, Benjamin, 69–71
  almanac of, 78–79, 119–21
  capital survey and, 66–67, 70–71, 78–80, 174, 254

Barbary pirates, 7, 93–94, 143, 188, 205–6

Bayard, James A., 257

Belgium, 164, 166

Bender, Lewis, 121

Benson, Egbert, 91

Biddle, Clement, 115

Big Jacob (slave), 241, 272

Black Codes, 112

Blagden, Thomas, 230

Blodget, Samuel, 95–97, 102, 150, 153–56, 157, 158, 168–69, 171

Bond, Phineas, 166

Boston, Mass., 107, 113, 154, 157

Bourne, Sylvanus, 162–64, 167

Bowling, Kenneth R., 4

Brent, Richard, 204

Bridges, Robert, 129

Brissot de Warville, Jacques-Pierre, 2, 113, 118

Brodsky, Alyn, 138

Bunker Hill, Battle of (1775), 17

Burke, Aedanus, 41, 51, 103, 116

Burr, Aaron, 249, 252, 256–57

Calhoun, John C., 111, 243

Callender, James, 247–48, 249, 250

Canada, 5, 6, 259, 264

Capitol, U.S., 4, 6, 9, 90, 213, 219, 274

burning of, 261–62

construction of, 174, 177, 189, 191, 195, 197–99, 203, 208–9, 214, 224, 225, 228, 237–38, 261, 270

dedication of, 149–52, 156, 157, 164, 171

designs for, 101–2, 105–6, 123–24, 135, 199, 213, 241

first session of Congress in, 252–56

Jefferson and, 99–102, 105, 124, 135, 246–47

L'Enfant and, 81–82, 99, 105

Thornton and, 105–6, 123–24, 135, 150, 199, 246–47, 254, 261, 262, 269, 275

Carey, Matthew, 138, 146

Carroll, Charles, 65

Carroll, Daniel, 48, 63, 86–87, 89, 170, 267

Census, U.S., 16, 22

Centinel of Liberty and George-Town Advertiser, 245, 247

Cherokees, 179, 183

Chickasaws, 179

Choctaws, 179

Clarke, Joseph, 151

Clay, Henry, 243

Cobbett, William, 146

Coit, Joshua, 204

Columbia, Pa., 15–16

Comprehensive Law of Suspects (1793), 164–65

Compromise of 1820, 52

Compromise of 1850, 52

Congress, U.S., 2–3, 64–65, 166
  Alien and Sedition Acts and, 231, 232
  appropriations for capital move by, 74–75
  Barbary pirates and, 93–94, 205–6
  capital location and, 7–8, 15–16, 21–29, 32, 40–44, 49–50, 54, 55, 77, 148, 152, 198, 201–6, 224–26, 273
  election of 1800 and, 256–57
  federal debt crisis and, 32–37, 40–44, 48–49, 50

Franklin, Benjamin, 39–40, 65, 66, 104, 119

Franklin and Armfield, 271

Free African Society, 131–32, 141–42

French and Indian War, 59–60, 65, 186

French Revolution, 46, 164–66, 167, 187, 211–12, 214

Freneau, Philip, 56, 249

Fugitive Slave Law (1793), 127–28, 148

fugitive slaves, 20, 24, 59, 67, 99, 113, 118, 121–22, 127–28, 148, 233–35, 245

Fuller, Lark, 191

Fuller, Thomas, 119

Gabriel's Rebellion (1800), 132, 132*n*, 248–49

Gallatin, Albert, 261

Garrison, William Lloyd, 21

Gazette of the United States, 38, 128–29

Genet, Edmond, 165–66

George Town, Md., 1, 28, 44, 48, 53, 54, 56, 60, 62, 63–64, 66, 71, 72, 74, 84, 155, 194, 208, 213, 226, 233, 254, 260

George Town Weekly Ledger, 71

Georgia, 16, 19, 178–79, 221

Germantown, Pa., 25, 27, 43, 118, 144, 146

Gerry, Elbridge, 42

Gleig, George, 261, 262

Grant, Ulysses S., 272

Great Britain, 6, 61, 92–93, 166, 178, 184

American Revolution and, 12, 14, 17, 224

French Revolution and, 164, 166

Jay Treaty and, 183–84, 205, 212, 247, 255

War of 1812 and, 259–64

Greenleaf, James, 9, 156–60, 162–63, 167–71, 172–74, 180–82, 194, 218–20, 222, 268

Griswold, Roger, 252

Grosvenor, Thomas P., 264–65

Hadfield, George, 198–99, 227

Haiti, 94–95, 108, 133

Hallet, Stephen, 102, 105, 106, 135

Hamilton, Alexander, 9, 13, 31–37, 40–51, 92, 96, 104, 143, 165, 176, 216, 220, 249, 257, 266

Adams and, 26, 210, 211, 232–33, 248

American Revolution and, 12, 17, 22, 34, 45, 95

Bank of the United States and, 64–65

capital location debate and, 40–44, 47–51

federal debt crisis and, 31–37, 40–51, 63

French war crisis and, 232–33, 255

Jay Treaty and, 184, 185

Hammon, Jupiter, 130

Hastings, Warren, 171

Hemings, James, 45–46

Hemings, Sally, 45, 46, 69, 247

Henson, Josiah, 68, 191–92

Hercules (slave), 234–35

Herschel, William, 104

Hoban, James, 101–2, 135, 150, 154, 190, 191, 193, 254

House of Representatives, U.S., 13, 37, 82, 105, 161, 238, 252

capital location and, 15–16, 21–23, 27, 48–49, 205

election of 1800 and, 256–57

federal debt assumption and, 43, 63, 203

proportional representation in, 20–21

slavery issue and, 37–40

Humphreys, David, 59

Hunt, Abraham, 122

Huntington, Benjamin, 38

India, 171, 172, 174, 181

Jackson, Andrew, 21, 263

Jackson, James, 2, 6, 38–39, 51, 99, 111, 273

Jackson, Jonathan, 251

Jay, John, 34, 47, 184–85, 186, 256